Warships After London

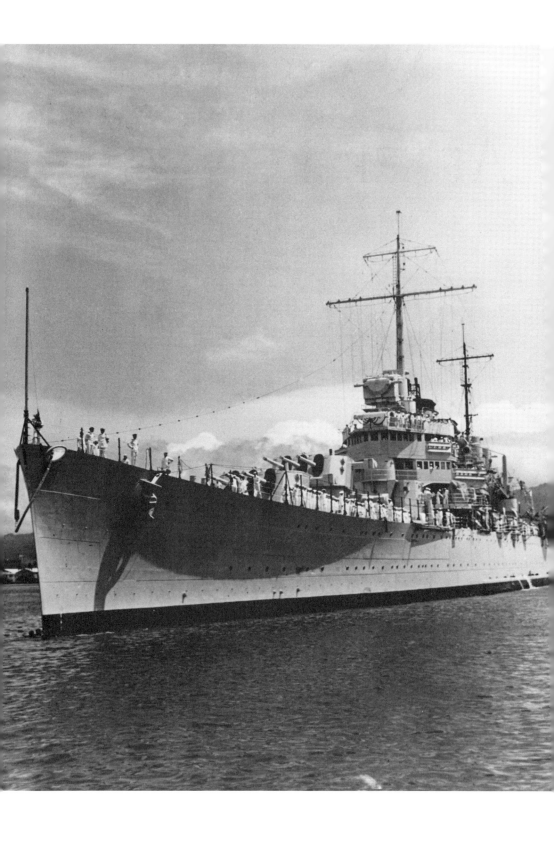

WARSHIPS
AFTER LONDON

JOHN JORDAN

Naval Institute Press
Annapolis, Maryland

Frontispiece: *Honolulu* (CL-48), one of seven 10,000-ton 'light' cruisers armed with fifteen 6in guns in triple turrets built for the US Navy as a response to the Japanese *Mogami* class during the mid-1930s. The photo was taken on the occasion of the ship's visit to the port after which she was named, Honolulu, Territory of Hawaii, on 14 July 1939. Note the 45ft flower garland (*lei*) suspended from the 'eyes' of the ship. (*NHHC, NH 80-G-451204*)

Copyright © John Jordan 2020

First published in Great Britain in 2020 by
Seaforth Publishing
An imprint of Pen & Sword Books Ltd
47 Church Street, Barnsley
S Yorkshire S70 2AS

www.seaforthpublishing.com
Email info@seaforthpublishing.com

Published and distributed in the United States of America and Canada by the
Naval Institute Press, 291 Wood Road, Annapolis, Maryland 21402-5043
www.nip.org

Library of Congress Cataloging Number: 2020939034

ISBN 978 1 68247 610 9

Pen & Sword Books Limited incorporates the imprints of Atlas, Archaeology, Aviation, Discovery, Family History, Fiction, History, Maritime, Military, Military Classics, Politics, Select, Transport, True Crime, Air World, Frontline Publishing, Leo Cooper, Remember When, Seaforth Publishing, The Praetorian Press, Wharncliffe Local History, Wharncliffe Transport, Wharncliffe True Crime and White Owl.

Typeset and designed by Stephen Dent
Printed and bound in Great Britain by TJ International Ltd, Padstow

CONTENTS

PREFACE

WARSHIPS AFTER WASHINGTON, covering naval developments in the five major fleets during the eight-year period that followed the signing of the Washington Treaty on 6 February 1922, was first published in late 2011. It was generally well received, and a second, corrected edition was published two years later, followed by a paperback edition in 2015. A number of reviewers of the book stated that they looked forward to a sequel covering the period 1930–36, following the signing of the London Treaty of 22 April 1930, which modified the Treaty provisions and extended the quantitative limitations imposed on capital ships and aircraft carriers to other categories of warship. *Warships After London* is that sequel.

My aim in writing the original book was to attempt to bridge the gap between the political and the technical. I also wanted to look at the very different ways in which the five major navies responded to the new limitations imposed by the Washington Treaty. The classification of all surface units outside the closely defined capital ship and aircraft carrier categories as 'auxiliary vessels' allowed considerable flexibility in the types of ship built, with heavily armed 'treaty cruisers' increasingly complemented by 'super-destroyers' and numbers limited only by national budgets. This had led to something of a free-for-all, which on the one hand promoted inventive solutions to problems of national security but which by the late 1920s was causing increasing concern. The London Treaty was an attempt impose order on chaos by defining three new categories of warship, cruisers, destroyers and submarines, which could then be kept in check by imposing qualitative and quantitative limitations similar in conception to those placed on capital ships and aircraft carriers at Washington.

This was to have a major impact on naval programmes. In the years that followed the signing of the Washington Treaty the five major navies did not have to concern themselves with the construction and financing of new capital ships due to the ten-year 'battleship holiday', and during the period 1922–30 not one of the high contracting powers opted to build up to its tonnage allocation for aircraft carriers; construction of lesser vessels continued unabated, without regard for unit displacement or numbers. However, the strict quantitative limits agreed at London instituted a completely different ball game. When reviewing the implications for the new categories, each of the major navies needed to look closely at its current inventory, assess how many of the ships could be replaced before the Washington Treaty expired on 31 December 1936, and calculate how to use the available tonnage to best advantage. It is these deliberations and their outcomes that constitute the primary focus of the present book.

Drawings and Data

Warships After London follows the same basic format as its predecessor. The fifty or so schematics have been specially prepared for this book, and are drawn and labelled in a uniform style to enable the reader to make an informed comparison between the different designs developed by the five navies within the parameters laid down by the Treaty. This has not been an easy task given the disparity in the quality of published material; where possible the author has used either official plans or drawings published in reliable secondary sources.

The tabulated data that accompanies the drawings and the text has been simplified for the purpose of making meaningful comparisons, with figures for dimensions rounded up or down to the nearest foot or metre and displacement figures – which often varied even between ships of the same class – to the nearest five tons. The British and American navies of the period used imperial units, the other three navies the metric system. Even within the metric system there were anomalies: the Italians and the French – at least in the post-Washington period – expressed gun calibre and torpedo diameter in millimetres, whereas the Japanese used centimetres and often rounded the figures up or down. Despite the author's wish to facilitate comparisons, there was an issue here of 'authenticity' and respect for the non-Anglo-Saxon navies. The solution adopted was inevitably a compromise: displacements, which are generally Washington standard for all ships and all navies, are given in long tons (tW); dimensions are in imperial units for Britain and the USA (with metric equivalents in parentheses), and in metric for Japan, France and Italy; for guns, torpedoes, armour thickness, boiler pressure, etc, the appropriate units for the navy concerned are used and conversion tables provided at the front of the book. Readers looking for more accurate and comprehensive data about a particular class of ship are referred to the specialist works cited in the bibliography.

There was a similar issue to resolve with regard to the different practices in programming and authorising construction. In all the countries concerned naval construction, together with the necessary funding, had to be authorised before ships could be ordered; in most cases there then followed a short interval before the ship was laid down. Naval 'estimates' were generally voted by the respective parliaments annually. However, in Japan construction programmes generally ran over several years. During the period covered by this book there were only two 'naval replenishment' programmes, dated 1931 and 1934. Ships approved in each of these programmes would be laid down to a schedule determined by the Navy, taking into account capacity in the naval dockyards, and some of the units within a single programme would be of improved design. The author has endeavoured to respect these cultural differences in drawing up the authorisation tables in Chapters 4–6.

Acknowledgements

The author wishes to thank Rob Gardiner of Seaforth Publishing for his support in bringing this project to fruition. Richard Worth provided a wealth of research material relating to the Treaty period and much encouragement. Many of the photographs published in this book are from the archives of the US Naval Historical and Heritage Command and the Kure Naval Museum. Friends and colleagues who kindly provided photographs include: Maurizio Brescia, Michele Cosentino, Norman Friedman, Ian Johnston, Leo van Ginderen, Jean Moulin and Conrad Waters.

   Finally, I would like to thank those authors who blazed a trail for the technical analysis I have attempted to apply to the five major navies of the period. Their influence is acknowledged in the selected bibliography published at the end of the book. One name stands out among the rest: Norman Friedman, who besides his detailed studies on the major categories of warship built for the British Royal Navy and the US Navy, has published a number of more general 'comparative' works illustrating the often very different choices navies make when designing ships for similar missions. While acknowledging these influences the author naturally accepts full responsibility for any errors of fact or judgement contained in this book.

John Jordan
Gosport, UK
March 2020

ACRONYMS & ABBREVIATIONS

AA	anti-aircraft
AP	armour piercing (shell)
A/S	anti-submarine
ASW	anti-submarine warfare
BD	between decks (gun mounting)
CP	centre pivot (gun mounting)
CT	conning tower
DC	depth charge
DCT	director control tower
	also depth charge thrower
DF	direction finding
DP	dual-purpose (gun)
FC	fire control
HA	high angle
HACS	high-angle control system
HACP	high-angle control position
HE	high explosive (shell)
HF/DF	high-frequency direction finding
HT	high tensile (steel)
IJN	Imperial Japanese Navy
mt	metric tons (tonnes)
MG	machine gun
NC	non-cemented (armour)
NTD	Navy Technical Department (Jap)
NGS	Naval General Staff
RPC	remote power control
SAP	semi-armour piercing (shell)
STCN	Service Technique des Constructions Navales (Fr)
STS	special treatment steel (US)
TDC	torpedo data computer (US)
TS	transmitting station
TSDS	two-speed destroyer sweep (RN)
tW	tons Washington ('standard' displacement)

CONVERSION TABLES

Length: feet to metres

ft	m	ft	m	ft	m	ft	m	ft	m	ft	m	ft	m
200	61	300	91	400	122	500	152	600	183	700	213	800	244
210	64	310	94	410	125	510	155	610	186	710	216	810	247
220	67	320	98	420	128	520	158	620	189	720	219	820	250
230	70	330	101	430	131	530	162	630	192	730	222	830	253
240	73	340	104	440	134	540	165	640	195	740	226	840	256
250	76	350	107	450	137	550	168	650	198	750	229	850	259
260	79	360	110	460	140	560	171	660	201	760	232	860	262
270	82	370	113	470	143	570	174	670	204	770	235	870	265
280	85	380	116	480	146	580	177	680	207	780	238	880	268
290	88	390	119	490	149	590	180	690	210	790	241	890	271

Note: conversion to the nearest whole metre

Beam and draught: feet to metres

ft	m	ft	m	ft	m
1	0.30	15	4.57	65	19.81
2	0.61	20	6.10	70	21.34
3	0.91	25	7.62	75	22.86
4	1.22	30	9.14	80	24.38
5	1.52	35	10.67	85	25.91
6	1.83	40	12.19	90	27.43
7	2.13	45	13.72	95	28.96
8	2.44	50	15.24	100	30.48
9	2.74	55	16.76	105	32.00
10	3.05	60	18.29	110	33.53

Note: conversion to two decimal places

Guns

in	mm	in	mm	in	mm
18in	457mm	(9.4in)	240mm	(5.1in)	130mm
16in	406mm	8in	203mm	5in	127mm
15in	381mm	(7.9in)	200mm	4.7in	120mm
14in	356mm	7.5in	190mm	4.5in	(114mm)
13.5in	(343mm)	(6.1in)	155mm	4in	102mm
(13.4in)	340mm	6in	152mm	(3.9in)	100mm
(13in)	330mm	5.5in	140mm	(3.5in)	90mm
(12.6in)	320mm	(5.4in)	138.6mm	3in	75/76mm
12in	305mm	(5.3in)	135mm	2pdr	40mm

Note 1: Parentheses indicate that this is simply an equivalent measurement; it does not represent an actual gun.

Note 2: The French and Italian Navies used millimetres, whereas the Japanese (like the Germans) expressed gun calibres as centimetres (457mm = 45.7cm); some calibres employed by the IJN were approximations (eg the 8cm HA gun – in fact a 76.2mm gun).

Note 3: In the text guns are frequently designated by a combination of calibre + the length of the gun in calibres, eg 305mm/50, 37/54.

Armour

in	mm	in	mm	in	mm
1in	25mm	3in	75mm	11in	280mm
1¼in	30mm	4in	100mm	12in	305mm
1½in	38mm	5in	125mm	13in	330mm
1¾in	45mm	6in	150mm	14in	355mm
2in	50mm	7in	175mm	15in	380mm
2¼in	55mm	8in	200mm	16in	405mm
2½in	65mm	9in	230mm	17in	430mm
2¾in	70mm	10in	255mm	18in	455mm

Note: conversion above 38mm to the nearest 5mm

Torpedoes

in	mm
(17.7in)	450mm
18in	(457mm)
21in	533mm
(21.7in)	550mm
(24in)	610mm
24.5in	(622mm)

Introduction:

THE LONDON TREATY
OF APRIL 1930

THE WASHINGTON CONFERENCE OF 1921–22 took place in the aftermath of the Great War of 1914–18. It was an attempt to impose order on the hitherto unregulated – and potentially ruinous – competition in naval armaments that was widely considered to have played a major part in the path to a devastating war and which, if left unchecked, would inevitably lead to further conflict. The resulting treaty, signed in February 1922, achieved many of its aims, of which arguably the most important was to confine national naval ambitions within a framework of 'collective security'. However, the wording of the Treaty left the five high contracting powers with considerable latitude in terms of the ships they could choose to build.

For US Secretary of State Charles Evans Hughes, who had initiated and led the conference, the principal unit of naval currency was the battleship, so the major focus of the discussions was on defining the maximum size (calculated using a new 'standard' displacement) and firepower of individual units and establishing a ceiling on the overall number of 'capital ships' (the term included battlecruisers) that could be maintained and built by each of the five powers. It proved possible at the conference to extend this concept of 'qualitative' and 'quantitative' limitations to the aircraft carrier, which was in its infancy, but not to other categories of surface vessel; these were grouped together under the term 'auxiliary vessels', which could be retained or built in unlimited numbers, and for which only an upper ceiling of 10,000 tons and 8in guns was established. Moreover, the British were unable to secure the abolition of the submarine in the face of vehement opposition from the French, who claimed that it was the naval weapon of choice for an inferior naval power that needed to defend its coasts and harbours against a surface blockade.

During the 1920s these loopholes were exploited by Japan and France to compensate for their dissatisfaction with the number of capital ships allocated to them by the Treaty. The Japanese, who had pushed for a 10:7 capital ship ratio *vis-à-vis* the US Navy but were compelled to accept a 5:3 (*ie* 10:6) ratio, embarked on a large compensatory construction programme of large cruisers, destroyers and submarines.

Takao, one of the powerful IJN cruisers armed with 8in (20cm) guns under construction at the time of the London Conference, during her trials in the spring of 1932. These ships were a major concern for both the British and the Americans. *(Fukui Shizuo collection)*

The eight cruisers of the *Nachi* and *Atago* classes were the most powerful ships permitted under the Treaty, armed with ten 8in guns and multiple torpedo tubes, and with a nominal displacement of 10,000 tons that was largely exceeded on completion. Large 'cruiser' and 'fleet' submarines developed using German technology were laid down in numbers, and from 1927 the IJN embarked on a series of powerful destroyers of the 'Special Type', armed with six 12.7cm (5in) guns and nine 61cm (24in) torpedoes. The French cruiser programme was more modest in its ambition, but France invested heavily in a new generation of flotilla craft and submarines; the new 'fleet' submarines were fast, with a maximum speed in excess of 19 knots on the surface, and the fleet scouts (*contre-torpilleurs*) were heavily armed and had twice the displacement of conventional destroyers.

An attempt to resolve some of these issues at Geneva in the summer of 1927 foundered when the Royal Navy and the US Navy were unable to find a common position on cruisers (see *Warships After Washington,* Chapter 11): the latter wanted a limited number of 10,000-ton fleet scouts armed with 8in guns that could operate in the western Pacific, while the Royal Navy wanted a larger number of ships to police the imperial trade routes and which, in order to be affordable, would need to have more modest dimensions and firepower. The political fallout from these failed negotiations was considerable, and when the date approached for a formal review of

The French *contre-torpilleur Bison* at Brest in 1933–34. These ships spanned the traditional cruiser and destroyer categories, thereby complicating international agreement on qualitative limitations. *(Leo van Ginderen collection)*

the Washington Treaty, the British Prime Minister of the day, James Ramsay MacDonald, resolved that a new push for more comprehensive naval arms limitation was required. The US Government readily agreed, and invitations were then extended to the other three contracting powers. The British and US governments were both anxious to exclude 'naval experts', who had been widely blamed for the failure of the Geneva Conference, from the negotiations; they would serve only as advisors to the civilian delegates.[1]

The London conference of January–April 1930 took place in the shadow of the Wall Street Crash of October 1929, which served to focus minds. The British economy had already been in trouble before the crash, resulting in postponements and cancellations within its naval programmes. In the United States, the wisdom and affordability of the large programme of cruiser construction recently agreed by Congress as a response to the British and Japanese programmes – five 10,000-ton ships were to have been authorised in each of the three fiscal years FY1929, FY1930 and FY1931 – were being questioned by the new Republican administration of President Herbert Hoover, who as a Quaker favoured reducing naval armaments to the minimum necessary for the country's security. And the large post-1922 French programme of submarines and flotilla craft had come to a grinding halt in the face of production bottlenecks in the factories and the shipyards.

However, leaving aside MacDonald's commitment to peace and collective security and Hoover's desire to minimise the US taxpayers' exposure to unnecessary defence expenditure, there were other issues that the conference needed to address. Both the British and the Americans were anxious to put a cap on Japanese naval ambitions, which posed an increasing threat to their interests in East and Southeast Asia. The

Imperial Japanese Navy was now seen as the chief potential adversary of both western navies, and failure to regulate the current unrestrained Japanese construction of large cruisers, destroyers and submarines would necessarily impact on the ability of the British and the Americans to curtail their own expenditure on naval armaments. There was little point in the Royal Navy building larger numbers of 7,000-ton cruisers armed with 6in guns for trade protection if the ships they were likely to face were 10,000-ton ships armed with 8in guns. Similarly, if the Japanese were allowed to continue to build heavily armed 1,700-ton destroyers – no fewer than twenty-four ships of the 'Special Type' had been laid down during the late 1920s – these would have to be matched by similar British and American ships, at considerable cost.

Discussions at the London conference of January–April 1930 were difficult and, at times, fraught (see *WAW* Chapter 11 for a detailed account). As expected, Japan pushed hard for a 10:7 ratio in large cruisers,[2] and Britain again failed to secure the abolition of the submarine. France, which favoured a system of 'global limitation' under which each country was allocated a figure for total tonnage based on its maritime obligations that it could then divide up in any way it saw fit, opposed the division of 'auxiliary vessels' into the separate categories that Britain and the USA insisted on imposing on the conference. The French delegation therefore declined to discuss overall tonnage limits for each of the new categories of cruiser, destroyer and submarine defined by the Treaty, and the Italians, whose primary position was parity with France, were unwilling to sign any agreement that was unacceptable to the French. These issues would be left to separate discussions between the two powers to be chaired by the British and to take place after the end of the conference. Thus all five of the contracting powers signed Parts I, II, IV and V of the resulting treaty, but only Britain, the USA and Japan signed up to Part III, which imposed quantitative tonnage limits on the newly defined categories. The Treaty was subsequently ratified by all three of the major naval powers – although not without considerable acrimony in Japan, where it was categorised by the increasingly influential 'fleet faction' as a further national humiliation[3] – but the Franco-Italian talks failed to establish a common position and broke up without agreement. Despite this, both the latter powers adhered broadly to the spirit of the London Treaty, and neither embarked on naval construction that might have been considered escalatory or destabilising.

It is always difficult to assess the relative success of an international conference. It is simplistic to talk of outcomes in terms of their benefit to 'Britain', 'the USA' and 'Japan', as opinion in each of those countries was deeply divided. The job of politicians is to ensure long-term peace and prosperity for their peoples, that of the military to prepare for the next war. The civilian politicians who organised the London conference of 1930 and conducted the negotiations returned to their respective countries broadly satisfied with the outcomes. None of the five powers concerned had walked out, and important (and hard-fought) compromises has been secured on the thorny issues of cruisers and submarines. The spirit of Washington lived on, and many of the holes in the original treaty had been patched over, if not completely sealed off.

There was less satisfaction with the outcomes of London 1930 on the part of the navies themselves,[4] which now had to review their existing programmes in the light of the new regulations affecting cruisers, destroyers, submarines and even the new 'treaty-exempt' category of 'small combatants and auxiliary vessels'. The US Navy would not now be able to complete the twenty-three 10,000-ton cruisers armed with 8in guns authorised by Congress[5] – it was restricted to eighteen – and would have to abandon its programme of large 'cruiser' submarines.[6] The Royal Navy's goal of seventy cruisers for the 'fleet' and 'trade' missions had to be abandoned and the lower figure of fifty quietly accepted as a 'temporary measure'; even this figure would be difficult to realise given the new limits on overall cruiser tonnage and the poor state of the British economy. However, the major impact of the new treaty regulations was undoubtedly on the IJN, which would be compelled to review not only its crucial 8in-gun cruiser programme, but its policies regarding the construction of large destroyers and submarines. Given the Japanese Naval General Staff's insistence on the 'qualitative superiority' of individual units over their western counterparts, this was a recipe for internal conflict between the NGS and the Japanese constructor corps, the NTD, with the result that many of the classes of warship designed and built under the 1931 'Circle 1' and the 1934 'Circle 2' programmes would have serious conceptual and technical flaws. These defects would prove costly to correct both in financial terms and in terms of the burden imposed on the dockyards by the need for reconstruction, which effectively delayed the building of new ships.

Chapter 1

The Implications of the London Treaty for the Five Major Navies

THE FINAL CHAPTER of the first volume of *Warships After Washington* (henceforth *WAW*) has a detailed account and analysis of the provisions of the London Treaty of 1930, and the full wording of the Treaty is published in the Appendix to the present volume. To avoid repetition, this chapter will therefore confine itself to the principal amendments to the original Washington Treaty of February 1922 and to the implications for the navies of each of the high contracting powers.

Capital Ships

The principal change was an extension of the ten-year 'battleship holiday' agreed at Washington for a further five years, until 31 December 1936, and the immediate reduction in the number of operational capital ships to the figures agreed for the longer term: fifteen for each of Britain and the USA, nine for Japan and five for each of France and Italy. This, however, was without prejudice to the right of France and Italy to lay down two new capital ships each of the maximum 35,000 tons standard permitted in the original treaty as replacements for their surviving dreadnoughts – a facility of which neither had hitherto opted to take advantage. This provision was to have unforeseen consequences when the French opted to utilise 53,000 tons of their 70,000-ton allocation to build ships intended to counter the new German *Panzerschiffe*, and were subsequently faced with an Italian decision to lay down two fast battleships of the maximum displacement allowed (see Chapter 2).

For the three major navies the principal consequence of the capital ship provisions was the impending obsolescence of their respective battle fleets. By January 1940 – the earliest date a vessel laid down in January 1937 might be expected to complete – the Royal Navy's oldest battleship, *Queen Elizabeth*, would be twenty-five years old, and even the latest US and Japanese battleships of the *Colorado* and *Nagato* classes would be seventeen to nineteen years old; only the British *Nelson* and *Rodney*, for which special permission had been obtained under Washington, would be under fifteen years old. Moreover, the average displacement of these older vessels (29,000–30,000 tons) was well below the maximum displacement permitted for new construction under the Treaty, so by December 1936 the overall capital ship tonnage figures for the respective navies would be well below the ceilings agreed in 1922.

The only practical solution was modernisation, but the Washington Treaty permitted the upgrading of capital ships currently in service or completing only to provide defence against air and submarine attack – bulges, deck armour and anti-aircraft weaponry – and this was subject to a maximum 3,000-ton increase in displacement. Although there was no further formal statement in the London Treaty, an informal understanding between Ramsay MacDonald and President Hoover was reached to the effect that, in view of the age of the surviving vessels, no objection would be raised to more radical reconstruction provided the 3,000-ton Washington allowance was respected.[1] Britain, which in the mid-1920s had formally objected to a proposed increase in the elevation of the main guns of the older US battleships (see *WAW* Chapter 5), would make no objection to the reconstruction post-London of the older Japanese and Italian battleships, which included new propulsion machinery, a lengthened hull (for higher speed) and much-increased elevation for the main guns (see Chapter 2). Indeed, from 1934 the Royal Navy would embark on a series of radical reconstructions of its own, beginning with the battleship *Warspite*.

Aircraft Carriers

The only significant amendment made to the original Washington provisions was the abolition of the 'treaty-exempt' category of air-capable vessels below 10,000 tons standard displacement. From this time, under Article 3 paragraph 1, all vessels 'designed for the specific and exclusive purpose of carrying aircraft', whatever their displacement, would be classified as aircraft carriers and would be subject to the overall tonnage limits laid down for this category. The change specifically targeted Japan, which was proposing to build a number of small treaty-exempt carriers to supplement the converted fleet carriers *Akagi* and *Kaga*, and which had a prototype, the 7,100-ton *Ryujo*, already on the stocks. In mitigation, landing-on or flying-off decks could now be fitted to cruisers (see below). However, while this was of potential benefit to the United States, which had cruiser tonnage to spare, this was not the case for Japan, which was already close to her maximum allocation.

Although aircraft carriers displacing 10,000 tons or less were now to be included in total carrier tonnage, under Article 4 paragraph 1 they were restricted to guns of a maximum 6.1in (155mm) calibre. This new provision was included to prevent a power classifying what was effectively a cruiser armed with 8in guns – now a restricted category (see below) – as an aircraft carrier. However, aircraft carriers above the 10,000-ton limit could still be armed with 8in guns, as in the original Washington Treaty provisions.

The overall tonnage limit for aircraft carriers was unchanged, which meant that just under 50 per cent of the US Navy's 135,000-ton allocation was taken up by the converted battlecruisers *Lexington* and *Saratoga*. While the latter were fine ships,

The IJN's *Ryujo*, laid down in 1929 with an declared displacement of 7,100tW, was designed as a 'treaty-exempt' carrier. This loophole was closed in the London Treaty of 1930, and *Ryujo* was redesigned with a double hangar and twice the complement of aircraft. *(Fukui Shizuo collection)*

since their completion they had been subjected to considerable criticism in the United States from within the naval aviation community,[2] which favoured a larger number of smaller (and therefore more flexible/survivable) flight decks – hence the US Navy's interest in the 'flying deck cruiser' proposed at the conference and allowed under the provisions of the Treaty.

Britain, France and Italy were relatively content with the new provisions for aircraft carriers, and the latter two powers showed little interest in taking up their existing allocation. However, following the abolition of the 'treaty-exempt' category, the IJN would have to rethink its current strategy. In order to get the full value from its investment in *Ryujo*, the Naval General Staff insisted on doubling the planned air complement from twenty-four to forty-eight aircraft; a second hangar was superimposed above the first, which not only increased displacement but would result in serious stability problems when the ship was completed in 1933 (see *WAW* Chapter 7).

Cruisers

The new restrictions on cruisers were arguably the most significant modification to the Washington Treaty and have historically attracted the most attention. The London Treaty decreed an end to 8in cruiser construction, although it proved impossible to secure a corresponding reduction in maximum displacement in the face of resolute opposition from the US delegation. Britain and Japan agreed that they would lay down no further 8in cruisers, and the USA would be permitted to lay down only three further sub-category (a) ships at prescribed intervals to arrive at their agreed ceiling of eighteen. All other future cruisers would mount guns with a maximum calibre of 6.1in (155mm). The various proposals and the discussions are detailed in *WAW* Chapter 11, and the overall tonnage totals finally agreed are set out in Table 1.1.

Table 1.1: **The New Tonnage Allocations by Category**

	Great Britain	United States	Japan
Cruisers:			
(a) with guns of more than 6.1in (155mm) calibre	146,800tW[1]	180,000tW	108,400tW (=60%)[2]
(b) with guns of 6.1in (155mm) calibre or less	192,200tW	143,500tW	100,450tW (=70%)
Destroyers	150,000tW	150,000tW	105,500tW (=70%)
Submarines	52,700tW	52,700tW	52,700tW (=100%)

Notes:
[1] tW = tons (Washington) standard
[2] percentage of US allocation

Britain and Japan were already close to the upper limits. New cruiser construction would therefore have to come from the scrapping of older vessels. This was less of a problem for Britain because of the decision at the conference to divide the cruisers currently in service into vessels laid down prior to 1 January 1920, which could be replaced sixteen years after completion, and those laid down after 31 December 1919, which would have to remain in service for twenty years. The theoretical justification for this clause was that cruisers in the latter category were necessarily of modern design that took into account the experience of the Great War of 1914–18. None of the thirty-nine existing British 6in cruisers fell into this category, having been laid down in or before 1918. However, eight of the ten American ships and ten of the twenty-one Japanese ships had been laid down after 1 January 1920, so could not be replaced before 1942–43, despite the fact that the US Navy's *Omaha* and the IJN's *Nagara* and *Sendai* types were dated designs, differing little in conception and capabilities from the cruisers being built by the Royal Navy at the end of the war. This posed a particular problem for Japan, which would have to wait until 1935 to release much of its existing tonnage for new construction (see Table 1.2).

Great Britain

For the Royal Navy, the issue was now to work within this statutory framework to secure the reduced overall figure of fifty cruisers deemed essential to support the fleet and protect trade. Although the ability to decommission large numbers of war-built cruisers at a comparatively early date favoured the Navy, the small turbine-powered 'fleet' cruisers that had scouted for Admiral Jellicoe in the North Sea had a unit displacement of around 4,000 tons, whereas their more modern replacements would be significantly larger. Trade protection, which was now the priority for the RN, required ships with good endurance, sufficient firepower to engage enemy cruisers operating on the high seas, and the ability to operate at least two aircraft; this required a ship with a minimum displacement of 6,000–7,000 tons – 50/75 per cent greater than that of the small 'fleet' cruiser.

Table 1.2: **Replacement Schedules for Existing Sub-category (b) Cruisers**

British Commonwealth of Nations

Number/Class	Unit Displacement	Gun Armament	Completed	Replacement
Laid down before 1 January 1920				
Dartmouth	4,800tW	8 – 6in	1911	1927
3 Chatham	5,120tW	8/9 – 6in	1914	1930
3 Caroline	3,895tW	4 – 6in	1915	1931
6 Cambrian	3,920tW	4 – 6in	1915–16	1931–32
2 Centaur	4,120tW	4 – 6in	1916	1932
3 Caledon	4,180tW	5 – 6in	1916	1932
5 Ceres	4,290tW	5 – 6in	1917–18	1933–34
5 Carlisle	4,200tW	5 – 6in	1918–22	1934–38
Adelaide	5,100tW	9 – 6in	1922	1938
8 'D'	4,850tW	6 – 6in	1918–22	1934–38
2 'E'	7,550t/7,580tW	7 – 6in	1926	1942
Laid down after 31 December 1919				
[None]				

Total: 39 ships of **177,625tW**

United States

Number/Class	Unit Displacement	Gun Armament	Completed	Replacement
Laid down before 1 January 1920				
2 Omaha	7,050tW	10 – 6in	1923	1939
Laid down after 31 December 1919				
8 Omaha	7,050tW	10 – 6in	1923–25	1943–45

Total: 10 ships of **70,500tW**

Japan

Number/Class	Unit Displacement	Gun Armament	Completed	Replacement
Laid down before 1 January 1920				
Tone	3,760tW	2 – 15cm, 8 – 12cm	1910	1926
3 Chikuma	4,400tW	8 – 15cm	1912	1928
2 Tenryu	3,230tW	4 – 14cm	1919	1935
5 Kuma	5,100tW	7 – 14cm	1920–21	1936–37[1]
Laid down after 31 December 1919				
Yubari	2,890tW	6 – 14cm	1923	1939[2]
6 Nagara	5,170tW	7 – 14cm	1922–25	1942–45
3 Sendai	5,195tW	7 – 14cm	1924–25	1944–45

Total: 21 ships of **98,415tW**

Notes:
[1] Article 20 allowed the Japanese to replace the cruiser *Tama* (completed 1921) by new construction to be completed during the year 1936, meaning that two of the five ships could be disposed of in that year.
[2] Because she displaced less than 3,000 tons, *Yubari* could theoretically have been replaced after sixteen years.

The British naval delegation at the London conference was well aware of these implications for numbers. Two of the four surviving large cruisers of the *Hawkins* class (which ironically had been a major influence on the 10,000-ton, 8in qualitative limit agreed at Washington) could be replaced under the sixteen-year rule in 1934–35, and Britain secured permission to dispose of their two sisters, *Frobisher* and *Effingham*, which had been laid down in 1916–17 but whose completion had been delayed until 1924–25, during the year 1936. The disposal of these four over-sized ships would release 39,416 tons, equivalent to six ships of 6,500 tons.

British post-London cruiser policy was coherent and detailed, with a set programme of construction to be completed by 31 December 1936. However, changes would be forced on the Royal Navy by developments abroad (see below and Chapter 4).

The United States of America
The US Navy was in a completely different situation. The General Board still favoured a long-range scouting force of twenty-three 10,000-ton cruisers, but the USA was now limited to eighteen ships armed with 8in guns. On the other hand, the US Navy now had a surfeit of tonnage available for the construction of sub-category (b) ships. Various proposals for cruisers armed with 6in guns, together with a separate proposal for a 'flying deck cruiser', would be considered in the wake of the London Treaty (see Chapter 4). However, following the IJN's declaration of its intention to lay down ships with an main armament of fifteen 6.1in guns (*Mogami* class), the US Navy would opt to complete its long-range cruiser scouting force with a class of similar ships, protection being on a par with the latest 8in cruisers of the *New Orleans* class.

Japan
Japan had been reluctant to abandon the construction of the 10,000-ton, 8in cruiser, which was a key element in its strategy to defeat the more numerous US fleet in the western Pacific. A new class of four ships derived from the latest *Takao* type was scheduled to be ordered under the 1931 Programme, and the IJN opted simply to replace the twin 8in turret of these ships with a triple turret armed with a new long-range 6.1in (15.5cm) 60-calibre gun. This was to have a major impact on both the US and the British cruiser programmes.

However, because Japan was close to the prescribed ceiling for sub-category (b) cruisers, new ships could be authorised only by using replacement tonnage, and many of the smaller cruisers currently in service had been laid down after 31 December 1919 and could not be replaced until 1942–43. The four elderly scout cruisers of the *Tone* and *Chikuma* classes could be disposed of immediately, releasing 16,960 tons. Even with the 2,035 tons currently available, however, this was barely sufficient for two new ships, and further units could not be completed until 1935–36, when the two 3,230-ton cruisers of the *Tenryu* class and two of the five 5,100-ton cruisers of the *Kuma* class became over-age (see Table 1.2). The displacement of the

As they were laid down after 31 December 1919, the Japanese cruisers of the *Sendai* class and eight of the ten 'scouts' of the US *Omaha* class would have to remain in service for 20 twenty years, despite their dated design. This was not a problem for the US Navy, which had more sub-category (b) tonnage than it knew what to do with, but imposed severe constraints on the construction of new ships armed with 15.5cm guns for the IJN. USS *Marblehead* (CL-12), seen here, was completed only in 1924, the Japanese ships in 1924–25, meaning that they could not be replaced until 1944–45. Both the Americans and the Japanese opted to employ these ships as leaders of the destroyer flotillas during the 1930s. *(NHHC, NH 67628 and NH 42152)*

Table 1.3: **The British and Japanese Destroyer Inventories 1930**

British Commonwealth of Nations

Number/Class	Unit Displacement	Armament	Completed	Replacement
Laid down before 1 January 1920				
11 'R' class	760–905tW	3 – 4in, 4 TT	1916–17	1928–29
50(+7)[1] 'S' class	790–905tW	3 – 4in, 4 TT	1919–20	1931–32
3(+1) *Saumarez*[2]	1,310tW	3/4 – 4in, 4 TT	1916–17	1928–29
48 'V'&'W'	1,090–1,120tW	4 – 4in, 6 TT	1917–18	1929–30
5 *Shakespeare*	1,310tW	5 – 4.7in, 6 TT	1917–25	1929–37
7 *Scott*	1,530–1,580tW	5 – 4.7in, 6 TT	1918–19	1930–31
16 Mod 'W'	1,140tW	4 – 4.7in, 6 TT	1919–24	1931–36
Laid down after 31 December 1919				
2 *Amazon*	1,173–1,352tW	4 – 4.7in, 8 TT	1927	1943
Codrington	1,520tW	5 – 4.7in, 8 TT	1930	1946
8 'A' class	1,330tW	4 – 4.7in, 8 TT	1930	1946
Keith	1,330tW	4 – 4.7in, 8 TT	[1931]	
8(+2) 'B' class	1,330tW	4 – 4.7in, 8 TT	[1931]	

Total: 150 destroyers of 157,585W in service; 18 ships of 24,130tW building.

new 15-gun cruisers therefore had to be kept to 8,500 tons. This was ambitious to say the least, and would lead to costly design errors (see Chapter 4).

France and Italy

France and Italy had not signed up to Part III of the London Treaty, so neither navy was subject to overall quantitative limits for its cruisers. Both embarked on 6in cruiser construction once their respective programmes of 8in 'treaty' cruisers were complete, but a combination of a world economic depression, the resumption of costly capital ship programmes, and a general desire not to embark on construction that might be considered by the other major powers to be destabilising or escalatory, meant that ships of modest displacement, built in modest numbers, resulted. Instead of concerning themselves with developments in the Far East, which were a major preoccupation for Britain and the USA, the French and Italian navies simply watched one another and responded when they felt the situation required.

Destroyers

The quantitative ceilings agreed at London 1930 for Britain and Japan were just below current levels: 150,000 tons (currently 150 ships of 157,585W, with eighteen ships of 24,130tW in build) for the former, 105,500 tons (currently 106 ships of 110,395tW, but with thirteen ships of 22,100tW in build) for the latter. The United States, which retained large numbers of the 1,000-ton mass-produced 'flush-deckers', had considerable excess tonnage, but most of these ships were in reserve and could be disposed of immediately. Japan had invested heavily in destroyers, which it

Japan

Number/Class	Unit Displacement	Armament	Completed	Replacement
Laid down before 1 January 1920				
[2nd class]				
2 *Sakura*	530tW	1 – 12cm, 4 TT	1912	1924
10 *Kaba*	595tW	1 – 12cm, 4 TT	1915	1927
4 *Momo*	755tW	3 – 12cm, 6 TT	1916–17	1928–29
6 *Enoki*	770tW	3 – 12cm, 6 TT	1918	1930
9 *Momi*	770tW	3 – 12cm, 4 TT	1919–21	1931–33
[1st class]				
2 *Umikaze*	1,030tW	2 – 12cm, 4 TT	1911	1923
Urakaze	810tW	1 – 12cm, 4 TT	1915	1927
4 *Isokaze*	1,105tW	4 – 12cm, 6 TT	1917	1929
2 *Tanikaze*	1,180tW	3 – 12cm, 6 TT	1919–20	1931–32
6 *Minekaze*	1,215tW	4 – 12cm, 6 TT	1920	1932
Laid down after 31 December 1919				
[2nd class]				
11 *Momi*	770tW	3 – 12cm, 4 TT	1919–21	1935–37
8 *Wakatabe*	820tW	3 – 12cm, 4 TT	1923–24	1939–40
[1st class]				
9 *Minekaze*	1,215tW	4 – 12cm, 6 TT	1921–22	1937–38
9 *Kamikaze*	1,270tW	4 – 12cm, 6 TT	1922–25	1938–41
12 *Mutsuki*	1,315tW	4 – 12cm, 6 TT	1925–27	1941–43
10 *Fubuki*	1,700tW[3]	6 – 12.7cm, 9 TT	1928–29	1944–45
10 *Ayanami*	1,700tW	6 – 12.7cm, 9 TT	1929–31	1945–47
4 *Akatsuki*	1,700tW	6 – 12.7cm, 9 TT	[1932]	

Total: 106 destroyers of 110,395tW in service; 13 ships of 22,100tW building.

Notes:
1 Number of Commonwealth ships in brackets..
2 Names in **Bold** were classified as 'Leaders' by the RN.
3 All 24 of the Japanese destroyers of the 'Special Type' were designated 'large destroyers' under the London Treaty.

divided into first class (generally 1,100+ tons) and second class (c.800 tons), so would need to dispose of many of its older vessels in order to keep within its 105,500-ton allocation.

Britain

British plans for a flotilla of eight new destroyers plus a flotilla leader in each successive financial year – three classes ('A', 'B' and 'C') were already authorised or building – were essentially unaffected, as the bulk of the destroyers currently in service had been laid down prior to 1 January 1920 and could be replaced twelve years after their completion. Moreover, no fewer than sixty-eight – the figure includes seven ships in service with the Royal Australian and Canadian Navies – of the 150 ships currently in service were of the smaller 'S' and 'R' types, which were approaching obsolescence.

The new generation of destroyers would all be 'fleet' units. In the event of war, it was envisaged that the older destroyers, which were fast and could be fitted with ASDIC, could be employed to form anti-submarine hunting groups, while convoy escort would be provided by a new generation of sloops built under the Treaty-exempt 'small combatants and auxiliary vessels' category (see Chapter 7).

The United States of America
The USA had not laid down a single destroyer during the period 1922–30 due to its surplus of war-built ships, but was preparing to embark on the construction of modern destroyers. By disposing of many of its over-age ships it would have more than sufficient capacity to build up to the newly established ceiling.

Japan
Japan currently had a fleet of fifty-six first-class destroyers (see Table 1.3) with a further thirteen in build, and of these no fewer than thirty-six were of modern design. There were nine 1,100-ton destroyers of First World War vintage that could be disposed of immediately in favour of new construction, and six of the fifteen ships of the *Minekaze* class had been laid down prior to 1 January 1920, so could be replaced during the 1930–36 time frame. The IJN had discontinued the construction of second-class destroyers in the early 1920s, but there remained fifty ships in the inventory, of which thirty-one could be disposed of in 1930–31; the remaining nineteen ships, which were of 770/820 tons and armed with three 12cm guns and four torpedo tubes, and were therefore comparable to the British war-built 'R' and 'S' classes, would have to remain in service until 1936.

There was an additional complication for the IJN. The London Treaty imposed a

The large Japanese destroyers of the 'Special Type', nominally of 1,700tW but overweight on completion, were a major concern for the British and the Americans. The provisions of London 1930 were specifically designed to preclude further construction of these powerful ships. This is *Amagiri* shortly after her completion in November 1930. *(Leo van Gineren collection)*

limit of 1,500 tons on 'standard' ships in the destroyer category, and only 16 per cent of destroyer tonnage could be allocated to ships of 1,500–1,850 tons displacement (Article 16, paragraph 4). The latter provision allowed for the larger British flotilla leaders, but effectively precluded the continued construction of the Japanese 'super-destroyers' of the 'Special Type', of which no fewer than twenty-four had been completed or were in build. These already accounted for a substantial proportion of Japan's destroyer tonnage allocation (40,800 tons, or just under 40 per cent), so there was no prospect of laying down further ships. The IJN would therefore opt to restrict the displacement of its next class of destroyers to 1,400 tons. Nevertheless, the Japanese Naval General Staff continued to insist on a gun and torpedo armament comparable to that of the 'Special Type'. As with the new 6.1in cruisers of the *Mogami* class, this would result in serious stability and structural issues, followed by a costly reconstruction.

France and Italy

France and Italy were again unaffected by the new quantitative limits, having opted out of Part III of the London Treaty. However, bottlenecks in industry and the ship-yards were now having a major impact on the French programme of flotilla craft. Authorisation for the six units of the *Le Fantasque* class (see *WAW* Chapter 10) had been delayed for one year; laid down in 1931–32, they would not enter service until 1936. The French would complete a series of thirty large fleet scouts (*contre-torpilleurs*) built in successive tranches of six, but only two further ships of the type would be authorised in the period 1930–36. These would be complemented by the first of a new generation of destroyers (*torpilleurs d'escadre*) intended to accompany the new fast battleships, but delays in construction were such that the name-ship, *Le Hardi*, entered service only in June 1940, when the Second World War was nine months old.

Italy was less affected by problems in the shipyards, but the economic downturn, together with expenditure on a new generation of capital ships, had an inevitable impact. Four large destroyers of a new type were authorised in 1930 and a repeat class of four in 1935, but it would be 1936 before Italy again embarked in earnest on the construction of fleet destroyers.

Submarines

Whereas 'standard' displacement for surface vessels had been defined at the Washington Conference, this was not the case for submarines, for which separate 'surfaced' and 'submerged' displacements were in general use. The new definition can be found in Part II, Article 6 paragraph 2 of the London Treaty (see Appendix), and had to be calculated retrospectively for all existing units.

The tonnage allocation agreed for each of the three major powers was a uniform 52,700 tons. On the face of it this was a remarkable *volte-face* in favour of Japan, which was permitted only 60 per cent of British and US tonnage in capital ships and 8in cruisers, and 70 per cent in the 6in cruiser and destroyer categories. However, in reality this was simply another move on the part of Britain and the United States to restrain Japanese ambitions. The IJN was the only one of the three major naval powers with an established and ongoing programme of large submarine construction, and regarded 78,000 tons as a *minimum* figure if its submarine arm was to successfully implement its twin strategies of long-range surveillance and attrition of the US Battle Fleet based at Pearl Harbor and on the West Coast. The British Royal Navy, on the other hand, which had embarked on a series of 1,400-ton overseas patrol submarines (OPS) from the mid-1920s, was at a point of transition, with new designs that included a large, fast 'fleet' submarine (*Thames*) for the Far East, a smaller boat designed for North Sea operations (*Swordfish*) and a minelayer (*Porpoise*) on the drawing board. The lead units of two of these types had been authorised under the 1929–30 Estimates, but orders had been postponed to await the outcome of the London Conference. The US Navy was likewise at a crossroads: having completed no fewer than fifty 800-ton boats of the 'S' class, designed during the First World War, during the early 1920s, the Navy had turned its attention to huge cruiser submarines which could transit the Pacific before embarking on their patrols. However, it was now having serious doubts about this programme (see *WAW* Chapter 9). At the conference the US naval delegation initially attempted to restrict the displacement of individual submarines to 1,800 tons – a proposal the British were happy to support, given that their new fleet submarine had a projected displacement of 1,760 tons – but this move was successfully resisted by the Japanese.

Most of the older British submarine construction dated from the end of the First World War, so could be steadily replaced by new construction. However, the current US Navy and IJN submarine inventories (see Table 1.4) largely surpassed the 52,700-ton figure. Many of these boats were small, relatively short-ranged types that would be of limited use in a Pacific war. However, submarines completed in the mid-1920s could not be replaced by new construction until well after the Washington Treaty expired. This initially created problems for both navies, but particularly for the Japanese. The IJN was faced with an additional complication: for every new fleet submarine (*Kaidai*) of 1,600 tons built, two older 800-ton boats would need to be scrapped, and for a new cruiser submarine (*Junsen*) the corresponding figure was 2.5. As a special concession, Article 20 paragraph (d) stated that 'Japan may anticipate replacement during the term of the present treaty by laying down not more than 19,200 tons (19,507 metric tons) of submarine tonnage, of which not more than 12,000 tons (12,192 metric tons) shall be completed by the 31st December, 1936.'

Although each of the high contracting powers was permitted to retain three 'oversize' submarines of 2,000–2,800 tons (Article 7, paragraph 2) – the provision was agreed to cover the US Navy's cruiser submarines *Narwhal*, *Nautilus* and *Argonaut* and the French *Surcouf* – it was made clear that these boats would need to be counted in the overall tonnage allocation. This would act as a powerful incentive to replace these submarines by smaller boats when they approached the end of their statutory thirteen-year lifespan. Consideration was given to excluding coastal submarines of 600 tons or less from the submarine allocation, and moving them into the Treaty-

Table 1.4: **Submarine Inventories 1930**

British Commonwealth of Nations

Number/Class	Unit Displacement	Armament	Completed	Replacement
1 'R' class	385tW	6 TT	1919	1932
14 'H' class	410tW	4 TT	1918–20	1931–33
2 'S' class	640tW	1 – 3in, 6 TT	[authorised]	
19 'L' class	760tW	1/2 – 4in, 6 TT	1917–19	1930–32
6 'L' class	845tW	1 – 4in, 4/6 TT	1919–26	1932–39
2 'M' class	1,450tW	a/c, mines, 4 TT	1920	1933
1 'K' class	1,710tW	3 – 4in, 10 TT	1923	1936
X 1	2,425tW	4 – 5.2in, 6 TT	1925	1938
1(+2) *Oberon*	1,311–1,354tW	1 – 4in, 8 TT	1927	1940
6 'O' class	1,475tW	1 – 4in, 8 TT	1929	1942
6 'P' class	1,475tW	1 – 4in, 8 TT	1930	1943
4 'R' class	1,475tW	1 – 4in, 8 TT	[1931]	
1 'River'	1,760tW	1 – 4.7in, 6 TT	[authorised]	

Total: 53 submarines of 45,534tW in service; 10 of 14,750tW building.

United States

Number/Class	Unit Displacement	Armament	Completed	Replacement
65 small	650tW or less	4 TT	[most 1918–20]	[most 1931–33]
50 'S' class	730–850tW	1 – 4in, 4 TT	1920–25	1933–38
3 'T' class	1,010tW	2 – 3in, 6 TT	1920–22	1933–35
V1–3	1,910tW	1 – 5in, 6 TT	1924–26	1937–39
V4	2,660tW	2 – 6in, 4 TT, mines	1928	1941
V5–6	2,760tW	2 – 6in, 4 TT	1930	1943
V7–9	1,550tW	1 – 3/4in, 6 TT	[authorised]	

Total: 122 submarines of 80,700tW, of which 31 of 16,120tW Listed for Disposal and 14 of 5,180tW over-age; 5 submarines of 10,170tW building or authorised.

Note that these figures are from the tables drawn up by the British delegation; the US Navy's *V8–9* would be completed to a smaller design in 1934 (see Chapter 6).

Japan

Number/Class	Unit Displacement	Armament	Completed	Replacement
[2nd class]				
15 K1–4 type	717–746tW	1 – 8cm, 6 TT	1919–24	1932–37
5 F1–2 type	682–686tW	5 TT	1920–22	1933–35
9 L1–3 type	889–893tW	1 – 8cm, 4/6 TT	1920–23	1933–36
9 L4 type	988tW	1 – 8cm, 6 TT	1923–26	1936–39
4 KT type	655tW	1 – 12cm, 4 TT	1923–27	1936–40

Total: 50 submarines of 36,610tW.

Number/Class	Unit Displacement	Armament	Completed	Replacement
[1st class]				
2 KD1–2	1,390tW	1 – 12cm, 8 TT	1924–25	1937–38
4 J1	1,955tW	2 – 14cm, 6 TT	1926–29	1939–42
4 KRS	1,142tW	1 – 14cm, 4 TT, mines	1927–28	1940–41
1 J1M	1,955tW	1 – 14cm, 6 TT, a/c	1930	1943
9 KD3	1,635tW	1 – 14cm, 8 TT	1927–30	1940–43
3 KD4	1,635tW	1 – 14cm, 6 TT	1929–30	1942–43
3 KD5	1,638tW	1 – 10cm, 6 TT	[1932]	

Total: 19 submarines of 29,883tW in service; 7 of 11,774tW building.

exempt 'small combatant' category as a complement to the 600-ton torpedo boat type (see Chapter 7); however, this proposal was not agreed. The 'size versus numbers' equation would impact on all three of the major navies, which were compelled to review their existing programmes of construction in the light of the new qualitative and quantitative limitations.

The French and Italian navies were only minimally impacted by the new qualitative limitations – planned successors to the French *Surcouf* had to be abandoned – as the Italian cruiser submarines and the French fleet boats had a standard displacement well below 2,000 tons. France and Italy refused to sign Part III of the London Treaty and were therefore free to build as many submarines as they wished; the French were constrained only by shipyard capacity and finance, as were the Italians.

Chapter 2

CAPITAL SHIPS 1930–36

THE EXTENSION OF THE 'BATTLESHIP HOLIDAY' by a further five years was greeted with a sense of relief by the major naval powers, all of which were now in the throes of a world economic recession that imposed its own limits on the funding of new construction. However, the international situation, which had remained relatively stable during the 1920s, was already beginning to deteriorate. Italy was endeavouring to manipulate an unstable political situation in the Balkans to its advantage, and was looking to increase its power and influence in the Eastern Mediterranean and in North and East Africa. Japan was in dispute with the government of China on a number of trade issues. During the early 1930s the prospect of military conflict between the major powers, which had been unthinkable in the era of Collective Security, appeared more likely, and in the longer term inevitable. In 1932 the British Government finally abandoned the 'Ten-Year Rule' that had dominated its military planning after Washington, and which assumed no major war for the next ten years.

In this climate it would have been folly to allow the existing battle fleets to fall into neglect. There were also two important new factors, one of which was a natural outcome of the London Treaty itself. In the absence of new construction, capital ships that would have been due for replacement over the next few years would now have to be modernised. Moreover, these upgrades would need to take into account a much-increased aerial threat. During the 1920s the threat posed by torpedo bombers had provided part of the rationale for bulges and liquid-loaded underwater protection systems, and for batteries of medium-range HA guns with specially developed fire control systems. By the 1930s there was a new aerial threat from the dive bomber, as yet in embryonic form but promising the accurate delivery of heavy ordnance from directly above the ship. Countermeasures would have to include heavily armoured decks, and quick-firing cannon and multiple machine guns with high speeds of elevation and training.

The additional passive and active defensive systems necessary to counter aerial bombing not only entailed a substantial financial investment, but there was a design cost in terms of topweight. This encouraged a trend towards a more fundamental reconstruction of older capital ships during the 1930s. The US Navy, the IJN and the French had installed new boilers in some ships in the years that followed Washington (see *WAW* Chapter 5), and in many cases a smaller number of large boilers had replaced a multitude of smaller boilers, but the primary motivation for these changes had been the substitution of modern oil-fired boilers for the older-type boilers with mixed or coal firing, thereby improving efficiency, facilitating maintenance and reducing the number of personnel required. During the 1930s, however, the advent of high-pressure steam conditions and lightweight turbines permitted more radical solutions, in which spaces formerly occupied by propulsion machinery could be freed up and used for additional magazines, fuel tanks or auxiliary machinery, while in some cases permitting an increase in speed by 3 or 4 knots.

Reconstructions in the Royal Navy

One unexpected benefit of the forced decommissioning under the London Treaty of the elderly battleships of the *Iron Duke* class was that these hulls were then available for trials and testing. It was decided that *Emperor of India* should be employed for tests against gunfire at longer ranges, and that *Marlborough* should be used to test the effects of aerial bombs. These tests took place during 1931, and demonstrated conclusively the inadequacy of the horizontal protection of ships designed prior to Jutland. It was noted that both the Americans and the Japanese had spent considerable sums on boosting the horizontal protection of their older capital ships, and it was decided that additional deck armour would be fitted above magazines and machinery spaces in all ships except *Hood* and the two *Nelson*s at their next major refit.

    Barham was the only ship of the *Queen Elizabeth* class yet to be modernised, and she would be the first to benefit from the more extensive upgrades proposed. She was duly taken in hand in January 1931. In addition to the bulges and the bridge/mast/funnel modifications of the ships modernised during the 1920s (see *WAW* Chapter 5) she was fitted with 4in NC armour on the original 1in plating above and just beyond the main magazines, at a cost of 500 tons in weight. She also received two of the new HACS Mk I fire control systems for her four single 4in HA guns, together with two of the new eight-barrelled 2pdr pom-pom mountings, and a powerful EIT catapult for a Fairey IIIF reconnaissance floatplane was fitted atop No. 3 ('X') turret. The refit at Portsmouth Dockyard took three years and cost £424,000, more than twice the figure for her sister *Warspite*.

    The next two ships to be taken in hand were the battleship *Malaya* and the battlecruiser *Repulse*, which received additional modifications. *Repulse*, taken in hand in April 1934, received 3¾in NC armour on 2in HT steel over the magazines and 2½in NC armour on 1in plating over her engine rooms – the latter decision having being taken on the basis of the *Marlborough/Emperor of India* trials. She was the first British capital ship to have purpose-built facilities for operating recce/spotter aircraft; these comprised a DIIH double-ended cross-deck catapult fitted at the level of the forecastle deck amidships, with twin hangars abreast the second funnel and cranes capable of handling the aircraft and the ship's boats. As in *Barham*, two HACS systems (Mk I*

The battlecruiser *Repulse* following her major refit in 1934–36. Note the twin aircraft hangars abeam the second funnel and the twin aircraft handling cranes. The Spanish Civil War recognition stripes on 'B' turret suggest that the photo was taken during 1937–38. *(RAN Seapower Centre)*

A close-up of the battleship *Malaya* taken at Malta in 1937. The photo shows clearly the twin aircraft hangars abeam the funnel with their handling cranes, and the heavy cross-deck catapult. Also prominent are the starboard-side twin 4in HA Mark XIX gun mountings and one of the two 8-barrelled, 2pdr pom-poms.

+ Mk II) were fitted for the four single 4in HA guns, and in addition to the latter there were two experimental twin 4in 'between decks' (BD) mountings aft; there were also two eight-barrelled 2pdr pom-pom mountings. The only weight compensation was the removal of the submerged torpedo tubes, the torpedo conning tower, and the sealed 'crushing tubes' from the bulges. Cost was a massive £1.4 million.

Malaya, which began her modernisation in October 1934, was similarly modified, except that the armour over the magazines was on the same scale as *Barham*. A smaller, lighter conning tower was fitted in place of the original to save 220 tons, but the ship was still expected to float 5in (13cm) deeper than her sister ship. As well as the latest HACS Mk III, *Malaya* received four of the new twin 4in Mk XIX mountings, the first installation of this mounting in a British capital ship; this would subsequently become standard on the older battleships. The anti-aircraft armament also included two eight-barrelled 2pdr pom-pom mountings. The cost of *Malaya*'s modernisation was just under £1 million, less than that of *Repulse* but more than twice that of *Barham*.

Table 2.1: Royal Navy Capital Ship Reconstruction 1930–1936

Ship	Date	Focus of modernisation
Barham	1931–34	bulges, horizontal protection, HACS
Repulse	1934–36	horizontal protection, HACS, twin 4in HA in BD mountings, cross-deck catapult + hangars
Royal Oak	1934–36	horizontal protection, HACS + twin 4in HA
Malaya	1934–36	horizontal protection, HACS + twin 4in HA, cross-deck catapult + hangars
Warspite	1934–37	new machinery, elevation main guns, horizontal protection, HACS + twin 4in HA, cross-deck catapult + hangars, new bridge structure
Renown	1936–39	new machinery, elevation main guns, horizontal protection, HACS + twin 4.5in DP, cross-deck catapult + hangars, new bridge structure

The only ship of the 'R' class to undergo a major refit was *Royal Oak*, which was refitted at roughly the same time as *Malaya*. She received 900 tons of deck armour, distributed as on the latter ship, together with the new HA outfit, but these ships were more compact and less spacious than the *Queen Elizabeth*s, so aircraft facilities were restricted to a heavy catapult on 'X' turret, as in *Barham*. The other 'R's were fitted with the twin 4in gun mounting and HACS, together with the heavy catapult, but were never taken in hand for the projected upgrade to their horizontal protection due to the demands of the new building and reconstruction programmes in the Royal Dockyards from 1936 to 1939.

By 1935–36 all of these ships were twenty years old, and despite extensive and costly reconstruction they retained their original machinery, which now required extensive maintenance and was inefficient, particularly at lower speeds. It was therefore decided to embark on a more radical reconstruction of the battleship *Warspite*, which might then serve as a model for further reconstructions. The refit was begun in March 1934 (*ie* seven months before the modernisation of *Malaya*), but was to take three years.

The original twenty-four large-tube Yarrow boilers were replaced by six modern

Warspite 1936 (GB)

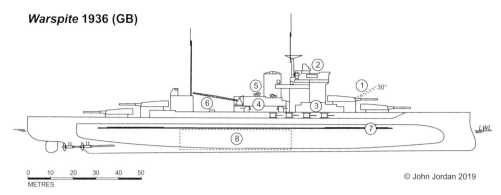

© John Jordan 2019

Warspite was the prototype for a planned major reconstruction of the five ships of the *Queen Elizabeth* class. The principal modifications were:

1 elevation of main 15in guns increased from 20 to 30 degrees, increasing range from 23,400 yards to 29,000 yards
2 new slab-sided bridge structure with armoured DCT for main guns; pole foremast in place of original tripod
3 only eight (four per side) 6in guns of the original 14-gun secondary casemate battery retained
4 four twin 4in HA mountings with sided HACS III fire control
5 four 8-barrelled 2pdr 'pom-pom' mountings atop hangar for close-in air defence
6 twin hangars either side of funnel with cross-deck heavy catapult for three/four large reconnaissance/spotter aircraft
7 2½in NC armour over machinery spaces and 4in NC over magazines fore and aft
8 new propulsion machinery: six of the latest Admiralty 3-drum boilers with single funnel and four sets of lightweight geared turbines.

Warspite: Machinery

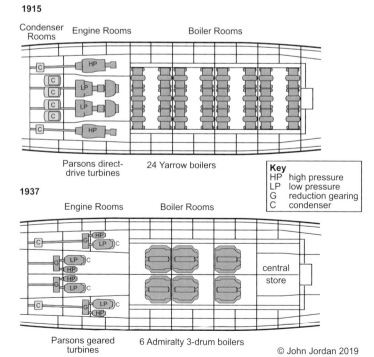

© John Jordan 2019

Admiralty three-drum boilers with a steam pressure of 400lb/in^2 (28kg/cm^2). These were installed in three of the four original boiler rooms, with new centreline bulkheads to improve subdivision. New lightweight turbines with single-reduction gearing replaced the original direct-drive models, and the engine room arrangements were likewise revised to improve subdivision, four turbine rooms and four separate gearing rooms being provided. These measures reduced machinery weight from 3,691 tons to 2,300 tons, and a further 675 tons was saved by reducing the 6in secondary battery to four guns on either side and thinning their protection to 2in plating, and by removing the original conning tower. These weight savings could then be invested in additional horizontal protection (the 2½in NC armour fitted over the engine rooms in *Warspite*'s sisters was extended to take in the boiler rooms as well), and into measures to improve the ship's fighting power.

The elevation of the main guns was increased from 20 to 30 degrees, and maximum range increased correspondingly from 23,400 yards to 29,000 yards with the older-type shell and to 32,200 yards with new shell. A completely new modern slab-sided bridge structure topped by an armoured director control tower (DCT) for the main guns was fitted, together with a heavy pole foremast, a light pole mainmast and a slim single funnel. There were four eight-barrelled 2pdr pom-poms abeam the funnel, atop the twin aircraft hangars, together with four quadruple 0.5in machine guns atop No. 2 ('B') and No. 3 ('X') turrets. The twin 4in HA mountings were at forecastle deck level with sided HACS III directors on pedestals at the after end of the bridge structure. Aviation arrangements were as in the other modernised ships.

The battleship *Warspite* in 1937 following her major reconstruction. The external evidence of the reconstruction can be seen in the massive bridge tower structure with its heavy pole foremast and the revised aircraft-handling arrangements amidships. However, equally important was the complete renewal of the propulsion machinery, with modern three-drum boilers and lightweight geared propulsion machinery.

This was a particular successful reconstruction, which would serve as a model for the battlecruiser *Renown* and for two sister ships, *Queen Elizabeth* and *Valiant*, in the late 1930s. Despite a marked increase in military capabilities, deep load displacement was only 500 tons in excess of that recorded before refit. A speed of 23.8 knots with 80,000shp was attained on trials, but even more striking was the fuel economy of the new machinery: fuel consumption at full speed was reduced from 41 tons per hour to 26.8t/h, and endurance at 10 knots increased from 8,400nm to 14,300nm.

Renown would be the last British capital ship to begin a total reconstruction before the end of the Washington Treaty period, and began refitting at Portsmouth Dockyard in September 1936. As with *Warspite*, the original machinery and superstructures were removed, and new lightweight machinery and a modern bridge fitted in their place. The new machinery installation was modelled on that of *Warspite*, but there were eight boilers occupying four of the original six spaces, the former forward boiler rooms being used for new auxiliary machinery. This enabled the twin funnels to be moved farther aft to keep smoke clear of the bridge. The new machinery saved 2,800 tons in weight and produced the same fuel economies as in *Warspite*; top speed (designed) was 30.7 knots with 120,000shp, and endurance 14,300nm at 10 knots.

The major difference from *Warspite* was the fitting of a completely new dual-purpose secondary armament, comprising ten twin 4.5in guns in a new between-decks mounting, controlled by no fewer than four HACS Mk IV directors. The 4.5in proved to be an outstanding weapon in the HA role, although there were some naval officers who felt that the 58lb (23kg) SAP shell it fired was too light to disable a destroyer. *Renown*'s horizontal protection had been upgraded in a refit in 1923–26, so additional armour was targeted at those areas that had not been so fitted: 2in NC armour over the engine rooms and 4in armour over the new 4.5in magazines, both thicknesses on existing 1in plating.

The cost of *Renown*'s refit, just over £3 million, set a new record. However, in an age of fast battleships she was to prove a very useful unit, more than capable of holding her own against the newer German battleships *Scharnhorst* and *Gneisenau* off Norway in April 1940 and serving as the flagship of Admiral James Somerville when operating with Force H in the Western Mediterranean.

The US Navy: Modernising the *New Mexicos*

The US Navy had spent large sums on the modernisation of its older dreadnought battleships during the 1920s.[1] However, of the six oldest ships of the *Florida*, *Wyoming* and *New York* classes only three would be retained in active service following the London Conference, and of the 'middle' group only four out of the seven had so far been upgraded. The priority now was to extend this modernisation to the three ships of the *New Mexico* class, none of which had a developed underwater protection system as first completed.

Between 1931 and 1934 the *New Mexico*s underwent the same basic modifications as their predecessors of the *Nevada* and *Pennsylvania* classes (see *WAW*

The US battleship *New Mexico* following modernisation. The original cage masts were landed, and the original bridge structure was replaced by a modern tower, the searchlights being grouped around the single funnel. The reconstruction involved the complete renewal of the propulsion machinery. *(NHHC, NH 60669)*

Chapter 5): deep bulges incorporating an air/liquid/air 'sandwich'-type underwater protection system were fitted, the elevation of the main guns was increased from 15 to 30 degrees, and 2in plating was fitted on the main armour deck; the splinter deck over the machinery was also reinforced from 1½ to 2⅜in (see section drawing). Catapults and an enhanced HA battery of eight 5in/25 single mountings, located atop the existing deckhouse for the secondary battery, had already been fitted during the late 1920s.

Whereas the older ships had been refitted with boilers from uncompleted ships of the 1916 programme but had retained their original turbines, the battleships of the *New Mexico* class were given completely new propulsion machinery. *Mississippi* and *Idaho* received six new Bureau Express boilers in place of their original nine older-type boilers, while *New Mexico*, which had been the trials ship for turbo-electric propulsion, received four larger White-Forster boilers. The original direct-drive turbines were replaced by new Westinghouse turbines with single-reduction gearing, which increased speed by about three quarters of a knot and improved fuel economy. The heavy tripod masts that gave the battleships of the *Nevada* and *Pennsylvania* classes their distinctive appearance were suppressed in favour of a modern tower bridge structure with light pole masts, the searchlight projectors being relocated around the single funnel. These ships were now easily distinguishable from any other US battleships in their appearance.

It was envisaged that the later US capital ships of the *Tennessee* and *Colorado* classes

Mississippi 1934 (US)

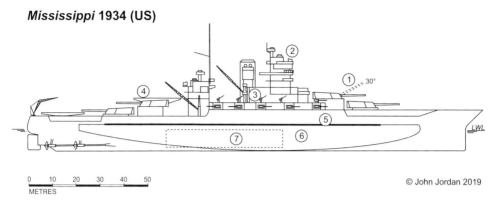

0 10 20 30 40 50
METRES

© John Jordan 2019

The three ships of the *New Mexico* class were the only US battleships to receive a major reconstruction during this period. The principal modifications were:

1 elevation of main 14in guns increased from 15 to 30 degrees, increasing range with new ammunition to 36,600 yards
2 new bridge tower with lightweight main/secondary battery directors; pole masts in place of original cage masts
3 eight (four per side) 5in HA guns (fitted 1920s) with modern HA fire control
4 catapults on turret No. 3 and quarterdeck (fitted 1920s) for three reconnaissance floatplanes
5 extra 2in NC armour over machinery spaces and magazines on original 3½in for total of 5½in
6 deep bulge with air/liquid/air 'sandwich' for underwater protection
7 new propulsion machinery: six of the latest small-watertube boilers (four of larger model in *New Mexico*) with single funnel and four sets of lightweight geared turbines.

Mississippi (US): Protection Following Reconstruction

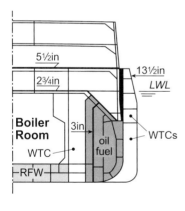

© John Jordan 2019

During their reconstruction 1932–36 the three battleships of the *New Mexico* class were fitted with deep bulges incorporating an air/liquid/air 'sandwich' system of underwater protection. The existing torpedo bulkhead was doubled in thickness..

(the 'Big Five') would receive a similar modernisation, with bulges, new machinery and new superstructures, but this was deferred at first due to the Depression and later because of the deteriorating international situation. They therefore retained their turbo-electric machinery and much of their original appearance at the outbreak of the Pacific War, by which time they were chronically overweight.

The Imperial Japanese Navy

Prior to the London Conference the Imperial Japanese Navy, like its Western counterparts, had actively planned for a new generation of capital ships to be laid down
once capital ship construction resumed, with a view to replacing the elderly *Kongo*s.
Competitive studies were produced by constructors Hiraga and Fujimoto for ships
with the maximum 35,000-ton Washington displacement armed either with nine
40.6cm (16in) guns in triple turrets or ten 40.6cm in two twin and two triple
turrets. A maximum speed of 25–26 knots was found to be possible (although at
what cost to protection is not clear), but the layout of the secondary batteries was
far from satisfactory, with a mix of casemate and turret-mounted guns in the Hiraga
design, and twin turrets mounted at the ends of the ship, outside the exceptionally
compact citadel, in the Fujimoto design. The aircraft facilities in both designs were
limited to catapults atop the main turrets. If these designs proved anything it was
that a satisfactory ship with 40.6cm guns, modern secondary and anti-aircraft
batteries, and high fleet speed could not be built on the 35,000-ton displacement
permitted under Washington.

In view of the London Conference, at which a new five-year pause in battleship
construction was agreed, the IJN's focus turned to upgrading its existing capital
ships. Under the Treaty the fourth ship of the *Kongo* class, *Hiei*, which had yet to be
modernised, would become a training ship. 'Demilitarisation' involved the removal
of No. 4 turret and the side armour belt; eleven of the original thirty-six boilers were
removed, so that she was capable of only 18 knots. Of the capital ships demilitarised
under the London Treaty, *Hiei* would be the only one to see further active service;
she would undergo a major reconstruction 1936–40 once the Washington Treaty
had expired.

In view of Japan's statutory inferiority in numbers, the emphasis was again on
qualitative superiority. For the battleships two qualities were seen to be essential: the
ability to outrange the enemy's guns, and higher tactical speed to enable the Japanese
battle line to choose the most advantageous angle of approach and to dictate the
range of engagement.

All the modernised battleships would receive extensive and costly turret modifications to permit a maximum elevation of 43 degrees. This was achieved by deepening
the gun pit and lowering the entire structure into it,[2] although loading could only be
carried out at lower angles. For the ships armed with 14in guns this meant a theoretical maximum range of 35,450m, as compared with around 31,300m for the
14in-gun ships of the US battleships, whose guns could be elevated only to
30 degrees. There was a parallel investment in the latest fire control systems: fire
control tables had been acquired from the British company Barr and Stroud for the
*Kongo*s when reconstructed in the late 1920s, and the IJN also developed its own fire
control instruments to compute target course and speed (*sokutekiban*); these complemented the standard *shagekiban* firing calculator. The IJN fire control instruments
were heavy and manpower-intensive, with manual rather than automatic inputs. In
the modernised battleships this was to result in high, top-heavy superstructures with

multiple platforms to accommodate the plethora of rangefinders and other fire control instruments.

Almost as soon as the London Conference ended, the super-dreadnoughts *Fuso* and *Yamashiro* were taken in hand for a thorough modernisation. Completed in 1915 and 1917 respectively, their twenty-four original Miyabara boilers were predominantly coal-fired. However, whereas the modernisation of the *Kongos'* propulsion plant during the 1920s had been limited to replacing the original boilers by more modern types, some of which were still coal-fired, a more radical solution was adopted for *Fuso* and her sister. It was decided to replace the entire propulsion machinery: six new Kampon ('Admiralty') oil-fired, small-tube boilers supplied the steam for four sets of Kampon geared steam turbines. This had the effect of reducing the weight of the machinery by 35 per cent while at the same time virtually doubling horsepower from 40,000shp to 75,000shp. Anti-torpedo bulges with a depth of 2.5m were fitted, but the additional drag was compensated by lengthening the stern by 7.6m, with the result that maximum speed was increased from 22.5 knots to 24.5 knots (*ie* close to that of the *Kongo* class as rebuilt in the late 1920s). The installation of modern geared turbines also meant that endurance was increased by a third.

Horizontal protection was improved as in the earlier *Kongo* modernisation by fitting additional armour to the upper and lower protective decks over the magazines and machinery; the turret roofs were also reinforced, so that the total weight of armour rose from 8,725 tonnes to 12,395 tonnes. The elevation of the main guns was raised from 33 to 43 degrees, and a modern HA battery of eight 12.7cm guns

Fuso 1935 (Jap)

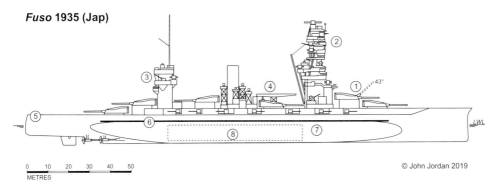

0 10 20 30 40 50
METRES

© John Jordan 2019

Fuso and her sister *Yamashiro* underwent a major reconstruction during 1932–35. The principal modifications were:

1 elevation of main 36cm guns increased from 30 to 43 degrees, increasing range to 35,450m
2 completely new superstructures: a 'pagoda'-style tower forward with multiple directors and optical fire control instruments, and a shorter tower aft with a pole mainmast
3 eight 12.7cm HA guns in twin mountings sided fore and aft with modern HA fire control
4 catapult on turret No. 3 (quarterdeck in *Yamashiro*) for three reconnaissance floatplanes
5 stern lengthened by 7.6m
6 additional NC armour over machinery spaces and magazines on main protective decks
7 deep (2.5m) bulge with multiple watertight compartments for stability and underwater protection
8 new propulsion machinery with almost double the horsepower: six of the latest Kampon small-watertube boilers with single funnel and four sets of Kampon geared turbines.

in four twin mountings was fitted, together with four twin 25mm light AA mountings when these became available.

A massive tower structure with multiple fire control platforms was built around the original tripod foremast, while the after tripod was replaced by a second, shorter tower structure topped by a pole mast; the searchlights were grouped around the remaining single funnel, and there was a single catapult atop No. 3 turret in *Fuso*, and at the stern in *Yamashiro*. These arrangements were necessary because the two widely spaced centreline turrets amidships precluded the fitting of any equipment outboard of them that might obstruct their training arcs or be subject to blast damage. The result was a precarious-looking ship in which the additional topweight can hardly have been compensated by the stability imparted by the bulges. A far better solution would have been to disembark No. 3 turret, which would have permitted the boats and the HA battery to have been located between the funnel and a smaller-scale bridge structure (as in the later conversions of the *Ise* and *Nagato* classes). However, the reduction of the main 35.6cm battery to ten guns, when many of *Fuso*'s US Navy contemporaries mounted twelve, would have been unacceptable to a Naval Staff imbued with the spirit of qualitative superiority.

The reconstruction of *Fuso* took three years, that of her sister five; the investment in terms of expenditure and dockyard labour was therefore huge. Even so, it was to

The IJN battleship *Fuso* running speed trials in 1933 following her reconstruction. Note the multi-platform tower structure built around the original tripod foremast. The propulsion machinery was completely renewed and the stern lengthened in order to increase maximum speed from 22.5 to 24.5 knots, and the elevation of the main guns was increased to 43 degrees. *(Kure Maritime Museum)*

Table 2.2: **IJN Capital Ship Reconstruction 1930–1936**

Ship	Date	Focus of modernisation
Fuso	1930–33	new machinery, elevation main guns, bulges, hull
Yamashiro	1930–35	lengthened, horizontal protection, twin 12.7cm
Ise	1935–37	HA, new 'pagoda' bridge structure, catapult +
Hyuga	1934–36	aircraft arrangements
Nagato	1934–36	
Mutsu	1934–36	
Kongo	1935–37	new machinery, elevation main guns, hull
Haruna	1933–34	lengthened, twin 12.7cm HA, new 'pagoda' bridge
Kirishima	1934–36	structure, catapult + aircraft arrangements
Hiei	1936–40	

be dwarfed by the follow-up programme, beginning in 1933, which saw all four remaining battleships together with the three active ships of the *Kongo* class taken in hand for a similar reconstruction in the space of two years. By the time this programme was under way it was becoming clear that Japan would withdraw from the Washington Treaty when the London Treaty expired in December 1936, so it was considered vital that the IJN's older battleships be brought up to standard before the workload of the naval dockyards was focused on a new generation of capital ships.

The two battleships of the *Ise* class were reconstructed on the same pattern as *Fuso* and *Yamashiro* between 1934 and 1937. More powerful machinery was fitted, with eight Kampon boilers supplying the steam for four sets of Kampon geared turbines, for the slightly higher maximum speed of 25 knots at 80,000shp. Otherwise the modifications were virtually identical, although the pairing of the 35.6cm turrets amidships abaft the single funnel made for a superior solution, and the height of the forward tower structure was less pronounced.

At the same time the two battleships of the *Nagato* class were taken in hand for a similar reconstruction, which took place in 1934–36. These ships were larger and of more recent design, so even more powerful propulsion machinery had to be fitted to enable them to keep pace with the other modernised ships; ten oil-fired Kampon boilers replaced the original twenty-one oil-fired and mixed types, supplying the steam for four sets of Kampon geared tubines rated at 82,000shp for a maximum speed of 25.5 knots. Horsepower was only slightly increased, and the fitting of more substantial bulges 2.8m deep[3] therefore meant a reduction in maximum speed from the original 26.5 knots, but this was acceptable given that the *Nagato*s were now expected to fight in the line of battle with the battleships of the *Fuso* and *Ise* classes. Even so, weight savings on the new propulsion machinery were substantially less than in the older ships: little more than 500 tonnes.

Nagato and her sister *Mutsu*, like the earlier IJN dreadnoughts, were completed with the graduated protection system common to British capital ships completed 1915–20 (*ie* up to and including HMS *Hood*). The upper deck above the casemates was increased from 25mm to 63mm, the upper armoured deck from 44mm to 69mm, and the lower armoured deck from 55mm to 75mm. A plunging shell pass-

Nagato during her major reconstruction of 1934–36. As with the other IJN reconstructions of the 1930s, new propulsion machinery was fitted, but the key features of the rebuild were the increased elevation of the main guns and the additional horizontal protection fitted to the decks, which was compensated by new bulges. *(Author's collection)*

ing through all three decks would therefore have a combined thickness of 207mm to negotiate, and although this was by no means equivalent to a single thickness of 207mm, it was anticipated that the lower armoured deck would need to deal only with splinters, any armour-piercing shell having been 'de-capped' by one or other of the upper two armoured decks.

The three active ships of the *Kongo* class had been extensively rebuilt during the late 1920s (see *WAW* Chapter 5), when they had been bulged and fitted with almost 4,000 tonnes of additional horizontal protection. Modernisation of the propulsion machinery had been restricted to replacing the older coal-fired boilers with a smaller number of oil- and coal-fired boilers of modern design. However, the bulges and weight additions meant a substantial reduction in maximum speed from 27.5 knots to 25 knots, effectively transferring the ships from the battlecruiser to the battleship category.

In 1933, barely two years after the completion of *Kongo*'s refit, it was decided that these three ships should undergo a second major reconstruction to fit them as 'fast battleships'. *Haruna* was duly taken in hand in 1933, *Kirishima* in 1934, and *Kongo* in 1935. In late 1936, when Japan had served notice of her intention to withdraw from the Washington Treaty, *Hiei* was also taken in hand to bring her up to the same standard as the other three ships.[4]

The original machinery, including the boilers fitted only a few years previously, was removed and replaced by eight powerful Kampon boilers and four sets of modern Kampon geared turbines. This saved more than 1,000 tonnes in weight, and at the same time delivered 136,000shp instead of 64,000shp, for a maximum speed of 30 knots. The elevation of the main guns was increased from 33 to 43 degrees. A modern HA battery of eight 12.7cm guns in twin mountings was also fitted, together with new fire control equipment and a tower bridge structure.[5] There was also a slight reinforcement of the armour on the barbettes of the main guns, and further modifications included the fitting of catapults and aircraft-handling equipment.

The dramatic increase in tactical speed would see these ships increasingly deployed away from the battle line, in support of the cruiser scouting forces and the carrier striking forces. Their place in the battle line would eventually be taken by the new 'super-battleships' of the *Yamato* class.

With the expiry of the Washington Treaty imminent, the Japanese showed little concern for the rules regarding permitted weight additions to these ships. Although much of the increase in displacement related to horizontal and underwater protection, and was therefore covered by the clause permitting reconstruction 'for the purpose of providing means of defence against air and submarine attack' of the Washington Treaty (Part 3, Section 1[d]), the maximum allowance for such modifi-

Between 1933 and 1935 three of the four former battlecruisers of the *Kongo* class were taken in hand to bring them up to the same standard as the battleships. The ships had received additional horizontal protection during the late 1920s, but were now given more powerful machinery, which together with the lengthening of the hull increased speed to a maximum 30 knots. This is *Haruna* running her post-refit trials in 1934. *(Kure Maritime Museum)*

cations was 3,000 tons, and this was largely exceeded in all cases, generally by
1,000–1,500 tons but in the case of the two *Nagato*s by more than 2,300 tons (see
Table 2.3). The increases in tactical speed and in the elevation of the main guns were
outside the Washington Treaty rules, but in mitigation it has to be said that increasing the elevation of the main guns in older battleships was now universally accepted.[6]
The Italians, who by now were admittedly operating on the edge of the Treaty, would
also secure a major increase in tactical speed in the reconstruction of their older
battleships (see below).

Table 2.3: **IJN Capital Ship Displacement After Reconstruction**

Ship	Standard displacement 1922	Standard displacement after reconstruction	Added weight
Fuso	30,600tW	34,700tW	+ 4,100 tons
Ise	31,260tW	35,800tW	+ 4,540 tons
Nagato	33,800tW	39,120tW	+ 5,320 tons
Kongo	27,500tW	31,720tW	+ 4,220 tons

Japan's failure to declare the new displacements should no longer be seen as an
attempt to conceal breaches of the Washington Treaty, which would have been due
to expire by the time most of the ships recommissioned. What was now most important for the IJN was to conceal the full extent of these modifications from the US
Navy, in the hope that the qualitative superiority they represented would not be
matched by a counter-programme of battleship modernisation. In this the IJN seems
to have been largely successful; the US Navy Intelligence handbook ONI 41–42[7]
credits the *Ise* and the *Nagato* classes with a displacement little greater than their
declared Washington displacements, while the figure given for the *Kongo*s
(30,000 tons) represents the displacement following their first and more 'public'
reconstruction of the late 1920s. The Japan of the 1930s remained a very closed soci-
ety, making espionage difficult, and it was only in 1936 that US cryptanalysts discov-
ered that the *Nagato* had achieved 26 knots on her original trials (she had previously
been thought capable of only 22 knots!).

France's Elderly Dreadnoughts
The three super-dreadnoughts of the *Bretagne* class had already undergone a limited
modernisation, first in the immediate post-war years and then during the mid-1920s
(see *WAW* Chapter 5). These had focused on improving their military capabilities, in
particular the main gunnery fire control, modifications to the machinery being
restricted to the replacement of four of the original twenty-four coal-fired boilers by
oil-fired models; the remaining (coal-fired) boilers had simply been refurbished. In a
further refit at Brest in 1929–31, *Lorraine* had four more boilers replaced, but it was
becoming very apparent that the machinery of these ships was on its last legs, and
once the 'battleship holiday' was extended at the London Conference it was decided
that they should undergo a major reconstruction to enable them to continue in service until 1944, when they would be almost thirty years old.

The first two ships, *Provence* and *Bretagne*, were taken in hand in 1931–32, and had their original boilers replaced by six Indret oil-fired boilers of modern design, and their original direct-drive turbines replaced by modern Parsons geared turbines. Other modifications included the renewal of the 340mm guns (using those intended for the *Normandie* class), the removal of the fore- and aftermost 138.6mm secondary guns and the submerged torpedo tubes, and the upgrading of the HA battery by adding a further four 75mm guns (for a total of eight), together with improvements to fire control systems. They were now more economical steamers, but they were still slow, and their hulls were too small and cramped to justify the fitting of bulges (which would have made them even slower), and consequently there was little that could be done about their horizontal protection.

The third ship of the class, *Lorraine*, was not reconstructed until 1934 and received additional modifications. It was realised that the only way of freeing up sufficient space for satisfactory aircraft handling arrangements and a battery of modern HA guns was to remove the centre turret (the French may have been influenced by the reconstruction of the Italian *Cavours*, which had begun a year earlier). The turret was replaced by a hangar for three aircraft, atop which was located a powerful trainable catapult; four twin 100mm mountings of the type fitted in the latest French cruisers of the *Algérie* and *La Galissonnière* classes were installed outboard of the hangar.

Table 2.4: **French Capital Ship Reconstruction 1930–1936**

Ship	Date	Focus of modernisation
Bretagne	1932–34	new machinery, re-gunned, new HA battery
Provence	1931–34	+ FC systems
Lorraine	1934–35	as above + turret removal, catapult + hangar, new twin 100mm HA

Lorraine was the only one of the elderly French dreadnoughts to receive more than an austere modernisation. She had the centre turret removed and replaced by a catapult and hangar for reconnaissance aircraft, and four twin 100mm mountings similar to those in *Algérie* were located outboard of the hangar. *Lorraine* is seen here at Le Havre in 1837, shortly after her reconstruction. *(Private collection)*

The older 305mm dreadnoughts of the *Courbet* class had undergone refits between 1927 and 1931, and were in any case due to be replaced by the new battleships currently projected (and which France was still permitted to build before the expiry of the 'battleship holiday'), so no major reconstruction was extended to them. In the event, because of delays in completing the new ships and the deteriorating international situation, two out of the three would soldier on into the late 1930s, being employed primarily as gunnery training ships from 1939; the third, *Jean Bart*, was in too poor a condition to be repaired and became an accommodation ship; she was renamed *Océan* to free up her original name for one of the new battleships.

New Battleships for the *Marine Nationale*

Under the London Treaty, France and Italy retained their right to complete the equivalent of two new 'Washington' battleships each of 35,000 tons displacement as replacements for their older dreadnoughts at any time between April 1930 and 31 December 1936. The *Marine Nationale* was still not inclined to build to the maximum displacement figure allowed because of the cost implications of providing the necessary infrastructure – building and docking facilities could not currently support a ship of this size. Studies for fast battleships of 35,000 tons suggested a length of up to 245m for a 30-knot ship, and infrastructure costs alone would total 130 million francs. However, the only other mathematical possibilities remained three ships of 23,333 tons or four ships of 17,500 tons, both types being the subject of a number of STCN studies.

Once the German Navy laid down the first of a planned series of 'armoured ships' (*Panzerschiffe*) in February 1929 the 17,500-ton *croiseur de combat* (see *WAW* Chapter 5) was dead in the water, as it was generally recognised that a ship of 17,500 tons could not be adequately protected against 280mm shell. With the approach of the London Conference, and in the knowledge that the British would be proposing a new limit for capital ships of 25,000 tons and 12in guns, designs for ships of this displacement – and preferably of 23,333 tons to enable three ships to be built within France's existing 70,000-ton allocation – were requested from the Service Technique.

The Navy Minister, Jean-Luc Dumesnil, was concerned that France should have the best ships permitted by the Treaty, and asked the Navy to justify its preference for smaller ships. However, when the additional infrastructure costs of building the 35,000-ton ship were pointed out, it was agreed that a ship of 23,333 tons based on earlier STCN studies should be submitted to parliament for approval during the following year. Like the earlier *croiseur de combat*, this ship was to have a main armament of eight 305mm/50 guns in two quadruple turrets forward, but protection would be far superior, comprising a vertical armour belt 215–230mm thick and a 100–130mm armoured deck. In a new departure, there would also be a dual-purpose secondary armament of twelve 130mm guns in three quadruple turrets, all mounted aft.

From January to March 1931 attempts were made to secure agreement with Italy on the construction of two battleships of 23,333 tons, but the Italians were unwilling to make this commitment despite earlier studies for a similar ship (see *WAW* Chapter 5). Time was now pressing; the first *Panzerschiff*, to be named *Deutschland*, was due for launch in May 1931, and a sister would be laid down in June. The first of the new French battleships was therefore included in the naval programme to be debated in June and July, and a heated debate ensued over the 23,333-ton proposed displacement, in which the new Minister, Albert Sarraut, conspicuously failed to satisfy critics of the project. When approval was finally granted on 10 July it was on condition that further studies be undertaken and submitted to the House for approval.

The STCN now undertook a detailed study of the characteristics of the new ships, taking into account the latest Naval Staff directive that stipulated that 26,000 tons was the minimum displacement to ensure adequate protection, and made a number of changes to the initial proposal. The new design was only slightly longer than the 23,333-ton project, but beam was increased by fully 3.5m in order to provide the necessary stability to accommodate a heavier main armament (330mm versus 305mm guns) and a major reinforcement of the horizontal protection. The increase in beam also provided the necessary depth for an effective system of underwater protection. The cost of these improvements was an increase in the displacement to 26,500 tons standard.

This left the *Marine Nationale* on the horns of a dilemma. If two ships each of 26,500 tons were built, this would leave only 17,000 tons of the 1931–36 treaty allocation for new capital ships unaccounted for. A third ship of 26,500 tons would bring France 9,500 tons over the Treaty limits – unthinkable in political terms – while 17,000 tons had already been deemed inadequate for an effective vessel. The end result was that the new ships had been 'designed down' to an artificial limit to little purpose. Moreover, even before the world's 'battleship holiday' finally ended in 1936, France would have to confront the infrastructure issue. In June 1934 Italy announced that it would begin construction of two battleships of 35,000 tons, and there was never any question that this would have to be met by an equivalent French response.

The first of the new ships, to be named *Dunkerque*, was finally approved in March 1932 and laid down on 26 October of the same year. The type was now officially designated *bâtiment de ligne* ('battleship'). A sister ship was to be included in the 1934 programme.

Dunkerque

In her general configuration and layout *Dunkerque* was reminiscent of the battle-cruiser designs projected for the British Royal Navy in the wake of the First World War, with the main armament all forward, the secondary armament aft, and a prominent tower structure housing the command spaces and carrying a comprehensive outfit of fire control directors. The major difference was that, whereas the British designs generally featured three triple turrets, of which two were positioned forward and one abaft the tower, the French opted for two quadruple turrets, which eliminated the mounting abaft the tower, thereby reducing the length of the armoured citadel. A further benefit of this arrangement was to enable the propulsion machinery to be placed more centrally, at the point of maximum beam, which enhanced underwater protection arrangements and gave the ships a more 'balanced' appearance, with a single broad funnel midway between the tower structure and a heavy pole mainmast around which the after FC directors were seated, and a quarterdeck available for aircraft operation.

In order to minimise the risk of both quadruple turrets being disabled by a single shell or torpedo, they were well spaced, being separated by a distance of 28.5m. The guns were paired and the turret partitioned by a 40mm bulkhead that extended down into the working chamber at a reduced thickness (25mm), so that damage from shell-fire could be isolated to one half of the turret. The 330mm/50 Model 1931 gun fired a 570kg shell with an initial velocity of 870m/s; maximum angle of elevation was 35 degrees, for a theoretical range of 41,500m.

The secondary armament comprised sixteen 130mm/45 Model 1932 guns, with three quadruple turrets mounted aft and two twin mountings amidships to cover the forward arcs. These were the first French dual-purpose mountings, and had a maximum elevation of 75 degrees. In anti-surface mode the 130/45 gun fired a 33.4kg AP shell to a maximum range of 20,800m; against aircraft it fired a 29.5kg time-fuzed HE shell. The fixed ammunition weighed 53kg, which was close to the maximum for comfortable handling by the gun crews. As with the quadruple turrets of

Dunkerque at her moorings in 1939. The all-forward main armament of eight 330mm guns in quadruple turrets was influenced by British design practice during the early 1920s. It had the advantage of reducing the length of the citadel, which in turn made it possible to maximise the thickness and weight of the deck and belt plates. *(J C Fargas collection, courtesy of Robert Dumas)*

A stern view of *Dunkerque* returning to Brest following the Naval Review of May 1937. Another advantage of the all-forward armament layout was that it freed up the quarterdeck for aviation facilities. Two Loire 130 reconnaissance aircraft could be stowed in the hangar, with a third on the catapult.
(Patrick du Cheyron collection, courtesy of Robert Dumas)

the main armament, the guns were paired (they shared a common cradle), and there was a 20mm steel bulkhead dividing the turret into two independent halves. The twin mounting resembled the quad half-mounting in layout, although the gun barrels were mounted farther apart. Whereas the quad mountings were fully armoured, the twins had only light 20mm plating. The quad mountings had their magazines located directly beneath them, but the twin mountings were 23m abaft their magazines, so ammunition had to be transferred horizontally between the upper and lower armoured decks.

Dunkerque was the first French battleship with a purpose-designed director control system for both the main and the secondary armament, and arrangements were particularly complete. The five main directors, each fitted with multiple stereoscopic rangefinders, were mounted one above the other atop the forward tower structure and at the base of the pole mainmast. The rangefinders for the main armament had a 12m base (8m in the after director), while those for the secondary armament had a 6m or 5m base.

Dunkerque (Fr)

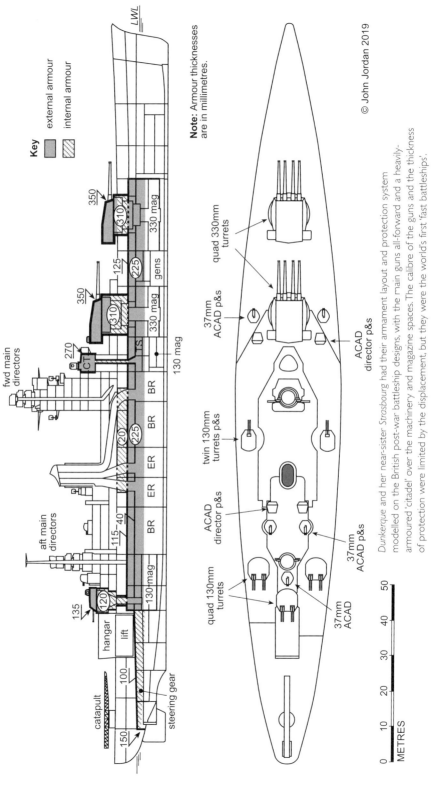

Key
- external armour
- internal armour

Note: Armour thicknesses are in millimetres.

© John Jordan 2019

LWL

fwd main directors

aft main directors

catapult

hangar   lift

steering gear

350   310

330 mag

350   310

125   225

gens

330 mag

330 mag

270   CT

TS

BR   BR

130 mag

20   225

ER   ER

BR

115   40

130 mag

135   120

130 mag

100

150

quad 330mm turrets

37mm ACAD p&s

ACAD director p&s

twin 130mm turrets p&s

ACAD director p&s

37mm ACAD p&s

quad 130mm turrets

37mm ACAD

METRES

0   10   20   30   40   50

Dunkerque and her near-sister Strasbourg had their armament layout and protection system modelled on the British post-war battleship designs, with the main guns all-forward and a heavily-armoured 'citadel' over the machinery and magazine spaces. The calibre of the guns and the thickness of protection were limited by the displacement, but they were the world's first 'fast battleships'.

A further innovation was that all the main and secondary turrets were fitted with remote power control (RPC) for training and elevation. However, the Sautter–Harlé–Blondel RPC training gear proved unreliable; synchronisation between the turrets and the directors was poor, and manual intervention was needed for fine adjustment. Moreover, the training mechanisms had insufficient power to cope with turrets of this weight and size, resulting in slow tracking speeds and frequent breakdowns. Major problems were experienced on trials, and even after modification the system never worked properly.

For close-in air defence *Dunkerque* was originally to have had five of the automatic twin 37mm Model 1935 (ACAD) guns then under development, together with eight quadruple 13.2mm Hotchkiss Model 1929 MG mountings. Major delays were experienced in the development and production of both these weapons. *Dunkerque* was fitted on completion with six single 37mm guns Model 1925 as a temporary measure, replaced in early 1939 by the twin 37mm Model 1933, the advanced Model 1935 having been further delayed.

A major advantage of the layout adopted for *Dunkerque* was that it freed the quarterdeck for the operation of aircraft, which were thereby protected from the blast of the main guns. Aviation facilities were particularly comprehensive and well-designed: they comprised a single powerful trainable catapult with a launch capacity of 3,500kg, and a two-tier hangar incorporating its own workshop, served by a system of deck rails and trolleys on which the aircraft were manoeuvred. A lift with a circular turntable set into the quarterdeck raised the aircraft to the level of the catapult, and to port of the hangar there was a crane with a 4.5-tonne capacity for lifting the aircraft aboard on landing. The bomb magazine and the aviation fuel tanks were located beneath the quarterdeck. The latter were directly beneath the stern, and incorporated a number of safety features, including the replacement of used fuel by an inert gas, and refrigeration and sprinkler systems.

The protection system was based closely on that of the British *Nelson* and *Rodney*, with an internal belt of 225mm cemented (face-hardened) armour secured to a 60mm teak backing and inclined inwards at 11°30. Because of concerns that a steeply plunging shell might pass beneath the armour belt and attack the ship's vitals, the inclined belt was extended farther beneath the waterline than in the British ships, albeit at a reduced thickness (the height of *Dunkerque*'s main belt was 5.75m as compared with 4m for the *Nelson*s). It was closed at its fore and after ends by transverse bulkheads with thicknesses of 210mm and 180mm respectively. The protection of the armoured conning tower, the quadruple turrets of the main and secondary armament and their respective barbettes was a match for any battleship built during the 1930s.

One important departure from contemporary British practice was the inclusion of a 'splinter deck' on the American model beneath the main armoured deck, covering the ship's vitals, and designed to keep out splinters when AP shells struck the main armoured deck above. The latter had a thickness of 125mm over the magazines and 115mm over the machinery. The lower armoured deck was of 40mm thickness on the flat, and was angled down on both sides to meet the bottom edge of the inclined armour belt.

The underwater protection system of *Dunkerque* was in line with the latest thinking, employing a combination of void compartments, light bulkheads and liquid loading to absorb the explosion of a torpedo warhead. A major innovation was the filling of the compartment outboard of the inclined armour belt, which had a maximum depth of 1.5m, with a rubber-based, water-excluding compound (*ébonite mousse*) to absorb the initial impact and to prevent uncontrolled flooding of the side compartments, which might otherwise have threatened stability. The total depth of the underwater protection system from the outer skin to the inner face of the torpedo bulkhead was 7.7m, an impressive figure – most contemporary foreign systems had a depth of around 5m.

The overall weight of protection in *Dunkerque* was 11,040 tonnes, equivalent to 40 per cent of standard displacement (see Table 2.5). These are impressive figures by any standard, even if the different accounting practices of the major navies are taken into account. The corresponding figures for the 35,000-ton *Nelson* were 10,250 tons and 29.5 per cent (see *WAW* Chapter 5).

The propulsion machinery, in which the latest Indret high-pressure superheated boilers were combined with lightweight geared steam turbines, was remarkably

Table 2.5: *Dunkerque*

Characteristics

Displacement:	26,500 tons standard (designed)
Dimensions:	215m x 31.1m x 8.6m
Machinery:	Six Indret small-tube boilers; four-shaft Parsons geared turbines; 107,000shp = 29.5 knots
Armament:	8 – 330mm/50 (2 x IV) 16 – 130mm/45 (3 x IV, 2 x II) DP 10 – 37mm/50 (5 x II) three Loire 130 recce seaplanes
Protection:	belt: 225mm decks: 125mm/115mm + 40mm turrets: 330mm faces, 250mm sides CT: 270–130mm
Complement:	1,300 (1,380 as flagship)

Breakdown of weights (as completed)

	weight (tonnes)	percentage of displacement
Hull + fittings:	9,778t	35%
Machinery:	2,214t	8%
Protection:	11,040t	40%
Armament:	4,858t	17%
Standard displacement:	27,890t (27,450tW)	100%

Dunkerque (Fr):
Protection

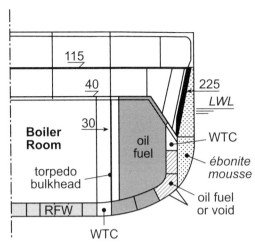

115
40
225
LWL

**Boiler
Room**

30

oil
fuel

WTC

torpedo
bulkhead

*ébonite
mousse*

oil fuel
or void

RFW

WTC

© John Jordan 2019

Dunkerque had a British-style protection system with an inclined armour belt topped by a thick protective deck. The underwater protection system was similar to that of the latest US Navy battleships, with an air/liquid/air 'sandwich' backed by a torpedo bulkhead. However, a peculiarly French innovation was to fill the outboard watertight compartment with a water-excluding rubber compound known as *ébonite mousse*.

compact for its power rating, and accounted for only 8 per cent of standard displacement. It was arranged on the unit principle, with the forward boiler room located directly beneath the tower (necessitating substantial angled uptake trunking above the armoured deck), and the other two boiler rooms directly beneath the single funnel, directly abaft the turbines driving the wing shafts. *Dunkerque* was the first battleship to adopt the unit layout, which had previously been confined to lightly protected cruisers.

Designed horsepower was 107,000shp for 29.5 knots, and *Dunkerque* attained 31.06 knots with 135,585shp on trials. The maximum fuel load for peacetime cruising was 4,500–5,000 tonnes, but in wartime this figure was reduced to 3,700 tonnes to maximise the effectiveness of the underwater protection system (filling the liquid loading compartments to the brim meant that instead of the fuel oil absorbing the pressure of the explosion it created additional pressure on the internal bulkheads). The lower figure gave an estimated range of 7,850nm at 15 knots.

To provide the ship with the necessary electrical power there were four turbo-generators each of 900kW distributed between the machinery rooms, and three diesel generators each of 400kW located low in the ship, for a total of 4,800kW. This was a remarkable figure for the period (the British *Hood* had a total generating capacity of 1,400kW, while the *Nelson*s had a capacity of 1,800kW), and reflected the increasing demands on electrical power of modern battleships equipped with power-operated control systems.

Given the innovative nature of their design it is not surprising that there were delays in bringing *Dunkerque* and her near-sister *Strasbourg* to full operational effectiveness, and some defects were to plague them throughout their all-too-brief service lives. North Atlantic operations during the winter of 1939–40 revealed that the long,

unprotected bow had insufficient sheer and flare, and tended to bury itself in a
seaway. This meant that speed had to be substantially reduced in heavy weather
conditions to prevent the forward 330mm turret being submerged. The lightly
constructed stern section also suffered from vibration, which frequently disabled one
or other of the servo-motors for the steering gear. The turbo-ventilators were noisy,
and both ships emitted palls of smoke when operating close to full power.
Underwater damage during the Second World War to *Dunkerque* and to the battleship *Richelieu*, which was of similar design and construction, was accompanied by
progressive flooding due to defective seals and glands around the electric cabling
where it passed through the watertight bulkheads.

However, the major weakness of these ships was their artillery, which like that of
other contemporary French warships was over-complex in operation and liable to
frequent breakdowns. Despite modification, the RPC for the main guns never
worked properly, and accuracy was further reduced by a dispersion of 200–1,000m
experienced when firing salvoes. This was later found to be due to the effect of firing
large shells simultaneously from the closely paired barrels of the quad mountings,
and the problem would be resolved by modifying the electrical firing circuits in the
later battleships so that there was an interval of a fraction of a second between the
firing of the paired guns.[8] Moreover, the dual-purpose secondary armament proved
to be effective neither in the anti-surface role, for which it was too lightweight, nor
in the anti-aircraft role, for which it was too cumbersome; it was also prone to
frequent breakdowns.

Italy's Response to *Dunkerque*

It is ironic that France's new capital ships should have been a response to a development completely outside the Washington Treaty: the German *Panzerschiffe*. Had
Germany not embarked on the construction of new armoured ships up to the
displacement and gun calibre limitations permitted by the Treaty of Versailles, and
had the *Reichsmarine* not opted for such a novel and unexpected solution (28cm
guns plus high speed and endurance at the expense of protection) it is doubtful
whether the French would have felt impelled to order new battleships at this point
in time. Neither France nor Italy was particularly anxious to be seen as the first to
embark on what was bound to be seen by its potential adversary as an escalation of
naval armaments, and neither was keen to commit itself to using any part of its
70,000-ton allocation without a firm indication of the intentions of the other; hence
the *Regia Marina*'s reluctance to commit itself to its own 23,300-ton design during
the late 1920s (see *WAW* Chapter 5), and France's belated attempt in 1931 to secure
a bilateral agreement with Italy on limiting their new generation of battleships to this
displacement. Once the die was cast and *Dunkerque* authorised, however, a chain
reaction was set off that was to take on a momentum of its own.

The Italians were by now inclining towards battleships of 35,000 tons, but
although various preliminary studies had been undertaken, these were not yet of
sufficient maturity to provide a firm basis for orders, and there were still doubts

surrounding the calibre of the main guns. The *Regia Marina* wanted ships with high tactical speed (29–30 knots), separate secondary and HA batteries, and well-developed protection against shells, bombs and torpedoes, and if the maximum calibre of 406mm (16in) permitted under the Washington Treaty was to be adopted, design studies suggested a maximum of six guns in three twin turrets. Six guns was considered less than ideal for salvo firing and the adoption of the 406mm calibre would mean a new gun, the development of which would be prolonged and costly. Serious consideration was therefore given to the 381mm (15in) calibre, of which Italy had already built examples for the uncompleted *Caracciolo* class.

In the interim, Italy needed to decide what to do about its ageing dreadnoughts, which were now nearly twenty years old and which were virtually unmodified since their completion in 1914–16. In the event the Italians opted for a complete reconstruction of the first pair of ships, *Conte di Cavour* and *Giulio Cesare*, to counter *Dunkerque* and her projected sister. Their declared standard displacement of 21,750 tons was only 4,750 tons short of the official figure for the new French ships, and under the Washington Treaty an additional 3,000 tons was available for bulges, horizontal protection and anti-aircraft guns. New high-performance lightweight steam turbine machinery could provide the horsepower for speeds in excess of 25 knots, while at the same time freeing up space for a modern underwater protection system. The main battery of thirteen 305mm (12in) guns was more than adequate in number, if not in calibre, to oppose the new French battleships. It was therefore possible to dispense with the centre triple turret altogether, thereby freeing up space amidships for a modern secondary armament in powered turrets and hull volume beneath for a rearrangement of the machinery spaces. *Cavour* and *Cesare* were duly taken in hand in 1933 for what was unquestionably the most radical reconstruction of any battleship between the wars.

The first stage of the reconstruction was to remove all the above-decks structures between the outer turrets, including the midships 305mm turret and the 120mm secondary casemate guns, and to strip out the original four-shaft machinery. The remaining ten 305mm guns were removed from the turrets; they were bored out to 320mm, and were refitted with new elevation, training and reloading mechanisms, then reinstalled in the original turrets, which were fitted with new rangefinders. The internal spaces formerly occupied by the midships 305mm magazine and the original four-shaft turbine machinery were used to fit two-shaft lightweight propulsion machinery similar in conception to that of the latest Italian cruisers: two rows of four Yarrow small-tube boilers either side of the centreline, each in its own compartment, with Belluzzo geared turbines forward driving the starboard shaft, and those driving the port shaft aft. This freed up hull volume for a new underwater protection system in the original outer machinery spaces. The latter was designed by the respected engineer Umberto Pugliese, and comprised a large-diameter sealed cylinder surrounded by liquid (fuel oil or feed water) backed up by a curved 25mm torpedo bulkhead (see drawing).

The upper part of the hull was rebuilt to improve sea-keeping qualities and to give

The Italian battleship *Conte di Cavour* at Taranto in 1938 following her reconstruction. She and her sister *Giulio Cesare* were completely rebuilt to create modern units. The two remaining Italian dreadnoughts of the *Duilio* class would undergo a similar reconstruction during the late 1930s. *(Courtesy of Erminio Bagnasco)*

a finer length to beam ratio. A new flared clipper bow, with a degree of sheer, was fitted on top of the original ram bow, and the forecastle deck was extended aft by plating in the original secondary casemates. Overall length was thereby increased by 10m, and the balance of the ship was shifted farther aft. Few modifications were made to the vertical protection, but the horizontal protection was strengthened considerably: 80mm plating over the machinery spaces, and 70mm plating on the original 30mm plating over the magazines fore and aft. The barbettes of the main guns received further protection in the form of 50mm 'spaced armour' outside the original 220–240mm armour, intended to 'de-cap' AP shell.

The superstructures were modelled on the latest cruisers of the *'Condottieri'* type (see Chapter 4). There was a new conical bridge tower with the main fire control director atop it and the secondary directors on tall pedestals to port and starboard, two short vertical closely spaced funnels with prominent cowlings, and a tall tripod mainmast that carried the after fire control director. A new secondary battery of twelve 120mm guns in six twin armoured turrets was fitted at forecastle deck level amidships, and a separate HA battery of four twin 100/47 guns was fitted at the four 'corners' of the ship, with twin 37mm mountings clustered around the funnels. Two catapults were to have been fitted abeam the funnels, with the aircraft stowed in the

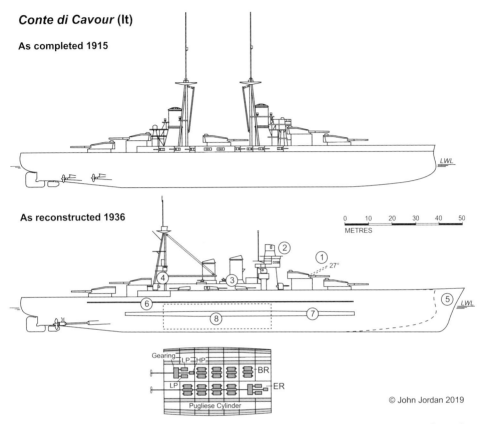

Conte di Cavour (It)

As completed 1915

As reconstructed 1936

0   10   20   30   40   50
METRES

© John Jordan 2019

The Italian *Conte di Cavour* and her sister *Giulio Cesare* underwent the most radical reconstruction of any of the battleships completed in 1914–18. The principal modifications were:

1   main guns in fore and after turrets bored out from 305mm to 320mm, and elevation increased from 20 to 27 degrees; maximum range 28,600m
2   completely new superstructures modelled on the latest Italian cruisers, with a conical forward tower carrying the fire control directors for the main and secondary guns and a tall tripod mainmast
3   centre 305mm turret removed and replaced by a new secondary battery of twelve 120mm guns in six twin turrets
4   four twin 100mm HA mountings installed at 'corners' of ship
5   new clipper bow with flare and sheer constructed over original; extended length by 10m, resulting in finer hull-form forward
6   80mm NC armour over machinery spaces, and 70mm plates added to existing 30mm plates over magazines fore and aft for total thickness of 100mm
7   Pugliese underwater protection scheme outboard of magazines and machinery
8   new cruiser-type propulsion machinery on two shafts with double the horsepower: eight Yarrow small-watertube boilers in individual boiler rooms with two sets of lightweight geared turbines.

open, but there proved to be insufficient space; when installed on *Cesare* on completion they were found to restrict the arcs of the anti-aircraft guns, and the aircraft were subject to damage when the secondary guns were fired.

When these ships recommissioned in 1937 they were virtually new units; only 40 per cent of the original construction remained. Apart from a trim problem that meant that the ships tended to bury their bows in a seaway, trials were generally very successful. The designed speed of 27 knots was comfortably achieved (*Cesare* attained 28.25 knots with some forcing of the machinery on trials). However, although they matched the French *Dunkerque* closely on paper, in reality the original hulls were too small for a really effective conversion. The innovative Pugliese underwater protection system had insufficient depth to resist the heavyweight torpedo warheads that were standard by the 1930s, and the horizontal protection, although a major improvement, remained markedly inferior to that of their French counterparts (100mm 'composite' versus 125mm single thickness over the magazines, 80mm versus 115mm over the machinery). Indeed, the total weight of protection for the Italian ships was 6,000 tonnes, little over half that for the *Dunkerque*. The French ships were also faster and had greater range.

The advantage of reconstruction as compared with new-build ships was that both *Cavour* and *Cesare* reached operational status at about the same time as *Dunkerque*, and some eighteen months before her half-sister *Strasbourg*. Moreover, there was no limit to how many existing ships could be rebuilt under Washington, and since the standard displacement of these ships as reconstructed was around 26,000 tons, Italy could afford to rebuild the two *Duilio*s and still have sufficient tonnage available to build two new battleships of 35,000 tons. This would in effect be the course the *Regia Marina* would pursue, *Caio Duilio* and *Andrea Doria* being taken in hand in 1937 for a three-year reconstruction similar to that of the *Cavour*s.

The New Italian Battleships

The design for the new battleships, drawn up under Chief Naval Engineer Pugliese, was ready by 1934, and two ships, *Littorio* and *Vittorio Veneto*, were laid down in October of the same year.

They were armed with nine 381mm/50 guns in three triple turrets, and had an elegant, well-balanced but powerful appearance. They were also exceptionally fast, with a designed speed of 30 knots that was comfortably exceeded on trials. Protection arrangements were particularly complete: there was a 280mm armour belt inclined at 12 degrees with an external 70mm 'de-capping' plate of NC steel at the waterline, and a vertical upper belt of 70mm NC. Horizontal protection comprised a 36mm upper deck and a main armoured deck with a thickness of 100mm over the machinery and 150mm over the magazines. The Pugliese underwater protection system, which extended the full length of the citadel, comprised a sealed cylinder with a maximum diameter of 3.8m backed up by a curved 40mm torpedo bulkhead. The boiler feed water or fuel oil that surrounded it, and which was intended to dissipate the force of the explosion in such a way that it acted on the entire surface of the cylinder, was replaced by seawater as it was consumed. The walls of the cylinder were thin, so that in theory the latter would absorb the pressure by distorting and would rupture before the torpedo bulkhead. The system, which had a maximum depth of 7.6m, was designed to resist a 350kg torpedo warhead, and was tested on the oiler *Brennero* during the early 1930s with excellent results.

As in the reconstructed *Cavour*s, separate anti-destroyer and anti-aircraft batteries

Littorio on early sea trials at full speed off Genoa on 21 December 1939, some months before commissioning. Only the main 380mm and secondary 152mm guns are in place. Note the visible inner structure of the conning tower, with the armoured tube around which the main fire directors would be fitted. *(M Cicogna collection, courtesy of Maurizio Brescia)*

were preferred to dual-purpose weapons. There were triple 152mm/55 in armoured turrets at the four corners of the forecastle deck, which extended beyond the after 381mm turret, and twelve 90mm/50 HA guns in quadraxial electrically stabilised mountings designed by Ansaldo grouped around the short capped funnels. The comprehensive anti-aircraft armament was completed by eight twin and four single 37/54 mountings plus sixteen of the new 20/65 guns, all in twin mountings. Four older-model 120mm/40 guns were also fitted amidships to fire illuminating shell.

The superstructures – and therefore the citadel itself – were compact, with the fire control directors for the main and secondary batteries being superimposed atop the bridge tower and in a smaller tower aft in similar fashion to the French *Dunkerques*, and with the four directors for the 90mm AA guns elevated on pedestals abeam the bridge tower and between the funnels. This left only the quarterdeck position available for the installation of a catapult for three Ro.43 floatplanes. This was less than ideal, as there was little freeboard aft, and there was no hangar so the aircraft were exposed to the elements. However, the third turret was at least raised in order to minimise blast damage when the main guns were fired.

The *Littorios* were powerful, well-designed ships that were to have a major impact on the new generation of battleships built by France and Great Britain. However, although their standard displacement was declared by the Italians to be 35,000 tons, weights as designed came out at just over 37,000 tons, and by the time they were completed in mid-1940 standard displacement was acknowledged to be around

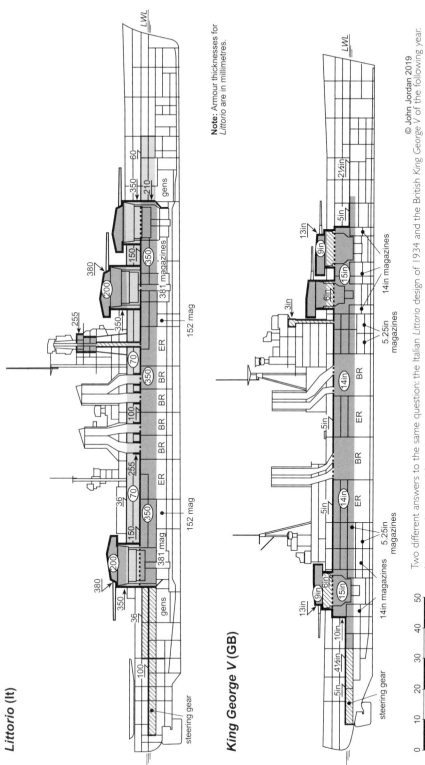

Littorio (It)

Note: Armour thicknesses for *Littorio* are in millimetres.

King George V (GB)

© John Jordan 2019

Two different answers to the same question: the Italian *Littorio* design of 1934 and the British *King George V* of the following year. *Littorio* was longer and faster but less heavily armoured. An unusual feature of Italian design was that the diesel generators were outside the main citadel and had only light protection above them. Note also the light upper belt topped by a 36mm deck.

Littorio at sea in the late summer of 1940. The separate LA and HA batteries are particularly prominent in this overhead view: the 152mm secondary guns are in triple turrets at the four corners of the ship with the 90mm HA guns in single quadraxial mountings amidships. *Littorio* has the distinctive red and white recognition stripes applied to the forecastle soon after the Battle of Punta Stilo. *(Istituto Luce, Maurizio Brescia collection)*

40,500 tons. While the construction techniques employed by the Italian shipyards lagged some way behind those being used elsewhere (all structures were of riveted steel), this provides further evidence that a fast modern battleship with 15/16in guns and protection sufficient to keep out similar shells could simply not be built on 35,000 tons.

In service the *Littorio*s proved to be particularly successful ships, despite the newness of many of their systems. The bulbous bow, which was adopted to facilitate high speed, combined with the substantial flare of the original clipper bow to generate excessive 'slamming', and the bow was modified following trials. There were also teething troubles with the complex stabilisation system of the 90mm HA mountings, and the salvo spread of the main 381mm guns was excessive – a common problem in Italian ships. The much-vaunted Pugliese underwater protection system proved less effective in practice than anticipated due to insufficient compartmentation of the bulge and poor structural connections. However, *Littorio* and her sister *Vittorio Veneto* were to prove tough opponents for the British Mediterranean Fleet during the Second World War, and successfully resisted damage from bombs and torpedoes on numerous occasions.

Action and Reaction: the French Response

The second ship of the *Dunkerque* class, *Strasbourg*, was due to be authorised under the 1934 Naval Estimates. The announcement by the Italian Government of the construction of two new battleships of 35,000 tons had the effect of throwing French plans into confusion. There was now little alternative but for the French to commit to new 35,000-ton battleships of their own, with all that implied for development delays and infrastructure costs. The latter would be much greater for France than for Italy, as the *Marine Nationale* had never built a gun above the 340mm (13.4in) calibre, whereas the Italians could call on their experience with the 381mm guns of the uncompleted 'super-dreadnoughts' of the *Caracciolo* class.

The *Marine Nationale* estimated the delays in beginning the construction of 35,000-ton battleships, which would require new plans and newly designed guns, at fifteen to eighteen months. A decision was therefore made to proceed with the construction of *Strasbourg*, and to incorporate whatever enhancements to her protection might be feasible within the overall constraints of the design. It was considered that these ships were still needed as an effective counter to the German *Panzerschiffe*, of which a further two had been laid down in 1931–32, and could more than hold their own against the reconstructed Italian *Cavour*s.

The main armour belt of *Strasbourg* was increased from 225mm to 283mm, and the end bulkheads of the citadel from 210mm and 180mm to 260mm and 210mm respectively. The horizontal protection, which impacted more on the stability of the ship, was left unchanged, but the thickness of the armour on the barbettes and the turret faces of the main guns was increased by 30mm, to 340mm and 360mm respectively. These modifications increased the standard displacement by 800 tons and draught by 0.16m.

The newly-completed French battleship *Richelieu* at Dakar in September 1940. Her derivation from the earlier *Dunkerque* is evident, but she was a much more powerful unit capable of confronting any contemporary foreign capital ship. *(Courtesy of Robert Dumas)*

Studies for the new 35,000-ton battleships began straight away, and although other alternatives, including various combinations of twin and triple turrets (all forward) were considered, the *Dunkerque* solution of two quadruple turrets forward was again preferred because it was the only one to meet protection requirements within the 35,000-ton Washington Treaty limit. It was also found that the 380mm/15in calibre was the maximum that could be successfully accommodated in a quadruple turret, due to weight and stress considerations.

The initial sketch designs all had five quad 130mm (5.1in) dual-purpose second-ary mountings, disposed as in *Dunkerque* with three aft and two amidships (to cover forward bearings). However, the Naval General Staff was concerned that the 130mm gun was too light to be an effective anti-destroyer weapon, and insisted on the substi-tution of a new triple 152mm (6in), based on the 55-calibre model adopted for the new generation of cruisers but with a genuine high-angle capability.

Staff requirements for protection were for a 360mm belt and a 160mm main armoured deck, backed up by a lower armoured ('splinter') deck 40/50mm thick over the machinery and magazines. Underwater protection was to be as for *Dunkerque*. In the event it proved impossible to provide this level of protection with-out exceeding the 35,000-ton displacement figure, despite a reduction of 4.85m in

Table 2.6: The New Generation of European Battleships

	Littorio class	Richelieu class	King George V class
Displacement:	35,000tW	35,000tW	35,500tW[1]
Dimensions:	238m × 32.4m × 10.5m	248m × 33.1m × 9.2m	745ft × 103ft × 29ft (227m × 31.4m × 8.8m)
Machinery:	Eight Yarrow small-tube boilers; 4-shaft Belluzzo geared turbines; 130,000shp = 30 knots	Six Indret small-tube boilers; 4-shaft Parsons geared turbines; 155,000shp = 32 knots	Eight Admiralty small-tube boilers; 4-shaft Parsons geared turbines; 100,000shp = 28 knots
Armament:	9 – 381mm/50 (3 × III); 12 – 152mm/55 (4 × III); 12 – 90mm/50 (12 × I) HA; 20– 37/54 (10 × II); three Ro.43 floatplanes	8 – 380mm/45 (2 × IV); 15 – 152mm/55 (5 × III) DP; 12 – 37mm/50 (6 × II); four Loire 130 seaplanes	10 – 14in/45 (2 × IV, 1 × II); 16 – 5.25in/50 (8 × II) DP; 32 – 2pdr (4 × VIII); four Walrus seaplanes
Protection:	belt: 350mm; decks: 36mm + 150mm; turrets: 380mm faces, 200mm sides; CT: 255mm	belt: 330mm; decks: 170/150mm + 40mm; turrets: 430mm faces, 300mm sides; CT: 340–170mm	belt: 15/14in; deck: 6/5in; turrets: 13in faces, 9in sides; CT: 3in
Complement:	1,865	1,570	1,420

Breakdown of weights

	Littorio weight in tonnes (percentage of displ)	Richelieu weight in tonnes (percentage of displ)	King George V weight in tons (percentage of displ)
Hull + fittings:	15,264t (40%)	12,982t (34%)	14,650t (40.5%)
Machinery:	2,303t (6.5%)[2]	2,865t (7.5%)	2,700t (7.5%)
Protection:	13,669t (36%)	16,045t (42%)	12,500t (35%)
Armament:	6,565t (17.5%)[2]	6,130t (16%)	6,050t (17%)
Displacement:	37,801t (100%)	38,022t (100%)	35,900tW (100%)

Notes:

1 This was the 'declared' displacement; it was anticipated that weight savings while building would keep displacement to 35,000 tons.

2 Note the comparatively light weight of the Littorio's 'cruiser'-type machinery; and the additional weight involved in having separate LA and HA batteries.

the length of the citadel made possible by using the novel and particularly compact SURAL[9] superheated boiler, and the main belt was reduced to 330mm thickness – the angle of incline was increased from 11 to 15 degrees to compensate – and the thickness of the armoured deck to 150mm; the thicknesses of the end bulkheads and the barbette armour for the 152mm turrets were also slightly reduced.

It proved difficult to find satisfactory positions for the six/eight 75mm HA guns that were originally to have complemented the dual-purpose secondary guns, so these were abandoned in favour of light anti-aircraft guns of 37mm and 13.2mm calibre grouped high around the superstructures.

Two ships, to be named *Richelieu* and *Jean Bart*, were duly authorised in 1935, and the first was laid down in October of the same year; her sister *Jean Bart* would be laid down seven months later. They would have the same virtues and the same defects as their predecessors of the *Dunkerque* class, except that the move to a heavier DP gun for the secondary battery served only to emphasise the priority accorded by the French Naval Staff to anti-destroyer capability over the defence against aircraft. Once early war experience revealed the inadequacy of the *Marine Nationale*'s anti-aircraft arrangements, a decision was taken to replace the midships 152mm triple turrets with six twin 100mm HA mountings, and these were in place by the time of *Richelieu*'s premature departure for North Africa in June 1940. The triple 152mm mounting, despite its theoretical 90-degree elevation and its highly automated loading and firing mechanisms, was to prove too cumbersome and too fragile to be effective in the anti-aircraft role, and its development was not matched by a capable high-angle fire control system.

Great Britain Joins the New European Arms Race

The orders for new Italian and French 35,000-ton battleships armed with 15in guns effectively put an end to the various Royal Navy studies undertaken during the late 1920s and the early 1930s for battleships of more modest displacement armed with 12in guns. All of these designs had been characterised by exceptionally heavy protection (required to resist the 14in and 16in shell of existing battleships), and none was capable of more than 23 knots. By 1935 studies for a new type of battleship to be laid down immediately after the expiry of the London Treaty (31 December 1936) had a uniform displacement of 35,000 tons, with an armament of 14in, 15in or 16in guns; nine out of the eleven variants proposed were capable of speeds of 27–30 knots. The high-speed designs were initially referred to by the Admiralty as 'battlecruisers' until it became clear that all the capital ships of the new generation were being designed for a minimum speed of 27 knots.

Although the Admiralty would have liked to have ships capable of matching the 30-knot speed of *Dunkerque* and the *Littorio*s, there was concern that this would inevitably result in a marked reduction in the level of protection. Although the other four Washington powers, whose primary operating environments were the Mediterranean and the Pacific, were contemplating long-range fleet engagements of 18,000m and beyond, the Royal Navy still regarded 12,000 to 16,000 yards as the 'decisive range', particularly in North European waters, and its new ships would have to be armoured accordingly. Director of Naval Construction (DNC) Goodall was himself very much an 'armour' man, and suggested that reducing speed from 30 to 27 knots would purchase a big increase in protection. Such a ship could be armed with nine 15/16in guns in three triple turrets, or twelve 14in in three quadruple turrets.

The *Nelson* layout with all three turrets forward was considered. However, Goodall was of the opinion that a ship with a modern anti-destroyer/anti-aircraft armament and aviation facilities would provide nothing like the weight savings that had been possible with the older battleships. It was also difficult to accommodate the propulsion machinery needed for a 27-knot ship if the three-turret main armament was all-forward, as the third turret and its magazine and shell rooms would be located amidships, at the point of maximum beam.[10]

By September 1935 the Admiralty was leaning towards a 29-knot ship armed with nine 15in guns to match the new French and Italian ships, but in the following month the US Government indicated to the Foreign Office that it was prepared to accept a new limit of 14in guns provided Japan agreed. This presented the Royal

The battleship *King George V* in October 1941. She is unmodified since completion except for the Type 271 'lantern'. Note the UP (unrotated projectile) mountings atop 'B' and 'X' turrets. In the event, the British would be the only Washington Treaty power to adopt the 14in gun specified as the maximum calibre under the London 1936 Treaty: the French and Italian ships, which were laid down prior to 31 December 1936, had 380mm/15in guns, the Americans 16in and the Japanese *Yamato* and *Musashi* 46cm/18in.

Navy with a dilemma: if it waited for the outcome of a conference due to take place in late 1935 it would be unable to place an order immediately for the new guns, and the projected completion of the new ships in 1940 would have to be put back. On the other hand, the US proposal (for which Britain had been pressing) could not be ignored, so in November the Admiralty sanctioned a 35,000-ton, 28-knot ship with an armament of twelve 14in guns.

The final design had exceptionally well-developed protection. The armoured deck, which was 6in thick over the magazines and 5in thick over the machinery, was raised to main deck level, and rested on top of a deep vertical side belt 15in thick over the magazines and 14in thick over the machinery. Although the armour protection conformed to the 'all-or-nothing' principle, there was some protection for the 'soft ends' of the ship: the lower of the three strakes of armour was continued for 40ft beyond the magazines fore and aft to protect the latter from raking gunfire, and there was horizontal armour up to 5in thick over the lower deck fore and aft. A new hard-ened steel plate with 25 per cent greater resistance had been developed by the British during the 1930s, and this was employed for the first time in the new ships, which became the *King George V* class.

The new arrangement of armour had considerable advantages. The height of the armoured deck meant that a much greater proportion of the internal volume was

Littorio (It): Protection   **King George V (GB): Protection**

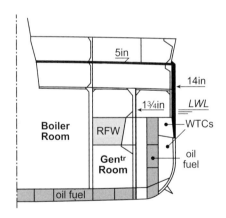

Note: Armour thicknesses for *Littorio* are in millimetres.

© John Jordan 2019

Again, two very different answers to the same question: the Italian *Littorio* had an inclined main belt with a 70mm 'decapping' plate in front of it, combined with a a novel underwater protection system devised by the distinguished naval engineer Umberto Pugliese, comprising a cylinder surrounded by fuel or water which in theory absorbed the explosive force of a torpedo warhead. The protection scheme of the British *King George V* was derived from the 'all-or-nothing' scheme of the late-WWI First World War US battleships. It featured a deep, vertical heavy belt over the machinery and magazines topped by a thick single thick protective deck. The underwater protection scheme was an air/liquid/air sandwich, backed by a conventional vertical torpedo bulkhead.

under armour, giving greater protection to electrical cabling, communications and fire control systems. The exceptionally deep vertical belt (23ft 6in/7.2m, compared with 5.75m for *Dunkerque* and only 13ft/4m for the *Nelsons*) was ideal for protecting reserve buoyancy (meaning that metacentric height could be reduced) and for keeping out a diving shell (a weakness of inclined belts). The new scheme was extensively tested up to 1936, when trials were carried out against a full-size reproduction of the midship section. It was estimated that the horizontal protection would keep out 15in shell up to 33,500 yards (29,500 yards for the machinery).

The underwater protection system was the classic air/liquid/air sandwich backed up by a vertical torpedo bulkhead, and was designed to resist a 1,000lb torpedo warhead. Given that one ship of the class, *Prince of Wales*, would succumb to only five much smaller aerial torpedoes with 450lb (205kg) or 330lb (150kg) warheads, claims for the system were probably optimistic, but there were extenuating circumstances to the ship's loss.[11]

In order to secure this level of protection the main armament had to be reduced from twelve to ten guns (nine would have probably been a better solution, but this would have resulted in a theoretical inferiority *vis-à-vis* the new Italian battleships that the Admiralty was reluctant to accept). Turret No. 2 ('B') now had only two guns, and this required some redesign of the ship to compensate for the reduction in weight forward (around 800 tons). The design of the turrets was based on the successful 15in/13.5in twin turrets designed by Vickers prior to the First World War. Fixed-angle loading was adopted to reduce complexity, but the more numerous safety interlocks caused teething troubles that were particularly marked during the engagement between the brand-new *Prince of Wales* and the *Bismarck*. A further problem was the requirement to pass ammunition into the quadruple turrets at any angle of train. This was resolved by adopting a transfer ring whose movement was independent of the ship and the turret; however, the designers did not allow sufficiently for the flexibility of the hull, and it frequently jammed. The 14in gun itself, which was 45 calibres long and fired a relatively heavy shell with a modest muzzle velocity, proved to be very successful in service, with a barrel life far superior to the 16in model of the *Nelsons*, and proved capable of penetrating more than 12in (305mm) of face-hardened armour at a range of 18,000 yards.

At a relatively late stage in the design process it was decided to replace the original dual-purpose secondary battery of twenty 4.5in guns (as in *Renown* and the two later *Queen Elizabeth* reconstructions) with eight of the new twin 5.25in mountings being developed for the cruisers of the *Dido* class (see Chapter 4). Doubts were expressed as to the efficacy of the 4.5in as an anti-destroyer weapon and the 5.25in gun, which fired a much heavier shell (80lb/36kg versus 58lb/23kg), seemed to provide the solution. The 5.25in twin mounting was completely self-contained, with its own electric motor for elevation, training, ramming and powering the ammunition hoists. The guns, which were widely spaced in separate cradles, could be elevated to 70 degrees. However, as with many contemporary dual-purpose mountings of the period, the designed firing cycle of 10–12rpm was never attained, 7–8rpm being the

Littorio (It): LA/HA Guns

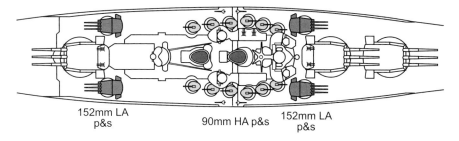

152mm LA
p&s

90mm HA p&s

152mm LA
p&s

King George V (GB): DP Guns

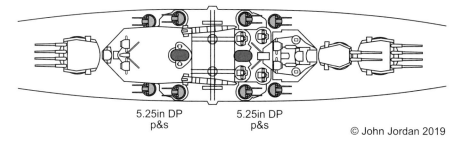

5.25in DP
p&s

5.25in DP
p&s

© John Jordan 2019

The Italians opted for a split battery for their low-angle and high-angle guns. There were heavy triple turrets for 152mm LA guns at the four corners of the ship, complemented by a new 90mm fully-automatic HA gun in twelve single turrets amidships. For *King George V* the British opted for a dual-purpose 5.25in twin mounting. This saved deck space and simplified magazine arrangements below decks, but although the 5.25in gun was effective in the low-angle, anti-destroyer role, the mounting was insufficiently 'agile' to provide effective anti-aircraft fire against the fast monoplanes that entered service during the late 1930s.

best achieved in service. The mounting was complex and difficult to maintain, and the training speed of 10–11 degrees per second was inadequate for effective fire against the latest monoplane aircraft.

The dual-purpose secondary mountings were arranged as four groups, the port and starboard pairings being located forward and aft of the heavy cross-deck catapult amidships. The latter, as in the latest battleship reconstructions, was served by twin hangars abeam the first funnel with handling cranes located at their outer corners. There were four eight-barrelled 2pdr pom-pom mountings grouped around the funnels, and control for the 5.25in mountings was provided by four HACS Mk IV director systems in a 'four-corner' arrangement that matched the disposition of the guns.

These were the first British battleships to adopt the unit machinery layout. There were four boiler rooms each with two Admiralty three-drum boilers and served by two vertical widely spaced funnels, separated by the turbines for the wing shafts. Each of the four sets of machinery was completely self-contained and could be isolated in the event of action damage, and the boilers could also be cross-connected to drive any of the turbines. Designed horsepower was 100,000shp for 28 knots.

Electrical power was provided by six 350kW turbo-generators and two 350kW diesel generators for a total of 2,800kW – a major advance on earlier British battleships, although still short of the figure for contemporary French capital ships.

The legend for these ships was ready in September 1936, standard displacement being estimated at 35,900 tons (which the DNC altered to 35,500 tons at the stroke of a pen). The first two ships, *King George V* and *Prince of Wales*, were laid down on 1 January 1937 – the first date available under the London Treaty. Three further ships of the class would be authorised under the 1937 estimates and laid down in May–July of the same year. A new European naval arms race was now in full swing.

The Pacific Powers

Sketch designs for new battleships for the US Navy had been prepared as a matter of course prior to the London Conference, and again during the early 1930s. All were essentially updated versions of the traditional US battleship, with firepower, protection and endurance prioritised over tactical speed. The US Navy favoured the 16in gun calibre and wanted armour against the same together with a deep underwater protection system, and like the British Royal Navy it considered 22–23 knots the maximum feasible speed on a displacement limited to 35,000 tons.

All this changed with the laying down of new battleships in Europe during the early 1930s, all of which were capable of speeds of 29–30 knots. Indeed there can

The first modern US battleships, *North Carolina* and *Washington*, were laid down only in 1937–38. They were designed to carry 14in guns in accordance with the London Treaty of 1936, but following the US invocation of the 'escalator' clause in March 1937 were rearmed with 16in guns. This is *Washington* (BB-56) off New York City on 21 August 1942. *(NHHC, NH 33803)*

be little doubt that the sudden American *volte-face* on maximum gun calibre in October 1935, when the US Government finally indicated to Great Britain that it would be prepared to accept a reduction to 14in, was the result of new US Navy studies for high-speed battleships that could match the new French and Italian ships and which would also be fast enough to operate with the new carriers. By this time the US Navy's General Board had already given serious consideration to a draft proposal for a 30-knot ship armed with nine 14in guns in triple turrets and with protection against 14in shellfire. Subsequent deliberations closely mirrored those of the Royal Navy, with a reduction to 27 knots buying an additional two or three 14in guns.

In the event, however, Japan was unwilling to agree the proposed reduction from 16in to 14in gun calibre, so the new US battleships were redesigned to accommodate nine 16in guns in triple turrets. Speed was 27–28 knots to enable them to operate with the fast carriers, but the protection system remained virtually unmodified. Due to strong pacifist and isolationist sentiments in the United States, President Roosevelt deferred *North Carolina* and *Washington* from the FY1937 Programme to FY1938 (July 1937–June 1938), so both were laid down long after the expiry of the Washington Treaty. Their most successful feature would be their dual-purpose battery of twenty 5in/38 guns in twin mountings, with HA fire control provided by the excellent Mk 37 tachymetric director system. They were otherwise everything one might expect from a ship designed under the Washington Treaty limitations.

This was far from the case, however, with the new Japanese battleships, for which design work began in earnest in 1934. Following the 1930 London Treaty, the Japanese Government had secured agreement for ratification from the Naval Staff largely by persuading them that a quantitative limitation did not necessarily imply a qualitative one. This argument provided the rationale for the IJN's massive battleship reconstruction programme of 1933–37, and for the upgrading of 'treaty' cruisers that had only recently been completed (see Chapter 4). It also laid the foundations for what has since become known as the 'Super-Battleship Strategy'.

In March 1934 Japan announced her intention to withdraw from the Washington Treaty when it expired at the end of December 1936. Although the British and Americans would attempt to hold on to the Treaty, which they would attempt to replace with a new updated model, Japanese withdrawal effectively marked the end of the Collective Security era.

From this point on the Japanese had no intention of re-engaging in the naval arms limitation process, and would pursue a policy of qualitative superiority, with quantitative levels determined solely by the capacity of the Japanese armaments industries. A detailed programme of new battleship construction was drawn up that stipulated the laying down of two ships in 1937, a further two in 1939, followed by three in 1942. These would be the largest and most powerful battleships in the world, armed initially with 46cm (18.1in) guns in three triple mountings, and later – once the US Navy had matched this gun calibre – with 51cm (20in) guns. They would be around

290m long, with a beam of 37m, and would have a standard displacement in excess of 60,000 tons. They would be built in the naval dockyards under the greatest secrecy in order to delay any effective American response. Moreover, even once the Americans became aware of the size and power of these ships they would be able to match them only if they were prepared to deny themselves the strategic flexibility that had underpinned US maritime operations since the turn of the century, as ships of this size would be too large to pass through the Panama Canal.

This project was to result in the battleships of the *Yamato* class, which were slightly shorter than in the initial design but were otherwise every bit as impressive. When the final design was approved in March 1937 only the Mitsubishi Shipyard in Nagasaki had a slipway large enough to accommodate the hull, and this had to be reinforced; the other vessels of the class were laid down on slipways that were either newly constructed or specially modified. The massive 46cm/45 guns of the main armament, each weighing 165 tonnes, were transported from the manufacturers to the shipyards aboard a purpose-built freighter. They fired shells weighing 1,460kg to a maximum range of 42,000m (the 16in guns on the *North Carolina* fired a 1,225kg shell to 33,750m). Construction began only in November 1937, when *Yamato* was laid down at the Kure Naval Dockyard. By this time the reconstruction of the older battleships was complete.

The first of the IJN 'super-battleships', *Yamato*, did not enter service until after Pearl Harbor, so Japan began the war with a fleet of six older battleships and four 'fast battleships' (formerly battlecruisers), all rebuilt to a uniform standard. The photo shows *Yamashiro*, *Fuso* and one of the fast battleships of the *Kongo* class in Tokyo Bay during the late 1930s. (*NHHC, NH 90773*)

Conclusions

The more radical capital ship reconstructions of the 1930s were made possible by the adoption of high-pressure steam conditions and lightweight geared turbines. The installation of new machinery freed up weight and space for horizontal and under-water protection, batteries of high-angle (or DP) guns for fleet air defence, and short-range cannon and machine guns for close-in defence against dive-bombing, together with more sophisticated fire control systems.

New high-performance machinery also made possible the design of a new generation of fast capital ships that did not need to sacrifice protection for speed. Whereas the 'treaty' battleship designs of the 1920s and early '30s were generally restricted to 22–23 knots, the 30-knot French and Italian battleships laid down in 1932–34 set down a marker and ensured that 27 knots would now be the *minimum* acceptable speed for battleships. From this point on the term 'battlecruiser' would be increasingly irrelevant, even though the Royal Navy continued to designate its older fast ships as such and the term has since been applied by some commentators – albeit incorrectly – to the French *Dunkerque* and *Strasbourg* (on account of the modest thickness of their armour belt) and to the German *Scharnhorst* and *Gneisenau* (on account of their less powerful main guns).

All the new ships had the 'all-or-nothing' protection system introduced by the US *Nevada* of 1916 and adopted for the British *Nelson*s post-Washington. The only capital ships laid down during the 1930s with a 'pre-Jutland' protection system were the German battleships of the *Scharnhorst* and *Bismarck* classes. The French, whose older surviving battleships were so dated that their complete, graduated armour belts are more accurately described as 'pre-dreadnought', became such enthusiastic converts to the new orthodoxy that their new ships were closely modelled on the British *Nelson*s, with a short, heavily armoured citadel made possible by carrying all the main armament forward in two quadruple turrets.

There were subtle differences, however, in the level of protection accorded to decks other than the main armoured deck (now seated on top of the armour belt to create a protective box or 'citadel'). The French opted for a 40mm 'splinter' deck on the American pattern to prevent fragments of AP shells that penetrated the main armoured deck or splinters from the deck itself from entering the machinery spaces and magazines. The Americans, who were increasingly concerned about the aerial threat, opted to add a 'bomb deck', the upper deck being reinforced to a similar thickness to ensure that bombs exploded outside the hull, where much of the force of their explosion would be vented freely into the atmosphere. In a slight variation of this, the Italians adopted a reinforced upper deck that was also intended to 'decap' an AP shell, complemented by a 70mm upper side belt, so that (in theory at least) only shell fragments reached the main armoured deck.

By the 1930s the inclined main armour belt, which was more difficult to penetrate for a given thickness, had become standard. Interestingly it was the British, who had pioneered this concept in the *Nelson*s, who first broke with the practice by adopting a much deeper, vertical belt for the *King George V* class.[12] Their concerns that a 'diving shell' might penetrate the soft underbelly beneath the armour belt were subsequently endorsed by the US Navy and the IJN. However, the latter two navies would make the mistake of continuing their inclined armour belts at a reduced thickness down to the double bottom, so that they effectively doubled as torpedo bulkheads. Because the bulkhead was now constructed of hardened armour steel, it tended to crack rather than deform when exposed to the shock of a torpedo warhead explosion, resulting in the very flooding of the machinery spaces that the torpedo bulkhead was intended to prevent.

There was less conformity with regard to underwater protection. The British, the French and the Italians came to favour the 'liquid layer' system introduced by the US Navy in its pre-Washington 'Big Five'. In general terms this comprised multiple thin longitudinal bulkheads with alternating void spaces and tanks filled with oil fuel or water in what is often termed an 'air/liquid/air sandwich'. In this system the thin-skinned outer (void) chamber served to vent the explosion, while the liquid in the centre compartment absorbed and distributed its force throughout the holding bulkhead, which if breached was backed up by a free-flooding space with a reinforced bulkhead inboard of it, thereby preventing flooding of the machinery spaces. Reconstructed battleships generally had this underwater protection system added on as a deep bulge (or 'blister'), but in the purpose-built ships of the 1930s it was generally more closely integrated with the upper hull to reduce resistance. The ingenious Pugliese system, adopted for all the new and reconstructed Italian battleships, and comprising a deformable cylinder surrounded by liquid, occupied only the lower corners of the hull and closely followed its contours, and was therefore attractive in terms of weight and space requirements.

Of the five Washington navies only the IJN persisted with 'dry' underwater protection systems, in part because of reservations about the threat posed to watertight integrity by liquid systems, which required extensive pipework to transfer liquids between compartments. Instead the Japanese preferred a system of heavy armoured bulkheads well inboard backed by holding bulkheads. Sealed 'crush' tubes, first employed by the Royal Navy in its underwater protection systems of the late war period, were retained for the older reconstructed ships.

Subsequent experience during the Second World War would show that all these approaches were valid, with the liquid layer system generally considered superior to the 'dry' systems, but that the key factors in the effectiveness of any of the systems adopted were their depth (necessary to absorb the full force of the explosion of a large torpedo warhead), and their ability to resist and contain flooding, which often depended on the quality of the detail design and construction.

A key issue for the new generation of capital ships was how to accommodate both a secondary 'anti-destroyer' battery and a high-angle anti-aircraft battery. The traditional 'battleship admirals' continued to insist on a gun with sufficient weight of shell to disable a destroyer before it could launch its torpedoes. Royal Navy theorists argued that a medium-calibre gun would only start hitting reliably below 10,000 yards, and that a modern destroyer would aim to launch torpedoes at around

6,000 yards. This meant a 'window of opportunity' of about two minutes (assuming destroyer approach speed as 30 knots). The destroyer would be approaching head on, making it difficult to obtain hits in the machinery spaces, and would need to be stopped if it were to be prevented from launching its torpedoes.

The implication was a relatively heavy secondary gun, the 6in calibre being preferred. There was a degree of unanimity over this, with 6in, 150mm, 152mm or 155mm guns mounted in twin or triple power-operated turrets being selected for the British *Nelson*s, the German *Scharnhorst* and *Bismarck* classes, the French *Richelieu* and Italian *Littorio* classes, and the Japanese *Yamato*s respectively. However, by the 1930s, the increase in the aerial threat meant that the new generation of battleships would also need to accommodate a powerful battery of high-angle guns, which competed for deck space with the turrets of the secondary armament, and which needed separate magazines and fire control directors, all of which implied additional cost, weight, hull volume and accommodation for gun and FC personnel.

The Italians, the Germans and the Japanese opted for separate anti-destroyer and anti-aircraft batteries, the deck-space problem being resolved in the latter two navies by mounting the anti-destroyer guns on the upper deck with the HA guns above them; in the Italian *Littorio* class the triple turrets of the secondary batteries were moved out to the corners of the ships, with the HA guns grouped around the funnels amidships at forecastle deck level (at some cost to bow and stern arcs). However, all of these ships emerged well above the Washington Treaty displacement of 35,000 tons, and the *Littorio*s had a complement of 1,830 officers and men, 400 more than the war complement of the British *King George V*s as first completed.

The only practical solution available to those navies who were more particular about adhering to treaty limits was the development of a viable dual-purpose mounting. In theory dual-purpose mountings saved topweight and deck space and were more economical on manning. However, there was a cost in terms of the complexity of the mounting, which ideally needed to be loaded at all angles of elevation and had to be capable of high training and elevation speeds. Moreover, the concept involved a compromise between a gun that could hit and stop a destroyer at a range of 10,000 yards (implying a large-calibre gun firing a heavy shell with a high muzzle velocity), and a gun that was sufficiently light and manoeuvrable to deal with the new generation of high-performance aircraft (implying a smaller calibre gun with a relatively short barrel length).

The British and the French opted for heavier guns better suited to anti-destroyer fire: the French for the 130mm (5.1in) calibre in *Dunkerque* and *Strasbourg*, followed by the 152mm (6in) calibre in the *Richelieu* class, the British for the intermediate 5.25in calibre. All these mountings were complex and prone to breakdown, and were capable only of long-range barrage fire in the anti-aircraft role. The Americans would opt for the lighter 5in DP gun, which had a relatively short 38-calibre barrel, was reliable and easy to maintain, and when paired with the tachymetric Mk 37 director was to prove the best medium-calibre HA gun of the Second World War. The US Navy's battle line was never to be subjected to torpedo attack by destroyers, so the effectiveness of the 5in/38 in this latter role was never put to the test. However, this was also true of the British and French battleships, so the theoretical superiority of their 5.25in and 152mm guns against destroyers proved to be of little practical value, while the inferior performance of these weapons against aircraft was a real disadvantage. Moreover, both the British and the French invested considerable resources in developing alternative dual-purpose guns; a modified variant of the 130mm fitted in the *Dunkerque*s was to have been developed for the later destroyers of the *Le Hardi* class, while older British capital ships undergoing reconstruction were fitted with the twin 4.5in mounting. At the same time, the US Navy was fitting the 5in/38 twin mounting in both battleships and cruisers, and the same gun in a single mounting in destroyers and aircraft carriers.

One curious anomaly in the thinking behind the new battleships was the general persistence with the thickly armoured conning tower. This had been a constant feature of battleship design since the pre-dreadnought era. However, the concept had evolved at a time when the standard range of engagement was around 2,000m, and battleships were vulnerable not only to the occasional hit by 11in or 12in shell, but were exposed to a hail of fire from quick-firing guns of 6in calibre and below that would quickly destroy most of the ship's upperworks.

Once engagement ranges increased beyond 15,000m, and hits were not only fewer and by heavier shells, but were also more likely to strike the broad hull rather than the unarmoured upperworks, the armoured conning tower became less important to the survival of the commanding officer of the ship and his key staff. In an era of treaty-limited displacements there was a considerable cost in weight in providing armour on the scale of a small gun turret for the conning tower and the communications tube that connected it with the key gunnery and machinery control spaces beneath the armoured deck. Moreover, the constricted internal volume of the conning tower was at odds with the much larger command spaces essential to modern warfare.

The Royal Navy began to question the value of the conning tower during the 1920s. Although an armoured conning tower was fitted in the *Nelson*s, it was not a feature of the British 'treaty' cruisers despite its retention in their foreign counterparts. Subsequently a number of older battleships in refit had their conning tower armour reduced in thickness, and the conning tower of the *King George V* class was a token box structure with 3–4½in protection. This remarkably courageous step was taken at a time when all the other major navies (with the exception of the Germans – another North Sea power) were contemplating battleship engagement ranges far in excess of the Royal Navy's anticipated 12,000–16,000 yards, engagements in which there would be far fewer and less frequent hits by large-calibre shells. Yet the conning tower was retained by all the other major navies despite its cost in armour and topweight.

One final observation remains to be made. Despite the lightweight, high-performance machinery that became available during the 1930s, none of the Washington navies was able to build a completely satisfactory battleship within the Treaty limits.

The tower of the French battleship *Richelieu* in 1940. The armoured conning tower with its multiple observation slits can be seen on the left of the photograph. *(Henri Landais collection, courtesy of Robert Dumas)*

The problem was that although a satisfactory capital ship armed with 16in guns could be built on a 35,000-ton displacement in 1922, this was no longer the case by 1935. A battleship at the time of the Washington Conference was a heavily armed, heavily armoured 'floating battery' designed to fight in a line of battle at a speed of 20 knots. By the mid-1930s battleships needed to be capable of independent operations and were more likely to be fighting in 'penny packets' of two or three ships (especially in Europe). They needed higher tactical speed to be able to intervene in support of the cruiser squadrons or to accompany fast aircraft carriers. They would face greater exposure to attack by modern high-performance aircraft, and would therefore need comprehensive layered anti-aircraft systems with ever more elaborate fire control in addition to their traditional main and secondary batteries.

With a maximum displacement limited by treaty these features could be purchased only by a reduction in firepower or protection, and once international relations again became clouded by fear and suspicion there was a marked reluctance on the part of the major powers to embark on any initiative that might place them at a military disadvantage. Once the Washington Treaty expired it was therefore inevitable that battleship displacement would again increase until 40,000–45,000 tons became the norm for a ship armed with 15in or 16in guns.

Chapter 3

AIRCRAFT CARRIERS 1930–36

THE LONDON TREATY left the Washington provisions with regard to aircraft carriers untouched with one significant exception: carriers displacing 10,000 tons or less now had to be counted in a country's overall tonnage allocation, and could be armed with guns up to a calibre of 6.1in (155mm). In compensation, newly designed capital ships and up to 25 per cent of cruisers could be fitted with a landing-on deck or flight deck, launch by catapult being assumed for ships equipped with just a short landing-on deck.

These were subtle differences that have received less critical attention than the new rules for cruisers, but they reflected a parting of the ways for the European and Pacific powers in terms of the way they perceived the future role of naval aviation.

In 1922 the only navy with a fully developed naval air arm and operational concepts to match was the Royal Navy. By 1930, however, the British had a force of three newly converted fleet carriers and the United States two even larger ships, which were themselves almost matched in size by the Japanese *Akagi* and *Kaga*. The first multi-carrier exercises had taken place in the Pacific, and were already making their impact on US Navy and IJN fleet organisation and operational procedures. New purpose-built carrier aircraft ordered during the early and mid-1920s were beginning to enter service, making possible powerful, balanced air groups that could provide long-range search and fleet fighter defence, and which could also deliver ranged bomb and torpedo attacks against enemy carriers and capital ships. As yet these aircraft were biplanes of traditional construction with relatively low speed and endurance; their low speed made them vulnerable to anti-aircraft fire, and their attacks generally had to be launched at less than 100nm range, making the carriers themselves vulnerable to cruisers screening or scouting for the enemy battle fleet, particularly when launching or recovering aircraft. However, the potential was clearly there for the future, given that the Washington and London Treaties imposed no limits on the capability or numbers of embarked naval aircraft.

Nowhere in this new scenario was there any perception that the aircraft carrier would or could replace the capital ship as the decisive unit of naval power. For both the Pacific navies the carrier would continue to be viewed as a 'force multiplier', a fragile unit with an important role to play in creating the conditions for a favourable battle line engagement, but one which would in all probability be disabled and out of the battle by the time the big guns fired. The British also saw the carrier as a force multiplier, but generally expected it to be tied more closely to the battle line so that it could provide spotter aircraft for the main gunnery engagement.[1] This would ultimately lead to a much greater emphasis on toughness and survivability of the platform (*ie* protection and anti-aircraft defence) at the expense of the offensive capabilities of the air component.

The British tried to impose further qualitative and quantitative restrictions on carriers both at Geneva and at the London Conference, at which a limit of 25,000 tons on individual carrier displacement and an overall tonnage limit of 100,000 tons were proposed. The proposal was as usual based on current Admiralty requirements, and although it would have suited Britain well – the three existing fleet carriers each displaced around 22,500 tons and only one further ship of 23,000–25,000 tons was currently projected – the United States and Japan, whose existing ships displaced 27,000–33,000 tons, were understandably less enthusiastic. The United States had already used up 80,000 tons of her current 135,000 tons allowance on *Lexington, Saratoga* and *Ranger*,[2] so under the new proposal would have only 20,000 tons available for new construction (implying a single carrier of an enlarged *Ranger* type). The Japanese would find themselves in a similar position; they had already used up 53,800 tons of their own 81,000-ton allocation on *Akagi* and *Kaga,* and if the latter figure were then to be reduced (using the 5:3 ratio) to 60,000 tons, the tonnage remaining would be barely sufficient to complete *Ryujo*, and would certainly preclude the building of further carriers.

The acceptance by the Pacific powers on the one hand of the future importance of the aircraft carrier to their operational strategy, and on the other of the inherent vulnerability of these ships, led both to favour multiple flight decks.[3] Both powers

Table 3.1: **Aircraft Carrier Tonnage Available after the London Treaty**[1]

Great Britain		United States		Japan	
Hermes	10,850tW	*Lexington*	33,000tW	*Akagi*	26,900tW
Eagle	22,600tW	*Saratoga*	33,000tW	*Kaga*	26,900tW
Furious	22,450tW	*Ranger*	13,800tW	*Ryujo*	7,100tW
Glorious	22,500tW				
Courageous	22,500tW				
Total	100,900tW	Total	79,800tW	Total	60,900tW
Remaining	34,100tW	Remaining	55,200tW	Remaining	20,100tW

Notes:
[1] HMS *Argus* (14,450tW), USS *Langley* (10,290tW) and the Japanese *Hosho* (7,470tW) have been omitted as, by the early 1930s, they were regarded by their respective navies as obsolescent and due for replacement. *Hermes* and *Eagle* (Great Britain) could also be replaced under the Washington rules despite being technically 'under-age'. Scrapping *Hermes*, which was regarded by the Royal Navy as too small to operate modern aircraft, would have given Britain sufficient tonnage for two new ships of just under 24,000 tons.

USS *Langley* (CV-1) was one of several aircraft carriers deemed to be 'experimental' under the Washington Treaty. These ships could be replaced at any time in order to boost the tonnage available for new construction. *Langley* is seen here in Hampton Roads in 1939; in October 1936 she underwent conversion as a 'seaplane tender' – a treaty-exempt category under London 1930 – and during the Second World War was employed as an aircraft transport. *(Leo van Ginderen collection)*

were therefore adamantly opposed to any reduction in the overall tonnage allocation, even though they were now more receptive to the reduction in individual carrier size. The Americans were particularly interested in building 'flying deck cruisers' as a means of boosting the number of available flight decks, hence the new rules permitting up to 25 per cent of overall cruiser tonnage to be so fitted.

The British had little interest in the flying deck cruiser, and acceded to pressure to accommodate this clause in the hope that the United States and Japan might be encouraged to fritter away a substantial part of their limited cruiser allocation on these hybrids. The Royal Navy's problem was that, with aircraft development now in the hands of the RAF and a major financial crisis, it had insufficient aircraft available for its existing carriers and cruisers. In 1929 it had been calculated that the current five carriers (the three newly converted fleet carriers plus *Eagle* and *Hermes*) required 175 aircraft, with a further seventy-five aircraft needed for existing battleships and cruisers; only 141 were available. By comparison, the United States had 229 aircraft and Japan 118. The Admiralty proposed that sufficient funding be provided for the purchase of two flights (*ie* twelve aircraft) per year, but none were ordered in 1929 due to the financial crisis, and funding for the 1930 batch was secured only after a fight.

Some Technical Issues

The first generation of fleet carriers had been built on capital ship hulls. This had a major influence on their configuration. They were generally well-protected (although only to hangar deck level) and well-armed; they were also exceptionally heavy in terms of their construction – hardly surprising when it is remembered that the American and Japanese ships were conversions of capital ships originally designed to displace 40,000–45,000 tons. This effectively limited the tonnage available for new carrier construction under the Washington and London Treaties, and consequently the number of available flight decks and the number of aircraft they could operate. The Japanese had already laid down, and the Americans just authorised, small purpose-built carriers (*Ryujo* and *Ranger* – see *WAW* Chapter 7), and although these would both prove too small to be operationally effective they would become the prototypes for ships of 15,000–20,000 tons laid down during the mid-1930s which would become central to their respective countries' war effort during 1941–42. These ships would be optimised for air operations; they would have modest protection, and would be armed only with anti-aircraft weapons.

USS *Ranger* (CV-4), completed in 1934, was the prototype for a new type of purpose-built US fleet carrier; the single-hangar design prioritised aviation capabilities above 'ship' qualities. She had a large, unobstructed rectangular flight deck, three aircraft lifts and an open hangar. The exhaust gases from her boilers were led up into hinged funnels on either side of the flight deck, and she was unarmoured and had no underwater protection. *Ranger* is seen here at Guantanamo Bay in November 1939. *(NHHC, 80-G-391559)*

The trend towards more lightly built ships would militate against the heavy anti-surface guns thought to be essential during the 1920s if the ships were to defend themselves against enemy cruisers. The change was made possible by the ever-increasing operational radius of modern aircraft, which meant that search and attack missions could increasingly be launched at a range that made direct contact with enemy surface forces less likely. It was a development undoubtedly welcomed by naval architects, who no longer had to concern themselves with how best to accommodate large power-operated gun mountings and their associated magazines in a lightly protected ship with a full-length flight deck. There were also considerable savings in weight, space and cost, so carriers could accommodate and operate more aircraft on a much smaller displacement.

Now that more experience with flying operations at sea was being accumulated, it was becoming apparent that island superstructures were less of a problem than had been anticipated, although the disposal of large quantities of hot, turbulent funnel gases was still an issue. The advantage of having a permanent raised island structure to port or to starboard of the flight deck for ship control and the management of flight operations was increasingly seen to outweigh the disadvantage of a disturbed airflow over the after part of the flight deck. Indeed, some pilots were now indicating a preference for an island, which provided a useful reference point during landing. The British had abandoned the flush-deck carrier after the conversion of *Furious*, an island structure would be fitted in the USS *Ranger* prior to her completion, and all the Japanese carriers designed or modernised during the 1930s would feature a small island. Subsequent British carriers would have their funnel uptakes integrated into the island structure, as would the US carriers that followed *Ranger*, but the Japanese preferred to dispose of these hot, corrosive exhaust gases via large downward-facing vents located to starboard, despite the unpleasant conditions this created for the gun crews manning the after anti-aircraft weapons.

Carrier design would also have to keep pace with developments in the performance of modern aircraft. By the early 1930s aircraft were larger and heavier, which meant higher take-off and landing speeds. Transverse arrester systems would be universally adopted to slow aircraft on landing (making a flush deck less attractive), and American and Japanese carriers would feature 'double-ended' systems to permit aircraft to land in the event of damage to the after end of the flight deck. Larger, heavier aircraft also signalled the end of the multi-deck layout adopted in the 1920s conversions for the Royal Navy and the IJN; the lower flying-off decks were too short to be useable by modern aircraft, and the length of the upper flight deck needed to be maximised to ensure that heavy torpedo bombers lined up on the after part of the flight deck could get into the air. A full-length upper deck, when combined with a system of arrester wires and a crash-barrier, also offered the possibility of flying off lightweight aircraft such as fighters from the forward part of the deck while simultaneously conducting landing operations aft. The alternative, particularly attractive for launching small numbers of reconnaissance aircraft or fleet defence fighters without having to turn into the wind, was the flush-deck 'accelera-

An F4F Wildcat fighter is prepared for launch on the cross-deck catapult at the edge of *Yorktown*'s hangar deck. Catapults and accelerators were fitted in the carriers completed during the interwar period to enable the carrier to launch fighters or reconnaissance aircraft without wind over deck.

tor' developed by the Royal Navy during the early 1930s or the cross-deck fixed catapults fitted at hangar-deck level in the new US carriers.

Aircraft size would also influence important aspects of carrier design such as hangar height and lift configuration. At first it was thought that future aircraft would continue to grow in size,[4] but this changed with the advent of high-performance monoplanes constructed of lightweight metal alloys during the late 1930s. These developments were to have a major influence on stowage and lift considerations. Biplanes designed for shipboard use generally had hinged wings that were folded back manually in line with the fuselage to maximize the number of aircraft that could be accommodated in the hangar, and lifts were often sized accordingly (especially in the British Royal Navy). However, wing folding for monoplane aircraft was normally close to the fuselage and was generally power-operated. The IJN was reluctant to accept the weight/performance penalty that was an unavoidable consequence of monoplane aircraft with folding wing mechanisms, and had to accept smaller air complements as a result.

Another development that would have a major impact on carrier design and operational tactics would be the advent of the dive bomber. These aircraft, which started to enter service with the US Navy from 1931, were specifically designed to put 500lb (later 1,000lb) bombs through the flight decks of enemy carriers by using a controlled dive that made a hit or near-miss far more likely. The impact of this development was considerable: greater attention now had to be paid to light, quick-firing AA guns that could fire at high angles of elevation, and to the protection of the hangar and flight deck. Purpose-built, carrier-based dive bombers would subsequently be developed by the Japanese, the British and ultimately the French, and would change the balance of air groups in the direction of offensive operations. Once air groups became dominated by strike aircraft the aircraft carrier itself would move away from its original battle fleet support function and would become capable of independent operations.

Finally, carriers were now designed to handle only wheeled aircraft, not float-planes. This meant an end to the British-style low quarterdeck with access to the (open) after end of the lower hangar, and the large stern handling cranes. With the demise of the separate flying-off deck and the stern seaplane handling arrangements, both ends of the ship could be plated up to the flight deck, line handling being performed via large rectangular openings. This had major benefits for sea-keeping, particularly in the hostile northern waters in which British ships had to operate. The US Navy and the IJN saw this as less important, and preferred to retain an 'open' bow and stern for line and boat-handling, and to mount light AA weapons to cover the bow and stern arcs.

The British *Ark Royal*

After the London Conference, work began again on the fourth fleet carrier projected for the Royal Navy since the late 1920s. By this time British carrier design thinking was evolving in response to developments in the Pacific. The large carriers completed for the US Navy and the IJN during the late 1920s were already operating much greater numbers of aircraft than their British counterparts (sixty in the case of the Japanese ships, seventy-four in *Lexington* and *Saratoga*, as compared with a theoretical maximum of fifty-two in *Courageous* and only thirty-six in *Furious* – see *WAW* Chapter 7). These numbers had previously been thought too large for effective aircraft management by the Royal Navy, which in the early days had struggled to fly off or land on more than six aircraft at a time. The higher tempo now being achieved by the US Navy, which in the 1929 Fleet Problem had demonstrated the ability to launch and land multi-plane strikes, was due to the adoption of a permanent deck-park with arming and refuelling performed on the flight deck, thereby obviating the need to strike aircraft down to the hangar on landing.

The Royal Navy gave the deck park solution serious consideration, and took all the necessary steps to acquire the technology that it deemed essential to facilitate the concept. The prototype for a new transverse arrester wire system was trialled in the carrier *Courageous* in January 1931, and it was subsequently decided to conduct trials using a twelve-plane deck park in the carrier *Eagle*.[5] At the same time development work began on the first 'accelerators', flush-deck catapults that used the carrier's hydraulics system to launch aircraft from the forward end of the flight deck. Production models capable of launching a 7,000lb (3,200kg) aircraft at 56 knots would be installed in *Courageous* and her sister *Glorious* in 1934, and more powerful models capable of launching 12,000lb (5,500kg) aircraft would follow. In theory these could be combined with a US-style 'crash barrier' strung between the island superstructure and the deck-edge that would divide the flight deck into a take-off area forward and a landing-on area aft.

When the preliminary design of the new carrier was discussed in earnest during the spring of 1931 there was initially strong support for a ship with a permanent deck park and a single hangar, but at a subsequent meeting it was decided that the ship would have a configuration similar to *Courageous*, with an island, a double hangar and no deck park. Nevertheless, both the accelerator and the arrester system would be features of the future *Ark Royal* and her armoured successors, making possible the adoption of larger air complements and US-style deck parks by the Royal Navy from 1941.

Other requirements agreed at the April meeting included: a speed of at least 27 knots for air operations and 32 knots for 'evasion' (to enable the ship to operate independently without the need to accommodate a heavy anti-cruiser gun armament); an air complement of sixty aircraft;[6] protection for the magazines against 6in cruiser shell, with horizontal protection at hangar deck level sufficient to keep out a 500lb SAP bomb, a flight deck capable of withstanding small 20lb bombs dropped by fighters, and underwater protection on a par with contemporary capital ships. Armament was to comprise four groups of dual-purpose guns, preferably of at least 4.7in calibre to deal with destroyer attacks, with four eight-barrelled 2pdr pom-poms and smaller multiple machine guns. There were to be three lifts, of which the after two were to be restricted in width (*ie* sized for aircraft with folded wings) and offset from the centre line, while the forward lift was sized to accommodate spread aircraft to enable planes to be struck down immediately on landing.

By October 1931 the separate flying-off deck had been suppressed in anticipation of likely developments in accelerators and arrester gear. It was hoped to include the new carrier in the 1933 estimates, but the ongoing financial crisis made this impossible, and authorisation was again delayed.

Work on the design began again in 1933, and characteristics were firmed up. Overall length was now 800ft,[7] and it was hoped to stow seventy-two aircraft in the double hangar, which at 58,200ft² had a significantly greater floor area than *Courageous*.[8] The three narrow lifts, powered by hydraulic rams and measuring 45ft by 22ft (the forward lift was slightly larger), were sized to accommodate the new torpedo/spotter/reconnaissance (TSR) Fairey Swordfish with wings folded, and were offset from the centre line to facilitate the movement of aircraft fore and aft at hangar and flight deck level. Unusually, the lifts had a double-platform configuration and travelled only one deck height, which meant that aircraft could not be transferred directly from the lower hangar to the flight deck (or vice versa). In operational terms this meant that aircraft were expected to be prepared for sorties in the upper hangar and maintained in the lower. There were to be two accelerators, as in *Courageous*, but with a 12,000lb launch capacity.

Preliminary sketches showed an armament of sixteen 5.1in guns in single DP mountings, arranged as four 'quadrant' groupings at hangar-deck level. However, the prototype 5.1in gun was not successful as the fixed round was too heavy to be manhandled comfortably, resulting in a firing cycle that was too slow for effective anti-aircraft fire. It would subsequently be replaced first by the 4.7in gun and finally

Ark Royal (GB)

Profile

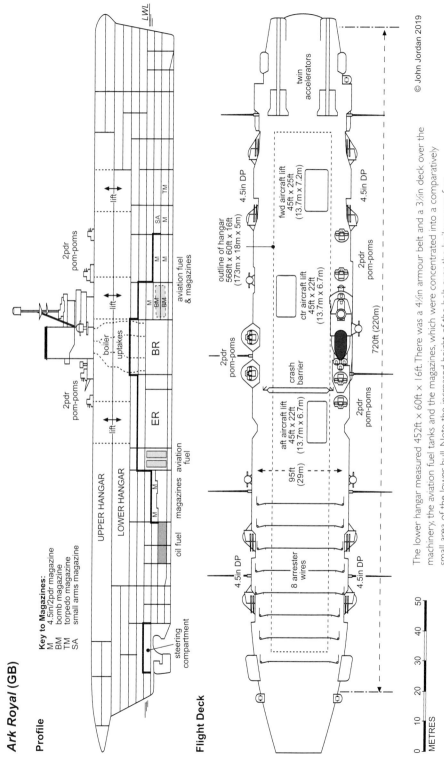

LWL

2pdr pom-poms

lift

2pdr pom-poms

lift

boiler uptakes

lift

2pdr pom-poms

UPPER HANGAR

LOWER HANGAR

ER

BR

SA M TM

M M

M M BM BM

M M

aviation fuel & magazines

aviation fuel

magazines

oil fuel

steering compartment

Key to Magazines:
M   4.5in/2pdr magazine
BM   bomb magazine
TM   torpedo magazine
SA   small arms magazine

Flight Deck

© John Jordan 2019

twin accelerators

4.5in DP

4.5in DP

outline of hangar 568ft x 60ft x 16ft (173m x 18m x 5m)

fwd aircraft lift 45ft x 25ft (13.7m x 7.2m)

ctr aircraft lift 45ft x 22ft (13.7m x 6.7m)

2pdr pom-poms

2pdr pom-poms

720ft (220m)

crash barrier

aft aircraft lift 45ft x 22ft (13.7m x 6.7m)

95ft (29m)

4.5in DP

8 arrester wires

4.5in DP

The lower hangar measured 452ft x 60ft x 16ft. There was a 4½in armour belt and a 3⅛in deck over the machinery, the aviation fuel tanks and the magazines, which were concentrated into a comparatively small area of the lower hull. Note the increased height of the belt over the boiler room fans.

0   10   20   30   40   50
METRES

by the 4.5in Mk 1 gun that went into the later capital ship reconstructions. The 4.5in guns were in twin DP mountings located at the four corners of the flight deck and just below it to enable aircraft on the opposite side of the ship to be engaged at higher levels of elevation; each of the paired mountings had its own fire control director.

Protection was now expected to take into account not only 500lb bombs but also the 1,000lb bombs reported to be projected for US Navy dive bombers. Horizontal armour was increased to 3½in over the magazines and machinery, while the armoured belt remained at 4½in to secure full protection from 6in shell. Underwater protection was on a par with contemporary British battleships (resistance to a 750lb torpedo warhead was demanded), and the aviation fuel tanks were isolated from the ship's structure and jacketed to enable them to survive distortion to structural members in the event of action damage. Fire containment measures on the hangar decks were exceptionally complete, comprising fire curtains and spray systems.

The major weakness of *Ark Royal* was her machinery layout, which would be largely instrumental in her loss when struck by a single torpedo fired by *U-81* in November 1941. The three engine rooms were in line abreast in order to keep the length of the citadel to a minimum, and were each supplied with steam by two boilers. The smoke ducts for the latter had to be led across the ship beneath the lower (armoured) hangar deck, and because these had not been fitted with baffles flooding spread to all boiler rooms after the torpedo hit. Equally significantly, a decision was made at the design stage to dispense altogether with diesel generators in favour of six 400kW turbo-generators; this meant that when steam pressure was lost so was the electrical power necessary for lighting and for powering the pumps.

HMS *Ark Royal* at Portsmouth during 1938–39. The effects of the adoption of a double hangar are evident in the high freeboard. Note also the enclosed bow and stern favoured by the Royal Navy for operations in the North Atlantic. *(NHHC 19-SB-2J-1)*

An aerial view of *Ark Royal* operating Fairey Swordfish aircraft dating from 1939. Note the twin hydraulic 'accelerators', which could be used for launching aircraft when the ship was at anchor, at the forward end of the flight deck. Note also the three narrow aircraft lifts, designed to minimise deck penetrations and offset from the centre-line to facilitate the movement of aircraft fore and aft at hangar and flight deck level; they could accommodate aircraft only with wings folded. *(NHHC, NH 79167)*

The sketch design and legend were finally approved in June 1934. However, even with extensive use of welding it was calculated that the ship would displace 22,800 tons, and this was a major concern, as the US Navy had indicated that it would be proposing a new limit of 22,000 tons for aircraft carriers at the upcoming London Conference of 1935. In the event this problem was resolved by the now-

Table 3.2: British Aircraft Carriers 1930–1936

	Ark Royal	*Illustrious* class
Built:	1935–38	4 ships 1937–41
Displacement:	22,000tW	23,000tW
Dimensions:	800ft × 95ft	753ft × 96ft
	(244m × 28.9m)	(230m × 29.2m)
Machinery:	Six Admiralty boilers;	Six Admiralty boilers;
	3-shaft geared turbines,	3-shaft geared turbines,
	102,000shp = 31kts	111,000shp = 30.5kts
Protection:	belt: 4½in	belt: 4½in
	hangar deck: 3½in	hangar sides: 4½in
		flight deck: 3in
Armament:	16 – 4.5in/45 (8 × II) DP	16 – 4.5in/45 (8 × II) DP
	48 – 2pdr (6 × VIII)	48 – 2pdr (6 × VIII)
Aircraft:	60 max	36

customary subterfuge of simply reducing the weight of munitions declared. The Royal Navy planned to build four more ships of this type, but following the London Conference of 1935 there was a change of direction.

Ark Royal was arguably the best carrier laid down for the Royal Navy in the inter-war period, and was in many respects superior to her Japanese and US Navy contemporaries. However, she was also a prime example of the extent to which 'ship' rather than aviation characteristics continued to dominate British carrier design during the 1930s. Although similar in size to the US Navy's *Yorktown* class, she operated fewer aircraft,[9] had an aviation fuel capacity of 100,000 tons compared with 187,000 tons, and had hangars with low ceilings and narrow lifts that could not accommodate spread aircraft.

New Carriers for the US Navy

The eye-catching performance of *Lexington* and *Saratoga* in Fleet Problem IX of 1929 had convinced the US Navy of the potential of the aircraft carrier as a strike weapon, but war games at the Naval War College continued to suggest that carriers were particularly vulnerable to counter-strikes by their own kind. An ongoing debate was therefore taking place between the advocates of large carriers, able to operate large air groups and with a degree of passive protection, and those who advocated a larger number of small flight decks, which although less capable of mounting decisive air strikes were more survivable because they were more numerous and could be spread over a wider area.

The US Navy's remaining carrier tonnage allocation following the completion of *Ranger*, which had a designed displacement of 13,800 tons, was 55,200 tons (see Table 3.1). This suggested a choice between two new carriers each of the maximum 27,000 tons permitted under Washington, three carriers of 18,400 tons, or adherence to the original proposal of four further ships of the *Ranger* type, each of 13,800 tons, A fourth possibility, given that the General Board was inclining towards the operation of carriers in tactical groupings of two, was a repeat *Ranger* plus two carriers each of 20,700 tons.

There was a general preference for three small or intermediate carriers, but there was also concern regarding the total absence of protection in the *Ranger* design. In May 1931 the Bureau of Aeronautics was suggesting that an increase in displacement to 18,400 tons would buy a speed of 32.5 knots (*Ranger*'s top speed was 29 knots), underwater protection intermediate between battleship and cruiser standards, horizontal protection over the magazines, machinery and aviation fuel tanks, improved defence against dive bombers, and increased internal operational facilities, with the hangar deck devoted exclusively to aircraft stowage and maintenance, changes in the number and layout of lifts, and improved bomb handling. Interestingly, the Bureau also favoured a separate 'flying-off' deck as in the British and Japanese carriers, which was surprising in view of the limitations this would inevitably impose on deck parks and multi-aircraft strikes.

Rear Admiral Moffett, chief of BuAer and a member of the US Navy delegation at the London Conference, was in favour of complementing a small number of large-deck carriers with a larger number of flying deck cruisers. In this he was supported by the Chief of Naval Operations, Admiral William V Pratt and by the Senate naval committee, which wanted the next cruiser to have a flight deck unless the Navy decided otherwise. A prototype design, discussed in Chapter 4, would go as far as the contract stage during 1931 before falling victim to the Depression.

Meanwhile, the debate about the new generation of purpose-built carriers intensified. BuAer still expressed a preference for a flush deck and a single hangar with either a separate flying-off deck or two cross-deck catapults at hangar-deck level. It also suggested that the larger (20,700-ton) ship might accommodate a second, shorter hangar amidships for the assembly of broken-down 'reserve' aircraft, served by two lifts and with a further two (outer) lifts serving the upper hangar.

Armament was still an issue, as without 8in guns the carrier was deemed incapable of operating independently of the battle line. Pratt considered that this problem could be addressed by operating 32.5-knot carriers with 8in-gun cruisers in combined scouting/offensive strike groups; he wanted one carrier for each of three four-ship cruiser divisions. It was acknowledged that flight decks would still be a prime target for hostile aircraft, so future carrier design would need to prioritise horizontal protection and heavy machine guns to protect against dive bombers. However, flight deck armour was impossible to achieve on the lower displacements being considered, so great emphasis would be placed in the US Navy of the 1930s on achieving air superiority by getting in the first strike against the enemy's carriers, protection against enemy bombers being limited to an armoured deck of modest thickness over the magazines and machinery.

The two-deck proposal was given serious consideration but was rejected in favour of a full-length flight deck with arrester wires at both ends. However, in compensation there were to be two cross-deck catapults at hangar-deck level for the launch of fighters and reconnaissance aircraft. Outriggers were to be fitted to maximise the size of the deck park. Designs for carriers of 15,200tW and 20,000tW were duly presented to the General Board in September 1931. It was proposed to order the two 20,000tW ships under FY1933 and a single 15,200tW ship (to complement *Ranger*) under 1934, but the orders were delayed by the Depression. The two larger ships, to be named *Yorktown* and *Enterprise*, would be built using industrial recovery funds and laid down in mid-1934. The smaller ship, *Wasp*, would be laid down in the spring of 1936, and would be the last US Navy carrier to be designed and built under the Washington Treaty.

All three would be designed to operate the new air group of seventy-two aircraft, which it was initially envisaged would comprise one squadron of dive bombers, one of scouts, one of single-seat, long-range fighters (for escorting strikes), and one of short-range fighters (for carrier defence). An alternative air group, which would be the one finally adopted, would have one of the fighter squadrons replaced by a squadron of torpedo attack/heavy bomber aircraft. Once the two-seat scout and dive bomber categories had been merged with the development of the SBD Dauntless,

Table 3.3: **US Navy Aircraft Carriers 1930–1936**

	Yorktown class	*Wasp*
Built:	2 ships 1934–38	1936–40
Displacement:	20,000tW	14,700tW
Dimensions:	809ft × 83ft	720ft × 82ft
	(247m × 25.3m)	(219m × 24.9m)
Machinery:	Nine B&W[1] boilers;	Six Yarrow boilers;
	4-shaft geared turbines,	2-shaft geared turbines,
	120,000shp = 32.5kts	70,000shp = 29.5kts
Protection:	belt: 4in	belt: none (see text)
	deck: 1½in	deck: 1¼in
Armament:	8 – 5in/38 (8 × I) DP	8 – 5in/38 (8 × I) DP
	16 – 1.1in MG (4 × IV)	16 – 1.1in MG (4 × IV)
Aircraft:	90	72

Notes:
[1] B&W = Babcock & Wilcox

the basis of the carrier air group that dominated the early period of the Pacific War would be firmly in place, and the US carriers would be operating seventy-two to ninety aircraft of only three distinct types.

The machinery required to drive the two 20,000-ton ships at their maximum speed of 32.5 knots was more than twice as powerful as that of *Ranger*, so it was decided that the hinged funnels of the latter would have to be replaced by a single large fixed funnel to starboard, and once this was accepted it was but a small step to a conventional island superstructure. *Wasp* would revert to a less powerful machinery installation (70,000shp versus 120,000shp for a maximum speed of 29.5 knots) but would retain the island superstructure, albeit with a smaller funnel.

Yorktown and *Enterprise* were given hull protection sufficient to resist 6in shell between 10,000 and 20,000 yards at a 60-degree target angle.[10] There was a vertical armour belt of a maximum 4in thickness on 0.75in standard construction steel with 4in bulkheads fore and aft, and 1.5in plating over the magazines and machinery. There was also an underwater protection system designed to resist a 400lb torpedo warhead. The contemporary standard for US battleships was a 700lb warhead; 400lb protection was sufficient against the smaller airborne torpedoes, but was not expected to cope with torpedoes launched by destroyers or submarines. The former were potentially less of a threat to a carrier than to a battleship, as at 32.5 knots the carrier would be capable of outrunning surface warships, whereas the battle line was expected to be specifically targeted by the enemy's destroyer flotillas. However, submarines remained a major threat and *Yorktown*, although disabled by aerial torpedoes, would be sunk by submarine torpedoes at Midway.[11] Her near-sister *Hornet*, on the other hand, remained afloat following severe damage inflicted by Japanese carrier aircraft at the Battle of Santa Cruz that included three aerial torpedo hits, and had to be dispatched by destroyer torpedoes.

Yorktown (US)

Profile

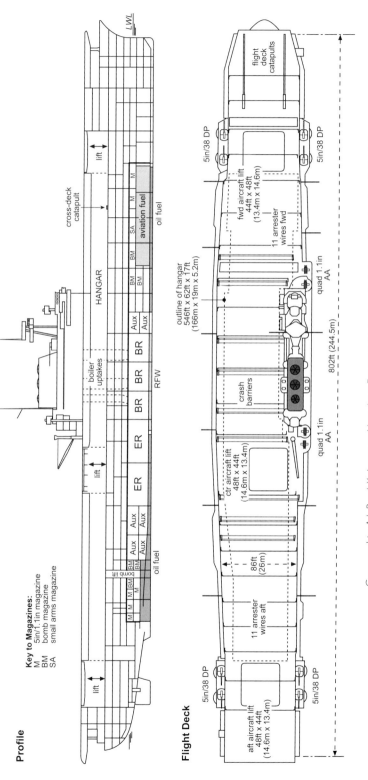

Key to Magazines:
M   5in/1.1in magazine
BM   bomb magazine
SA   small arms magazine

Flight Deck

Compared to *Ark Royal*, *Yorktown* and her sister *Enterprise* had only a single hangar, broader aircraft lift platforms, and a longer, shallower armour belt over the machinery, aviation fuel tanks and magazines. Note the arrester wires fore and aft, which enabled these carriers to land aircraft over the bow as well as the stern. The short flight deck catapults and the cross-deck catapult in the hangar were rarely used and were later removed.

© John Jordan 2019

It proved impossible to provide even this modest level of protection for the displacement-limited *Wasp*, which had only 1.25in plating over the magazines and machinery and no underwater protection system. There was provision for fitting external belt armour at a later date, once Treaty limits were no longer applicable, but this was never fitted due to operational demands and the workload in the shipyards.

Yorktown and *Enterprise* had an 800ft flight deck served by three large evenly spaced lifts each 48ft by 44ft. *Wasp*'s flight deck was significantly shorter at 727ft, and only the centre and after lifts were retained, the forward lift being replaced by a 'T'-shaped folding model on the deck edge to maximise hangar space. The smaller flight deck made the simultaneous launch of large numbers of aircraft difficult, so the air group was smaller (initially by a full eighteen-plane squadron). All three ships were fitted from the outset with two flight deck catapults; *Yorktown* and *Enterprise* had a single cross-deck catapult of the same type at hangar-deck level, while *Wasp* had two. These were somewhat underpowered compared with the later British models, which made the launch of heavy modern aircraft from the hangar, where launches could not benefit from wind over deck, difficult. The catapults were seldom used, as it took about three times as long to launch small groups of aircraft as was possible using a conventional 'rolling' take-off, and they were later removed for installation aboard escort carriers.

Anti-aircraft provision was the same in both carrier types, and was oriented for

Yorktown off Haiti during 1938–40 with a full deck-load of aircraft. Note the large black 'Y' on the funnel used for identification purposes. *(NHHC, 80-G-5132)*

USS *Yorktown* (CV-5) in Hampton Roads in October 1937, shortly after her completion. Like *Ranger*, she had a only a single hangar, although clearance was significantly greater than in *Ark Royal* and her IJN contemporaries. Note the hinged doors used to close the open hangar in adverse weather conditions. *(NHHC, NH 50330)*

the first time towards small-calibre quick-firing machine guns for defence against dive bombers. In addition to eight single 5in guns of the new 38-calibre dual-purpose model, there were four quadruple 1.1in mountings and six quadruple 0.5in machine guns. Both the latter guns had a very short range and would prove relatively ineffectual against fast monoplane aircraft; they would be replaced first by massed single 20mm Oerlikon cannon and then by twin and quadruple 40mm guns as the war progressed.

The two *Yorktown*s would prove very successful ships, and their design would form the basis for the later *Essex* class that would dominate the final two years of the Pacific War. *Wasp* would subsequently be criticised as too small and too slow for effective carrier operations. All three of the new US fleet carriers were less well-protected than the British *Ark Royal*, but the *Yorktown*s proved very resistant to combat damage, and were difficult to sink – *Enterprise* survived the war, despite

USS *Wasp* (CV-7) at Guantanamo Bay in October 1940. Although heavily influenced by the *Yorktown* class, she was effectively a reversion to the *Ranger* design, with modest speed and little in the way of protection. The 'reduced' design was necessary to ensure that the US Navy stayed within its carrier tonnage allocation under the Washington and London 1930 Treaties. *(NHHC, NH 43463)*

being frequently hit. It is difficult to make any proper assessment of the survivability of the unprotected *Wasp*, as she was never subjected to a sustained aerial attack by the Japanese, and no other carrier would have survived being struck on the same side by three submarine torpedo warheads of 405kg (900lb).[12] On the other hand, the US carriers were far better equipped for large-scale air operations than their British counterparts, and by the early 1940s were operating far more capable carrier aircraft.

The Japanese *Soryu* and *Hiryu*

Like the US Navy, the Imperial Japanese Navy entered the 1930s fully convinced of the future potential of naval aviation. The carriers *Akagi* and *Kaga* had been completed during the late 1920s and *Akagi,* operating alongside the smaller *Hosho*, had already played a major role in fleet exercises. Air groups had been trained, and new types of purpose-built carrier aircraft were now rolling off the production lines in increasing numbers.

However, the London Treaty had been by no means favourable to Japanese plans. In particular, the option of building an unlimited number of small carriers below 10,000 tons based on *Ryujo* had been foreclosed; such ships would now count under Japan's overall tonnage allocation. The flying deck cruiser, as permitted under Article 16 of the London Treaty, was an option, but although hybrid carrier/cruiser designs received serious consideration by the IJN during 1931–32, no such ship was authorised or laid down.

The G6 design of 1932 was armed with three twin 20cm/8in guns forward,[13] and had a waterline length of 240m, a standard displacement of 12,000 tons (trial displacement 17,500 tonnes[14]), propulsion machinery rated at 150,000shp for a speed of 36 knots, and an air complement of seventy fighters and torpedo bombers. The ship would have been far too large to qualify as a 'flying deck cruiser' (10,000 tons maximum), and the latter category was in any case restricted to 155mm/6.1in guns (see *WAW* Chapter 11). It could have been built only using Japan's remaining available carrier tonnage, which was 12,630 tons – assuming *Hosho* was retained. Drawings of the G6 design show many of the features of *Akagi*, including the same two-way incline of the flight deck and the large downward-facing funnel vent on the starboard side, but with the short 'flying-off' decks forward replaced by superimposed 20cm gun turrets on the centre line.

The G8 design dating from 1933, which is reported to have been the initial design for what would become the medium carrier *Soryu*, was for quite a different type of ship: a modern carrier with a full-length flight deck and a stern plated up in the manner of the British *Ark Royal*, with a prominent vertical funnel amidships to starboard and a substantial island farther forward. The island carried the fire control directors for five 15.5cm (6.1in) guns – the same model fitted in the *Mogami* class cruisers (see Chapter 4) – in one twin and one triple turret mounted back-to-back beneath the forward end of the flight deck. Capabilities were otherwise similar to those of the G6 design, with a designed air complement of twenty-four Type 90 fighters and forty-eight Type 89 torpedo bombers. Again, it is difficult to see how such a ship could have been built on the comparatively small displacement claimed. The final design, initially designated G9, would be a true carrier with the anti-surface guns eliminated.

The IJN currently had four carriers (*Hosho*, *Akagi*, *Kaga*, *Ryujo*), the US Navy three (*Saratoga*, *Lexington*, *Ranger*). However, the operational value of *Hosho*, the Japanese prototype for this category, was limited, and *Akagi* and *Kaga*, prior to their mid-1930s conversion, were essentially experimental. In contrast, the US Navy carriers were all modern, powerful ships, and there were plans to build two carriers of an improved *Ranger* type. In view of the reinforcement of the US Navy and the increasingly fraught relationship with the United States, the IJN deemed it essential to maximise the total tonnage available and to build two medium-sized carriers. The 12,630 tons available could be increased to 20,100 tons by the decommissioning of *Hosho* (nominally 7,470 tons) in accordance with Article VIII of the Washington Treaty, which treated all carriers in existence or building on 12 November 1921 as 'experimental'.

The displacement of each of the new ships was therefore to be limited to 10,050 tons – an extremely ambitious figure, given that the original staff requirements drawn up in 1931 stipulated an air complement of sixty-eight and protection for the magazines against 8in shell. This 10,050-ton figure was a mathematical necessity born of a perceived need to match US carrier numbers and treaty limitations that limited Japan to three-fifths of US carrier tonnage. Despite the modifications made to the original *Ryujo* design, Japan continued to declare the displacement of this ship as 7,100 tons,[15] while *Akagi* and *Kaga* had a declared combined displacement of 53,800 tons. Thus the standard displacement of each the two new carriers in the 1934 'Circle 2' Programme, which predates Japan's official announcement of her withdrawal from the Washington Treaty, was declared to be 10,050 tons.

The final design for the new carrier, which was laid down in November 1934 as *Soryu*, was larger than anticipated but was still radically different from the G8 sketch. It was essentially an enlarged *Ryujo*, with a cruiser hull powered by a *Mogami*-type propulsion plant, no anti-surface guns, and an identical anti-aircraft armament of six twin 12.7in/40 HA guns. The hot exhaust gases were vented to starboard via two downward-facing funnels, and forward of these there was a small island structure for the ship and flying control spaces, atop which one of the two main fire control directors for the 12.7cm guns was mounted. The bow and stern were open, as in the earlier IJN carriers, to facilitate line and boat handling. The flight deck, although shorter than in the G8 design, extended almost the full length of the ship and was 220m long. There was a double hangar capable of accommodating a maximum of seventy-three aircraft, including reserve aircraft in a broken-down condition, served by three well-spaced lifts of adequate dimensions (the forward lift could accommodate the largest aircraft currently in service with wings spread). The initial plans envisaged an air group comprising only fighters and dive bombers. This was revised four times before *Soryu*'s completion, and in the final version torpedo bombers were included. *Soryu* was now to embark a total of fifty-seven (+ sixteen reserve) aircraft:

The two 'medium fleet' carriers of the *Soryu* class were remarkably capable ships for their size, able to accommodate a a useful complement of attack aircraft and with a good turn of speed. However, they had limited protection against shell and bombs and none against torpedoes. *(Kure Naval Museum)*

The Japanese carriers showed a mix of British and US practice. The aircraft were normally struck down and stowed in the twin hangars but the flight deck, with its three large aircraft lifts and fore-and-aft arrangement of arrester wires, was broadly similar to that of US carriers. Protection for the two medium carriers of the *Soryu* class was comparatively light.

Soryu (Jap)

Profile

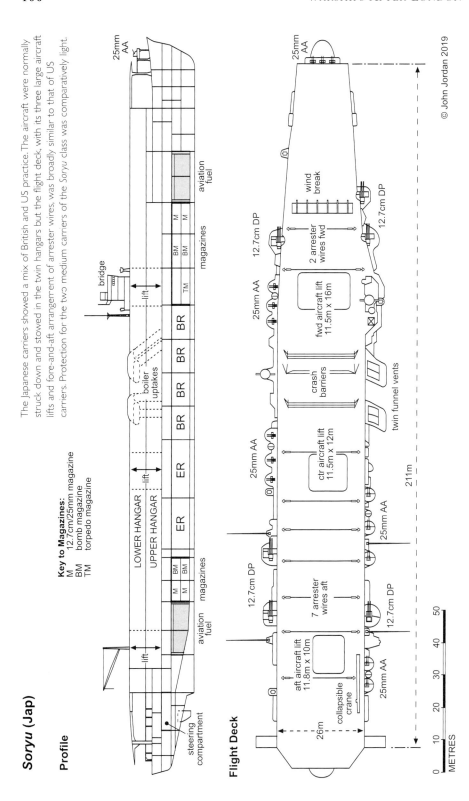

Key to Magazines:
M   12.7cm/25mm magazine
BM   bomb magazine
TM   torpedo magazine

25mm AA

bridge

lift

LOWER HANGAR

UPPER HANGAR

lift

boiler
uptakes

| M | BM | | ER | ER | BR | BR | BR | BR | | TM | BM | M |
| M | BM | | | | | | | | | | BM | M |

magazines   magazines

aviation
fuel   aviation
                                                             fuel

lift

steering
compartment

Flight Deck

25mm AA

12.7cm DP

12.7cm DP

aft aircraft lift
11.8m x 10m

7 arrester
wires aft

25mm AA

25mm AA

ctr aircraft lift
11.5m x 12m

crash
barriers

twin funnel vents

211m

25mm AA

25mm AA

fwd aircraft lift
11.5m x 16m

2 arrester
wires fwd

wind
break

12.7cm DP

12.7cm DP

25mm
AA

collapsible
crane

26m

© John Jordan 2019

0 10 20 30 40 50
METRES

twelve (+ four) Type 96 fighters, twenty-seven (+ nine) Type 96 dive bombers, nine (+ three) Type 97 torpedo bombers and nine (+ zero) Type 97 reconnaissance planes.

As with the smaller American carriers, only minimal protection could be fitted in. There was 140mm vertical armour over the magazines with a 40mm deck, but only 35mm with a 25mm deck over the machinery spaces. The level of protection was sufficient to protect only the magazines against cruiser shell at ranges in excess of 12,000m, and the relatively fine hull, adopted with a view to maximising tactical speed, precluded an effective underwater protection system. When completed in late 1937 *Soryu* displaced 15,900 tons standard, slightly more than the US Navy's slower and virtually unprotected *Wasp*.

Her projected sister-ship, authorised under the same 1934 'Circle 2' Programme but not laid down until July 1936, incorporated a number of modifications. Some of these were the result of operational experience with *Ryujo*, which suffered badly in the Great Storm off Honshu in 1935; other changes, notably the strengthening of the armour protection, were possible because from 31 December 1936 Japan would no longer be subject to Washington and London Treaty restrictions.

Following the problems experienced with *Ryujo*, the hull structure of the new ship, to be named *Hiryu*, was generally strengthened and the height of the forecastle deck raised to improve sea-keeping in adverse conditions. There was also an increase of 1m in beam, which improved stability and increased fuel stowage from 3,700 tonnes to 4,400 tonnes. The thickness of the armour belt was increased to 85mm over the machinery and 150mm over the magazines, although the horizontal protection remained unchanged, presumably because of stability concerns. The reinforcement of the armour protection was costly in terms of weight, and contributed to a 1,000-ton increase in displacement compared with *Soryu*.

Soryu's sister, *Hiryu*, seen here running trials in April 1939, featured a number of improvements, which included an increase in the height of the bow and improved protection against shellfire. However, the most striking difference visually was the relocation of the island bridge to the mid-point to port. *(NHHC, NH 73063)*

During the mid-1930s a Japanese Naval Aviation study suggested that the opti-mum position for the island from an aircraft handling point of view was amidships, and not forward as in *Soryu* and the reconstructed *Kaga*. These recommendations were duly adopted for both *Hiryu* and for *Akagi,* which was undergoing reconstruc-tion at the same time that *Hiryu* was building. As the exhaust vents for the boilers were located in this position on the starboard side, the island had to be located to port. The new position was not a success; it was found to create an even greater degree of turbulence over the after part of the flight deck than the islands on *Soryu* and *Kaga*, and was not repeated on later ships.

Soryu and *Hiryu* were remarkable ships for their displacement: they could accom-modate and operate a useful air group, and both achieved 34 knots on trials. However, they were lightly built and on the small side for effective air operations; their successors of the *Shokaku* class, which were designed following Japan's with-drawal from the Washington Treaty, would be larger and better protected.

Reconstruction of *Akagi* and *Kaga*

At the same time that the *Soryu* design was being finalised, it was decided that the two existing fleet carriers should be modernised and upgraded. The reconstruction of these ships mirrored the extensive modernisation programme for the older battle-ships and the early 'treaty' cruisers undertaken by the IJN during the last three years of the Washington Treaty period in readiness for a new construction programme free from treaty limitations. Although *Akagi* and *Kaga* had been in service for only a few years, numerous defects in their original conversion had become apparent during that period, and both ships had spent regular periods in refit or reserve.

 Of the two ships, *Kaga* was the one most urgently in need of reconstruction, despite the fact that she had entered service only in November 1929. The horizon-tal funnel arrangement modelled on the British *Furious* was considered a total fail-ure, and because *Kaga* had been converted from a battleship hull her maximum speed of 27 knots was considered marginal for the operation of modern aircraft and made it difficult for her to operate tactically with the 31-knot *Akagi*.[16]

Kaga's reconstruction was approved in May 1933 but was subsequently delayed by funding difficulties; it was undertaken by the Sasebo Naval Dockyard between June 1934 and June 1935 and was as radical as any of the battleship conversions described in Chapter 2. In order to preserve stability, which would otherwise have been threat-ened by the planned topweight additions, the original torpedo bulge was extended upwards outboard of the inclined belt and the bulges were compensated for, as in the older battleships, by extending the hull aft by 11m, thereby restoring the length/beam coefficient. The original machinery was also replaced: there were now eight modern oil-fired boilers in place of the original oil- and mixed-fired models, and new Kampon geared turbines. Horsepower rose from 91,000shp to 127,400shp, and maximum speed from 27.5kts to 28.3kts. The original horizontal funnel ducting was removed and the boiler exhausts trunked to starboard, being vented through a single large downward-facing funnel amidships as in other contemporary IJN carriers. The space

Table 3.4: IJN Aircraft Carriers 1930–1936

	Soryu class	Kaga	Akagi
Built:	2 ships 1934–39	rebuilt 1934–35	rebuilt 1935–38
Displacement:	15,900tW[1]	38,200tW	36,500tW
Dimensions:	228m x 21.3m	248m x 32.5m	261m x 31.3m
Machinery:	Eight Kampon boilers; 4-shaft geared turbines, 152,000shp = 34.5kts	Eight Kampon boilers; 4-shaft geared turbines, 127,400shp = 28.5kts	Nineteen Kampon boilers; 4-shaft geared turbines, 133,000shp = 31kts
Protection:	belt: 140/35mm deck: 40/25mm	belt: 150mm deck: 38mm	belt: 150mm deck: 38mm
Armament:	– 12 – 12.7cm/40 (6 x II) HA 28 – 25mm (14 x II)	10 – 20cm/50 (10 x I) 16 – 12.7cm/40 (8 x II) HA 22 – 25mm (11 x II)	6 – 20cm/50 (6 x I) 12 – 12cm/45 (6 x II) HA 22 – 25mm (11 x II)
Aircraft:	57	72	66

Notes:
[1] Details for *Soryu*; near-sister *Hiryu* had a displacement of 17,300tW and had heavier armour protection (see text).

to the sides of the upper hangar formerly occupied by the funnel ducting was converted into additional accommodation for maintenance personnel and air crews.

The aviation facilities were also completely revised. The short flying-off platform at upper hangar deck level was removed and the main flight deck extended to the bows; it was now 248m in length where previously it had been 170m, enabling a full strike of modern aircraft to be ranged and launched. At the same time, a new transverse arrester system developed and manufactured in Japan (Kure Type 1) was fitted.

The original conversion of *Kaga* from a battleship hull proved less than successful, mainly due to the problems experienced with the disposal of the exhaust gases from the boilers via large-diameter lateral pipes. She is seen here after reconstruction, which featured a single large flight deck served by three aircraft lifts, and large downward-angled vents to starboard for the boiler exhausts. *(NHHC, NH 73060)*

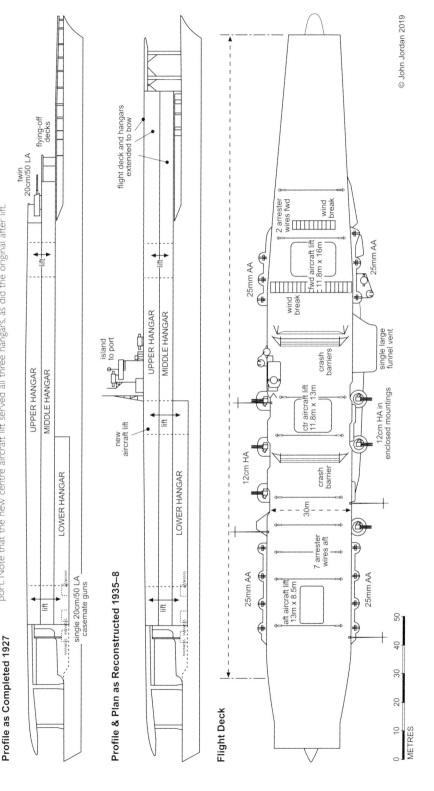

Akagi (Jap)

Profile as Completed 1927

Akagi as built and as reconstructed in 1935–38. The flight deck and hangars were extended to the bow, the original twin 20cm suppressed, and a new island bridge was located amidships to port. Note that the new centre aircraft lift served all three hangars, as did the original after lift.

Profile & Plan as Reconstructed 1935–8

© John Jordan 2019

flying-off decks

twin 20cm/50 LA

lift

UPPER HANGAR

MIDDLE HANGAR

LOWER HANGAR

single 20cm/50 LA casemate guns

flight deck and hangars extended to bow

island to port

new aircraft lift

lift

UPPER HANGAR

MIDDLE HANGAR

LOWER HANGAR

lift

Flight Deck

2 arrester wires fwd

wind break

25mm AA

25mm AA

fwd aircraft lift 11.8m × 16m

wind break

wind break

crash barriers

single large funnel vent

ctr aircraft lift 11.8m × 13m

12cm HA in enclosed mountings

12cm HA

crash barrier

30m

7 arrester wires aft

25mm AA

aft aircraft lift 13m × 8.5m

25mm AA

0 10 20 30 40 50
METRES

Both main hangars were extended forward beneath the new section of flight deck, raising the theoretical capacity to more than ninety aircraft (of which seventy-two were operational with the remaining aircraft in broken-down condition in the lower hangar, which was also slightly enlarged). By this time the deck loads being operated by the IJN were approaching the size of those aboard US Navy carriers, so a third lift was required to ensure that aircraft could be struck down quickly on landing, and this was located forward of the original two in the new flight deck/hangar section. The ammunition transfer and aircraft refuelling arrangements were also revised and renewed, and the original conning positions beneath the forward end of the flight deck were removed and replaced by a small island superstructure to starboard similar to that projected for *Soryu*.

The original armour protection was largely unmodified, but the two twin 20cm turrets fitted forward were removed, and the guns reinstalled in casemates forward of the original casemate guns at main deck level aft. The 20cm guns were by now of questionable utility, given their proximity to the waterline, but were still considered important to protect the ship against enemy cruisers. In place of the original HA armament of twelve 12cm guns there were sixteen 12.7cm/40 in the new twin mounting currently being fitted in the modernised cruisers and battleships. These would be supplemented during the late 1930s by the new twin 25mm mounting being manufactured under licence from Hotchkiss to provide a close-in and anti-dive bomber capability.

When *Kaga* emerged from refit her standard displacement had risen to a massive 38,200 tons, more than 8,000 tons greater than her displacement as first completed and 11,300 tons greater than her official displacement under the Washington Treaty. The change was not declared, as Japan had already notified the other Washington powers of her intention to withdraw from the Treaty when it expired in December 1936.

Akagi was taken in hand at Sasebo in late 1935 following the completion of *Kaga*'s refit. Work was again delayed by funding problems, with the result that, although *Akagi*'s reconstruction was far less extensive than *Kaga*'s, it was almost three years before the ship emerged from the Sasebo Navy Yard. The original boilers were replaced by modern oil-fired units, but *Akagi* retained her original turbines, and horsepower was therefore little changed. As in *Kaga* the original torpedo bulge was extended upwards outboard of the inclined armour belt, but the increased water-plane area appears to have had only a minor effect on maximum speed, which remained at just over 31 knots.

The major changes were in the aviation facilities, which were modified as in *Kaga*. The main flight deck was extended to the bow and both main hangars enlarged to provide a similar aircraft capacity, and a third lift was added, although as the distance between the original lifts was greater in *Akagi* than in *Kaga* the new lift was installed amidships, between the other two. *Akagi* was rebuilt at the same time that *Hiryu* was under construction, so she had the same port-side island structure amidships, opposite the single large vent for the exhaust gases. Because of the shortage of funding for

Akagi received a less extensive modernisation due to budgetary problems, and retained her original HA guns and propulsion machinery. However, aviation facilities were now on a par with *Kaga*: a single large flight deck replaced the original multi-deck configuration forward and was served by three aircraft lifts. *Akagi*, seen here in 1941 with three Zero fighters at the forward end of the flight deck, had the same port-side arrangement of the island as *Hiryu*. (NHHC, NH 73059)

the refit, the original 12cm guns were retained, although the starboard-side mountings were fitted with enclosed gas-tight gunhouses to protect the gun crews from the funnel exhaust. The 20cm turrets were removed altogether, so that only the original six casemate guns remained.

As rebuilt, *Akagi* displaced 36,500 tons standard, less than *Kaga* but considerably more than when first completed. Both ships would serve with distinction in the Pacific War before their loss at Midway in June 1942.

The British Armoured Carriers

When, in a desperate attempt by Britain and the United States to resuscitate the naval arms limitation process, the Second London Conference was convened on 9 December 1935, all efforts to impose further size and gun-calibre restraints on capital ships were stymied by Japan's decision to withdraw from the Washington Treaty and the failure to engage her in a new treaty. In effect there was little point in discussing new limits that might be agreed by Britain and the USA, whose rivalry was a matter of pride and status, when these limits would not apply to Japan, which was by now regarded by both as a potential enemy.

The carrier issue was slightly different, in that Japan seemed to have little interest in building large carriers, and since the late 1920s had indicated a distinct preference for large numbers of small air-capable ships – of the last carriers laid down under the Washington Treaty, *Ryujo* had been declared as 7,100 tons, and *Soryu* and *Hiryu* as 10,050 tons. It was therefore possible for Britain, the United States and France – Italy declined to participate in the conference – to agree a maximum individual displacement of 23,000 tons for future carriers, since none of them wished to build a larger ship. However, Britain was by this time becoming concerned about 'over-stretch' in the Royal Navy's commitments. A rapidly deteriorating political situation made it conceivable that Britain might in the near future be faced with a resurgent German Navy in the North Atlantic, by a modern and increasingly powerful Italian Navy in the Mediterranean, and by an expansionist Japan looking towards Southeast Asia. Consideration began to be given to smaller 'trade protection' carriers, and even to aircraft depot ships similar in conception to the French *Commandant Teste*. It was therefore proposed and agreed at the conference that the quantitative limits on carriers should be abolished; in future each of the contracting powers could build as many 23,000-ton ships as they required.[17]

Once the limits on overall carrier tonnage were abolished it made sense for the Royal Navy to abandon the planned force level of five carriers each with maximum aircraft capacity, in favour of a larger number of fleet carriers each with fewer aircraft. *Ark Royal*, rather than becoming a prototype for a new generation of carriers as first anticipated, now became a conceptual 'dead end'. This *volte-face* was welcomed by the Navy for a number of reasons. In the current political climate, with the RAF still responsible for the development and supply of naval aircraft, it was easier for the Navy to secure funding for ships than for the aircraft those ships might require. Moreover, British experience suggested that forty-two to forty-eight aircraft was the maximum that could be effectively operated from an aircraft carrier using current procedures, and a reduction in air complement would facilitate the design of a ship more survivable and resistant to damage than the current flimsy carriers with their unprotected flight decks and hangars.

During the late 1920s and even the early '30s it was possible to envisage that an aircraft carrier could be defended against hostile air strikes by its own fighters. Surface pickets stationed 10nm from the capital ships were succeeded by aerial sector patrols employing two-seat reconnaissance aircraft and posted in the direction of possible hostile attacks. A standing fighter patrol would orbit above the fleet to be vectored out as soon as a visual sighting was made, and this could be boosted by scrambling fighters from the flight deck. However, as bomber speeds increased this tactic was undermined, and it became an accepted maxim that the bomber would penetrate any form of aerial defence. In the pre-radar era the Royal Navy would therefore come to rely more and more on radio-controlled AA fire and 'passive' protection. At the same time RN fighters would evolve from small, agile single-seat biplanes into two-seat monoplanes with a long-range strike escort or dive bomber function.

Until the mid-1930s the range of land-based bombers was limited, and there were large expanses of open water where a surface fleet could expect to encounter only aircraft operating from carrier flight decks. British carriers would normally operate outside the range of land-based aviation, and it was not expected that they should conduct strikes against airfields. This doctrine not only underpinned carrier and air group configuration, but it made high-performance aircraft capable of holding their own against land-based types unnecessary. However, by the late 1930s, with the

Illustrious (GB)

Profile

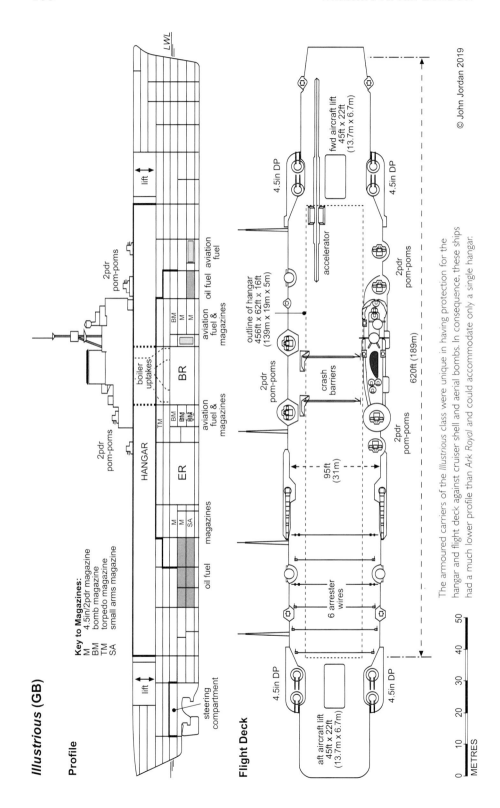

Key to Magazines:
M   4.5in/2pdr magazine
BM bomb magazine
TM torpedo magazine
SA small arms magazine

LWL

2pdr
pom-poms

2pdr
pom-poms

boiler
uptakes

HANGAR

ER

BR

oil fuel   aviation
fuel

aviation
fuel &
magazines

aviation
fuel &
magazines

magazines

oil fuel

magazines

steering
compartment

lift

lift

Flight Deck

4.5in DP

4.5in DP

fwd aircraft lift
45ft x 22ft
(13.7m x 6.7m)

accelerator

outline of hangar
456ft x 62ft x 16ft
(139m x 19m x 5m)

crash
barriers

2pdr
pom-poms

2pdr
pom-poms

2pdr
pom-poms

2pdr
pom-poms

620ft (189m)

95ft
(31m)

6 arrester
wires

4.5in DP

4.5in DP

aft aircraft lift
45ft x 22ft
(13.7m x 6.7m)

© John Jordan 2019

The armoured carriers of the *Illustrious* class were unique in having protection for the
hangar and flight deck against cruiser shell and aerial bombs. In consequence, these ships
had a much lower profile than *Ark Royal* and could accommodate only a single hangar.

0   10   20   30   40   50
METRES

advent of long-range, land-based aircraft capable of high approach speeds and armed with bombs or torpedoes, the sea areas in which there was no significant land-based threat had contracted considerably, and the aircraft to which carrier planes might be exposed were much more capable. Worse still, whereas during the 1920s the Royal Navy's most likely opponent was the Imperial Japanese Navy and the most likely venue the relatively open waters of the South China Sea, by the mid-1930s it was becoming apparent that British carriers might have to operate against a powerful and modern Italian land-based air force in the Mediterranean.

It was these considerations that underpinned the 'armoured carrier', the last carrier type designed by any of the Washington powers before the Treaty expired in December 1936. Fundamentally different in conception from the American and Japanese carriers and also from the Royal Navy's own *Ark Royal*, with which they nevertheless shared a number of technical features, the aircraft carriers of the *Illustrious* class had an armoured flight deck and hangar designed to resist 500lb (250kg) aerial bombs and 6in cruiser shell. The flight deck above the hangar was constructed of 3in NC armour plates, while the hangar walls were protected by 4½in cemented armour. Beneath the hangar there was a standard 4½in armour belt over the magazines and machinery, covered by a 2½in deck outboard of the hangar walls.

The cost in terms of topweight of such heavy armour so far above the waterline was enormous, and meant that only a single hangar could be accommodated. The two lifts, identical in size to those of *Ark Royal*, were of a very different single-tier design with a higher 6-ton capacity and a faster cycle. They could not be armoured so had to be located at the outer ends of the hangar, which could be closed off from the lift wells by 4½in armoured shutters during action. This effectively precluded air operations while the carrier was under attack, the ship being 'closed down' and defended by fighters already in the air and by a formidable anti-aircraft battery, which comprised eight twin 4.5in/45 guns in enclosed Between Deck (BD) mount-ings[18] and six eight-barrelled 2pdr pom-poms.

The hangar, 458ft long and 62ft wide with a height of 16ft, was divided by fire curtains into three equal areas, each for a squadron of twelve aircraft. The air comple-ment initially envisaged was thirty TSR Albacore biplanes and six FDB (fighter dive bomber) Skuas, half that of the standard American or Japanese fleet carrier of the period. The single hangar, the relatively short flight deck with its long round-down, and the narrow lifts were to make it difficult to operate a larger air complement incorporating modern high-performance fighter aircraft during the Second World War, and the later armoured carriers had to be extensively modified during their construction. The reduction in hull volume as compared with *Ark Royal* would also make it more difficult to accommodate the increased complement of aircrew and maintenance personnel implicit in a larger air group, to which had to be added the radar technicians and the gun crews for new light AA weapons fitted in wartime.

The three-shaft machinery layout was broadly similar to that of *Ark Royal* but with the boiler and engine rooms more widely spaced and with the auxiliary machinery outside the main machinery compartments for improved damage control. The ships

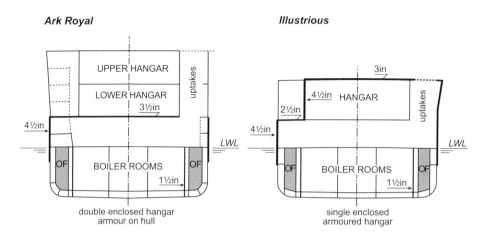

Ark Royal

Illustrious

© John Jordan 2019

The box protection for the hangar of *Illustrious* was extended out to the sides amidships in order to enclose the boiler uptakes to starboard and the boiler room ventilation trunking to port (not shown here).

The armoured carrier *Victorious* operating Fairey Albacore TSR and Fairey Fulmar reconnaissance/fighter aircraft in 1941, shortly after she entered service. Note the low freeboard compared with *Ark Royal*; these ships had only a single hangar, which reduced the potential air complement by almost 50 per cent. *(NHHC, NH 73690)*

proved impressively resistant to action damage as anticipated, albeit at the expense of what was arguably their primary function, the operation of modern high-performance aircraft.

Two ships, *Illustrious* and *Victorious*, were authorised under the 1936 programme and laid down in 1937, following the expiry of the Washington Treaty, with a further pair to follow under the 1937 estimates. The final design was approved on 14 December 1936. The Royal Navy considered the armoured carrier a revolutionary development, and took great trouble to conceal its qualities from the other major powers, to the extent that it declared a much higher air complement (the theoretical justification was a US-style deck park!) in order to persuade the United States and Japan that these ships were simply a further development of *Ark Royal*.

France and Italy

While these significant developments in naval aviation were taking place in the navies of Britain, Japan and the United States, the other two Washington powers were effectively left on the sidelines. Italy had long taken the view that aircraft carriers were of limited value in the land-locked Mediterranean (see *WAW* Chapter 7), and large modern air bases were developed not only on the Italian mainland, but on Sicily, Sardinia and the Dodecanese Islands. The dramatic improvements in the speed and endurance of land-based aircraft during the 1930s meant that any naval force operating in the central Mediterranean would be subject to attack by heavy land-based bombers, and that friendly surface forces could, at least in theory, be provided with fighter cover.

Although the *Regia Marina* still toyed with the occasional carrier project, these were never seriously pursued, and with the improved performance of modern aircraft the French *Marine Nationale* was increasingly inclining towards the same viewpoint. How could carrier planes, whose performance was limited by the operational constraints of a short, narrow runway, limited hangar capacity, and the constant vertical movement of aircraft between hangar and flight deck, hope to compete with high-performance, land-based aircraft operating from broad, uncluttered runways and air bases capable of accommodating an air wing of perhaps a hundred aircraft?

Advocates of French naval aviation were not helped by the limitations of their single fleet carrier, *Béarn*, which was to prove the least successful of the 1920s capital ship conversions. *Béarn* was too slow to accompany the new generation of capital ships laid down during the 1930s, and it was difficult for the *Marine Nationale* to justify funding for suitable carrier aircraft when the numbers to be purchased would be so pitifully small. *Béarn* was generally attached tactically to the older battleships of the *Bretagne* and *Courbet* classes throughout the period, following them from the Mediterranean to the Atlantic and then back to the Mediterranean.

Béarn entered service with a twelve-plane squadron of Dewoitine D1 high-wing monoplane fighters and two twelve-plane recce/bomber squadrons of Levasseur PL.4 folding-wing biplanes, only half of which were normally embarked during peacetime. The bomber squadron would be replaced by a torpedo bomber squadron flying

The converted *Béarn* remained in service throughout the 1930s, but modernisation was limited and she was too slow to accompany the new generation of battleships. The photo shows two Levasseur PL.101 reconnaissance aircraft of 7S1 squadron being brought up to the flight deck during the late 1930s using the centre and after lifts. Note the heavy clamshell doors, which ensured the flight deck remained in operation when the lifts were lowered to hangar level. *(Courtesy of Philippe Caresse)*

the PL.7 from 1930, but derivatives of these high-wing monoplane fighters and lumbering biplane reconnaissance and torpedo bombers would continue in service until the late 1930s, when they were due to be replaced by French-built Nieuport dive bombers and American Vought torpedo planes.

Wind-over-deck speed was inadequate by contemporary foreign standards, and in 1931 studies were undertaken with a view to replacing the entire propulsion machinery. Shaft horsepower would have virtually tripled to 60,000shp, but the anticipated increase in speed from 21.5 knots to 23.4 knots (only 22.3kts with bulges) hardly seemed to justify the cost and an estimated three years out of service, so it was decided to replace only the boilers, for better fuel economy and ease of maintenance. The decision not to upgrade *Béarn*'s machinery made the operation of modern aircraft from her relatively small flight deck increasingly marginal, compelling the *Marine Nationale* to think more seriously about new purpose-built ships.

Studies for the conversion of the oldest two 'treaty' cruisers, *Duquesne* and *Tourville*, to fast carriers were undertaken in 1935–36, but it was found that the hulls were too narrow to accommodate a hangar of sufficient breadth; even with three of the four original 203mm gun turrets removed the air complement would have been only twelve to fourteen aircraft. Eventually this project was abandoned, and it was decided instead to build two purpose-built carriers of 18,000 tonnes with double hangars to accommodate a more satisfactory total of forty aircraft; these were duly authorised under the 1938 programme. Only one of the ships, named *Joffre*, would be laid down and her construction proceeded slowly before being abandoned in 1940.

The low priority accorded to these programmes was a reflection of current theories prevalent in the *Marine Nationale* that saw carriers as useful only outside the range of land-based aircraft. With the political developments of the late 1930s, which saw the French taking on primary responsibility for the English Channel and the Western Mediterranean while the British Royal Navy looked after the North Atlantic and the Eastern Mediterranean, new carriers were considered less important than new capital ships with which to oppose the increasingly powerful Italian Navy.

Conclusions

The aircraft carriers built or converted during the 1920s were largely experimental ships, designed to test untried theories; the ships laid down or projected during the latter part of the Treaty period were purpose-built ships that responded to clear requirements and which incorporated the tactical and technical lessons learned from operations with the early ships.

However, whereas during the early/mid-1920s all five of the major naval powers had envisaged using their carriers in similar ways, by the 1930s a major rift, at first tactical and ultimately strategic in nature, had opened up between the Pacific powers on the one hand and the European powers on the other. Although the US Navy and the IJN still clung to the concept of a 'decisive battle' conducted between two battle lines, both now envisaged that the main battle would be preceded by a struggle for air supremacy over the battle area, waged by aircraft carriers operating in advance of (and tactically independent of) their respective battle fleets. In this scenario fast carrier divisions, accompanied by cruisers and cued into position by a combination of cruiser submarines and long-range seaplanes, would range over the vast and open expanses of the Pacific to prepare the ground for the final fateful encounter between the capital ships.

The European powers, whose navies would be operating not in open expanses of ocean but relatively close to the continental land mass, had a completely different perspective. The Italians envisaged operating fast and relatively light surface forces against French (and eventually British) communications in the Mediterranean, with air support – both offensive and defensive – being provided from land bases. France would aim to frustrate these tactics by the deployment of similar forces. Indeed, there were elements in the *Marine Nationale* that were increasingly unconvinced of the value of aircraft carriers in sea areas dominated by land-based air and even in the North Atlantic, where the weather and sea conditions were frequently unfavourable to the operation of carrier aircraft.

In 1922 the British had been the world leader in naval aviation, and remained just as committed to the aircraft carrier during the 1930s as they had in the early days. However, British ideas regarding the tactical employment of the aircraft carrier remained virtually unchanged throughout the period, and naval aviation never acquired the strategic dimension that it would increasingly assume in the Pacific navies. The core function of the British carrier remained reconnaissance for the battle fleet, the shooting down of enemy reconnaissance aircraft over the battle fleet, spotting for the battle fleet, and torpedo strikes against the enemy battle line to slow it and bring it to action. The carrier was tied to the battle fleet tactically and was expected to accompany the battleships, not to operate independently in advance of them. The standard Royal Navy tactical grouping of the early period of the Second World War would generally comprise a squadron of two or more capital ships plus a carrier, whereas in the Pacific aircraft carriers would constitute the main advanced strike forces following the destruction of the US battle line at Pearl Harbor, and carrier aviation would dominate the early stages of that war.

There can be little doubt that the development of naval aviation in Britain during the interwar period was adversely affected by the need to agree policy with the Air Ministry, which has been widely blamed for its 'continental' outlook and a lack of empathy with the Navy's legitimate requirements. It was this organisational and philosophical divide between the two services rather than inter-service rivalry that had the greatest impact between the wars. Generally speaking the Royal Navy got the aircraft it wanted, albeit not in the numbers it would have liked. The problem was that during the 1930s the Navy would become increasingly out of touch with the rapidly advancing technology of modern aircraft, and because of its lack of an influential aviation community within the service opted for rugged, low-performance aircraft that would struggle to cope against land-based monoplanes and the new generation of carrier aircraft developed by the US Navy and the IJN.

The Royal Navy persisted with large, specialised three-seat spotter aircraft aboard carriers until the mid-1930s, thereby reducing the number of strike aircraft that could be accommodated and increasing the maintenance load. The development of multi-role aircraft such as the Fairey Swordfish (TSR) and Blackburn Skua (FDB), which rarely performed well in more than one of their multiple functions, was a consequence not only of limited funding but of small air complements and a conservative operating doctrine.

Because it was assumed (and accepted, arguably too readily) that aircraft designed for carrier operation would necessarily be inferior in their performance characteristics to land-based types, the Royal Navy increasingly failed to design ships that were well-adapted to operating high-performance aircraft, often in the face of Air Ministry advice. Aircraft dimensions were limited by hangar and lift constraints, and similar constraints on all-up weight and take-off/landing speeds were imposed by lift, accelerator and arrester wire limitations. The armoured carrier of the late 1930s, with its relatively small single hangar and narrow lifts, was the ultimate expression of the Royal Navy's 'ship first, aircraft second' philosophy. The poor performance of the available two-seat fighter aircraft, useful only for chasing away reconnaissance aircraft and for escorting torpedo strikes, meant that the only possible defence against fast land-based bombers was to drain the carrier's aircraft of fuel, lock them down in an armoured hangar, and put up a supposedly 'impenetrable' anti-aircraft barrage using the massed HA guns of the fleet. This meant that when radar became available, making it once again possible to intercept hostile bombers before they entered gun range, the Royal Navy had no suitable single-seat fighter aircraft, and land-based types with unsuitable airframes and insufficient range for maritime operations had to be hurriedly adapted.[19]

How much of this would have been different had there been an established aviation community within the Navy during this period, rather than a naval Observer Corps with pilots on loan from the RAF, must remain a matter for debate. Such communities were undoubtedly far more influential in the US Navy and the IJN during the interwar period than was the case in the Royal Navy, but it should not be forgotten that even the American and Japanese aviators had to fight for influence against more powerful and established 'Big Gun' elements in their respective navies, and that the US Navy came to regard the aircraft carrier as the primary weapon in the war against Japan only because it had no other option following the sinking of its battle fleet at Pearl Harbor.[20]

This increasing divergence in tactical thinking was reflected in the design and configuration of the carriers laid down during the latter part of the Treaty period. The British *Ark Royal*, although similar with regard to size and displacement, was a very different ship from the American *Yorktown*, and these conceptual differences was even more marked in the armoured carriers of the *Illustrious* class, with their heavy hangar and flight deck protection and their small air groups. The Japanese persisted with operational doctrine that was essentially adapted from Royal Navy practice, and the size of the air group therefore continued to be equated with hangar capacity – hence the double hangars and the restricted deck heights, but with an air group composition that increasingly resembled that of US carriers: high-performance, single-seat fighters, dive bombers and torpedo planes. Because the enemy battle line remained a primary target there was, as in the Royal Navy, a heavy weighting in favour of torpedo attack aircraft, whereas the US Navy for a time contemplated replacing all its torpedo planes with dive bombers. Where the IJN increasingly diverged from the Royal Navy was in the procedures it developed to match the large deck loads and the high tempo of air operations characteristic of carrier operations in the US Navy.

Japanese carriers, although more lightly built that their British counterparts, had similar internal hangars with workshops and accommodation to the sides, whereas US Navy carriers from the USS *Ranger* onwards had open hangars, which meant that aircraft could be warmed up on the hangar deck before being raised by the lifts for spotting. The IJN ships had similar fire precautions as their British counterparts, with fire curtains separating off sections of the hangars, but there was less attention to detail. In particular, the aviation fuel tanks were not isolated from the hull structure, and were therefore vulnerable to indirect action damage. The build-up of fumes from aviation fuel leaking into the enclosed hangars would lead to the loss of more than one Japanese carrier during the Second World War.

Chapter 4

CRUISERS 1930–36

DESPITE THE IMPORTANT NEW DEVELOPMENTS in capital ship and carrier design during the early 1930s, it was on cruiser design and construction that the London Treaty would have its greatest impact. The Washington Treaty, while placing a relatively high qualitative limit on the individual cruiser, had conspicuously failed to set any quantitative limit that might have restrained construction. The result had been a mini-arms race in cruisers armed with 8in guns and with a displacement

USS *Vincennes* (CA-44) was the second of three additional 8in-gun 'treaty' cruisers which that the US Navy was permitted to lay down after 1930. She would be the last of the *New Orleans* type to be built, the third ship being completed to a modified design. She is seen here off Rockland, Maine, on 12 January 1937 during her sea trials. *(NHHC, NH 50844)*

116

of 10,000 tons. All five of the Washington powers had built to the limit in qualitative terms, and the 'treaty' cruiser had become a 'catch-all' type of ship, capable of performing as a fleet scout (both strategic and tactical), as a trade protection vessel, or as a high-speed raider threatening the enemy's sea lines of communication. By the 1930s the fleet organisation of four out of the five powers was evolving into a scouting force for advanced operations built around 8in-gun cruisers and a Battle Force[1] built around the older capital ships and destroyer flotillas, supported by the 6in/14cm-gun cruisers laid down pre-1922. The exception was the British Royal Navy, which was less convinced of the value of cruisers as an advanced scouting force than the other powers,[2] and which after an initial bout of enthusiasm now considered the 10,000-ton cruiser armed with 8in guns too large and costly to be affordable in the numbers it required to protect the trade routes of the Empire.

The new qualitative and quantitative limits introduced by the London Treaty, largely in response to British pressure, were to prompt a major review on the part of all the major powers of their cruiser requirements. The United States and Japan were no longer permitted to continue building the 8in cruisers both would have preferred, yet the former now had a considerable allocation of tonnage with which to build new 6in-gun ships. The US Navy would give serious consideration to using some of this tonnage to build cruisers with flight decks, as permitted by the London Treaty.

Now that quantitative limits had been established and the major navies could no longer build as many of the largest possible types as they could afford, there would be a trade-off between individual size and the number of hulls, and the reduction to a maximum gun calibre of 6in effectively increased flexibility by making ships of 5,000–6,000 tons a viable proposition. Moreover, by the early 1930s the smaller cruisers completed in the aftermath of the First World War were ageing and becoming due for replacement. For most of the major navies this would increase the tonnage available for new construction, but the demise of these ships would leave a role in direct support of the battle fleets that needed to be filled, leading to studies of smaller designs intended to lead or support the fleet's destroyers, to protect the battle line against the enemy's flotilla craft, to be available for tactical scouting, and to boost fleet air defence.

Whereas the 'treaty' cruisers had been relatively uniform in terms of size, armament and tactical speed (see *WAW* Chapter 6), the trade-off between speed and protection being the major design issue, the new cruisers would vary considerably in size and capability according to the mission assigned to them. This disparity would complicate the issue of comparability, which as ever was an important consideration for all five navies. Besides designing ships that fitted its own tactical concepts, the US Navy would have a constant eye on how those ships might perform against their Japanese counterparts; the Italians would keep a close watch on the French and vice versa, and the British would have to consider the very different requirements of war in the Far East (against Japan), in the Mediterranean (with Italy the potential adversary) and, towards the end of the Washington Treaty era, in the North Sea and North Atlantic (against a newly resurgent Germany).

The *Leander* and *Arethusa* Classes

For the Royal Navy, light cruiser requirements had been discussed in detail as early as 1921, but these discussions had been superseded by the Washington Conference, following which the Navy embarked on the construction of 8in cruisers to the exclusion of all other types. When it became clear that the latter were not affordable in the numbers required to police the trade routes, attention turned again to smaller cruisers, first the 8,200-ton *York* and *Exeter* with their reduced main 8in batteries, then to a 7,500-ton Convoy Defence Cruiser with the same armament as *York*, heavy protection to enable it to take on a fully fledged 'treaty' cruiser but a speed of only 21 knots, and finally to a cruiser of 6,000–7,000 tons that would necessarily be armed with guns of smaller calibre, the preferred armament being eight 6in guns in twin power-operated mountings.

A displacement of at least 6,000 tons was considered necessary to provide an endurance of 7,000nm at 16 knots, the minimum requirement for trade protection and operations against Japan, and as the design was fleshed out it became clear that even this displacement was on the small side for an effective ship. The legend/sketch design approved in June 1929 was for a ship of 6,500 tons with four twin 6in turrets, a speed of 32.5 knots and an endurance of 6,500nm at 16 knots. These figures became the basis of the British proposals for new limits on cruiser displacement (7,000 tons maximum) and gun calibre (6.1in/155mm) at the London Conference, and the first of the new cruisers, *Leander*, was authorised prior to the Conference with a view to setting an example and influencing the negotiations. The reduction in maximum gun calibre from 8in to 6.1in was duly secured but the US Navy, which insisted on a trans-Pacific capability for cruisers operating with the scouting force, baulked at any reduction in maximum displacement.[3]

Leander would not be laid down until September 1930, by which time many changes had been made in the detail design. In order to secure improved subdivision, a third boiler room and a separate gearing room were added, which increased the length of the machinery spaces by 17ft.[4] The boiler uptakes were combined into a single broad funnel, which could then be moved well clear of a new, streamlined bridge. There were also modifications to the protection system and to the aviation provision. These changes required an increase in power, first to 63,000shp and finally (using new higher-pressure boilers) to 72,000shp. Standard displacement rose first to 7,000 tons and finally to 7,150 tons as approved in June 1931. It was estimated that displacement might grow by a further 300 tons during building, although this latter estimate was to prove pessimistic; increasingly extensive use of electric welding in the shipyards saved weight, and although *Leander* displaced 7,290 tons on completion the second batch of three ships were completed at 7,030–7,070 tons and the last of the type, *Ajax*, at 6,840 tons.

The ship that emerged was precisely what might have been expected given the self-imposed restraints on displacement and *Leander*'s projected role as a trade protection cruiser: a moderately sized and moderately armed cruiser with good all-round capabilities and good endurance for her size. The twin 6in mounting, which unlike the

Leander (GB)

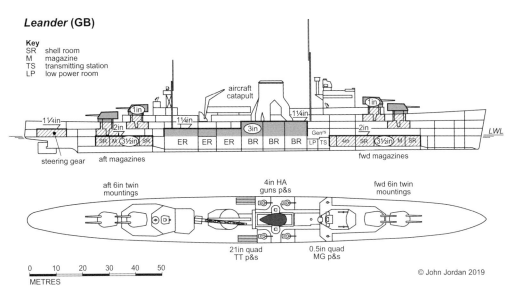

Key
SR   shell room
M   magazine
TS   transmitting station
LP   low power room

Leander was intended as the model for the post-London cruiser. All the subsequent Royal Navy cruiser designs of the 1930s had *Leander* as their starting point. Note the split ammunition supply system, with fixed lower hoists feeding 'ammunition lobbies'; the cordite cartridges were transferred manually to the turret and the shells to an upper hoist that rotated with the turret.

mountings in the *Nelson*s had manual ramming and breech operation, was reliable with a good rate of fire (generally six rounds per minute); it also provided far better protection for the gun crews than the single open mountings of the war-built ships. There was a heavy 53ft catapult amidships for the Fairey IIIF reconnaissance/spotter aircraft, but this large, ungainly aircraft was found to be unsuitable for operation from cruisers, and was subsequently replaced by the smaller Osprey, launched from a lighter 46ft catapult. Cost considerations resulted in the suppression of a proposed second director control tower (DCT) aft for main battery fire, and there was only an austere fixed after fire control position. Even so, the cost of each individual unit was around £1.6 million as compared with £2 million for a 'County', so savings were not as great as had been anticipated; only five smaller and less-capable *Leander*s could be purchased for the cost of four 'Counties'.

Following the conclusion of the London Conference, the Admiralty calculated that, with the scrapping of over-age, war-built cruisers, a total tonnage of 90,720 tons was available for new construction up to 31 December 1936. This would have been sufficient for fourteen ships of the *Leander* class had displacement been kept to the 6,500-ton design approved in June 1929, and would have delivered the fifty cruiser hulls the Navy considered the bare minimum to fulfil its missions in support of the fleet and trade. However, the growth in size to 7,000 tons by September 1930 implied a reduction to thirteen ships. A batch of three was authorised under the 1930 Estimates, but the programme was then re-evaluated in the light of internal requirements and developments abroad.

Before 1930 the Royal Navy could take for granted an inexhaustible supply of

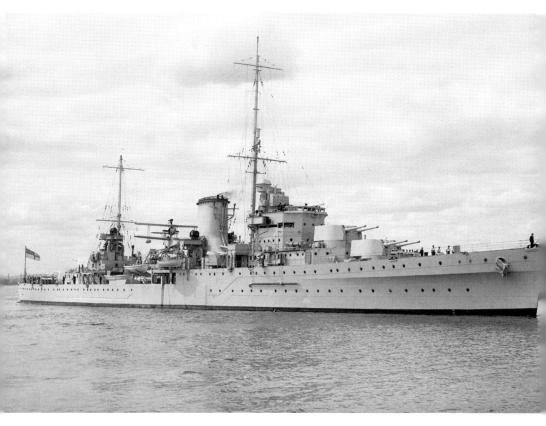

HMS *Leander* visiting Melbourne while serving with the New Zealand Division of the Royal Navy in early 1938. The original Mark V 4in HA guns abeam the funnel have been replaced by Mark XVI guns in the twin Mark XIX mounting; she is otherwise largely unmodified since her completion. *(Allan C Green collection, State Library of Victoria)*

small 6in gun cruisers completed or laid down during the First World War, and was therefore able to focus on larger ocean-going types. However, by the late 1920s it was becoming clear that the war-built 'C's and 'D's would have to be replaced at some time in the near future. The 6,000/7,000-ton cruiser that would become the *Leander* was not manoeuvrable enough to work with the destroyer flotillas, and was considered too large for scouting and screening at night. A 'fleet' cruiser displacing less than 6,000 tons would therefore have to be considered alongside the 'trade' cruiser. Both the Home and Mediterranean Fleets (especially the latter) were pressing for ships of this size, and it was correctly pointed out that more hulls could be built for the same overall tonnage allocation and the same financial outlay. Since the ships would be operating primarily with the destroyer flotillas they would need protection only against 4.7in destroyer shell and would not require costly and space-intensive aircraft operating facilities.

Several designs comparable in size and capabilities to the French *contre-torpilleurs* were produced, with high tactical speed (36–38 knots), single open mountings and minimal protection, but eventually the Royal Navy settled on a ship intermediate between the *Leander* and the older fleet cruisers of the 'C' and 'D' classes with the following characteristics: six 6in guns in twin power-operated turrets plus two/three 4in HA, two triple torpedo tube mountings, a speed of 32 knots, moderate protection for magazines and machinery, and an endurance of 5,000nm at 15 knots. The machinery installation was to be intermediate between the destroyer (lightweight/performance) and cruiser (heavier/endurance + reliability) types, with only two shafts.

It was initially estimated that all this could be achieved on 4,800 tons, and by the autumn of 1930 it was envisaged that ten *Leanders* would be built for trade protection, to be complemented by four of the smaller cruisers for fleet work. However, following improvements made during the detail design stage, the displacement of the new fleet cruiser rose first to 5,000 tons (four shafts) and ultimately to 5,500 tons (unit machinery layout, which cost 20ft in length).

Table 4.1: **British Cruisers 1930–1936**

	Leander class	*Arethusa* class
Built:	5 ships 1930–34[1]	4 ships 1933–37
Displacement:	7,000tW (designed)	5,200tW (designed)
Dimensions:	555ft × 56ft	506ft × 51ft
	(169m × 17.0m)	(154m × 15.5m)
Machinery:	Six Admiralty boilers;	Four Admiralty boilers;
	4-shaft geared turbines,	4-shaft geared turbines,
	72,000shp = 32.5kts	64,000shp = 32.5kts
Armament:	8 – 6in/50 (4 × II)	6 – 6in/50 (3 × II)
	4 – 4in/45 (4 × I) HA	4 – 4in/45 (4 × I) HA
	8 – 0.5in MG (2 × IV)	8 – 0.5in MG (2 × IV)
	8 – 21in TT (2 × IV)	6 – 21in TT (2 × III)
Protection:	mach: 3in belt, 1¼in deck	mach: 2¼in belt, 1in deck
	mags: 3½in sides, 2in crowns	mags: 3in sides, 2in crowns
	turrets: 1in	turrets: 1in

Notes:
1   They were followed by three modified ships with a revised machinery layout, built 1933–36 (see text).

Long-term requirements were for eight ships: four for the Home Fleet and four for the Mediterranean Fleet. However, this would amount to 44,000 tons – virtually half the tonnage allocation available for new cruiser construction up to 31 December 1936. A meeting of the Admiralty Board on 14 January 1932 considered two possible options: ten *Leanders* at 7,000 tons plus three of the new fleet cruisers at 5,500 tons, leaving 4,220 tons for a smaller design; or nine *Leanders* plus five of the new ships. This was the option eventually selected, with a single fleet cruiser to be ordered in each of the years 1931–35. Two *Leanders* and one fleet cruiser (*Arethusa* class) were duly authorised under the 1931 Estimates, and this pattern would be repeated in 1932.

Arethusa (GB)

Key
SR shell room
M   magazine
TS transmitting station
LP low power room

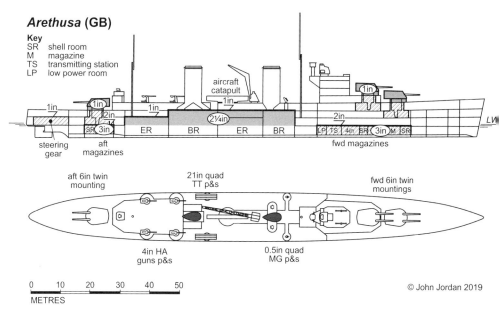

The small 'fleet' cruisers of the *Arethusa* class were a reduced version of the *Leander* design, with three instead of four 6in turrets and lighter protection. The aircraft catapult was retained to enable the ships to be employed in the trade protection role. Note the light protection for the 6in ammunition lobbies associated with the British 'short-trunk' turret, which featured split ammunition hoists.

The last unit of the four-ship *Arethusa* class, *Aurora*, running her trials out of Portsmouth in 1937. She is in an incomplete state: the HA director and the 4in HA guns have yet to be fitted. *Aurora* was completed as the flagship of Rear-Admiral Destroyers, and had a deckhouse amidships in place of the aircraft catapult. *(Conrad Waters collection)*

Arethusa as completed was essentially a scaled-down version of *Leander* with three 6in twin turrets instead of four, an identical HA armament of four single 4in guns, and triple torpedo tubes instead of quad mountings. She was also the first British cruiser to have the unit propulsion system, in which the two boiler and two engine rooms were alternated to give two self-contained units, with the forward unit driving the outer shafts. This layout was a feature of the early US 'treaty' cruisers, and had the advantage of continuing to provide power to the ship in the event of two adjacent machinery compartments being flooded during action, as was likely in the event of a torpedo hit amidships.

Both the Admiralty Board and the Controller insisted that the ship should be able to operate one or two reconnaissance aircraft for the eventuality that the ship might be employed for trade protection. The Controller wanted the heavyweight 53ft catapult, but space and cost constraints resulted in the lighter 46ft type being fitted amidships. Aircraft operation from fleet cruisers was not popular with the C-in-Cs of the Home and Mediterranean Fleets, each of whom would normally have at least one carrier to provide aircraft for reconnaissance, and the catapults and aircraft would be removed in 1940–41. Two of the four ships completed served as flagships of the destroyer squadrons of the two main fleets before the war, with the Mediterranean being the primary theatre of employment for the remaining units.

At about the same time as the legend for *Arethusa* was approved (February 1932), there was growing concern over developments abroad, particular in the Far East. These developments could not be ignored, and the Admiralty Board considered qualitative improvements to the *Leander* design, primarily focused on armament and protection, to be desirable. However, there was a parallel concern that any improvement would imply a larger ship, which could then not be built in sufficient numbers to deliver the totemic fifty-ship figure. Despite this, the Director of Naval Construction (DNC) was instructed to prepare a design for a modified *Leander* of 7,750 tons with improved protection, armed with either nine or ten 6in guns. Both of these solutions implied a new triple turret, and development of the latter was also set in train.

Work on the new design began in March 1932; it incorporated the unit propulsion system adopted for the new fleet cruisers. Ultimately, largely because of concerns that the triple turret would not be ready in time for the 1932 ships, only the new machinery arrangement was adopted. There was a cost to this: a unit layout implied longer machinery spaces, which then needed to be protected by a greater weight of armour; it also reduced the accommodation space available to the crew, and the additional weight of protection meant an extra 1ft on the beam of the ship. The lack of centre-line space between the twin funnels initially precluded fitting the heavyweight 53ft catapult, and the second of the two funnels had to be moved aft by 6ft to accommodate it. However, the cost in weight was little over 100 tons.

Two of the modified ships were ordered (together with the second unit of the *Arethusa* class) under the 1932 Estimates, and it was found that one of the two 1931 *Leanders* could be completed to the same specifications. Of the two 1932 ships,

Phaeton was subsequently purchased by the Royal Australian Navy while under construction and renamed *Sydney*, and the remaining two, completed for the Royal Navy as *Amphion* and *Apollo*, would also be transferred to the RAN shortly before the Second World War – they became *Perth* and *Hobart* respectively – by which time they were effectively outclassed by the new 'Town'-class cruisers built as a response to the Japanese *Mogami* (see below).

European Echoes

Although much has been made of the failure of the French and the Italians either to agree to the provisions of Part III of the London Treaty or to ratify the remainder of the Treaty, both navies were in the event broadly compliant with its provisions and anxious not to be seen to be undermining the arms limitation process. The two 8in-gun 'treaty' cruisers planned for 1930, the French *Algérie* and the Italian *Pola*, were duly ordered, but these would be the last of their type built for either navy. They would bring the total number of sub-category (a) cruisers built for France and Italy to seven. On a strict 5:3:1.75 Washington ratio this was equivalent to twenty cruisers for the two major powers and twelve or thirteen for Japan, but this could hardly

One of three Modified *Leanders* subsequently purchased by Australia, *Sydney* is depicted here during a visit to Melbourne in September 1938. She retains the single Mark V 4in HA guns with which she was completed. The aircraft on the catapult is a Supermarine Seagull V amphibian. *(Allan C Green collection, State Library of Victoria)*

be viewed as escalatory, particularly as there was no intention to persist with construction of the 10,000-ton, 8in/203mm-gun type.

In fact, both the French and Italian navies were quite happy with their respective seven 'treaty' cruisers, equivalent to two fast three-ship divisions with a seventh ship in refit. Italy was already building 6in-gun cruisers, albeit of a fast, lightly protected type intended to counter the French *contre-torpilleurs* (see *WAW* Chapter 8), and the French, although suspicious of Italian ambitions, were politically committed to the disarmament process and viewed the qualitative restrictions on cruiser displacement and gun calibre proposed by the British during the late 1920s as inevitable in the longer term. In the 1930 estimates, alongside *Algérie*, was a new cruiser of 5,900 tons standard displacement armed with nine 152mm (6in) guns in triple turrets, *Emile Bertin*. This ship would become the prototype for a new series of 'light cruisers' (*croiseurs légers*) once the implications of the London Treaty were fully digested.

For the France of the late 1920s not only was there the prospect of a new arms limitation treaty, but also a new threat from an old enemy, Germany. From 1925 onwards the German Republic, despite the crippling constraints of the Versailles Treaty, began to rebuild the *Reichsmarine*, and one of its priorities was the replacement of its six elderly light cruisers, completed just after the turn of the century, by modern units. The first of the new cruisers, *Emden*, was a coal-fired ship of dated design, but between 1926 and 1928 the Germans laid down four radically different ships[5] with a nominal displacement of 6,000 tons (the maximum permitted under the Versailles Treaty), moderate protection and an armament of nine 15cm guns in triple turrets. It was these ships, rather than the Italian '*Condottieri*', which inspired *Emile Bertin*. Like the German ships, she was fitted for minelaying, trading her modest protection for high speed (34 knots).

The principal implications of the London Treaty for France and Italy were that their existing light cruisers, which were virtually unprotected, would now be faced not only by lightly built flotilla craft armed with 120mm and 138mm guns, but by 'fighting cruisers' similar to the British *Leander*s, armed with 6in/152mm guns and protected against guns of the same calibre. This led to a serious reappraisal of light cruiser designs. The next series of Italian '*Condottieri*' would be significantly larger and heavier than their predecessors, despite an almost identical armament, and would have well-developed protection against 6in shells. Their French counterparts, the *croiseurs protégés* of the *La Galissonniére* class, would sacrifice high speed for protection almost on a par with the 'treaty' cruiser *Algérie*.

Montecuccoli and Duca d'Aosta

The two ships of the third group of '*Condottieri*', *Raimondo Montecuccoli* and *Muzio Attendolo*, marked a distinct change in direction from the lightly protected ships of the first two groups, to which they bore little physical resemblance. Length between perpendiculars was increased by 7 metres and beam by 1 metre, freeboard was increased and the bow given pronounced sheer and flare for improved sea-keeping. The aviation arrangements, which in the first two groups had caused major design

Montecuccoli (It)

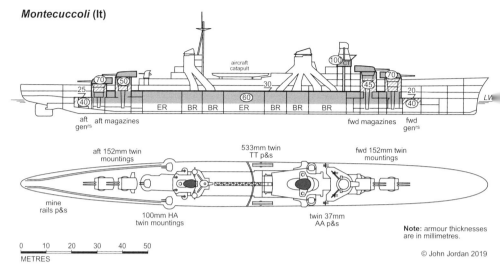

aircraft catapult

70 50
25
40
ER BR BR ER BR BR BR
aft gen^rs
aft magazines
100
61
70
45
30
60
20
40
LV
fwd magazines
fwd gen^rs

aft 152mm twin mountings

533mm twin TT p&s

fwd 152mm twin mountings

mine rails p&s

100mm HA twin mountings

twin 37mm AA p&s

Note: armour thicknesses are in millimetres.

0   10   20   30   40   50
METRES

© John Jordan 2019

Italian light cruiser designs of the early 1930s continued to emphasise high speed. Compare the length of the machinery spaces with the British *Leander*, which had a similar displacement. One consequence of this was the increased length of the 'citadel' and the reduced thickness of the armoured belt. Note that the diesel generators were outside the citadel, as in the contemporary Italian battleships, and were protected only by a 40mm internal turtle deck.

Raimondo Montecuccoli was the first of a series of four fast, lightly-armoured cruisers built post-London for the Italian *Regia Marina*. Completed in June 1935, she was superior in every respect to the early 'Condottieri', and had the classic Italian silhouette of the period, with a conical forward tower structure and a tripod mainmast. *(Allan C Green collection, State Library of Victoria)*

problems, were completely revised. A Gagnotto 22m trainable catapult was located between the funnels atop a long deckhouse extending aft from the forecastle, the uptakes for the after funnel being trunked back sharply to provide the necessary centre-line space. Finally, the traditional bridge of the earlier ships was replaced by a conical structure incorporating the armoured conning tower and topped by the DCT for the main battery. A tall tripod mainmast stepped around the after funnel supported a derrick that handled the aircraft and the ship's boats, an economical arrangement and one that contributed to the elegant, 'racy' appearance of these ships.

Protection was a major advance on the earlier two groups. Outboard of the machinery spaces there were deep cofferdams, with a 60mm nickel-chrome belt on the outside backed by a 25mm internal 'splinter' bulkhead, each 'box' being completed by 20mm plating top and bottom. Inside the twin cofferdams there was 30mm horizontal protection directly over the machinery spaces and the magazines, which had an additional 40mm bulkhead inboard of the main belt. The conning tower had 100mm sides, and the turrets were protected by 70mm plating. The layered side armour was in theory reasonably effective against 6in HE shell, but could still easily be penetrated by AP and SAP shell.

The cost of these improvements was 2,000 tonnes, of which 800 tonnes was additional protection (1,380t versus 580t in the *Di Giussano* class). Shaft horsepower had to be increased from 95,000shp to 106,000shp to provide a designed speed of 37 knots; even so the trial speeds of 37–38 knots were obtained only with forcing of the machinery.

The Italian *Eugenio di Savoia* tied up alongside her sister *Duca d'Aosta* and *Muzio Attendolo* in July 1939. Note the close spacing of the twin 152mm/53-cal guns, which shared a common cradle. *(NHHC, NH 80947)*

Table 4.2: French & Italian Cruisers 1930–1936

	Emile Bertin (Fr)	*Montecuccoli* class (It)	*La Galissonnière* class (Fr)	*Abruzzi* class (It)
Built:	1 ship 1931–34	2 ships 1931–35	6 ships 1931–37	2 ships 1933–37
Displacement:	5,890tW	7,400tW	7,600tW	9,440tW
Dimensions:	177m × 15.8m	182m × 16.6m	180m × 17.5m	187m × 18.9m
Machinery:	Six Penhoët boilers; 4-shaft geared turbines, 102,000shp = 34kts	Six Yarrow boilers; 2-shaft geared turbines, 106,000shp = 37kts	Four Indret boilers; 2-shaft geared turbines, 84,000shp = 31kts	Eight Yarrow boilers; 2-shaft geared turbines, 100,000shp = 34kts
Armament:	9 – 152mm/55 (3 × III) 4 – 90mm/50 (1 × II, 2 × I) HA 4 – 37mm/50 (4 × I) 6 – 550mm TT (2 × III)	8 – 152mm/53 (4 × II) 6 – 100mm/47 (3 × II) HA 8 – 37mm/54 (4 × II) 4 – 533mm TT (2 × II)	9 – 152mm/55 (3 × III) 8 – 90mm/50 (4 × II) HA 8 – 13.2mm/76 (4 × II) 4 – 550mm TT (2 × II)	10 – 152mm/55 (2 × III, 2 × II) 8 – 100mm/47 (4 × II) HA 8 – 37mm/54 (4 × II) 6 – 533mm TT (2 × III)
Protection:	mags: 30mm sides deck: 20mm turrets: none CT: 30mm	belt: 60mm + 25mm deck: 30mm turrets: 70mm CT: 100mm	belt: 105mm deck: 38mm turrets: 100mm faces CT: 95mm	belt: 100mm + 30mm deck: 40mm turrets: 135mm CT: 140mm

Notes:
1 They were followed by two similar but larger ships of the *Duca d'Aosta* class, built 1932–36 (see text).

The fourth group of 'Condottieri', Duca d'Aosta and Eugenio di Savoia, were slightly enlarged versions of the Montecuccolis, with armour thicknesses increased throughout: the cofferdams outboard of the machinery were 70mm + 35mm with 30mm roofs, the protective deck over the machinery was 35mm, and there was 100mm armour on the turrets. The twin trainable torpedo mountings of the earlier ships were replaced by triples and there were additional light AA guns, but the armament was otherwise unchanged. The Aostas weighed in at 8,300tW, an increase of 1,000 tonnes over the Montecuccolis – 300 tonnes of which were for additional protection – and 3,000 tonnes over the ships of the first two groups. Although there would still be legitimate doubts regarding their ability to absorb heavy punishment, the Aostas were clearly quite different ships from the 'cartoni animati'[6] of the Di Giussano and the Cadorna classes.

The French La Galissonnière Class

Although the new Italian cruisers were larger and better protected than the earlier 'Condottieri', their primary mission, that of countering the French contre-torpilleurs, remained essentially unchanged. They were lightly constructed and fast, with two-shaft, destroyer-type machinery better suited to short bursts of high speed than to lengthy patrols.[7]

Laid down in August 1931 as a fast minelaying cruiser with a maximum speed of 34 knots, Emile Bertin became the prototype for a series of six light cruisers designed in the wake of the London Treaty. These ships would have an identical main armament of nine 6in guns, but would be slower and better protected. Emile Bertin is photographed here at Brest in 1937. (Author's collection)

La Galissonnière (Fr)

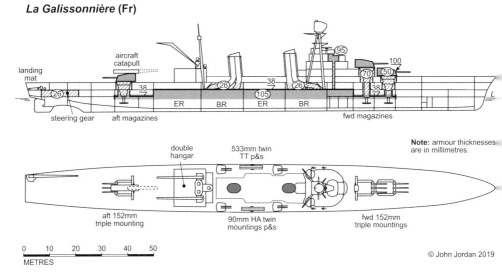

The French light cruisers of the *La Galissonnière* class had the 'unit' machinery arrangement of earlier French cruisers but a protection system adapted from the last French 'treaty' cruiser, *Algérie*. Note the extending catapult atop No. 3 turret and the capacious aircraft hangar that formed the after superstructure.

In the wake of the London Treaty, the French *Marine Nationale* was interested in quite a different type of cruiser. Although the design would be based on that of *Emile Bertin*, which had similar characteristics to the Italian '*Condottieri*',[8] the French wanted a 'fleet' cruiser capable of operating with the projected fast battleships, for which design work was nearly complete. The new ships, designated 'protected' cruisers (*croiseurs protégés*), were to be employed for tactical scouting, for support of the *contre-torpilleurs* operating on the flank of the battle squadrons against the smaller Italian cruisers, and for protection of the battle line against enemy flotilla craft; there was no requirement for minelaying. The General Staff wanted a ship with the armament of *Emile Bertin*, but which sacrificed high speed for protection on a par with the latest French 'treaty' cruiser, *Algérie*. It also wanted a low silhouette, as in the latest *contre-torpilleurs* of the *Le Fantasque* class (see *WAW* Chapter 8), and the ability to operate four aircraft (two reconnaissance planes plus two float fighters). In anticipation of future naval arms limitation agreements – and as a mark of political support for the British proposals made at Geneva and London – standard displacement was to be kept within 8,000 tonnes.

The result was one of the most successful cruiser designs of the interwar period. Standard displacement was 7,720 tonnes (7,600tW), of which 1,884 tonnes (24 per cent) were given over to protection. The 105mm belt and 38mm deck were considered adequate to defeat 138mm shell from 9,000m, and gave an 'immune zone' of 14,000–19,000m against 6in/152mm shell. The turrets and barbettes were also heavily armoured. Consideration was given to increasing the thickness of the horizontal armour to 80mm for protection against bombs and providing a 60mm

The French cruiser *Georges Leygues* arriving in New York in July 1939 for the World's Fair with the Statue of Liberty behind her; she was accompanied on the visit by her sisters *Gloire* and *Montcalm*. Note the prominent hangar aft, which could accommodate two Loire 130 reconnaissance amphibians side by side. A third aircraft could be stowed atop the hangar and a fourth on the catapult. *(NHHC, NH 81771)*

torpedo bulkhead, but these measures would have cost 1,420 tonnes and would have raised standard displacement above 9,000 tonnes, so they were rejected.

Originally the new cruisers, which were subsequently known as the *La Galissonnière* class, were to have had an HA gun armament comprising only four 90mm, as in *Emile Bertin*, but this was subsequently doubled, the triple torpedo mountings being reduced to twins in compensation. It was also decided to provide a capacious twin hangar for the new Loire 130 reconnaissance seaplane. This effectively displaced the catapult, so a new telescopic type (14.6m extending to 22.2m) was fitted atop the after 152mm turret. This was the first time a hangar had been provided in a French cruiser; however, the benefits were slightly outweighed by the exposure of the aircraft to blast and vibration when located on the catapult.

The French attempted to resolve the customary problem of aircraft recovery by equipping the ships with landing mats deployed from a narrow aperture in the transom stern. These systems were manufactured in Germany by Hein and Kiwull, and comprised a rectangular sheet of ribbed canvas measuring approximately 12m by 8m. With the mat deployed, the floatplane approached the mother ship from the stern, and once safely on the mat could be lifted via a stern crane onto the quarterdeck.

Trials of the mat took place during 1938 but were less successful than had been hoped. It took some fifteen minutes to deploy, during which speed was limited to 10–15 knots, and the recovery operation, which included hoisting the aircraft aboard and ramp stowage, took a further twenty-three to thirty minutes. The stern aperture was relatively close to the waterline, and operations in heavy seas often resulted in the flooding of the mat handling room. It also proved difficult to dry out the mats after use, and after two years the fabric had deteriorated to such an extent that it was decided to remove them and to plate in the stern aperture.

At 84,000shp shaft horsepower was identical to that of the cruiser *Algérie*, but there were only four boilers and two sets of turbines driving two shafts, for a saving

La Galissonnière:
Aviation Facilities

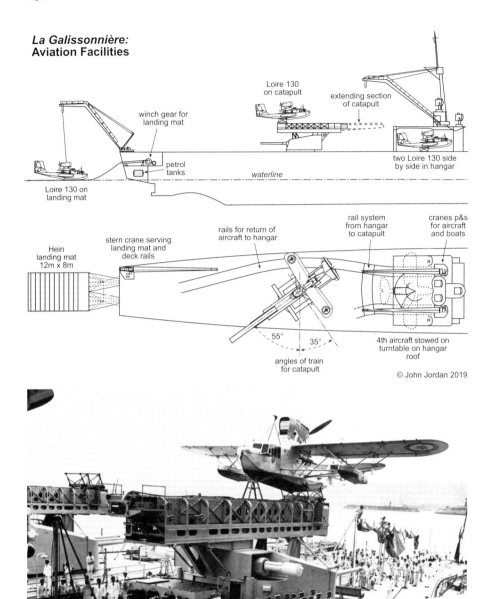

A Loire 130 amphibian atop the extending catapult of *Georges Leygues* during the visit to New York in July 1939. The catapult beam was less than 15m long when retracted but 22m when fully extended. *(NHHC, NH 91633)*

of 80 tonnes in weight and an increase in endurance of 500nm at 18 knots. Unfortunately, despite the designed speed being only 31 knots, the machinery contractors were encouraged to achieve a trials speed of 35 knots, to be rewarded by a 300,000FF prize. Speed trials were therefore conducted in similar conditions to those that prevailed in the Italian *Regia Marina*, with the ship in light condition and considerable forcing of the machinery. *Gloire* attained the remarkable figure of 36.8 knots with 116,174shp (an overload of 38 per cent!) at the expense of later problems, which culminated in a total machinery breakdown while being shadowed by an Allied (and potentially hostile) cruiser off North Africa during September 1940.[9]

Two ships of the *La Galissonnière* class were authorised under the 1931 Estimates, followed by four in 1932. When completed they would be organised in two three-ship divisions: one attached to the Atlantic Squadron and the other based at Toulon in the Mediterranean. The new cruisers were highly regarded by the *Marine Nationale*: they proved to be excellent sea-boats, and their 152mm guns, which were highly automated, were capable of five rounds per minute once their over-complex reloading mechanisms and defective hoists had been modified.

The Italian Response

The *Regia Marina* felt it necessary to respond to the new French cruisers. The next pair of '*Condottieri*', which were due to be authorised in 1933, were quite different to their predecessors in that high tactical speed was sacrificed for protection and a main battery of ten 152mm guns, to enable the ships to operate as 'fleet' cruisers in direct support of the battleships and to oppose the *La Galissonnière* class.

One of the fundamental problems in providing armour of sufficient thickness over the magazines and machinery of the earlier Italian light cruisers was the length of their machinery spaces. Because of the fine lines of the hull – adopted to secure high speed – the boilers had to be installed in line, as in destroyers; in the *Montecuccoli*s the machinery spaces (comprising no fewer than five boiler rooms and two engine rooms) were 78.5m long and the armoured citadel 120m long, these two figures representing 47 per cent and 72 per cent of the ship's length between perpendiculars respectively. In *Duca degli Abruzzi* and her sister, *Giuseppe Garibaldi*, the adoption of a fuller hull-form and a slight reduction in shaft horsepower (designed speed was 34 knots) meant that it was possible to accommodate eight smaller boilers side by side in only four boiler rooms. The length of the machinery spaces was now only 57m and that of the citadel 94m (equivalent to 33 per cent and 55 per cent respectively). The armoured citadel was therefore much more compact than in the earlier '*Condottieri*'.

The protection system adopted was unique in that it combined a 30mm 'de-capping' layer that followed the convex configuration of the outer hull with a concave belt of cemented armour 100mm thick inside it, the two forming virtually an ellipse in cross section (see drawing). Horizontal protection was provided by a 40mm NC deck, there was 100–105mm protection for the turrets and barbettes, and there was protective plating for the first time over the boiler uptake trunking

Abruzzi (It): Protection

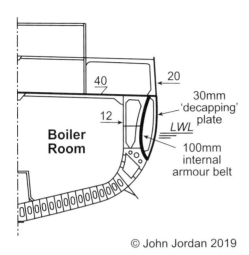

40

20

30mm
'decapping'
plate

12

LWL

**Boiler
Room**

100mm
internal
armour belt

© John Jordan 2019

The two Italian cruisers of the *Abruzzi* class had armour protection on a par with the French *La Galissonnière* class. The side protection system was unusual in having a convex 30mm 'de-capping' plate of high-tensile steel, and an internal concave plate 100mm thick, the stand-off between the two plates being greatest at the waterline.

and the steering gear aft. The total weight of protection was 2,130 tonnes, 22 per cent of standard displacement. This was an increase of some 400 tonnes over the *Aosta*s, and the armour could be applied at much greater thicknesses because of the shortened citadel.

There were four turrets for the main guns, as in the earlier '*Condottieri*', but turrets

The two ships of the *Abruzzi* class were the *Regia Marina*'s response to the French *La Galissonnière* type. They were slower and more heavily armoured than their predecessors and mounted two more guns. This is *Abruzzi* in 1938, shortly after her completion pre-war. Note the closely spaced funnels that distinguished these ships from earlier Italian light cruisers. *(Erminio Bagnasco collection)*

Nos. 1 and 4 were triples, giving the ships a one-gun advantage over their *Marine Nationale* counterparts. The 152mm/55 fitted in these ships was a new model, with improved range and hitting power. As in the French ships there was an HA battery of four twin mountings, using the standard Italian 100/47 gun, and the ships retained the two triple torpedo mountings of the *Aostas*. The major drawback with compressing the machinery spaces was that there was no longer sufficient space amidships to mount a catapult on the centre line. The *Abruzzi*s therefore had the somewhat cramped arrangement projected for the reconstructed battleships of the *Cavour* class (see Chapter 2), with twin catapults angled outboard of the second funnel; four aircraft were to have been carried (two atop and two alongside the catapults), but only two could be comfortably accommodated in service.

Like their French counterparts, the *Abruzzi*s were of robust construction and proved very successful in service. With war approaching, the *Regia Marina* proposed the construction of two further lightly modified units (the *Ciano* class), but these were never laid down.

The US Flying Deck Cruiser

Although the three major European navies adapted comfortably to the 8,000-ton 6in-gun cruiser, there was markedly less enthusiasm for the type among the two Pacific nations. In particular, the United States, which had insisted on parity with Britain from the standpoint of national prestige rather than from operational considerations, found itself with more sub-category (b) cruiser tonnage than it knew what to do with. The US Navy had only a limited requirement for cruisers armed with guns below the preferred 8in gun calibre, but under the Treaty had been allocated 143,500 tons for sub-category (b) cruisers, of which only 71,000 tons were already accounted for by the ten *Omaha*s, leaving 72,500 tons remaining for new ships. This represented less than 25 per cent of total US cruiser tonnage, so in theory all of this could be used to build cruisers with flight decks (see London Treaty Part III, Article 16), to be used for tactical battle scouting and fleet support.

Constructors attached to the US naval delegation[10] during the Treaty negotiations had demonstrated that an effective flying deck cruiser could be built on 10,000 tons, and that such a ship could have an armament of nine 6in guns in triple turrets, a speed of 31 knots, a 234ft flight deck, and could operate twenty aircraft. Following the conclusion of the conference, the idea was further developed by Preliminary Design, and the concept was tested in 'restricted deck' trials aboard the carrier *Saratoga*. The trials established that the flight deck should be as large as possible, ideally 350ft by 65ft, that there should be arresting gear over the whole length of the flight deck with additional barriers forward, and that all aircraft should be struck down on landing (as in Royal Navy practice) using the single lift forward, the landing process being speeded by cranes that could transfer aircraft from the flight deck to the open forward end of the hangar.

There was considerable enthusiasm for the project in Congress, and in December 1930 the Bureau of Construction and Repair (C&R) produced several studies, one

Flying Deck Cruiser 1931 (US)

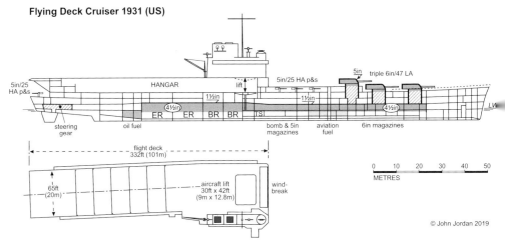

The US flying deck cruiser design would have provided the US Navy with a distributed aviation capacity to complement the larger carriers, but its comparatively short flight deck would have struggled to cope with the larger, heavier, faster aircraft that would enter service in the late 1930s.

of which had a double hangar. However, at this point the various US Navy bureaux began to present contradictory demands. The aviators of BuAer wanted a ship optimised for air operations with the longest possible unobstructed flight deck and hinged funnels; BuOrd and C&R insisted that cruiser characteristics (*ie* gunnery, fire control and protection) should be prioritised, while BuEng and C&R wanted a fixed funnel.

The design finally selected was inevitably a compromise, with the guns and their associated magazines all forward, and the flight deck, hangar and machinery occupying the after end of the ship; the aviation fuel tanks and the magazines for aircraft ordnance were located amidships (see drawing). The flight deck was 332ft long with a single lift capable of accommodating a spread aircraft at its forward end, and there was a fixed funnel and an island carrying the fire control directors to starboard. The three triple 6in turrets were close to the bow, with the third turret superimposed, the main HA battery (comprising eight single 5in/25 guns) was

Table 4.3: **USN Flying Deck Cruiser**

	Cruiser No 39
Built:	(projected)
Displacement:	10,000tW
Dimensions:	645ft × 63ft
	(168m × 19m)
Machinery:	4-shaft geared turbines;
	80,000shp = 32.5kts
Armament:	9 – 6in/47 (3 × III)
	8 – 5in/25 (8 × I) HA
	24 aircraft
Protection	belt: 4½in
	deck: 1½in

amidships, and there was to be an air group of twenty-four dive bombers or fighters. All the aircraft could be spotted on deck, and could then be flown off in the 130ft remaining with 30 knots of wind over the deck (although the dive bombers would have to be under-fuelled).

War games at the Naval War College established that in a contest between the flying deck cruiser (CLV) and a conventional gun-armed cruiser the aircraft-carrying ship would generally fare better because of its ability to strike first and at longer range. Also, unlike a fully fledged carrier, the CLV would still be a useful fleet unit even after the destruction of its flight deck. It was judged to be particularly valuable for scouting and convoy escort missions. The General Board had strong reservations about this hybrid type of vessel, which did not have the balanced air group necessary to allow it to scout independently, and which it considered vulnerable even to destroyer fire. However, there was sufficient interest and enthusiasm to justify building a prototype, and this went as far as contract plans before the Depression intervened. In 1934 a new project for a cruiser with a less substantial flight deck, the CF, was undertaken, but by this time the General Board had lost interest in the type and it was abandoned.

At the same time that the initial studies for flying deck cruisers were undertaken, there were preliminary studies for conventional cruisers armed with 6in guns. Despite the London US naval delegation's insistence that cruisers of less than 10,000 tons were of little value in trans-Pacific operations, the designers were given a less stringent set of requirements than might have been anticipated: a speed of 32.5 knots as in the sub-category (a) ships, a cruise radius as close to the latter as possible, a main armament of 6in guns and a displacement between 6,000 tons and 10,000 tons. It was further stipulated that the largest designs should have protection against 8in shell.

In November 1930 Preliminary Design came up with six designs (see Table 4.4), of which the largest could accommodate fifteen 6in guns in three quadruple turrets and one triple turret and had armour protection comparable to the latest sub-category (a) cruisers of the *New Orleans* class. Schemes 2 and 3 were both armed with twelve 6in guns in four triple turrets, the principal difference being that the former had the same level of protection as Scheme 1, whereas Scheme 3 was protected only against 6in shell. Scheme 4 had nine 6in guns in three triple turrets and similar protection to Scheme 3, and was similar in size and overall capabilities to the new European 6in-gun cruisers (the British *Leander*, the French *La Galissonnière* and the later Italian '*Condottieri*' – see above). The last two schemes were an attempt to produce a successful 'fleet' cruiser on the minimum specified displacement of 6,000 tons: Scheme 5 had the same main armament as Scheme 4 but was protected only against destroyer shell, while in Scheme 6 one of the three triple 6in turrets was traded for protection on a par with Schemes 3 and 4.

Despite support for a smaller cruiser from C-in-C Battle Force, the 6,000-ton designs were not liked; Scheme 5 was felt to be over-gunned, while the sacrifice in firepower in Scheme 6 was considered unacceptable given that contemporary

Table 4.4: **USN Light Cruiser Studies Nov 1930**

	Scheme 1	Scheme 2	Scheme 3
Displacement:	10,000tW	9,600tW	8,350tW
Speed:	32.5kts	32.5kts	32.5kts
Armament:	15 – 6in (3 × IV, I × III)	12 – 6in (4 × III)	12 – 6in (4 × III)
	8 – 5in (8 × I) HA	8 – 5in (8 × I) HA	6 – 5in (6 × I) HA
	6 – 21in TT (2 × III)	6 – 21in TT (2 × III)	6 – 21in TT (2 × III)
Protection:	(as *New Orleans*)	(as *New Orleans*)	moderate

European light cruisers were to be armed with eight or nine 6in guns. Scheme 1 was undermined by a refusal of BuOrd to guarantee a quadruple mounting, so the General Board favoured Scheme 2, which had the necessary endurance for independent scouting and trade protection operations and was the only practical design capable of standing toe-to-toe with a Japanese sub-category (a) cruiser armed with 8in guns. A 1930 analysis by the Naval War College also backed the Scheme 2 cruiser, but wanted to use the first 80,000 tons of the US Navy's 143,500-ton allocation for the construction of eight flying deck cruisers and the remaining 63,500 tons (plus 3,700 tons transferred from the destroyer category) to build seven 9,600-ton types. Pratt, now CNO, also advocated building eight flying deck cruisers, but felt that Scheme 4 represented the best solution to the 6in cruiser problem, as the smaller ship responded better to the needs of the Battle Force and could be built in greater numbers (nine against only seven Scheme 2 cruisers). Pratt even suggested that the US Navy might reconsider its decision to build three further 8in cruisers, as this would have provided a considerable boost to available 6in cruiser tonnage, but the proposal was effectively vetoed by the General Board.

These discussions were effectively halted by the Depression, which precluded the laying down of the prototype flying deck cruiser and put the plans for 6in cruisers on hold. When the cruiser issue came to be reviewed again in 1933 there was an important new development: the announcement by the Japanese in February of that year of plans to build four new sub-category (b) cruisers of moderate displacement armed with no fewer than fifteen 15.5in (6.1in) guns.

The Japanese *Mogami* class

If there was one aspect of the London Treaty that caused the greatest disruption to the Imperial Japanese Navy's future plans it was the statutory termination of 8in cruiser construction. If for the US Navy the 8in-gun 'treaty' cruiser was prized for its ability to conduct independent strategic scouting over the vast expanses of the Pacific Ocean, for the IJN it had become a sub-capital ship, capable of operating on the flanks of the battle fleet in such a way as to compensate for Japan's inferiority in capital ships, much as the squadron of armoured cruisers had done against the nominally superior Russian battle squadrons at the Battle of Tsushima in 1905. Much money had already been lavished on the eight 10,000-ton sub-category (a) cruisers[11] of the *Myoko* and *Takao* classes, and a further class of four would most

Scheme 4	Scheme 5	Scheme 6
7,175tW	6,000tW	6,000tW
32.5kts	32.5kts	32.5kts
9 – 6in (3 × III)	9 – 6in (3 × III)	6 – 6in (2 × III)
4 – 5in (4 × I) HA	4 – 5in (4 × I) HA	4 – 5in (4 × I) HA
6 – 21in TT (2 × III)	6 – 21in TT (2 × III)	6 – 21in TT (2 × III)
moderate	light	moderate

certainly have been ordered under the 1931 Naval Programme had not the London Conference intervened.

Japan's 8in-gun cruiser quota of twelve ships as defined by the London Treaty (it included the smaller *Furutaka* and *Aoba* classes) had already been fulfilled, which placed the IJN in the frustrating situation of seeing its existing superiority in this category progressively eroded as the US Navy continued to build towards its permitted quota of eighteen ships – the second of its own 'treaty' cruisers was commissioned only during the London Conference!

The only option available to Japan if it was to continue to compete with the US Navy was to use its sub-category (b) tonnage to build cruisers comparable in every other respect to the *Myoko*s and *Takao*s but armed with 15.5cm guns – the maximum gun calibre permitted under the Treaty. The problem with this course of action was that the overall tonnage allocated to Japan for sub-category (b) cruisers was only 100,450 tons, much of which was already invested in light cruisers completed postwar that could not be replaced until the late 1930s. Thus began a series of elaborate and detailed calculations to determine what was possible within the constraints of treaty rules.

If the four oldest cruisers were scrapped straight away an additional 16,960tW would be available for new construction, which if added to the unused 2,035 tons of Japan's allocation under the London Treaty was equivalent to two ships of 9,500tW (see Table 4.5). The next ships up for replacement were the two *Tenryu*s, which could be replaced in 1935, and the first two units of the five-ship *Kuma* class, which could be replaced in 1936. This would make available a further 16,660 tons, equivalent to two ships of 8,330tW. Finally, the remaining three *Kuma*s (15,300 tons) would be due for replacement in 1937, and could therefore be replaced by a further two ships each of 7,650tW to be laid down in 1934. Rather than accept three different types of ship, the IJN made the logical decision to distribute the overall total of 50,955 tons (the equivalent of half its sub-category (b) cruiser allocation) as evenly as possible: four ships of 8,500tW would be completed before the end of 1936, with two being laid down as soon as design work was complete and the second pair to be laid down in 1933 for completion in 1936; and two ships of 8,450 tons would be laid down in 1934 as replacements for the last three *Kuma*s.

These were sensible, rational decisions that were once again undermined by the impossible demands of the Naval Staff, which wanted ships comparable in firepower,

Table 4.5: Japan's Navy List: Sub-category (b) Cruisers 1 April 1930

	Displacement	Replacement date	Tonnage available
Tone	3,760tW	1930	18,995tW[1]
3 *Chikuma*	3 × 4,400tW	1930	
2 *Tenryu*	2 × 3,230tW	1935	31,960tW
5 *Kuma*	5 × 5,100tW	2 × 1936	
		3 × 1937	
Tonnage available for replacement cruisers by 31 Dec 1936			50,955tW

Note:
1   Includes 2,035tW available following London Treaty.

protection and performance to its existing 'A-class' cruisers of the *Myoko* and *Takao* classes. Although the 15.5cm gun calibre had to be accepted, the Naval Staff wanted five triple turrets to compensate for the reduction in hitting power compared with the 20cm gun; it also wanted provision made for the eventual replacement of the 15.5cm triple turrets by 20cm twin turrets, thereby regaining lost fighting capabilities and bringing about the desired parity with the US Navy's 8in cruiser force level. Nor was the Naval Staff prepared to countenance any reduction in torpedo armament, particularly in view of the investment in new long-range, oxygen-propelled torpedoes it had set in train. Capabilities in this respect were actually to be increased, with four triple torpedo mountings replacing the twin mountings of the *Takao*s. In addition, the Naval Staff wanted protection for the magazines against 8in shell and for the machinery against 6in shell, a maximum speed of 37 knots, and endurance comparable to the 'A-class' ships.

The task of meeting these exacting requirements on a displacement of only 8,500 tons proved beyond the capacity of the Japanese constructors, who initially also attempted to accommodate the massive bridge structure and aircraft hangar of the *Takao*s into the design. Radical weight-saving measures were attempted, including the adoption for the first time of electric welding for the hull and fittings, and a less complex protection system in which the inclined armour belt was continued at reduced thickness to the double bottom, where it doubled as a torpedo bulkhead (see drawing and caption). The Japanese would by now have been aware of the benefits of electrical welding in the early US 'treaty' cruisers, which had each turned out 900 tons underweight; nevertheless, they would also have been acutely conscious that their own 'treaty' cruisers as completed were *overweight* by a similar margin, so there was never the remotest possibility that welding alone would bring displacement down to 8,500 tons.

An elevation of 75 degrees for the main guns was intended to give a dual-purpose capability, so the original HA armament comprised only four 12cm single guns – two fewer than in the *Myoko*s, although there was no change from the *Takao*s, whose main guns likewise had a high-angle capability. Despite the increase in shaft horsepower from 130,000shp in the *Takao*s to 152,000shp in the *Mogami*s the machinery weighed less, combining higher steam pressures (23kg/cm^2) and superheating with

Suzuya (Jap)

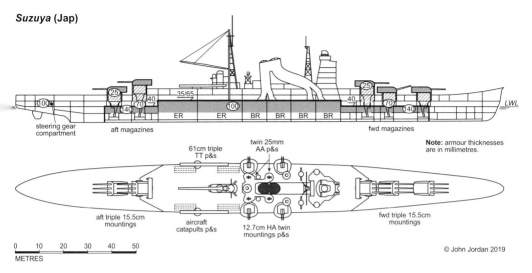

Suzuya and her sister Kumano had only eight boilers in four boiler rooms compared with ten boilers in five boiler rooms for the first two ships; the length of the central part of the armoured citadel was thereby slightly reduced. However, in contrast to the British cruiser designs of the period, which had internal 'box' protection for the magazines, the external belt was continued at a reduced height over the magazines fore and aft.

lightweight geared turbines; the new machinery was rated at 61.5shp/tonne compared with 48.8shp/tonne in the earlier 'A-class' cruisers.[12]

When approved in the summer of 1931 the definitive design had an anticipated nominal displacement of 9,500tW – it was still to be officially declared as 8,500tW for Treaty purposes, as any increase on this figure would have threatened the legitimacy of the larger programme. By 1932–33 it had risen further, as the training and

Suzuya (Jap): Protection

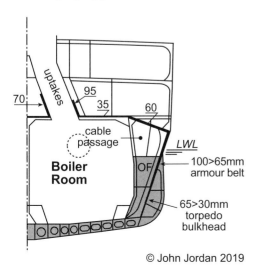

© John Jordan 2019

The cruisers of the Mogami class had an unusual protection system in which a graduated inclined belt of non-cemented (NVNC) armour was continued downwards to the double bottom to form an internal torpedo bulkhead of high-tensile steel, which was likewise steadily reduced in thickness. The purpose of this arrangement was not only to protect against torpedoes but to defeat 'underwater trajectory' shells that might otherwise plunge beneath the inclined waterline belt; it would be a feature of the later IJN cruisers of the Tone class and of the 'super-battleships' of the Yamato class. The 35mm protective deck over the machinery spaces was sloped down to the upper edge of the belt and reinforced to 60mm thickness. There was also comparatively thick protection for the boiler uptakes where they penetrated the protective deck.

The IJN cruiser *Mogami* on her speed trials in the Bungo Channel on 20 March 1935. Although she attained a mean speed of just under 36 knots, the trials revealed major structural weaknesses that proved costly and labour-intensive. *(Fukui Shizuo collection)*

Mogami following her reconstruction 1936–38. All four twin 12.7mm HA mountings are now in place. Note the Nakajima reconnaissance floatplanes on the 'flight deck' forward of No. 4 15.5cm gun mounting. *(Fukui Shizuo collection)*

elevation speeds of the new 15.5cm mounting were found to be inadequate for use against modern high-performance aircraft. Maximum elevation was reduced to 55 degrees, and it was decided to compensate by replacing the four single 12cm HA guns (weight of mounting: 10 tonnes) by twin 12.7/40 mountings (4 x 24.5 tonnes), a decision that also implied extending the shelter deck to the sides of the ship.

Soon after the launch of *Mogami* and *Mikuma*, the capsizing of the torpedo boat *Tomozuru* led to a review of the stability of recent IJN construction, and the design was recast to incorporate recommendations, a reduction in topweight being paramount. The massive bridge was lowered and reduced in size (weight was now 59 tonnes versus 160 tonnes in the original design), and the high tetrapod foremast replaced by a lightweight tripod. The after structures were reduced and the hangar eliminated; in compensation, the broad HA gun deck was extended aft, and the reconnaissance floatplanes stowed on a rail transfer system between the catapults. The triple torpedo mountings could now be moved aft away from the bridge and beneath the aircraft deck, the rapid transfer mechanisms for their reloads being fitted to the underside of the deck. Other measures to improve stability included a reduction in deck heights, and the fitting of a liquid ballast pumping system to compensate for empty fuel bunkers in the light condition.

These measures effectively resolved potential stability problems; modifications to the superstructures alone saved 135 tonnes in topweight. Even so, by the time *Mogami* was first completed in March 1935 she exceeded her planned trial displacement by a massive 1,800 tonnes. This made nonsense of the constructors' original calculations, particularly with regard to longitudinal strength, and when *Mogami* ran her trials she suffered serious damage to her welded hull. High-speed trials in March/April 1935 resulted in buckling and distortion of the frames and side stringers in the vicinity of the propellers; fuel bunkers were ruptured and bow plates buckled. Distortion of the hull from the wave action was so severe that it resulted in deformation of the roller paths of turrets Nos. 3 and 4, the barbettes of which were structurally connected to the shelter deck. Repairs were subsequently carried out at Kure, but when a typhoon struck the Fourth Fleet in September 1935 both *Mogami* and *Mikuma* suffered further deformation of the hull, with rupturing of some of the electrically welded joints in the fore part of the ship. An Investigation Board was appointed in October 1935, and the ships were placed in reserve at Kure pending reconstruction.

By this time the third unit of the class, *Suzuya*, was nearing completion, and underwent reconstruction in 1935–36 at Yokosuka. Construction of the fourth ship, *Kumano*, was temporarily suspended, then resumed in the spring of 1936. The Ducol shell plating amidships was now riveted instead of welded, with welded mild steel being used for the ship's ends. Additional 'strengthening' plates of Ducol steel were fitted on either side of the keel and at the level of the upper deck to prevent longitudinal deformation of the hull, and the raised barbettes separated from the superstructure decks. These modifications resulted in an increase in weight of more than 1,000 tonnes, so new bulges were fitted over the original ones to preserve buoy-

Table 4.6: The IJN *Mogami* and the US and British Response

	Mogami class (Jap)	*Brooklyn* class (US)	*Southampton* class (GB)
Built:	4 ships 1931–37	7 ships[1] 1934–38	8 ships 1934–39
Displacement:	8,500tW[2]	9,770tW	9,000tW[3]
Dimensions:	202m × 18m	608ft × 62ft (185m × 18.8m)	592ft × 62ft (180m × 18.8m)
Machinery:	Ten[4] Kampon boilers; 4-shaft geared turbines, 152,000shp = 37kts[1]	Eight B&W[5] boilers; 4-shaft geared turbines, 100,000shp = 32.5kts	Four Admiralty boilers; 4-shaft geared turbines, 75,000shp = 32kts
Armament:	15 – 15.5cm/60 (5 × III) 8 – 12.7cm/40 (4 × II) HA 8 – 25mm (4 × II) 12 – 61cm TT (4 × III)	15 – 6in/47 (5 × III) 8 – 5in/25 (8 × I) HA 8 × 0.5in MG (8 × I)	12 – 6in/50 (4 × III) 8 – 4in/45 (4 × II) HA 8 – 2pdr (2 × IV) 6 – 21in TT (2 × III)
Protection:	mach: 100mm belt, 35mm deck mags: 140mm belt, 40mm deck turrets: 25mm	mach: 5in belt, 2in deck mags: 3/4.7in sides, 2in deck turrets: 6.5in faces, 1½in sides CT: 6in	mach: 4½in belt, 1½in deck mags: 4½in sides, 2in crowns turrets: 1–2in

Notes:
1 Two modified ships were ordered under FY1935.
2 Designed – see text for actual displacement and speed following reconstruction.
3 Declared displacement; the early ships were slightly heavier, and designed displacement of the three 1935 ships was 9,400tW.
4 The second pair of ships, *Kumano* and *Suzuya*, had eight.
5 B&W = Babcock & Wilcox

ancy and stability. When completed in October 1937 *Kumano* had a trial displacement of 13,723 tonnes, equivalent to a standard displacement of 11,890tW, which represented an increase of 25 per cent over the designed displacement of 9,500tW (and a 40 per cent increase over the declared displacement of 8,500tW!). Maximum speed was reduced to 35 knots – still an impressive figure for ships of this size.

Mogami and *Mikuma* would be rebuilt to the same standard in 1936–38. Following refit only six reload torpedoes were carried, but this figure was again increased to twelve following modifications to enable the ships to fire the Type 93 oxygen-fuelled 'Long Lance' torpedo in 1938. All four ships would subsequently have their triple 15.5cm gun mountings replaced by 20cm twin mountings in 1939, although 20cm turrets of new design would have to be built to accommodate the larger-diameter roller path of the 15.5cm triples.

The two ships to be ordered under the following 'Circle 2' Programme of 1934 were to have been virtual repeats of the *Mogami* class, but with a designed radius of 10,000nm at 18 knots. When they were authorised there was as yet no inkling of the problems that would be experienced with the *Mogami*s, and the design would be recast in early 1936 when both ships were already on the stocks (see below).

The American and British Responses

The serious technical problems the IJN experienced with of the *Mogami*s were very much in the future when their construction was announced to the world in February 1933. The key issue as far as the British and the Americans were concerned was that Japan was to build cruisers armed with fifteen 6.1in/15.5cm guns on a displacement of only 8,500 tons. For the British, already committed to a programme of light cruisers of moderate displacement armed with only six or eight 6in guns, this constituted a very serious development, as the new Japanese cruisers would pose just as serious a threat to trade routes in the Far East as their 8in/20cm-gun predecessors. The US Navy, on the other hand, which had virtually settled on a well-balanced 9,600-ton cruiser with good protection but only twelve 6in guns, would be compelled to re-evaluate its existing proposals; despite their recent preference for heavy protection, the Americans were simply not prepared to be outgunned by the Japanese, and if the latter could fit fifteen 15.5cm guns into a ship displacing only 8,500 tons standard, then a US Navy cruiser of 10,000 tons ought at least to be able to match them in firepower.

The US Navy's *Brooklyn* Class

The US Navy's reaction to the 15-gun *Mogami*s was immediate. On 10 March 1933, less than a month after the Japanese announcement, the General Board requested studies of cruisers with fifteen 6in guns in five triple turrets or sixteen 6in in four quadruple turrets, with reduced protection to compensate for the increased weight of armament. The adoption of longitudinal construction, long after it had become standard practice in most other navies, was estimated to give a potential weight saving of 280–290 tons; even so the cost of an additional triple turret with its asso-

Brooklyn (US)

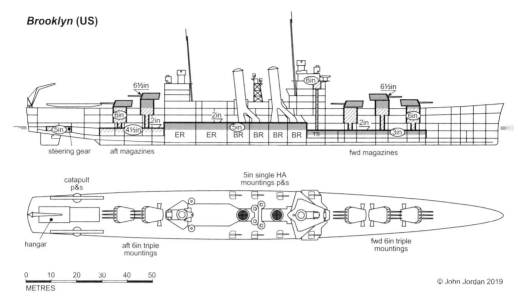

© John Jordan 2019

The 6in cruisers of the *Brooklyn* class had a machinery layout and protection system derived from the late 'treaty' cruisers of the *New Orleans* class. The shallow 3in armour belt over the forward magazines was external, whereas the after magazines, the crowns of which were closer to the waterline, had thicker internal 'box' protection.

The US cruiser *Brooklyn* (CL-40) in the Hudson River in 1939. The US Navy opted to match the 15 fifteen guns of the Japanese *Mogami* and *Mikuma*. ((NHHC, 80-G-10223213)

ciated hoists and magazine would cost 18 per cent of armour weight, making protection against 8in shell marginal. However, the alternative solution, the quadruple turret, was considered a risky development, and was rejected by the General Board.

The general configuration of the *Brooklyn* class was based, as in its Scheme 2 predecessor, on the late 'treaty' cruisers of the *New Orleans* class, with the boiler rooms grouped together, two closely spaced slim funnels and pole masts raked at the same angle as the funnels. However, the need to accommodate an additional turret aft and now an additional turret forward effectively compressed the superstructures, and made it difficult to accommodate the aircraft and their handling gear amidships. The solution adopted was to extend the forecastle deck to the stern to accommodate a hangar beneath the quarterdeck. Twin catapults were relocated on either side of the quarterdeck, with a single heavy handling crane at the stern (see photo of *Nashville*). This arrangement proved successful, and would be repeated in all subsequent US cruiser construction. Consideration was also given to deploying a framed canvas landing mat similar to that adopted for the new French cruisers from the stern, but this was ultimately rejected. Although the quarterdeck position was more exposed to the elements, the relatively high freeboard made it acceptable, and it had the additional

This 1943 photograph of *Nashville* (CL-43) at Mare Island shows the aviation arrangements favoured by the US Navy for its post-London cruisers. A capacious hangar beneath the quarterdeck, covered when not in use with a sliding hatch, is flanked by twin catapults powered by explosive charges. The aircraft were handled by a centre-line crane. ((NHHC, 19-N-49143)

advantages of removing the threat of an aviation fuel fire from the superstructures and of freeing up the midship section for anti-aircraft weapons with unobstructed arcs.

The 6in/47 Mk 16 gun adopted for this class was a new weapon firing semi-fixed ammunition,[13] and its firing cycle of 8–10rpm per gun was in marked contrast to the 8in/55 of the 'treaty' cruisers, which were capable of only 2 rounds per minute. When firing the new 130lb (59kg) 'super-heavy' projectile it would have almost twice the penetration of the 6in gun fitted in the *Omaha* class, and would have a range of 26,100 yards (23,870m) at its maximum elevation of 47.5 degrees. Like their linear 8in-gun predecessors of the *New Orleans* class, the *Brooklyn*s would have no torpedo tubes, an indication that they were not intended for 'fleet' work.

Despite concerns expressed regarding the inability of these ships to withstand 8in shell, they were more heavily armoured than any contemporary cruisers with the exception of the Italian *Zaras*; they were to prove particularly resistant to battle damage, and the last of the US Navy's 8in-gun 'treaty' cruisers, *Wichita* (see below), would be virtually a repeat design. They proved to be excellent sea-boats, and even in a heavy Atlantic swell they were dry, with a smooth, easy roll. However, there was subsequent evidence that some structural integrity had been sacrificed in the drive to save weight, and several ships were to suffer damage to the bow section in heavy weather.

Four *Brooklyn*s were ordered on 3 August 1933 under Fiscal Year 1934, of which one ship was counted as having been authorised (as an 8in 'treaty' cruiser) in 1929, the other three being funded under the National Industrial Recovery Act. A further three units, all counted as 1929 authorisations, were ordered the following year under FY1935. By this time the light cruisers of the *Omaha* were becoming due for replacement, and studies were initiated for smaller cruisers better suited to work with the destroyers of the Battle Force. However, the General Board, concerned about Japan's continuing construction of large 6in-gun cruisers, opted in favour of repeat *Brooklyn*s and two modified ships, with four twin 5in/38 DP mountings in place of the eight single 5in/25 mountings of the earlier units, were duly ordered as replacements for the two over-age ships of the *Omaha* class under FY1936.

The British were predictably upset by the construction of the *Brooklyn*s. In September 1933 a formal note was despatched claiming that, together with the new Japanese ships, they would be seen as the first step in a new and ruinous arms competition in large cruisers. The implication of the note was that the blame for this state of affairs lay squarely on the United States for refusing to countenance a reduction in individual displacement below 10,000 tons at the London Conference. It was suggested that a new upper limit on cruiser displacement needed to be agreed between Britain, the United States and Japan. In response the United States stated that the size of the new ships was driven by operational requirements (*ie* the need to cross the Pacific to protect its interests in Southeast Asia). This dismissive American response would compel the British to embark on the construction of comparable large light cruisers, while simultaneously pressing at the political level for a new agreement on restricting cruiser size.

The British 'Town' Class

The Japanese announcement in February 1933 that it would build four *Mogami*s and the US Navy's response led to a dramatic change in British cruiser policy, which was formalised at a meeting of the Admiralty Board in late July and approved by the Prime Minister in August. Design work began immediately. Staff requirements envisaged a cruiser with a displacement of 7,800 tons, armed with twelve 6in guns in four triple turrets, with protection against 6in gunfire but a moderate speed of only 30 knots. The ship would have a range of 7,000nm at 16 knots, an HA armament of three twin 4in HA mountings, one of which would be on the centre line with good all-round arcs, and would operate no fewer than five TSR-type aircraft, of which two would be stowed in hangars; these would be able to search for and attack enemy surface raiders and provide a limited strike force. A torpedo armament was not considered essential, but as the ships could be called on to work with the fleet there would be provision for rapid embarkation. It was accepted that the larger ship would mean a reduction to a total force of forty-nine cruisers by 31 December 1936, but it was hoped to make up for this in future, once the Washington Treaty had expired.

The staff requirements were comfortably met in four studies based on the eight-gun Modified *Leander* that ranged in displacement from 7,800 tons to 8,835 tons, the differences largely relating to hull size and propulsion (the smaller two designs could accommodate only three aircraft). The largest and fastest ('D') was selected as the most promising for further development; it became even larger as discussion proceeded on the detail of the design, which was now designated 'M'. For the first time in a British post-Washington cruiser the armour belt over the machinery was extended forward by 45ft to cover the transmitting station, switchboard and W/T offices. In compensation, the thickness of the belt had to be reduced from 5in to 4½in; however, there was now protection for a greater part of the waterline. After much discussion, aircraft arrangements similar to the modernised battleships would also be adopted, comprising a double-ended heavy cross-deck catapult with aircraft hangars on either side of the fore-funnel. Two of the new quad 2pdr pom-pom mountings were substituted for two of the light quad 0.5in MG, and the armour on the sides of the magazines was to be cemented. The legend was submitted in late February 1934 and approved on 2 March 1934.

There would be further changes. It soon became apparent that the requirement for one of the twin 4in mountings to have all-round arcs was difficult to fulfil given the pressure on centre-line space, and two sided mountings had to be accepted in its place. HA fire control was provided by HACS III directors on either side of the bridge.[14] The TSR aircraft was to be replaced by the larger Walrus, the complement being reduced to three. The final modification was the raking back of the twin funnels and tripod masts, which helped to keep the bridge clear of funnel smoke and contributed to the handsome lines of the ships.

By the end of this process, standard displacement had risen to 9,110 tons, although the 'official' figure declared under the Treaty was 9,000 tons (figures for ammunition and other supplies were regularly pared down by this time).[15] Cost was

Southampton (GB)

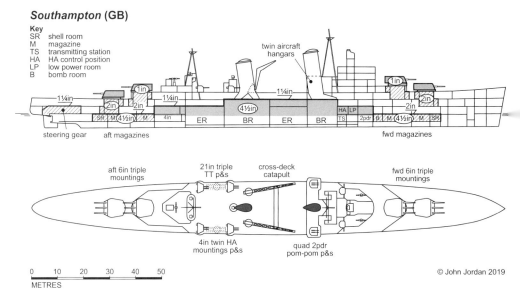

Key
SR   shell room
M   magazine
TS   transmitting station
HA   HA control position
LP   low power room
B   bomb room

twin aircraft hangars

steering gear   aft magazines

fwd magazines

aft 6in triple mountings

21in triple TT p&s

cross-deck catapult

fwd 6in triple mountings

4in twin HA mountings p&s

quad 2pdr pom-pom p&s

0   10   20   30   40   50
METRES

© John Jordan 2019

The protection system of the 6in cruisers of the *Southampton* class was derived from that of the Modified *Leander* and *Arethusa* classes but with forward and after extensions to the armour belt to cover the transmitting station (forward) and the magazines for the 4in HA and 2pdr guns. The magazines for the main 6in guns continued to have thick internal 'box' protection, and there was 2in protection for the sides of the ammunition lobbies.

around £2.1 million, slightly higher than the cost of an 8in-gun cruiser of the 'County' class. Thus the attempt by the British to limit the cost of individual cruisers by seeking treaty reductions in displacement and gun calibre ultimately came to nothing. On the other hand, the cruisers of the 'Town' class were arguably the most balanced large cruisers built by any of the major navies during the 1930s, capable of a high rate of fire from their triple 6in turrets and with well-developed protection against similarly armed ships. Moreover, by 1935, with a fast-deteriorating international situation, more money was being made available to the Royal Navy, and the high cost of these ships would be less problematical.

Two units, initially to be named *Minotaur* and *Polyphemus* (thereby continuing the mythological theme of the *Leander*s and *Arethusa*s) but subsequently renamed *Newcastle* and *Southampton*, were ordered under the 1933 estimates, together with a single 'fleet' cruiser of the *Arethusa* class. The following year, three more were authorised alongside the last of the four *Arethusa*s. Three further units of a slightly modified design with thicker deck protection and improved protection for the turrets and hoists were authorised under the 1935 estimates.

With the release of funding for new naval construction from 1935 and the imminent possibility that new, lower displacement limits might be agreed at the next London Conference, the Royal Navy investigated the possibility of matching the new Japanese and American cruisers with an enlarged 'Town'-class design with four quadruple turrets,[16] but the latter proved difficult to design (dispersion was a major problem) and had to be abandoned. With the May 1936 deadline for ordering the ships fast approaching, it was decided that they should be rearmed with triple turrets, which allowed the hull to be shortened by 10ft, and that the thickness of the horizontal protection would be increased. 'Box' protection for the magazines, which had been a feature of all British cruisers since Washington, was abandoned in favour of an extension of the side belt fore and aft and protected decks which extended to the ship's sides. The heavier HA armament of six twin 4in mountings remained from the original design, and the fore-funnel was now separated from the bridge with the catapult on the open expanse of deck forward of it and aircraft hangars port and starboard integrated with the after part of the bridge structure.

These changes increased the legend displacement to 10,300 tons, a figure that was exceeded by 250 tons on completion. Two ships, *Belfast* and *Edinburgh*, were ordered under the 1936 Estimates, and they were to remain the only ships of their type. Although sea-keeping qualities were even better than in the earlier 'Towns', design weaknesses made them inferior in other respects. The magazines for the 4in guns were forward of the machinery, so ammunition had to be transported to them horizontally from the after end of the forecastle using a system of three-tiered conveyors. There was also a major point of structural weakness at the end of the forecastle itself, which was common to other British interwar light cruisers but which in this class was exacerbated by the stepping down of the side armour (and with it the armoured deck) within a few feet of the forecastle break. When mined during the Second World War *Belfast* would break her back at this point, by which time her sister *Edinburgh* and a number of the earlier 'Towns' were already suffering stress fractures

The 'Town'-class cruiser HMS *Southampton* in 1937, shortly after her completion. This class was Britain's answer to Japan's *Mogami* class. The extension of the waterline belt at a reduced height fore and aft of the machinery spaces can be clearly seen. *(Conrad Waters collection)*

HMS *Belfast* on 3 September 1939, the day war was declared. *Belfast* and her sister *Edinburgh* were the ultimate development of the 'Town' class. They had heavier protection and two additional 4in HA twin mountings. *(Courtesy of Conrad Waters)*

in this area, and remedial work involving stiffening and the extension of the forecastle aft had to be undertaken in all units.

The Last of the US Navy's Treaty Cruisers

The London Treaty of 1930 had permitted the US Navy to complete a further three cruisers armed with 8in guns according to a predetermined schedule. *Quincy* (CA-39) was duly ordered under the FY1933 estimates, *Vincennes* (CA-44) under FY1934, and *Wichita* (CA-45) under FY1935. All had technically been authorised by Congress under the 1929 programme, and funding was easy to secure. The first two ships were virtually repeats of the *New Orleans* type (see *WAW* Chapter 6), but *Wichita* was built to a new design that took into account the improvements made in the *Brooklyn* class.

By this time it had become apparent that dispersion was a serious problem with the earlier triple 8in mounting, which had its guns closely spaced in the same sleeve. A salvo spread of 1,000 yards was not uncommon at 25,000 yards range, and given that at these longer ranges the shells would be plunging at a steep angle it was quite possible with dispersion of this magnitude for the target to be 'bracketed' by a salvo without a single hit or near-miss. The solution for the older mounting was to fit electrical delay coils to the centre gun-tube, for a reduction in salvo spread to 700 yards; alternatively ships could fire split salvoes, but this would reduce the firing cycle even further in ships with a notoriously slow rate of fire. For *Wichita*, which would in any case not follow the standard *New Orleans* design, it made sense to develop a completely new turret with increased spacing of the gun barrels and independent loading and firing (implying a larger, heavier barbette).

With the reduction from five turrets in the *Brooklyn* class to three in *Wichita* it proved possible to devise a superior layout for the 5in HA guns, which as in the modified *Brooklyns* were of the new 38-calibre, dual-purpose model, with single mountings on the centre line fore and aft and three on either side. The guns most exposed to blast and the elements were fitted with shields. Armour thicknesses were slightly increased to give protection against the current 8in shell from 10,000 yards at a 90-degree target angle, making *Wichita* the most heavily armoured cruiser of the interwar period. However, there was a cost, and when completed in 1939 *Wichita* was overweight; she entered service without two of her 5in gun mountings, and when these were eventually fitted the topweight had to be counterbalanced by 200 tons of fixed keel ballast.

Wichita (CA-45) was the third of three additional 8in-gun 'treaty cruisers' the US Navy was permitted to lay down during the period 1930–36. Unlike *Quincy* (CA-39) and *Vincennes* (CA-44) she was built to a completely new design derived from the *Brooklyn* class. She is seen here in close-up in 1940. Note the secondary battery of eight (initially six) 5in/38-cal HA guns. *(Ted Stone collection, NHHC, NH 66793)*

Modernisation and Reconstruction

By the end of 1932 all the 8in-gun cruisers laid down for Britain, Japan and Italy during the 1920s had entered service, and of the French ships of the type only *Algérie* was still fitting out. By contrast, only ten of the US Navy's permitted eighteen 'treaty' cruisers were in service, and the first five heavily armoured ships of the *New Orleans* class had only recently been laid down. The British, who had completed seven ships of the *Kent* class and four of the *London* class before the first US 'treaty' cruiser even entered service, were concerned that these early examples of the type were under-protected compared with the latest American and European ships

In 1933 the Royal Navy began studies for reconstruction of the *Kent*s. All ships of the class had been completed below the 10,000-ton limit: *Kent* completed at 9,850 tons, *Suffolk* at 9,800 tons, and the other units of the class at 9,750 tons. This meant that 150–250 tons of weight was already available for additional protection. Further proposed weight reductions included cutting down the hull aft of No. 4 ('Y') turret (45 tons), removing the torpedo tubes (32 tons), and removing obsolete fittings such as the original catapult, the HA guns, and the after control structure (133 tons). These savings provided a theoretical total of 360–460 tons for improved protection, new anti-aircraft guns and new aircraft arrangements.

It was estimated that a 5½in belt over the machinery rooms, the dynamo room and the transmitting station would give limited protection against 8in shell beyond 10,000 yards and immunity beyond 15,000 yards, whereas 4½in armour would give no immunity against 8in shells but immunity to 6in shells beyond 8,000 yards. However, the weight of a 5½in belt could be accommodated only at the expense of aircraft, which were considered essential on the trade routes, so the reduced thick-

The cruiser *Suffolk* following her rebuild. Weight was saved by cutting down the quarterdeck. She now has a prominent hangar with a cross-deck catapult and a modern HA battery.

ness had to be accepted. The recommendations were approved in September 1934, and reconstruction of all except the two Australian ships took place in 1935–38.

In addition to the 4½in armour belt, new Mk XIX twin 4in mountings were fitted in place of the original singles, together with two HACS Mk I control systems, and the close-in AA now comprised two quadruple 2pdr pom-poms and two quadruple 0.5in MG. All ships were fitted with a double-ended SIIL cross-deck catapult abaft the third funnel, and all except *Kent* had a large double hangar abaft the catapult.

The additional armour cost 286 tons, the new anti-aircraft weapons 34 tons, and the aviation facilities 120 tons for a total of 442 tons. The torpedo tubes were landed and put into storage for possible re-installation during wartime; not all ships were cut down aft, but weight savings should have totalled 165–210 tons, thereby compensating for the added protection and new equipment. However, the first ship to complete refit weighed in at just over 10,300 tons, and the figure for other ships of the class was slightly higher.[17]

It was originally envisaged that all of the Royal Navy's 8in-gun cruisers would undergo a similar reconstruction, but with increasingly onerous workloads in the naval dockyards associated with the rearmament programme of the late 1930s, which was closely followed by the outbreak of war, only *London* was taken in hand.[18]

Reconstruction of the *Myoko* and *Furutaka* Classes

The IJN 'treaty' cruisers, including the earliest 8in-gun types, were generally better protected than their British counterparts. However, the Japanese were equally anxious that these ships should not be outclassed by the more recent US cruisers, so they were to be upgraded in line with the general modernisation decision of July 1930. In particular, the armament and fire control systems of the *Myoko*s, completed in 1928–29, would need to be brought up to date, and even more radical reconstruction would be necessary for the older six-gun *Furutaka* and *Aoba* classes, the design of which pre-dated the Washington Treaty.

All of these ships had been completed with fixed torpedo tubes between decks at the insistence of the Naval General Staff in the face of strong opposition from their designer, Constructor Captain Hiraga. However, a mine explosion aboard the minelayer *Tokiwa* in 1927 bore out Hiraga's concerns, and it was subsequently decided that in future cruisers would have trainable tubes at upper deck level, as in the *Takao*s, with the torpedo warheads protected by Ducol steel plates. The anti-aircraft armament would also need to be upgraded in the light of the latest developments.

During the early 1930s the original 20cm (7.9in) guns of the *Myoko*s were replaced by the newer 20cm Type 3 no. 2 model fitted in the *Takao*s, which had the slightly larger 20.3cm (8in) bore of British and American 'treaty' cruisers. New shells and charges were embarked, so the hoists had to be modified, for an overall increase in weight of 45 tonnes.

From 1934 to 1936 all four ships were rebuilt. The original fixed torpedo tubes, the aircraft hangar and the original catapult were removed. A new deckhouse extending the full width of the hull was constructed aft on the same level as the orig-

inal shelter deck forward; it extended from the second funnel to the barbette for
No. 4 turret, and housed quadruple trainable torpedo mountings with quick reload
systems. It was eventually planned to fit four sets of tubes, but only the after pair
was initially fitted, the eight reloads being stowed in a special 'shed' on the centre
line. There was an overhead rail system on the deckhead for moving the reloads to
the tubes.

Atop the deckhouse was a rail system capable of accommodating three reconnais-
sance/spotter floatplanes, with two of the latest Kure Type no. 2 catapults port and
starboard. Four of the new twin 12.7/40 HA mountings were fitted, and these were
complemented by two Type 91 fire control directors. Other modifications included
improved communications systems, more spacious accommodation for the crew (the
former torpedo room was utilised), and air conditioning in some key spaces.

Additional bulges had to be fitted on top of the original ones to maintain buoyancy and stability; it was still envisaged that in wartime that the upper part of this
bulge would be filled with steel tubes. In contrast to the British, who with the *Kent*
modernisation were keen to counterbalance new equipment to be fitted with the
removal of an equivalent weight of older items of equipment, the IJN was quite
happy to add weight topsides and to compensate for this by bulging. This resolved
the buoyancy/stability problem at the expense of longitudinal strength, which in
these ships as originally designed was already marginal. Following the 4th Fleet incident of 1935 plates of Ducol steel were riveted along the hull sides on both sides of
the keel, as with the rebuilt *Mogami*s. This cost a further 500 tonnes in weight on
top of the 680 tonnes added during rebuilding. Trial displacement was now around
14,500 tonnes, equivalent to a standard displacement of 12,300tW. Maximum speed
was reduced to 34 knots – still an impressive figure for ships of this size – and
endurance was reduced to 4,000nm at 16 knots, approximately half that of comparable British and American cruisers.

The last Japanese 'A-class' cruisers to be taken in hand for modernisation during
the Treaty period were the two *Furutaka*s, which in 1935–36 suffered serious blade
failures in their turbines. Because these and the *Aoba*s were the smallest and least
capable of the 8in-gun cruisers, having been designed prior to the Washington
Treaty, it had originally been envisaged that they would be replaced by new construction following Japan's withdrawal from the Treaty system, but in 1936 the pressure
of new construction on the shipyards resulted in a decision to modernise them in line
with the other 'A-class' ships.

The original single 20cm gun mountings were replaced with three twin mountings for the 20cm Type 3 no. 2 gun fitted in more recent ships, and the fire control
systems were modernised. The *Furutaka*s were too small to accommodate the new
twin 12.7cm HA mountings, so they retained four 12cm single mountings, the after
pair being moved forward to make room for two quadruple trainable torpedo
mountings with their reloads in adjacent lockers on the upper deck. The original
torpedo rooms for the fixed tubes were converted to accommodation, as in the
*Myoko*s. The original twelve boilers with mixed firing were replaced by ten modern

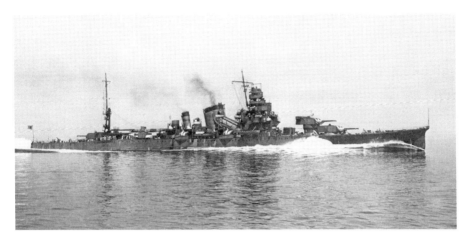

The IJN cruiser *Furutaka* running her full-power trials in the Bungo Channel on 9 June 1939. The reconstruction involved the replacement of the original single 20cm turrets by three twins, as in the *Aoba* class, and the fixed torpedo tubes by two quadruple trainable deck mountings with reloads for each of the tubes. *(Fukui Shizuo collection)*

oil-fired boilers, freeing up No. 1 boiler room for additional accommodation, and the defective turbine blades renewed. The bridge was rebuilt, and a single trainable Kure Type 2 catapult for two floatplanes was installed abaft the second funnel. New close-range AA weapons were fitted, and generating power increased.

These modifications brought the two *Furutaka*s up to the same standard as the more modern IJN 'A-class' cruisers. However, they again involved a significant increase in topweight, and the *Furutaka*s had to be fitted, like the *Myoko*s, with additional bulges to restore buoyancy and stability. The bulges themselves were constructed of Ducol steel plates in order to improve longitudinal strength, and were to be filled with steel tubes at the waterline. Trial displacement was now 10,500 tonnes, as compared with 9,500 tonnes when first completed in 1926. Again there was a cost: maximum speed was reduced by 2 knots to 33 knots, and there was a corresponding reduction in endurance. The two ships of the *Aoba* class, which had been completed with twin 20cm turrets from the outset, would receive a less complete modernisation from 1938.

Tone and *Chikuma*

In early 1936 the Japanese Naval General Staff took the decision to modify the two 'B-class' cruisers recently laid down as a follow-on to the *Mogami* class. These modifications were aimed not only at correcting the serious structural defects experienced in trials with *Mogami* and *Mikuma*, but at a change of role. By the mid-1930s Japanese operational doctrine had shifted perceptibly with regard to the employment of its 'A-class' cruisers. The fifth revision of Battle Instructions in 1934 gave much greater prominence to night battle prior to the decisive action. While attrition of the US battle fleet during its passage across the Pacific remained a primary requirement for a Japanese victory, it was recognised that this had been made more difficult by the latest US Navy cruising formation, which envisaged an outer ring of 8in cruisers. The IJN's response was to create powerful night combat groups comprising the 'A-class' cruisers and the destroyer flotillas belonging to the Second (Scouting) Fleet, supported by the reconstructed fast battleships of the *Kongo* class. The heavy ships, which were specially equipped and trained for night fighting, were to break through the outer ring, creating gaps through which the destroyer flotillas could be infiltrated to make their massed attacks against the enemy battle line.[19]

This advanced force would require accurate and detailed aerial scouting information during the late afternoon and evening in order for the night combat groups to take up their positions on the flanks of the enemy fleet, and this would have to be provided by the battleships and cruisers themselves. The Naval General Staff therefore decided that the new cruisers were to operate between two and four three-seat floatplanes (useful also for spotting during the main fleet action) plus four two-seat floatplanes. It was not possible to stow all these aircraft in a hangar, but the aircraft would need to be protected from the blast of the main guns, so one of the five triple 15.5cm turrets was suppressed and the other four grouped together forward, leaving the entire after part of the ship clear for the operation of aircraft. The original aircraft deck, with its twin side-mounted catapults and its elaborate system of rails, was slightly enlarged to accommodate four aircraft, and a centre-line rail extended via a ramp onto the quarterdeck where a further two to four aircraft could be ranged. As the aircraft were exposed to damage from the elements, spare wings were carried. The rails and the ramp were served by a 24m handling crane, and a command post from which launch and recovery was directed was provided at the foot of the tripod mainmast.

The ships were otherwise similar to the *Mogami*s, except that the longitudinal strengthening measures applied to the latter when they were rebuilt in 1936–38 were incorporated while building; hull weight was 4,690 tonnes, as compared with 3,680 tonnes for *Mogami* as designed and 4,490 tonnes for *Kumano* as completed in 1937.

Tone (Jap)

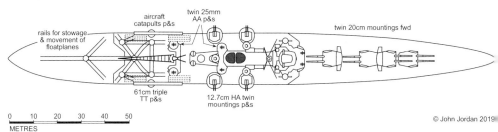

The drawing shows the cruiser *Tone* as completed in November 1938, with the original 15.5cm triple turrets replaced by twin 20cm turrets. The unusual all-forward main armament layout was adopted to free up the after part of the ship for an air group of six reconnaissance floatplanes, for which two trainable catapults and an elaborate system of rails and turntables was provided. In the original design there was to to have been a fifth twin 12.7cm HA mounting aft, but this was suppressed in favour of the large, centre-line aircraft-handling crane.

The reduction to four turrets also enabled thicker armour to be fitted, particularly around the magazines, which had 145mm sides with a 56mm deck, and the conning tower. Following the expiry of the London Treaty on 1 January 1937 it was decided to replace the triple 15.5cm turrets by 20cm twins, and as construction was not too far advanced these were easily incorporated into the design.

Tone and *Chikuma* were probably the best of the Japanese interwar cruisers, largely because of the reduction in the main armament, which made for a well-balanced design with superior protection for the magazines and excellent habitability. Standard displacement on completion was, nevertheless, close to 12,000 tons, well above the Treaty limit and also well above their designed displacement. With the reorganisation of the IJN's carriers into the First Air Fleet in April 1941 these two units would be attached to Admiral Nagumo's force throughout the early phase of the war, providing aerial reconnaissance for Japan's elite carrier force up to and including the disaster at Midway.

The London Treaty of 1936 and its Impact on the Royal Navy

Most of the negotiation at the London Conference of 1935–36 (for detail see Chapter 8 Postscript), as at the earlier London conference, focused on the cruiser category. It was agreed that future cruisers should be limited to a standard displacement of 8,000 tons, and although the British refused to have a quantitative ceiling imposed, there was to be an informal agreement to the effect that the British would maintain a force of seventy cruisers, of which ten would be over-age, while the US Navy would be permitted to build up to a force of sixty under-age cruisers. Since current projected US force levels were only thirty-seven ships, of which two *Omaha*s were shortly due for replacement,[20] this would mean twenty-five new cruisers, which because of the new 8,000-ton limit would necessarily be 'fleet' ships.

The London Treaty of 1936 had minimal impact on the Royal Navy's plans, which is perhaps unsurprising given that the proposals adopted by the conference were largely those put forward by the British. By this time Britain was becoming increasingly concerned that it might have to fight in two theatres simultaneously, hence its attempt to secure acceptance for a new 'two-power' standard embracing a minimum figure of seventy cruisers.[21]

In order to attain a force level of seventy ships within the necessary time frame, it would be necessary to at least double the figure of three cruisers laid down per year that had prevailed during the early 1930s, and to retain some of the over-age ships that would otherwise have been scrapped.

The problem with the retention of the over-age ships, particularly the small cruisers of the 'C' and 'D' classes completed during the latter part of the First World War,[22] was that they were no longer regarded as suitable for fleet work due to their relatively low speed and obsolescent armament. In their place the Royal Navy wanted to build modern units capable of matching the French *contre-torpilleurs* and the Italian 'Condottieri' in performance, so during late 1934 seven small cruiser designs were drawn up with a view to providing a 'C'/'D' replacement. All except two of these designs were in the 4,500–5,500 displacement range (*ie* comparable to the 'C's and 'D's), with moderate protection, a speed of 31–33 knots and an armament of six 6in guns, generally in single mountings.[23] The sixth was a small unprotected cruiser of 3,500 tons, with 'destroyer' machinery capable of 38 knots, and there was also an attempt at an 1,850-ton ship, designated the Scout 'V', which was intended as a counter to the French and Japanese 'leaders' (in fact the *contre-torpilleurs* and 'Special Type' destroyers respectively); the latter was to be armed with five twin 4.7in guns, and would provide the basis for the destroyers of the 'Tribal' class (see Chapter 5). All of the larger ships had protection adequate to take on other 6in cruisers, and there was an emphasis on anti-aircraft capabilities at the expense of aviation facilities, long-range reconnaissance being the function of the carrier(s) accompanying the fleet.

As the London Treaty of 1930 was still in force when these designs were first considered, the Admiralty Board felt it needed to get the maximum capability from the minimum tonnage. It decided that trade cruisers were the priority, and that the 'C' and 'D' classes could adequately be replaced by the small Scout 'V' design. This view was strongly opposed in the fleet, where the C-in-C Mediterranean in particular felt that larger, more powerful ships were needed for tactical scouting, to support the destroyer flotillas, to perform general duties, and to boost fleet anti-aircraft defences. This last factor was to become an increasingly important issue as the design evolved. Ideally guns of 5.5–6in calibre were required for surface engagement, but this implied a low-angle main armament, and on only 5,000 tons it was then difficult to provide an HA battery of adequate size. On the other hand, the dual-purpose main armament of 4.7in guns in twin mountings proposed as an alternative would be inadequate in the anti-surface role, as 4.7in was the standard calibre for British and Italian destroyers, and the ships would be outgunned not only by the French *contre-torpilleurs* and the Italian '*Condottieri*', but even by the large French destroyers of the *1,500-tonnes* type, which were armed with 130mm (5.1in) guns.

In the event it was decided to opt for a 5.25in gun in a twin dual-purpose mounting – the same mounting that would be fitted in the battleships of the *King George V* class (see Chapter 2). This weapon offered a shell heavy enough to disable light cruisers and destroyers, but was light enough to permit handling at a rate sufficient to provide a useful barrage against aircraft. A firing cycle of 10–12rpm and an elevation of 90 degrees were demanded, and these were almost met[24] at the cost of some complexity in the mounting. The semi-fixed round was the largest that could be comfortably handled, and because it was important to keep down the weight of the mounting the gunhouses were small and cramped. However, in theory the 5.25in dual-purpose gun was a solution to the otherwise insoluble problem of providing an effective anti-surface capability and a valuable addition to fleet air defence in a small cruiser, and the *Dido* class would influence the later US Navy small fleet cruisers of the *Atlanta* class.

Five ships were ordered under the 1936 Estimates, and like their predecessors of

Table 4.7: **The Last Cruisers Authorised Under the Treaty**

	Wichita (US)	Tone class (Jap)	Dido class (GB)
Built;	1 ship 1935–39	2 ships 1934–39	11 ships 1937–42
Displacement:	10,000tW (designed)	11,215tW[1]	5,450tW
Dimensions:	608ft × 62ft	202m × 18.5m	512ft × 51ft
	(185m × 18.8m)		(156m × 15.4m)
Machinery:	Eight B&W boilers;	Eight Kampon boilers;	Four Admiralty boilers;
	4-shaft geared turbines,	4-shaft geared turbines,	4-shaft geared turbines,
	100,000shp = 33kts	152,000shp = 35kts	62,000shp = 32kts
Armament:	9 – 8in/55 (3 × III)	8 – 20cm/50 (4 × II)[1]	10 – 5.25in/50 (5 × II) DP
	8 – 5in/38 (8 × I) HA	8 – 12.7cm/40 (4 × II) HA	8 – 2pdr (2 × IV)
	–	12 – 61cm TT (4 × III)	6 – 21in TT (2 × III)
Protection:	mach: 6in belt, 2¼in deck	mach: 100mm belt, 31mm deck	mach: 3in belt, 1in deck
	mags: 3/5½in sides, 2¼in deck	mags: 145mm belt, 56mm deck	mags: 3in sides, 3in crowns
	turrets: 8in faces, 1½in sides	turrets: 25mm	
	CT: 6in		

Notes:
[1] As redesigned in 1936.

the *Leander* and *Arethusa* classes were given names from classical mythology. By June 1936 the design had been finalised: displacement was to be 5,300 tons,[25] with a main armament of ten 5.25in guns in twin centre-line mountings. A high-pressure steam plant (400lb/in^2), using the by-now customary unit machinery layout, gave a top speed of 32 knots and a moderate endurance of 5,500nm at 16 knots, and there was

HMS *Dido* shortly after completion. Due to a shortage of 5.25in twin mountings, many of the ships in this class received a single 4in star shell gun in place of 'Q' mounting. *(Courtesy of Stephen Johnston)*

a 3in side belt and a 1in deck with 3in crowns for the magazines. Two further ships would be ordered under the 1937 Estimates, a further three under the 1938 Estimates, and no fewer than six under the emergency 1939 Programme, for a total of sixteen ships.

In parallel with the development of the *Dido* class, serious consideration was given to what to do with the older 'C' and 'D' classes should the Royal Navy be permitted to retain these ships.[26] In their current configuration they were of limited use as fleet cruisers in the North Sea or the Mediterranean because of their dated and inadequate anti-aircraft armament; on the other hand their limited endurance made them unsuitable for trade protection. There was little that could be done about the latter given their small size, but in 1934 it was proposed that they be rearmed as anti-aircraft cruisers to boost fleet air defences, using 4in HA single mountings freed up by the current round of battleship modernisations. *Coventry* and *Curlew* were duly taken in hand in 1935–36 for a prototype conversion in which the original armament was replaced by ten single 4in guns in open mountings controlled by two HACS Mk III installations, with 8-barrelled, 2pdr pom-poms superimposed on the centre line fore and aft. The mainmast was removed and replaced by a short pole to clear AA arcs in the after part of the ship.

The conversion required few structural alterations and involved minimal costs due to the utilisation of existing equipment. Weight additions were roughly the same as

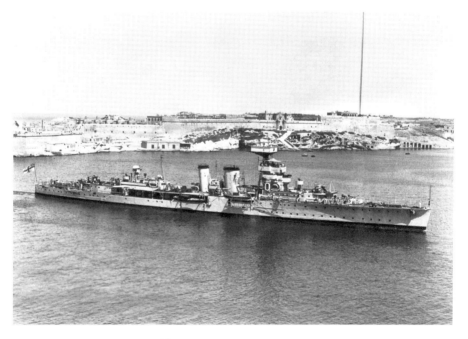

HMS *Curlew*, seen here at Malta in 1938, was one of two prototype AA conversions of the older British 'fleet' cruisers. Her original 6in guns were replaced by ten 4in Mark V HA single mountings, controlled by two HACS III HA directors, and these were complemented by two 8-barrelled 2pdr pom-pom mountings superfiring over the 4in guns fore and aft. *(Leo van Ginderen collection)*

removals; however, weights were now distributed somewhat differently, and there was an increase in topweight that required 100 tons of permanent ballast in the double bottom. The conversion was successful, and in June 1936 it was decided to proceed with reconstruction of the eleven remaining 'C's, but a shortage of funding and dockyard capacity was to delay this programme until 1938–39, when four further ships were taken in hand. It was also decided in 1936 that the eight-ship 'D' class should undergo a similar conversion with four of the new 4.5in DP twin mountings replacing the original main armament, but this proposal was a victim of the rearmament programme, which extended the naval dockyards to their limit.

Although these elderly AA cruisers would prove their value during the Second World War, particularly in the Mediterranean theatre, they were costly in terms of manpower. Nevertheless, their reconstruction was influential, and demonstrated that the Royal Navy was still capable of innovatory schemes and concepts. The IJN contemplated a similar conversion of the small fleet cruisers *Tenryu* and *Tatsuta* in the mid-1930s, when it was proposed that their original armament of four 14cm guns be replaced by four 12.7cm/40 twin mountings with Type 94 HA control; funding was proposed under the 'Circle 3' Programme of 1937, but the proposal had to be abandoned, again because of the heavy workload in the dockyards.

Conclusions

With the continuing 'holiday' in battleship construction, it was cruisers that set the pace for change during the period 1930–1936. The new restrictions on gun calibre and overall tonnage were instrumental in promoting various schemes for utilising the available tonnage, resulting both in a constant jockeying for position between the major navies and also in frequent internal disagreements regarding the characteristics of the ships to be built, the number of hulls required, and the balance between the different types. In general terms the French and the Italians – and initially the British – opted to build moderately armed and moderately protected cruisers of around 7,000–8,000 tons, whereas the Japanese and the Americans preferred to continue building ships of 9,500–10,000 tons with similar general characteristics to their earlier 'treaty' cruisers but armed with multiple 6in/15.5cm guns. This compelled the British to review their own policies, and to respond with the twelve-gun cruisers of the 'Town' class.

The position had been far simpler during the 1920s, when in the wake of the Washington Treaty all five navies had embarked on serial construction of the largest and most powerful cruisers permitted, with a standard displacement of 10,000 tons and an armament of between eight and ten 8in/20.3cm guns. Rather than continuing to build these ships in numbers limited only by what the respective countries could afford, the London Treaty compelled all five navies to look much more closely at what they required to create a modern, balanced fleet, rather than simply chasing funding for 'treaty' cruisers.

The other factor that complicated the cruiser issue during the 1930s was the impending obsolescence of the large numbers of war-built and post-war 'fleet' cruis-

Table 4.8: Cruiser Authorisations 1930–1936

Programme	Great Britain	USA	Japan	France	Italy
1930	3 Leander			Algérie Emile Bertin	Pola 2 Montecuccoli
1931	1 Leander 1 Amphion 1 Arethusa		4 Mogami	2 La Galissonnière	2 Aosta
1932	2 Amphion 1 Arethusa			4 La Galissonnière	2 Abruzzi
1933	2 Southampton 1 Arethusa	1 New Orleans			
1934	3 Southampton 1 Arethusa	1 New Orleans 4 Brooklyn	2 Tone		
1935	3 Southampton	Wichita 3 Brooklyn			
1936	2 Belfast 5 Dido	2 Mod Brooklyn			
Total	26 category (b)	3 category (a) 9 category (b)	6 category (b)	1 category (a) 7 category (b)	1 category (a) 6 category (b)

ers that would need to be replaced. After Washington all five major navies had been able to focus their attention on building large cruisers designed for strategic scouting or trade protection because of their existing large inventories of these smaller ships. However, from the early 1930s serious consideration would need to be given to building small fleet cruisers capable of operating with the battle fleet; these would need to be fast enough and manoeuvrable enough to turn away from trouble if they encountered enemy heavy forces when employed for tactical scouting, and to operate with or in support of the destroyer flotillas.

The British accepted at an early stage that new fleet cruisers would have to be built alongside the larger, more powerful cruisers needed to protect trade, and for the Royal Navy the issue was the balance between the two, given the London restrictions on overall cruiser tonnage. The French, whose only war-built cruisers were the German prizes transferred in 1920, opted to build a larger modern fleet type from the outset, and the Italians would follow suit. The IJN's focus was on large cruisers that despite (provisionally) mounting the 15.5cm gun could match the US Navy's 8in-gun ships; their numerous post-war fleet cruisers received only the most basic modifications to enable them to continue in their role as flagships for the destroyer flotillas and the submarine squadrons. However, for the US Navy the small fleet cruiser was the subject of considerable internal debate. In general terms the Battle Force, supported by the CNO, wanted them, but the General Board was unconvinced of their value. Only when the US Navy had built up to its original goal of twenty-five large cruisers was it prepared to contemplate smaller types.

These debates were taking place at a time when naval warfare was changing. Aviation capabilities in particular – both land-based and carrier-borne – were increasing exponentially, opening up new opportunities but also posing a greater threat to traditional fleet operations, and therefore asking new questions about cruiser missions and characteristics. In a 1936 paper to the Institute of Naval Architects entitled 'Uncontrolled Weapons and Warships of Limited Displacement', which dealt specifically with the growth in some features of cruisers between 1920 and 1935, the British Director of Naval Construction Stanley Goodall commented that by 1935 anti-aircraft armament accounted for 3 per cent (versus 1 per cent in 1920) of displacement, deck protection 10 per cent (versus 2 per cent) and the weather deck area occupied by aircraft and their associated equipment 20 per cent (versus 0 per cent). Goodall pointed out that all these increases had to be accommodated in a hull limited in size by the treaties.

The problem highlighted in this paper is crucial to any analysis of why the Treaty system ultimately failed. The essence of Goodall's criticism appears on the surface to be that the Treaty limitations were too tight for the constructors to be able to build effective ships, which has been the viewpoint taken by many naval historians. However, Goodall's point is more subtle, and has wider implications. The problem was arguably not the displacement limits themselves; it was that naval staffs still expected to pack the same firepower (in terms of gun calibre, number of main guns, torpedoes, etc) into a ship designed in the 1930s to modern standards as they would have expected to do in a ship designed in 1920 to fight at relatively short battle ranges in a maritime environment over which aircraft held little sway. In fact, the Japanese NGS fully expected modern construction techniques such as welding and modern high-pressure steam machinery to enable them to pack even more hardware into a hull of limited displacement.

The result was that virtually all the cruisers built during the 1930s were over-gunned for their displacement. The *Mogami*s provide the ultimate cautionary tale, but over-gunning was a common problem. During the Second World War it would prove difficult to fit the required anti-aircraft weaponry and the newly developed radars used for air/surface warning and fire control, or to accommodate the additional personnel needed to man them. Treaty limits on displacement encouraged navies to dispense with margins, which had they been retained during construction could have been used for future growth. Enhanced AA armaments would not only increase displacements, but overloading would bring with it corresponding reductions in stability, speed and endurance, and accommodating the new equipment would frequently require the removal of part of the original armament.

Chapter 5

DESTROYERS 1930–36

BY THE TIME OF THE LONDON CONFERENCE of 1930 there were major disparities between the major navies, not so much in terms of destroyer strength but of destroyer renewal. The British, having inherited a numerically strong force of large modern destroyers completed during the period 1916–21, had only recently embarked on the construction of new-build units. These were now being built at the rate of nine per year (a flotilla of eight identical vessels plus a larger flotilla leader), the first flotilla having been authorised under the 1927 Estimates.[1] The new British destroyers were conventional gun-and-torpedo boats derived from the types building at the end of the First World War, the only concessions to technological progress being the introduction of superheated steam and improved fire control systems.

The US Navy had inherited an even larger force of destroyers from the late war period, but this had proved to be a mixed blessing. The 'flush-deckers' were not good ships: too small and fragile for oceanic operations and with poor sea-keeping qualities, they were also inferior in firepower to their British and Japanese counterparts. Moreover, the huge financial investment they represented meant that Congress was unwilling to fund new destroyers – even the 'Leaders' that the US Navy insisted were necessary if the 'flush-deckers' were to be fully effective as fleet units (see *WAW* Chapter 10) – until their useful lifespan had expired. No new destroyers had therefore been laid down for the US Navy during the period 1922–30.

In 1922 the French *Marine Nationale* did not have a single fleet destroyer of modern design. As soon as the Washington Conference ended, it embarked on the construction of a series of large, powerful ships of 1,500 tonnes armed with 130mm (5.1in) guns. The twelve *Bourrasque*s of the 1922 Programme were closely followed by fourteen similar units of the *L'Adroit* class. The other major navies were duly impressed: the IJN promptly laid down the even larger destroyers of the 'Special Type', armed with six 12.7cm guns, and the British would experiment with the installation of a 5.1in/50 QF gun in the 'C'-class Leader *Kempenfelt* during the early 1930s (see below). However, this increase in firepower was purchased at the expense not only of stability, which was at best marginal, but of speed. The *1,500 tonnes* had a designed maximum speed that was 3 to 4 knots slower than their foreign contemporaries, and while this was adequate to accompany the older dreadnoughts that constituted the French battle divisions of the 1920s, it did not give a sufficient margin to enable them to operate with the new generation of fast capital ships; the next class of French *torpilleurs d'escadre* would be of radically different design.

The Italian Navy found itself in a far better position than the French with regard to fleet destroyers in 1922. The Italian destroyers built post-Washington were therefore evolutionary in design, building on the not-inconsiderable strengths of their predecessors. They were of moderate displacement, were generally armed with two twin 120mm (4.7in) gun mountings and two triple banks of torpedo tubes, and had a maximum designed speed of 35 knots or more when new. A consistent level of funding had seen a batch of four authorised in each year between 1923 and 1925, and again in 1928 and 1929 (the two-year gap in authorisations being due to the construction of the larger *esploratori* of the '*Navigatori*' class – see *WAW* Chapter 8). The latest destroyers of the *Freccia* and *Folgore* class incorporated major improvements in fire control and command facilities, but in consequence suffered from stability problems that would be resolved only by a significant increase in hull size and displacement in their 1930s-built successors.

All of the destroyers built by Britain, France and Italy during the 1920s fell comfortably within the new qualitative and qualitative limits agreed at the London Conference in terms of unit displacement and gun calibre. This is unsurprising, as the British-inspired proposals to limit standard destroyers to 1,500 tons standard and 5.1in guns were clearly formulated to take into account current (and possible future) developments in the Royal Navy and the *Marine Nationale*; the US Navy had yet to embark on a new programme of destroyers, and the Italian ships were well within the limits. However, the same was not true of Japan, whose twenty-four fleet destroyers of the 'Special Type' now came into the category of 'Leaders' (1,501–1,850 tons), which were allowed to account for a maximum 16 per cent of overall destroyer tonnage. The new qualitative and quantitative limits were clearly directed at nipping in the bud the aggressive large destroyer programme of the IJN, and were therefore readily endorsed by the United States. They would, equally predictably, be yet another source of resentment for the Japanese Navy, which would now have to revise its entire destroyer strategy. All new destroyers built during the remainder of the Treaty period would have to be designed for a maximum displacement of 1,500 tons standard, which had implications for the number of guns and torpedoes that could be carried. Given the reluctance of the IJN Naval General Staff to accept any reduction in military capabilities and their conviction that new technology such as welding would provide the necessary weight savings, this was a recipe for disaster.

More of the Same for the Royal Navy

There can be little doubt that the destroyers authorised for the Royal Navy between 1927 and 1930 were the most successful ships of the type built by any of the major navies during the post-Washington period. With a balanced armament of guns and torpedoes, a useful turn of speed and excellent sea-keeping qualities, they also represented good value for money, and many of them would go on to serve with distinc-

HMS *Fortune*, seen here in October 1938, was one of a series of standard destroyers laid down by the Royal Navy from the late 1920s. Ordered as flotillas of eight ships plus a 'leader', they were particularly successful ships and constituted the bulk of the British destroyer fleet at the outbreak of war. *(Leo van Ginderen collection)*

tion during the Second World War. If anything they were too successful; their success, together with the increasing conservatism in the Admiralty's tactical thinking and the difficulty of securing funding for new developments, meant that this particular series of fleet destroyers, built to essentially the same design for a largely unchanged mission, extended from 'A' to 'D' (1927–30 Estimates) through 'E' and 'F' (1931–2 Estimates) to 'G', 'H' and 'I' (1933–5 Estimates).

Naturally there were incremental improvements along the way. Operational Asdic sets were now available and were housed in retractable domes, and all the fleet destroyers from the 'D' class were so equipped. In the 'E' and 'F' classes the larger after boiler room was subdivided so that all three boilers were now in separate boiler rooms, thereby improving survivability in the event of torpedo or shell hits. The elevation of the main guns was also increased to 40 degrees by locating shallow wells in the deck – this obviated raising the height of the trunnions, which would have impaired loading at low angles of elevation. Light anti-aircraft weapons were now coming into service in the form of the quadruple 0.5in MG mounting, of which two would be fitted in place of the former single 2pdr guns. In the last series the two forward boiler rooms were combined to save length. The 'H' class introduced a new

CP (Centre Pivot) main gun mounting that enabled the shallow wells to be dispensed with, and the 'I' class introduced a new quintuple torpedo mounting (or 'pentad' in RN parlance).

All of the post-London ships were fitted with Asdic from the outset, and it was envisaged that alternate classes would now be fitted either for sweeping ahead of the fleet (using the Two-Speed Destroyer Sweep, or TSDS) or for minelaying. Two of the 'E' class were duly fitted as minelaying prototypes with rails for sixty mines from abeam the after funnel to the stern. The 'I' class would be similarly fitted out, the two upper-deck gun mountings and the torpedo tubes being landed in compensation for a full mine load. The latter class would also have an improved layout of the bridge and command facilities.

By this time the basic fleet destroyer design was having trouble accommodating all the incremental improvements. Besides the new quintuple tubes, the 'I' class was fitted with a full ASW outfit (two depth charge throwers plus two racks for sixteen additional charges) and TSDS. The quintuple torpedo mountings in particular were found to have an adverse effect on stability, and the class had to use liquid ballast in the half-oil condition.

The 'Tribal' class

Despite general satisfaction with the standard destroyer design the Admiralty was concerned that the British ships were inferior in terms of firepower to the latest Japanese destroyers of the 'Special Type', which were armed with six 12.7cm guns in twin enclosed gun mountings. An experimental 5.1in/50 QF single mounting was trialled in the 'C'-class leader *Kempenfelt* in 1932, but the 108lb fixed ammunition was found to be too heavy for comfortable handling and the mounting itself was considered too heavy for the ship, even though standard displacement was some 100 tons greater than the declared figure for the *Fubuki* class – this in itself was indicative of the different stability standards prevailing in the RN and the IJN!

One of the designs considered during 1934 as a replacement for the small fleet cruisers of the 'C' and 'D' classes (see Chapter 4) was a 1,850-ton ship armed with five twin 4.7in guns, designated Scout 'V', which was intended as a counter to the French *contre-torpilleurs*, the Japanese 'Special Type', and the Italian '*Navigatori*' class. Although one of the larger designs was eventually adopted for the cruiser replacement programme – it became the *Dido* class – the Scout 'V' would provide the basis of a new large destroyer.

The 'Tribal' class, seven units of which would be authorised alongside the 'I' flotilla under the 1935–36 Estimates with a further nine authorised under the 1936–37 Estimates, differed fundamentally in conception from the standard British destroyer, which by this stage had evolved into a 'fleet torpedo boat'. There were no fewer than eight 4.7in guns – double the standard battery – and only a single quadruple bank of torpedo tubes. The 4.7in guns were in a new twin mounting with hydraulic training and elevation and power ramming, which ensured that each barrel had a firing cycle that almost matched the hand-worked single mounting in fair-

'Tribal' Class (GB)

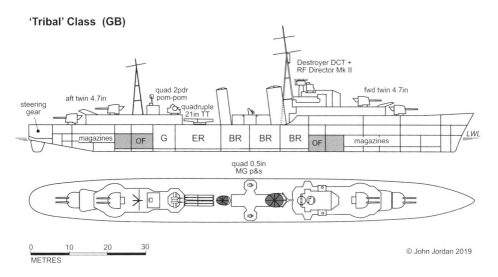

steering gear · aft twin 4.7in · quad 2pdr pom-pom · Destroyer DCT + RF Director Mk II · fwd twin 4.7in · quadruple 21in TT · quad 0.5in MG p&s

magazines | OF | G | ER | BR | BR | BR | OF | magazines | LWL

0   10   20   30
METRES

© John Jordan 2019

The 'Tribal' class broke with traditional British destroyer practice in having a heavy gun armament and only a single torpedo mounting. Note the separate gearing room abaft the engine room.

weather conditions and was superior in rough seas. The fifth twin mounting of the original design was suppressed during development in favour of a quadruple 2pdr pom-pom mounting located on the centre line at the forward end of the after deck-house, which was supplemented by two of the now-standard quadruple 0.5in MG mountings between the funnels.

The 'Tribals' were not only significantly larger than earlier British destroyer types

Mohawk, seen here at Portsmouth on 10 September 1938, was one of sixteen large destroyers laid down for the Royal Navy at the end of the treaty period. They were fast and powerfully armed, but although their displacement put them into the 'leader' category they were grouped into two conventional eight-ship destroyer flotillas. (Conrad Waters collection)

but they were much more sophisticated in technological terms than their predecessors. They were the first British destroyers with an anti-aircraft predictor (although the AA fire control arrangements still fell short of a full HACS), and in addition to their technically advanced twin gun mountings they had power operation for the single bank of torpedo tubes. Subdivision was also far superior to the standard destroyer, with each of the three boilers in a separate boiler room and the reduction gearing in a separate room to the turbines.

There was, as always, a cost to all of this. There was a substantial increase in the weight of the various systems: the twin 4.7in mounting weighed 25 tons – the weight of the single hand-worked model installed in the standard RN destroyer was 9.5 tons; more electrical generating power was required; and in financial terms each ship had a total projected cost of £515,000, a 45 per cent increase over the contemporary 'I' class. Yet despite all this expenditure the main guns were restricted to 40-degree elevation, the quadruple 2pdr mounting as originally fitted was hand-worked and therefore had problems following high-speed modern aircraft, and there was no effective long-range HA fire control system. This would prove a major disadvantage when ships of this class operated in the Mediterranean during 1940–42.

The New Generation

It was never envisaged that the 'Tribal' class would set the standard for the next generation of British destroyers. These sixteen ships, which are probably best described as the Royal Navy's 'Special Type', were intended to bridge the gap between the destroyer and the light cruiser as a counterweight to the larger French, Italian and Japanese flotilla craft, and were ordered as the equivalent of two flotillas over two years alongside the mainstream types. However, they also bridged a technological gap between the first generation of British interwar destroyers and the second, which commenced with the 'J' class.

The 'J' class introduced longitudinal construction to the Royal Navy destroyer,[2] had

---

Table 5.1: **British Destroyers 1930–1936**

	'E'/'F' classes	'Tribal' class	'J' class
Built:	16 + 2L 1933–35[1]	16 ships 1936–38	8 ships 1937–39
Displacement:	1,350tW	1,850tW	1,690tW
Dimensions:	329ft × 33ft	377ft × 37ft	357ft × 36ft
	(100m × 10.1m)	(115m × 11.1m)	(109m × 10.9m)
Machinery	Three Admiralty boilers;	Three Admiralty boilers;	Two Admiralty boilers;
	2-shaft geared turbines,	2-shaft geared turbines,	2-shaft geared turbines,
	36,000shp = 36kts	44,000shp = 36kts	40,000shp = 36kts
Armament	4 – 4.7in/45 (4 × I)	8 – 4.7in/45 (4 × II)	6 – 4.7in/45 (3 × II)
	8 – 0.5in (2 × IV)	4 – 2pdr (1 × IV)	4 – 2pdr (1 × IV)
	8 – 21in TT (2 × IV)[2]	4 – 21in TT (1 × IV)	10 – 21in TT (2 × V)

Notes:
1   The 'E' and 'F' classes were followed by the 'G', 'H' and 'I' classes, built to a slightly modified design.
2   Two of the 'E' class were fitted for minelaying.

only two boilers instead of the standard three, and introduced the twin 4.7in mounting (already adopted for the 'Tribals') to the standard fleet destroyer. The design would
have been even more radical had the 4.7in dual-purpose single mounting originally
projected materialised; this would have brought the 'J's closer in conception to the
latest US Navy destroyers (albeit without the remarkable Mk 37 tachymetric director).

There was considerable opposition within the Navy to many of these innovations.
Longitudinal construction of the hull was arguably long overdue, and brought with
it substantial weight savings that could then be used to increase military capabilities.[3]
However, the reduction from three to only two boilers was more controversial, and
was opposed by both the Naval Staff and the Engineer-in-Chief, who pointed out
that using two boilers (generally considered to be the minimum to ensure safety at
sea) meant using *all* boilers, that peacetime boiler cleaning routines would be more
difficult, that in the event of damage to a single boiler the ship would be left with
only half power, and that there would be lower economy at cruising speed.

Against this, equally compelling arguments were made in favour of the two-boiler
solution by the Director of Naval Construction (DNC): there were significant reductions in weight, space, personnel and cost; increased survivability would result from
the reduction in flooded length; extra space would be created directly beneath the

The destroyer *Jupiter* photographed in the Clyde shortly after her completion. She marked a break with
earlier RN destroyer design in having only two boilers and a single funnel, and in having her 4.7in main guns
paired in twin mountings. *(Yarrow, courtesy of Conrad Waters)*

A close-up of the destroyer *Jackal* while building at John Brown's on the Clyde. One of the quintuple torpedo mountings ('pentads') is prominent, as is the after twin 4.7in gun mounting which, unusually, was aligned on forward bearings. *(National Records of Scotland via Ian Johnston)*

bridge – an area becoming increasingly congested; and it offered the possibility of either a cheaper unit cost or a ship with increased military capabilities. These arguments were eventually to carry the day, and the result was a silhouette similar to the latest Italian destroyers, with a single broad funnel. This simpler layout, together with the weight savings that resulted, made it possible to boost the AA armament by fitting a quadruple 2pdr pom-pom abaft the funnel, where it enjoyed clear arcs over the after part of the ship; the now-standard quadruple 0.5in MG mountings were moved to the bridge wings to cover forward arcs.

The twin mounting was likewise opposed by the Naval Staff as too complex and costly for a standard fleet destroyer; there was concern that a relatively small destroyer hull did not make for a good gunnery platform, and that a single hand-worked mounting, manned by a well-trained crew, was handier and could deliver a higher rate of fire under most conditions. The success of the 4.7in twin mounting

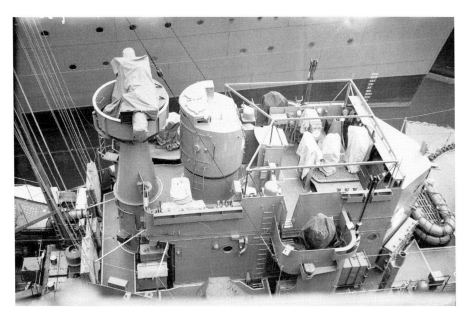

Close-up of *Jackal's* bridge, showing the Destroyer DCT and the Three-man Rangefinder adopted for this class. The combination did not prove particularly successful. *(National Records of Scotland via Ian Johnston)*

'J' Class (GB)

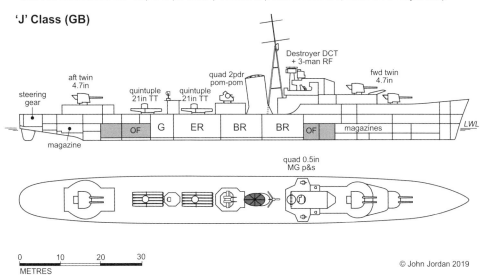

© John Jordan 2019

In the destroyers of the 'J' class steam for the turbines was supplied by only two boilers in two boiler rooms. Weaponry was similar to the larger 'Tribals' but with a completely different balance between guns and torpedoes.

overruled these arguments, and the fitting of three twins – two forward, one aft – effectively increased firepower by 50 per cent, albeit at significantly increased cost and a doubling of weight compared with the 'A' to 'I' type. However, the fire control arrangements in the 'J' were a step backward, with the separate Rangefinder Director Mark II for AA fire control in the 'Tribals' abandoned in favour of a Destroyer DCT modified to accept AA inputs working in conjunction with a simple 'Three-man Rangefinder'. This was to prove unsatisfactory, and led to wartime modifications. The failure to develop an effective anti-aircraft fire control system for destroyers is further evidence of the Admiralty's prioritisation of surface engagement over fleet air defence duties; when war began British destroyers would prove barely capable of defending themselves, let alone other vessels, against air attack by modern high-performance aircraft.

The 'J' class would be the first 'standard' destroyer flotilla without a larger 'leader'; instead, one of the eight ships would be fitted with a longer deckhouse aft to provide the additional accommodation required (TSDS was omitted). Eight units were authorised under the 1936 Estimates, with eight repeat units of the 'K' class to be authorised the following year. Despite initial hopes that the new design would result in a cheaper destroyer, at a total cost of £595,000 per unit the 'J's were even more expensive than the 'Tribals'.

New Destroyer Designs for the US Navy

The period 1928–31 saw intensive discussions within the US Navy regarding the size and configuration of the new destroyers to be built during the 1930s to replace the ageing 'flush-deckers', and the Americans initially looked very much to the British Royal Navy for its ideas. The British had proposed qualitative limits of 1,850 tons/ 5.1in guns for destroyer leaders and 1,500 tons/5.1in guns for standard destroyers at the Geneva Conference, and as the Royal Navy was already building within these limits it was clear that these figures would be the benchmark for any future agreement. The US Navy's respect for British prowess in destroyer design extended even to a proposal in 1928 that two 1,500-ton prototypes should be built that might serve as leaders to the smaller flush-deckers and which would provide experience for later ships, just as *Amazon* and *Ambuscade* had done for the Royal Navy (see *WAW* Chapter 10).

The primary initial focus in the US Navy continued to be on Leaders, and 1928 characteristics called for an 1,850-ton ship armed with four 5in/51 single mountings and twelve torpedo tubes, capable of 35 knots and with an endurance of 6,000nm at 12 knots. This and other destroyer projects remained dormant during the lead-up to the London Conference, but discussion began again in earnest in early 1930.

Throughout this period, and indeed right up to the Second World War, the US Navy continued to see the destroyer as a fleet torpedo boat in the Jutland mould. Moreover, the Americans saw destroyer 'endurance' not only in terms of fuel oil and stores, but also in terms of the number of torpedoes carried (*cf* the similar emphasis laid on this for submarines – see Chapter 6 and *WAW* Chapter 9). While the British would be content with eight torpedoes for the 'A' to 'H' classes, many of the new US Navy designs would feature twelve or even sixteen torpedo tubes – generally 'sided' to provide two salvoes of six or eight torpedoes. The US Navy was also in accord with British thinking regarding the unsuitability of the destroyer as a gunnery platform. All the early American designs featured four single 5in guns, and an initial preference for the 51-calibre model, which had greater range and penetration than the short 25-calibre gun, was overturned because officers serving with the fleet felt that the latter was a much handier weapon for a rolling, pitching destroyer, and had little confidence that effective control could be provided for the 51-calibre model out to its maximum range. Sea-keeping remained a serious consideration given the poor performance of the 'flush-deckers' in this respect, and all of the new designs would feature a British-style raised forecastle.

By November 1930 C&R had produced sketch designs for two alternative standard destroyer types, of 1,375 tons and 1,500 tons respectively, and a Leader of 1,850 tons. All three had a raised forecastle and were armed with four single 5in/25 low-angle mountings. The Leader had two quadruple torpedo tubes on the centre line, the destroyers four triple tubes disposed as in the 'flush-deckers'. All had a speed of 35–35.5 knots, and endurance for the destroyers was 6,500nm at 12 knots, and for the Leader 8,100nm.[4] The General Board naturally wanted to pack more guns into the Leader to justify the additional 350 tons displacement, and this would eventually lead to important conceptual differences between the two types. Equally significantly, BuOrd was now proposing to replace the 5in/51 and the 5in/25 by a new 38-calibre weapon, which besides being intermediate between the two older models in accuracy and hitting power offered a genuine dual-purpose capability.

Following further debate a decision was made in favour of a 1,500-ton destroyer armed with five 5in/38 guns in single DP mountings and two quadruple banks of

USS *Farragut* (DD-348) was the first modern destroyer built for the US Navy since the First World War. She had a raised forecastle to improve sea-keeping characteristics, superheated steam propulsion, and director control for her 5in/38-cal DP guns. *Farragut* is seen here in 1935, shortly after her completion. *(NHHC, 19-N-14753)*

tubes, and this was duly approved in April 1931. The Secretary of the Navy was concerned that there was no provision for anti-submarine warfare, so the quarterdeck was strengthened for the future fitting of ASW weaponry,[5] and a QC sonar, together with JL hydrophones, was worked into the design.

The result would be the eight ships of the *Farragut* class authorised under FY1931 and built in 1932–35. In technological terms they represented a quantum leap over the 'flush-decker' design. The design featured superheated steam propulsion, director control and powered ammunition hoists, and the guns and torpedoes were on the centre line. The *Farragut*s had 35 per cent greater weight of armament, 3 knots more speed, improved habitability and greater endurance, all for a 22 per cent increase in displacement. Ship characteristics included greater stability, a smaller turning circle and improved sea-keeping.

There was some concern about weights when the design was finalised, and in order to reduce these to a minimum only the forward two gun mountings, which were the ones most exposed to the elements, were provided with shields. However, so much weight was saved in construction that they turned out 40 tons light, with a standard displacement of only 1,360 tons. Subsequent experience with the ships following their completion suggested that weight saving in the shipyards had been overzealous, and the fragility of this and subsequent US destroyer classes would be much criticised in the fleet. However, the combination of the 5in/38 dual-purpose gun and the Mk 33 director would prove particularly successful, and would set the pattern for all future US destroyers.

The Leaders

Having settled on a new type of standard destroyer the US Navy's attention was again focused on the Leader it had long desired. The early post-London studies had placed the emphasis on a commonality of systems with the smaller destroyers, as in the Royal Navy, and when discussions resumed in earnest in early 1932 the General Board still seemed to hold to the view that the Leader would have a similar armament to the *Farragut*s, but would have light protection for the bridge and the machinery, and improved sea-keeping and stability. However, when C&R presented the Board with a design that had a similar torpedo armament to the *Farragut*s and six 5in/38 single DP mountings, concern was expressed that the limited gain in firepower (one 5in gun) at a cost of 450 tons in displacement could not be justified.

In the end it was decided to arm the ships with eight 5in/38 guns in *low-angle* twin mountings, and to compensate for the reduction in air defence capability by fitting a quadruple 1.1in mounting – then under development as the US counterpart to the RN's 2pdr pom-pom – fore and aft. There were two problems with this solution: there was no longer commonality of systems between the standard destroyer and the Leader; and there was a massive increase in topweight, which threatened stability and precluded the fitting of even the desired light protection. The Leader had begun life as an enlarged destroyer with enhanced – and protected – command facilities; it had emerged as a sort of 'super-destroyer', a scaled-down version of the contemporary

Porter (US)

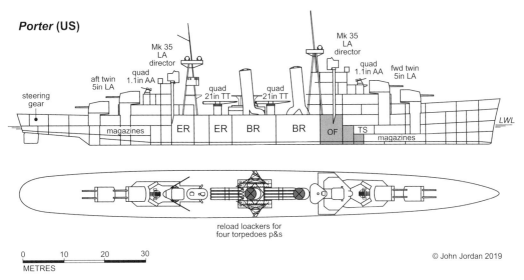

The US Leaders of the *Porter* class had a heavy gun and torpedo armament. Eight reload torpedoes for the eight trainable, centre-line tubes were stowed in lockers on either side of the second funnel. Note the elaborate gantry structure employed for reloading.

The US Leader *Balch* (DD-363) is seen here running trials on 23 September 1936; the Mk 35 directors for the main guns and the quad 1.1in mountings have yet to be fitted. Eight ships of the class were authorised under FY1933. Unusually, their eight 5in/38-cal guns were in twin low-angle mountings. *(NHHC, NH 61695)*

French *Mogador* type (see below) comparable in terms of firepower with a small light cruiser. The final design for these ships featured heavy Mk 35 fire control directors and tripod masts, and there were eight reloads for the two quadruple banks of tubes, stowed in lockers on either side of the second funnel and handled using an overhead framework of steel bars.

Eight Leaders of the *Porter* class were authorised under FY1933, and they were to be followed by five ships of the *Somers* class (two under FY1934, three under FY1935). The latter were initially to have been repeats of the *Porter* class, but the General Board compounded its initial error by demanding that the torpedo reloads of the *Porters* be replaced by a third quadruple bank of torpedo tubes. This required the trunking of the boiler uptakes into a single broad funnel to create the necessary centre-line space. By this time the ships were seriously overweight; the after Mk 35 director was suppressed and the tripods replaced by simple pole masts. However, this still left no margin of weight or stability, and this would become a serious problem when it became clear during the Second World War that AA capabilities would have to be enhanced.

When completed the *Porters* would be employed in their designed role as leaders of the destroyer flotillas. However, their single-purpose main battery was found to be of limited use during the Pacific War; initially No. 3 gun mounting would be landed and replaced by light anti-aircraft weapons, and in 1944 they would be completely rearmed with five dual-purpose guns – ironically one fewer than the General Board had rejected as inadequate in 1932! The *Somers* class, which had even more serious stability problems, had one bank of tubes as well as No. 3 mounting removed, and would be similarly rebuilt late in the war.

The Benefits of High-pressure Steam

When discussions on the characteristics of the next class of standard destroyer began in early 1933, there was considerable pressure from the Fleet and from the General Board, who would no doubt have been fully aware of the latest developments in the IJN, to mount the largest possible battery of torpedoes. The General Board favoured an increase in the torpedo armament from two quadruple banks of tubes to three, even at the cost of one of the 5in guns. However, given that the IJN Special Type was armed with six 12.7cm guns, and that even the latest pared-down ships of the *Hatsuharu* class would have five, the US Navy was reluctant to accept only four guns. This became such a big issue that at one point C&R declared that an armament of five guns and three banks of tubes was possible only if there were a reversion to single-purpose (LA) mountings, as in the Leaders. However, both the Fleet and the CNO were anxious to retain a dual-purpose gun capability in fleet destroyers, so a compromise solution in which the two after torpedo tube mountings were moved to the waist of the ship, with No. 3 gun mounting on an extension of the after deck-house between them, was agreed.

The most striking innovation of the new destroyers, led by the eighteen-ship *Mahan* class, would be their lightweight, high-pressure steam machinery. Taking

Mahan (US)

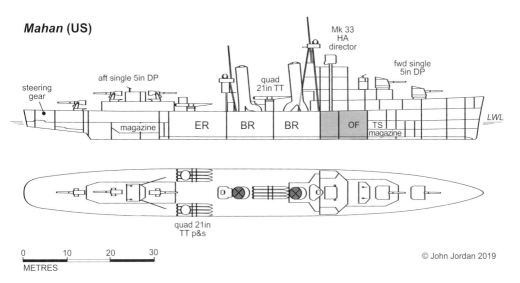

In the *Mahan* class two of the three quadruple torpedo mountings were in the waist. Later ships of the class had the modified gun shield that became characteristic of the US Navy's 5in/38 DP mountings.

The destroyers of the *Mahan* class introduced high-pressure steam and lightweight, fast-running turbines to the US Navy. A class of eighteen was authorised in the same financial year as the eight leaders of the *Porter* class. This is the name-ship, *Mahan* (DD-364) in 1938. Note the early-model shields for the 5in/38 DP guns. *(NHHC, 80-G-466572)*

Table 5.2: US Destroyers 1930–1936

	Farragut class	*Porter class Leaders*[1]	*Mahan class*	*Bagley class*[2]
Built:	8 ships 1932–35	8 ships 1933–37	18 ships 1934–37	8 ships 1935–37
Displacement:	1,360tW	1,830tW	1,490tW	1,650tW
Dimensions:	341ft × 34ft (104m × 10.4m)	381ft × 37ft (116m × 11.3m)	341ft × 35ft (104m × 10.7m)	341ft × 36ft (104m × 10.8m)
Machinery:	Two Yarrow boilers; 2-shaft geared turbines, 42,800shp = 36.5kts	Four B&W[3] boilers; 2-shaft geared turbines, 50,000shp = 37kts	Four B&W boilers; 2-shaft geared turbines, 49,000shp = 36.5kts	Four B&W boilers; 2-shaft geared turbines, 49,000shp = 38.5kts
Armament:	5 – 5in/38 (5 × I) DP; 4 – 0.5in MG (4 × I); 8 – 21in TT (2 × IV)	8 – 5in/38 (4 × II) LA; 8 – 1.1in (2 × IV); 8 – 21in TT (2 × IV)	5 – 5in/38 (5 × I) DP; 4 – 0.5in MG (4 × I); 12 – 21in TT (3 × IV)	4 – 5in/38 (4 × I) DP; 4 – 0.5in MG (4 × I); 16 – 21in TT (4 × IV)

Notes:
1   The *Porter* class was followed by five similar ships of the *Somers* class.
2   Similar to the *Bagley* class were the four ships of the *Gridley* class and the ten ships of the *Benham* class.
3   Babcock & Wilcox.

advantage of the latest commercial developments in technology, as it had with its submarine diesels (see Chapter 6), the US Navy contracted its new generation of boilers and turbines to land-based companies – previously the machinery had been built by the shipyards under licence. Boiler pressures were raised to 600lb/in^2 (42kg/cm^2) in the Leaders of the *Somers* class, an increase of 50–60 per cent on the latest European superheated models, and the fast-running turbines were simpler, easier to build, more robust and more efficient; a typical GE Curtis turbine had 1,750 blades versus 17,500 in a Parsons lower-speed type; the rotor was 25 per cent shorter, and was machined from a forging rather than built up. The only downside of the new fast-running turbines was that they required double-reduction gearing to generate the correct shaft speed and to ensure fuel economy.

The benefits of the new machinery were immense. They included: major savings in boiler/engine room space – machinery for 49,000shp in the *Mahan*s could be accommodated in the same space as the 42,800shp plant in the *Farragut*s; better fuel economy, and therefore greater endurance; and increased reliability combined with a reduction in maintenance.

Even as the *Mahan*s were being built there were demands for an even heavier torpedo armament in the next series of ships. It was proposed that a fourth quadruple bank of tubes be accommodated at the expense of a single 5in gun. All torpedo tubes would now be mounted in the waist, as in the 'flush-deckers', in order to lower the centre of gravity – the centre-line tubes of the early 1930s destroyers had been raised to ensure that the torpedoes cleared the deck edge on firing. It was even suggested that rather than treating the torpedo load-out as two separate broadsides of eight, all sixteen torpedoes might be fired in a single salvo using the latest gyro technology.[6]

These proposals were duly approved, and the next series of destroyers would have four guns and sixteen torpedo tubes, the boiler uptakes being trunked into a single funnel to create the necessary topside space. Ten ships would be authorised under FY1934 and twelve in FY1935. They would be divided into three classes purely on the basis of their machinery: the eight *Bagley*s (FY1934) would be built to a Navy design and would have the same machinery as the *Mahan*s; the four *Gridley*s (FY1934/35) were designed and built by Bethlehem Steel; and the ten *Benham*s (FY1935) were a Gibbs & Cox design with three boilers in place of four. All three classes came out overweight, with the *Benham*s exceeding their designed standard displacement by 160 tons. It was becoming prohibitively difficult to design a destroyer for Pacific operations within the 1,500-ton limit agreed at London, and the later Leaders of the *Somers* class would likewise emerge grossly overweight.

Even so, trials with the recently completed *Farragut*s revealed the new generation of US Navy destroyers to be fragile vessels, prone to sustain structural damage in adverse sea conditions. There was concern that such a large investment was being made[7] in large but flimsy ships that could be easily disabled by small bombs or strafing, yet studies featuring protective plating for the bridge and machinery suggested that weight for this could be found only by adopting even lighter hull construction.

With a fundamental revision of the upper qualitative limits for destroyers in

The series of US destroyers that followed the *Mahan* class had the number of torpedo tubes increased to sixteen, in four quadruple sided mountings port and starboard, and had their boiler uptakes trunked into a single funnel. This is *Blue* (DD-387) during the late 1930s. *(NHHC, NH 616680)*

prospect as a result of the upcoming London Treaty, the opportunity was taken for a major review of US destroyer design in 1936. Dual-purpose firepower, to counter Japanese torpedo attack planes, was prioritised over torpedoes in the twelve-ship *Sims* class authorised under FY1936, and a slightly larger, more robust hull was adopted. However, despite the reduction to three quadruple torpedo tube mountings as in the *Mahan*s, four reloads were provided and the dual-purpose fire control director for the guns was the new, more capable Mk 37, which was combined with a below-decks computer. Three of the five guns (Nos. 1/2/5) were in fully enclosed weather-proof mountings and there were, for the first time, depth charge racks on the stern. Other improvements included more powerful emergency generators to keep the main guns operating in the event of machinery damage, and ½in STS protective plating on the wheelhouse and the director.

These modifications meant that, despite the original intention to produce a robust, seaworthy ship, the *Sims* class turned out seriously overweight (1,690 tons versus 1,570 tons designed) and top-heavy. Short-term remediation included the removal of one of the waist torpedo tubes on completion (the other was moved to the ship's axis), the suppression of the splinter protection, and the embarkation of 60 tons of fixed ballast. Subsequent classes would be redesigned, and waist torpedo tubes would be abandoned altogether in favour of two quintuple centre-line mountings.

The main problem with the US Navy destroyers built during the 1930s was that they were over-armed for their size – a feature encouraged by a perceived need to compete with the destroyers being built for the Imperial Japanese Navy, which were similarly over-gunned and overweight, and whose true displacement was in any case being understated. When the US Navy finally got round to building destroyers with the full range of capabilities it required for trans-Pacific operations, it had to adopt a much larger hull. Despite having a gun/torpedo armament comparable to the *Mahan* and *Sims* classes, the destroyers of the *Fletcher* class laid down in 1941 had a hull with 10m more length and 2m more beam, and a designed displacement of 2,100 tons (which was grossly exceeded once they received a full complement of light AA and ASW weapons).

The IJN, the Quart and the Pint Pot

Japan had been the principal loser from the London Treaty when it came to destroyers. The new qualitative limits of 1,500 tons standard displacement for a fleet destroyer (84 per cent or more of global tonnage) and 1,850 tons for a 'leader' (maximum 16 per cent of global tonnage) were intended to call a halt to the new generation of large IJN destroyers, considered to be escalatory, and construction of the 'Special Type' was duly terminated after the last four ships of the *Akatsuki* sub-group were laid down during 1930. Since the displacement of the twenty-four ships of the *Fubuki* and *Akatsuki* classes was being declared as 1,700tW, the Japanese already had 40,800 tons of destroyers in the 1,501–1,850tW bracket built or building – almost 40 per cent of their total destroyer tonnage allocation. No further ships above 1,500 tons would be permitted until the later units of the 'Special Type' were due for replacement in the mid-/late-1940s.

The Japanese were aware that the latest British destroyers of the 'E' and 'F' classes had a designed displacement of 1,350 tons standard, and that the US Navy was looking at a similar figure for its own new destroyers – the *Farragut*s were designed for 1,400 tons. It was therefore decided that the destroyers to be included in the 1931 Programme would likewise have a (nominal) displacement of 1,400tW. Eighteen were initially requested by the Navy, but by November 1930 this figure had been reduced to twelve.

The usual problem presented itself. The Naval General Staff was reluctant to reduce gun firepower below that of the new American destroyers, which would be armed with five 5in guns. On the other hand, it not only insisted that the torpedo armament of the 'Special Type', comprising three triple mountings all on the centre line, be retained, but that a full set of reload torpedoes be provided. As the latest 61cm Type 90 torpedo weighed 2.6 tonnes, the torpedoes alone represented 47 tonnes, all carried as topweight, and this did not take into account the weight of the trainable tubes or of the additional lockers and their quick-reload gear.

Not only was this armament to be carried on a hull that displaced only 1,400 tons – a reduction of 300 tons from the 'Special Type' – but it was a hull that was necessarily 10 metres shorter (*ie* with 10m less centre-line space). Fitting in three fully enclosed 12.7cm mountings as in the 'Special Type' (the third was a single mounting), together with three banks of centre-line tubes each with an adja-

Hatsuharu (Jap)

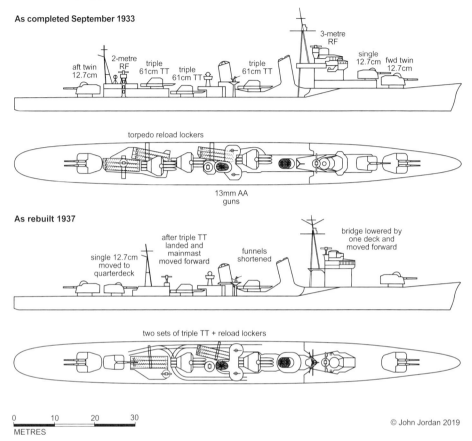

As completed September 1933

aft twin
12.7cm

2-metre
RF

triple
61cm TT

triple
61cm TT

triple
61cm TT

3-metre
RF

single
12.7cm

fwd twin
12.7cm

torpedo reload lockers

13mm AA
guns

As rebuilt 1937

single 12.7cm
moved to
quarterdeck

after triple TT
landed and
mainmast
moved forward

funnels
shortened

bridge lowered by
one deck and
moved forward

two sets of triple TT + reload lockers

0   10   20   30
METRES

© John Jordan 2019

cent set of quick-reload lockers, tested the ingenuity of the Japanese constructors to the limit. The third bank of tubes had to be mounted at the forward end of the after deckhouse so that it was effectively 'superimposed' above the second, and the reload lockers were accommodated abaft it by moving the single gun mounting to a new deckhouse forward of the bridge, where it fired above the twin mounting on the forecastle (see drawing).

As with the 'B-class' cruisers of the *Mogami* class, the necessary weight savings were supposed to be achieved by adopting an all-welded hull. This had the unfortunate effect of combining a lightweight hull with a massive increase in topweight. The superimposed gun mountings forward of the bridge meant that not only was No. 2 gun higher than any of the three gun mountings on the 'Special Type', but it had to be located atop a new deckhouse, and the bridge structure raised accordingly. Add to this the weight of the three triple torpedo mountings, the third of which was mounted on the roof of the after deckhouse, and the reload lockers with their nine reserve torpedoes, and the *Hatsuharu* design was simply not feasible. When the first two ships were completed in 1934, shortly before the capsizing incident with the

The IJN destroyers *Hatsuharu* and *Nenohi* (seen here) experienced serious stability problems on trials. Note the superimposed single 12.7cm gun mounting forward and the high bridge. *(NHHC, NH 75417)*

Nenohi following her reconstruction. The after triple torpedo mounting was landed, the single 12.7cm mounting relocated on the upper deck aft, and the bridge lowered. The photo was taken at Shanghai in August 1938. *(NHHC, NH 75418)*

torpedo boat *Tomozuru*, it was immediately apparent that the stability of the new ships was a serious issue, and they were subsequently rebuilt, while the other four ships of the class were similarly modified while building.

The third torpedo tube mounting, which was at the root of the ships' design problems, was removed, together with its reload lockers. This allowed the after deckhouse to be shortened, which in turn made space for the single gun mounting, which was moved from its original position forward of the bridge to the quarterdeck, immediately forward of the after twin mounting. This eliminated the extra deckhouse forward of the bridge, and the bridge structure itself could then be lowered. Even these drastic measures were insufficient to provide stability to the revised standard. Like the destroyers of the 'Special Type' (see *WAW* Chapter 10), the *Hatsuharu*s had their hulls strengthened and permanent keel ballast added, increasing standard displacement to 1,715 tons. These modifications resulted in a reduction in maximum speed from 36.5 knots (designed) to little more than 33 knots, and the ships were now significantly over the 1,500-ton limit.

This was a salutary lesson to the IJN, and compelled the Naval Staff to rethink its destroyer requirements. The remaining six destroyers of the 1931 Programme were redesigned along similar lines to the rebuilt *Hatsuharu*s, becoming the *Shiratsuyu* class. Some attempt was made to claw back performance: the two triple triple torpedo mountings became two quads – the current British and US Navy standard for a torpedo broadside – and speed was increased to 34 knots. However, it had to be accepted that given conservative Japanese steam propulsion technology and the need for more robust construction, standard displacement would be in the region of 1,650–1,700 tons – 1,400tW remained the declared figure for foreign consumption.

Table 5.3: IJN Destroyers 1930–1936

	Hatsuharu class[1]	Asashio class
Built:	6 ships 1931–35	10 ships 1935–38
Displacement:	1,490tW	1,960tW
Dimensions:	110m × 10m	118m × 10.35m
Machinery:	Three Kampon boilers; 2-shaft geared turbines, 42,000shp = 36.5kts	Three Kampon boilers; 2-shaft geared turbines, 50,000shp = 35kts
Armament:	5 – 12.7cm/50 (2xII, 1xI) 2 – 13mm (2 × I) 9 – 61cm TT (3 × III)	6 – 12.7cm/50 (3 × II) 4 – 25mm (2 × II) 8 – 61cm TT (2 × IV)

Notes:
[1] Data for first two ships as completed. The *Hatsuharu*s were followed by ten modified ships of the *Shiratsuyu* class (see text).

The 1934 Programme

Fourteen new destroyers were approved under the 1934 Naval Programme. To keep Japan's global destroyer tonnage to the minimum these were officially announced to displace 1,380 tons, a further reduction of 20 tons over the *Hatsuharu* class. In a slight adjustment to the balance of the armament, there was to have been a return to three twin 12.7cm gun mountings, but with only two trainable torpedo mountings, albeit each of four tubes; as in the *Hatsuharu* class, a full set of reloads would have been carried in lockers adjacent to the tubes.

It was at this point that the full extent of the stability problems with the *Hatsuharu*s revealed itself, and the 1934 Programme was thrown into disarray. In order to minimise delay the first four ships would be built as repeat *Shiratsuyu*s, with the quad torpedo mountings but only five 12.7cm guns. However, with the end of the London Treaty qualitative restrictions in prospect, it was now possible to draw up a new design incorporating all the military qualities deemed essential by the Naval General Staff. The result was the ten-ship *Asashio* class, which were laid down in 1935–36 and would form the basis of all subsequent IJN destroyers.

Asashio (Jap)

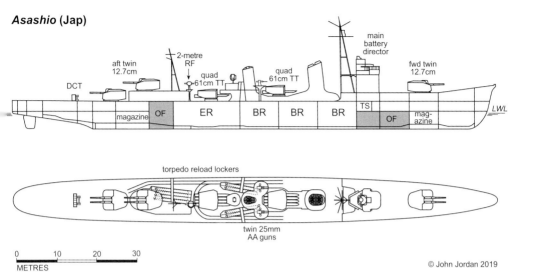

The *Asashio* class, laid down from September 1935, had a similar armament to the 'Special Type' of the late 1920s, the principal difference being that the number of torpedo tubes was reduced from nine to eight.

Asashio on her full power trials in July 1937. This class marked a return to the size and armament of the 'Special Type', a development made possible by Japan's withdrawal from the treaty system. (Fukui Shizuo collection)

The gun arrangement duplicated that of the 'Special Type', with one enclosed 12.7cm twin mounting forward and two aft, No. 2 mounting being again superimposed above No. 3. However, the torpedo arrangement was essentially that adopted for the *Shiratsuyu* class, with two quadruple mountings on the centre line, each of which could be replenished from quick-reload lockers. This meant that although there was one fewer tube than in the 'Special Type', there were sufficient torpedoes for two salvoes of eight; moreover, by the time the *Shiratsuyu*s and the *Asashio*s entered service, the torpedo was the formidable 61cm Type 93 'Long Lance', an oxygen-fuelled model with a 490kg warhead and a range of 20,000m at the unprecedented speed of 48–50 knots. This torpedo, which left no telltale wake, largely outclassed the torpedoes of all the other world navies in performance, and was to be one of the major surprises of the Pacific War, proving devastating in the night-time actions around the Solomon Islands in late 1942.

The rebuilt units of the *Hatsuharu* class had to accept a reduction in their maximum speed to just over 33 knots – less than in the latest cruisers. The *Shiratsuyu* class was more carefully designed, so speed increased to 34 knots with an identical propulsion plant, but this was still 1 knot short of the original designed speed due to the enforced increase in the ships' displacement. The *Asashio*s had a hull comparable in size to the earlier 'Special Type', so it was necessary to increase shaft horsepower from 42,000shp to 50,000shp to provide the required 35 knots. New, more advanced turbines were adopted for this class, and these initially gave problems. The stern and rudder arrangements also proved unsatisfactory, and the ships had an abnormally large turning circle. However, both these problems were largely resolved before the Second World War.

As we have seen with the US Navy, the IJN found that it could build a satisfactory destroyer for Pacific operations only on a larger displacement than permitted by the London Treaty. The *Asashio*s displaced 1,960 tons standard, and their successors of the *Kagero* and *Yugumo* classes, which would be built to the same basic design, would be even heavier (2,030tW and 2,080tW respectively).

A New Generation of Flotilla Craft for the *Marine Nationale*

During the 1920s French flotilla craft belonged to one of two strands: the 2,400–2,800 tonnes *contre-torpilleurs* and the 1,500-tonne *torpilleurs d'escadre* ('fleet torpedo boats'). Twenty-six of the latter had been completed – the last six were fitting out at the time of the London Conference – and the full programme of thirty *contre-torpilleurs* had been authorised (six under the 1922 Naval Programme, twenty-four under the 1924 Programme). The early *contre-torpilleurs* and *torpilleurs d'escadre* of the 1922 Programme had a large degree of commonality in terms of weapon systems and equipment, but with the later series of *contre-torpilleurs*, which were armed with heavier guns and more torpedoes, and which were capable of ever-higher speeds, the two types had steadily moved farther apart.

Following the London Conference France, fearful that Britain might otherwise invoke the escalator clause enshrined in Article 21 of the Treaty,[8] accepted the general principle of no increase in naval forces beyond current levels, so from this point on only 'replacement' construction would be authorised. The *Marine Nationale* initially envisaged a request for two repeat *Le Fantasque*s under the 1931 Estimates, with a third in 1932. However, from October 1930 major budgetary restraints were imposed as a result of the economic crisis in Europe and many existing light vessels were placed in reserve. Given the new perceived threat from the German *Panzerschiffe* of the *Deutschland* class, funding was to be concentrated on the new *croiseur de combat* (CC-1 – subsequently *Dunkerque*) – and on light cruisers to counter the new German *Köln* and *Leipzig* classes (see Chapter 4).

In reality there was little impetus for a new programme of flotilla craft due to the massive backlog of work in the shipyards. Work had begun on the first two hulls of the penultimate class of *contre-torpilleurs*, the *Vauquelins*, only during the London Conference, leaving a further twelve ships already authorised still to be laid down. The 1932 Estimates would include a single *contre-torpilleur* of a new design, which was to replace the ex-German *Amiral Senès*, and the prototype of a new *torpilleur d'escadre* intended to accompany the new fast battleships of the *Dunkerque* class. Both ships were authorised, but construction would be delayed for both political and technical reasons.

The *contre-torpilleur type 1931* was originally to have been an improved *Le Fantasque*, with six 138.6mm Mle 1929 in a twin mounting of new design. The *torpilleur d'escadre* was to be similar in concept, with six 130mm in twin mountings and much higher speed than the 33-knot *Bourrasques*, which had been designed to accompany the elderly French dreadnoughts. Besides the increase in

Although designed during the late 1920s, the six *contre-torpilleurs* of the Le Fantasque class (see WAW Chapter 8) were delayed by budgetary problems and bottlenecks in the French shipyards and dockyards; they were laid down only in 1931–32, and were not completed until 1936. This is Le Triomphant on 30 May 1938. *(Author's collection)*

the number of guns carried, the key advantages of the twin mounting over the single for the *Marine Nationale* were:

– a reduction in the height of the bridge structure (and therefore in the silhouette of the ship)
– a reduction in topweight (and therefore improved stability)
– a reduction in the blast effect of the forward guns on the bridge because the twin mounting was located farther forward.

The new *contre-torpilleur* was duly allocated the name *Mogador* and the *torpilleur* the name *Le Hardi*, but construction of both types was suspended in July 1932 pending negotiations between France and Italy that took place under the aegis of the League of Nations, and which aimed to stabilise the size of the two fleets at a level acceptable to both parties.

The delay allowed further work to be done on the plans for the new ships. By October 1932 there was an alternative sketch for *Mogador* in which four twin 130mm guns – the same model as in the *torpilleur* – were substituted for the three 138.6mm twin mountings. However, development work on the twin 138.6mm mounting, which had begun in 1930, continued throughout this period, and eventually a fully enclosed 'pseudo-turret' designed by Saint-Chamond was adopted first for the 130mm, and subsequently the 138.6mm gun. This featured a central pusher hoist that brought up the ammunition from the magazine to a rotatable tipping drum on the mounting axis, from which it was shunted onto waiting trays and loaded into the guns. These arrangements were originally designed for the fixed ammunition of the 130mm gun, but separate ammunition had to be used for the heavier 138.6mm, which resulted in additional complexity. There were superimposed trays for the shells and the propellant cartridges; a catapult rammer was used for shells, but the cartridges were manually loaded.

The new *contre-torpilleur* and *torpilleur* designs, initially so close in conception, would once again move farther apart. As the strategy for hunting down the German *Panzerschiffe* developed, a requirement was established for a light vessel capable of operating in the Atlantic swell to provide scouting, and the *Mogador* design was again revised in early 1933 to take account of this. Developments in propulsion suggested that the horsepower necessary for a larger hull could be provided without any increase in weight. It was initially proposed that a centre-line catapult for a fighter/reconnaissance aircraft should be fitted, but this had to be abandoned because there was insufficient reserve stability when the catapult was trained on the beam. However, a further increase in firepower was considered essential for this role, and when STCN reported that an additional twin turret could be accommodated at a cost of 100 tons displacement and 0.7 knots in speed, this was the option pursued.

Protection of the superstructures by 22mm plating (*cf* contemporary proposals for the US Navy's Leaders) and even a cruiser-type conning tower were considered, but both these solutions would have cost 100 tons and resulted in an unacceptable loss

Mogador (Fr)

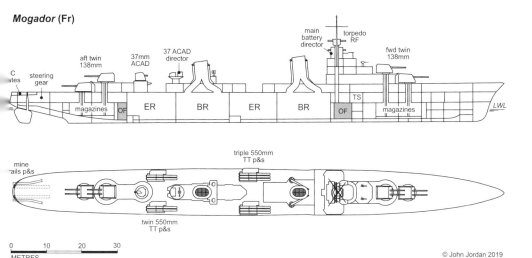

The French *contre-torpilleur Mogador* as designed. Note the 37mm ACAD fully-automatic twin mounting on the after deckhouse and its FC director abaft the second funnel.

The *contre-torpilleur Mogador* in late 1939. Only two of these powerful ships were completed; the complexity of their twin gun mountings meant that they never achieved their designed rate of fire. (*NHHC, NH 86543*)

of stability. New drawings were produced in late 1933 and these were approved in March 1934 (by which time displacement had grown by a further 110 tons to 2,880tW) subject to the following modifications: an additional torpedo tube, a 50 per cent increase in ammunition (for prolonged firing in action), and additional light AA weapons. Despite these demands the *Marine Nationale* was insistent that displacement be kept below 3,000tW, as anything above that would place these ships in the London category for 'cruisers', which would mean that they could be replaced only after twenty years instead of sixteen. This was achieved by the now-customary procedure of reducing the declared weight of liquids and other consumables.

With the German *Panzerschiff* programme ongoing – a third unit, *Admiral Graf Spee*, was laid down in October 1932 – the *Marine Nationale* countered with a second *Dunkerque* in the 1934 Estimates (see Chapter 2), accompanied by a second 'scout', *Volta*.

The programme for the new *torpilleurs d'escadre* would take even longer to bring to fruition. A report by the Fleet Trials Commission presented in June 1932 was strongly critical of the 1,500-tonne destroyers of the *Bourrasque* and *L'Adroit* classes, which it considered insufficiently robust, with inadequate margins of stability and with insufficient speed to operate with the new capital ships. As approved in August 1934 the new design had a reinforced bow and forecastle for operations in the Atlantic, an improved distribution of oil fuel tanks to lighten the bows, improved habitability, and a reduced silhouette with superstructures and masts modelled on the latest *contre-torpilleurs*. The layout of the main guns, which were in three twin 'pseudo-turrets', was reminiscent of the IJN 'Special Type', with one mounting on the forecastle and two aft. The *Le Hardi* was also similar in size to the Japanese ships,

The French destroyer *Epée* comes alongside the cruiser *Dupleix* in the autumn of 1940. Although the name-ship of the class, *Le Hardi*, was authorised in 1934, none of the ships had completed their trials before the Armistice of 1940, and they were rushed into service with a number of unresolved technical issues. *(Conrad Waters collection)*

Le Hardi (Fr)

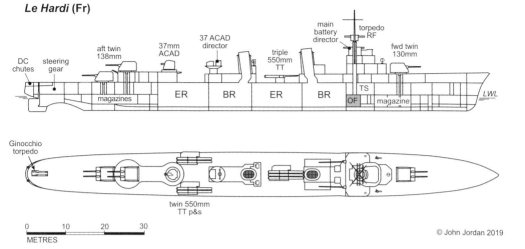

The fleet destroyers of the *Le Hardi* class were similar in size and capabilities to the Japanese destroyers of the 'Special Type'. As designed, they were to be fitted, like the *Mogadors*, with a 37mm ACAD twin mounting aft.

with a 117m overall length and a standard displacement of 1,770 tons.

There were seven 550mm torpedo tubes, disposed as in the *contre-torpilleurs* of the *Vauquelin* class (see *WAW* Chapter 8), with a triple mounting on the centre line between the funnels and paired wing tubes aft. Shaft horsepower was almost double that of the *1,500-tonnes* type, and maximum speed was 37 knots for a service speed of 34–35 knots at normal load. Despite this, the weight of the machinery accounted for a smaller proportion of displacement than in the *L'Adroit* class due to the adoption of high-pressure steam conditions with superheating, using the new, compact Sural boiler designed by Indret.

Two more units would be authorised under the 1935 Estimates, with a further three under the 1936 Estimates, but *Le Hardi* would be laid down only in May 1936, and although the other five quickly followed her onto the building ways, none had formally entered service by the time of the Armistice in June 1940, and only the name-ship had run trials.

The new generation of French flotilla craft were impressive ships that suffered from over-complex weapon and propulsion systems. The 'pseudo-turrets' of the *Mogador* class turned in a disastrous performance on trials in 1938, with frequent jams and breakdowns. The spring-loaded rammers were insufficiently powerful when the guns were elevated, so the guns had to be returned to the horizontal for reloading. The result was a firing cycle of only 3–5rpm maximum, less than half that envisaged. Radical modifications were subsequently carried out, but even so a firing cycle of 8rpm could be achieved only with considerable effort from the loading numbers, and then only at angles of elevation up to 10 degrees.

The pseudo-turrets of the *Le Hardi* class suffered similar problems, although these were less acute because the 130mm gun used the fixed ammunition for which the central hoist and tilting bucket had originally been designed. However, frequent breakdowns in the power rammers and regular malfunctions in the electrical firing mechanism meant that the theoretical firing cycle of 14/15rpm was achieved only after radical modifications to the mounting, and when achieved was unsustainable.

The high-pressure boilers of both types were subject to frequent breakdown and were difficult to maintain. The turbine machinery, on the other hand, generally proved robust and reliable. Speeds in excess of 40 knots[9] were achieved on trials, but endurance at cruise speed was disappointing. The *Mogador*s had been designed for long range in view of their intended employment as Atlantic scouts; in theory their 710 tonnes of oil fuel (versus 580 tonnes in the *Le Fantasque*s) should have given them a range of 4,350nm at 15 knots, but this was never attained in service. The endurance figures calculated for *Le Hardi* following trials suggested that 2,000nm at 16 knots was the best that could be expected.

Finally, both types were originally to have been fitted with a new fully automatic twin 37mm AA mounting, the Model 1935 ACAD, which featured remote power control and the impressive rate of fire of 200rpm per barrel. However, development of this weapon was protracted, and when it failed to materialise the semi-automatic Model 1933, which was capable of only 30–40rpm per barrel, had to be substituted. These failures meant that the modern French flotilla craft, whose main guns were limited to an elevation of 30–35 degrees and which had only rudimentary AA fire control arrangements, were poorly equipped to deal with modern, high-perform-ance aircraft.

Larger Destroyers for the *Regia Marina*

The first unit of the *Freccia* class (see *WAW* Chapter 10) ran trials during 1931, and it was only then that the full extent of their topweight problems became apparent. However, there were already concerns that too much was being attempted on their

---

Table 5.4: **Italian and French Flotilla Craft 1930–1936**

	Maestrale class[1] (It)	*Mogador* class (Fr)	*Le Hardi* class (Fr)
Built:	4 ships 1931–34	2 ships 1934–39	8 ships 1935–40[2]
Displacement:	1,420tW	2,880tW	1,770tW
Dimensions:	107m x 10.3m	138m x 12.6m	117m x 11.1m
Machinery:	Three Yarrow boilers; 2-shaft geared turbines, 45,000shp = 38kts	Four Indret boilers; 2-shaft geared turbines, 92,000shp = 39kts	Four Penhoët boilers; 2-shaft geared turbines, 58,000shp = 37kts
Armament:	4 – 120mm/50 (2 x II) 2 – 40mm (2 x I) 6 – 533mm TT (2 x III)	8 – 138.6mm/50 (4 x II) 2 – 37mm (1 x II) ACAD 10 – 550mm TT (2xII, 2xIII) 16 DC in twin chutes	6 – 130mm/45 (3 x II) 2 – 37mm (1 x II) ACAD 7 – 550mm TT (2xII, 1xIII) 8/12 DC in twin chutes

Notes:
1 The *Maestrale* class was followed by the four slightly-modified ships of the *Oriani* class, then by the twelve ships of the 'Soldati' class, the standard Italian destroyer of the Second World War.
2 Four further ships of this class were ordered under the 1938 and 1938 *bis* Programmes, but were never completed.

displacement and the first destroyers ordered after the London Conference, the four ships of the *Maestrale* class, were significantly larger while retaining the same basic armament of two twin 120/50 gun mountings and two triple 533mm torpedo tube mountings.

The *Maestrale*s fully utilised the 1,500 tons available for standard destroyers under the new treaty; their designed displacement was 1,440 tons – more than 200 tons in excess of the *Freccia/Folgore* series, and there was a 10-metre increase in length and a 1-metre increase in beam. They had a stronger hull, with a stern modelled on the older Italian destroyers designed by Thornycroft and Pattison. Sea-keeping was thereby improved, and they were more stable with a stern quarter sea. Despite having essentially the same propulsion plant as their predecessors, they were just as fast on trials, with *Libeccio* achieving more than 41 knots for a short period with forced draught. Sea speed, as with other Italian ships of the period, was another matter, and as weight increased with later additions this came down to around 33 knots.

These were solid, successful ships with an internal compartmentation which was both rational and well-developed for the period. The light anti-aircraft armament was adequate when completed, and was improved by the fitting of more modern 37/54 and 20/65 weapons after 1936. Mine rails aft enabled them to embark thirty-six to forty mines, with a maximum capacity of fifty-six to sixty-six if the after torpedo tubes were immobilised. There was, however, no anti-submarine capability

Maestrale, the lead ship of a class of large destroyers, was laid down for the Italian *Regia Marina* after the conclusion of the London Treaty. She is seen here in October 1934 during her early sea trials. (*G Parodi collection, courtesy of Maurizio Brescia*)

Maestrale (It)

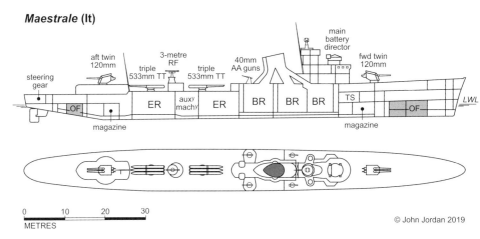

steering gear

aft twin 120mm

triple 533mm TT

3-metre RF

triple 533mm TT

40mm AA guns

main battery director

fwd twin 120mm

magazine   OF   ER   auxy machy   ER   BR   BR   BR   TS   OF   LWL   magazine

0   10   20   30
METRES

© John Jordan 2019

The *Maestrale* class had a similar armament to the Italian destroyers laid down during the late 1920s: four 120mm guns in twin mountings and two banks of triple torpedo tubes. Layout was similar, but they were much more successful ships due to their greater size.

When first commissioned, the four units of the *Maestrale* class were considered part of the light scouting force of the *Regia Marina* and did not have identification letters painted on the bows and on the stern as did destroyers and torpedo boats, As scouts, they were visually identified by funnel bands, with the flotilla leader (*Maestrale*) having no bands and *Scirocco*, *Grecale* and *Libeccio* one, two and three bands respectively. They are seen here at Venice, with two light cruisers of the '*Condottieri*' type in the background. (*Maurizio Brescia collection*)

as completed, and the fitting of depth charge throwers and detection systems during the Second World War would mean a reduction in both speed and stability.

The *Maestrale* class would be the last destroyers authorised for the Italian Navy for some years. As with the *Marine Nationale*, the renewal of the battle fleet would require a huge investment at a time when budgets were under pressure from the poor economic situation in Europe. The first of the next group of four destroyers, *Oriani*, would be laid down only in October 1935, although in contrast to the new French fleet torpedo boats of the *Le Hardi* class she would be completed in little over two years.

The four *Oriani*s – also known as the *Poeti* because they bore the names of famous Italian poets – were essentially repeats of the *Maestrale* class, being virtually identical in respect of hull dimensions, external appearance, main armament and much of their equipment. The principal difference lay in their more advanced machinery, which utilised higher steam conditions and more advanced superheating. Shaft horsepower was increased from 44,000shp to 48,000shp with machinery of the same weight and volume, and although this had little impact on trials speeds there was less fall-off when the ships were operating at deep load.

The last Italian destroyers to be authorised during the Treaty period were the '*Soldati*' ('Soldiers') class, an initial batch of twelve being authorised in 1936 and laid down from January 1937. This dramatic escalation in the Italian destroyer building programme was made in the secure knowledge that there would be no further

The *Maestrale* class was followed, after an interval of four years, by the similar *Oriani* class. This is *Vittorio Alfieri*, of the *Oriani* sub-group, at Taranto in 1939, passing from the Mar Piccolo to the Mar Grande via the *canale navigabile*. Unlike the *Maestrale* class, the four '*Poeti*' – the ships were named after poets – were classified as destroyers from the outset and had identification letters painted on the bows and at the stern. (*Erminio Bagnasco collection*)

restraints on global tonnage. The '*Soldati*' design was essentially a repeat *Oriani* with an additional single 'short' 120/15 gun for illuminating shell between the torpedo tubes. Designed displacement increased to 1,620 tons standard. All twelve ships would be completed before the outbreak of war in Europe in September 1939, and they proved so successful that six repeat ships would be laid down in late 1940. Together with the large destroyers of the *Maestrale* and *Oriani* classes they would be grouped tactically with the fast cruisers of the *Trento/Bolzano* and *Montecuccoli/Duca d'Aosta* classes, while the older, slower destroyers were attached to the battle fleet.

Conclusions

The destroyers authorised and laid down during the period 1930–36 were still essentially 'fleet torpedo boats'. However much forward-thinking officers might stress the future importance of fleet air defence and anti-submarine warfare, the major fleets were unified in their belief that the weapon of choice for the destroyer was the torpedo, to be used against the enemy line of battle, and that powerful low-angle guns with well-developed fire control systems were essential in order to protect the battle line against hostile torpedo craft; anything else was a luxury that added to both cost and weight. Only the US Navy opted for a dual-purpose main gun, and even this far-sighted decision did not meet with universal approval – single-purpose mountings were adopted for the Leaders to boost their anti-surface firepower. The installation of anti-submarine sensors and weaponry was spasmodic and half-hearted; ships were often fitted 'for' but not 'with' these weapons, which would invariably be the first items to be deleted if the design experienced a weight problem.

The London Treaty limits on destroyer displacement, gun calibre, and global tonnage were framed with this philosophy in mind. The standard 'post-Jutland' destroyers built for the Royal Navy during the late 1920s displaced 1,350 tons, and their French counterparts, which had the heavier 130mm (5.1in) gun, 1,460 tons, so a displacement limit of 1,500tW and 5.1in guns seemed perfectly reasonable at the time; it left a 150-ton margin for the growth of British destroyers and put a cap on further escalation. The largest Italian destroyers authorised during the 1920s, the *Freccia* and *Folgore* classes, were well within the limit, and there was a general feeling that the Japanese destroyers of the 'Special Type' constituted an escalatory step that needed to be stamped on before it got out of hand. The 1,800-ton 'Leader' category, capped at 16 per cent of global destroyer tonnage, had the advantage of embracing the destroyers of the 'Special Type' while putting a premature end to their construction; at the same time it allowed the Royal Navy to continue on its traditional course, and the US Navy to build the British-type destroyer leaders to which it aspired.

The essential problem with the agreed qualitative limits was that they imposed a technical and philosophical straightjacket on destroyer development. The general view was that developments such as welding, high-pressure steam conditions and lightweight turbines would allow destroyers to stay within London Treaty limits while at the same time providing greater firepower and more highly developed control systems. However, this view failed to take into account that the weight-saving measures lightened the lower hull while the added weaponry and control systems were mounted high in the ship, where they threatened stability.

In order to accommodate dual-purpose guns (which were more complex and heavier than their single-purpose counterparts), highly developed HA fire control systems and an increasing number of close-range AA weapons, hulls had to become larger. The British Royal Navy was initially opposed to DP guns and complex fire control systems in destroyers not because it failed to see their value for fleet air defence – particularly in the land-locked Mediterranean – but because it held to the view that these systems, and their size and cost, would change the nature of the destroyer, making of it a large, complex and valuable unit that could not be hazarded in massed torpedo attacks against the enemy fleet and which would become unaf-

The primary weapon of the destroyers built during the 1930s continued to be the torpedo. The is the US Navy's *Dunlap* (DD-384), launching a torpedo from her starboard after quad mounting. *(NHHC, 80-G-413482)*

Table 5.5: Destroyer Authorisations 1930–1936

Programme	Great Britain	USA	Japan	France	Italy
1930	8 'D' +FL (1931–33)			6 *Le Fantasque* (1931–36)	4 *Maestrale* (1931–34)
1931	8 'E' +FL (1933–34)	8 *Farragut* (1932–35)	6 *Hatsuharu* (1931–35) 6 *Shiratsuyu* (1933–37)		
1932	8 'F' +FL (1933–35)			1 *Mogador* (1934–39) 1 *Le Hardi* (1936–40)	
1933	8 'G' +FL (1934–36)	8 *Porter* (1933–37) 18 *Mahan* (1934–37)			
1934	8 'H' +FL (1935–37)	2 *Somers* (1935–38) 2 *Gridley* (1935–38) 8 *Bagley* (1935–38)	4 *Shiratsuyu* (1935–38) 10 *Asashio* (1935–39)	1 *Mogador* (1934–39)	
1935	7 'Tribal'[1] (1936–38) 8 'I' +FL (1936–38)	3 *Somers* (1936–39) 2 *Gridley* (1936–39) 10 *Benham* (1936–39)		2 *Le Hardi* (1936–40)	4 *Oriani* (1935–37)
1936	9 'Tribal'[1] (1936–39) 8 'J' (1937–39)	12 *Sims* (1937–40)		3 *Le Hardi* (1936–40)	12 *'Soldati'* (1937–39)
Total	6 Leaders 72 Destroyers	13 Leaders 60 Destroyers	26 Destroyers	8 Contre-torpilleurs 6 Destroyers	20 Destroyers

Note:
[1] Although not classed as a 'Leader' by the Royal Navy, the displacement of the 'Tribal' class was that of a 'large destroyer' (maximum displacement 1,850tW) as defined by the London Treaty.

fordable in the numbers required. In the event only the two Pacific powers would go down this road, and both had to accept that the resulting ships would inevitably be larger and costlier.[10]

A full anti-submarine warfare outfit was equally costly in terms of topweight, hull space and deck space. All submarines built following the Washington Conference were designed with a primary mission of making torpedo attacks on warships, yet despite this ASW in destroyers was initially a low priority for the major navies. Only the British and the Americans were prepared to invest significant sums in the development of effective underwater sensors, and by the late 1920s Asdic and Sonar equipment was operational with their respective navies, but in British fleet destroyers the accompanying depth charge racks and throwers had to compete with two-speed sweep gear (and in some later ships minelaying rails) for a very limited amount of quarterdeck space. The new generation of US Navy destroyers built during the 1930s were completed without A/S weapons; quarterdecks were strengthened for the future installation of depth charge racks, but ASW weaponry was regarded by the US Navy as an 'add-on', permissible in wartime overload conditions but not to be counted in a standard displacement limited by treaty.

Japanese destroyer designs had a handful of stern chutes for single depth charges – generally half a dozen – and depth charge throwers copied from the US 'Y'-gun, but there was no properly funded development of anti-submarine detection systems. For the Italian destroyers, minelaying rather than ASW was the priority, and the *Oriani*s laid down in 1935–36 were the first ships to be fitted with depth charge throwers.

The French *Marine Nationale* started off with the best of intentions – in fact the French flotilla craft were the only post-Washington ships to be designed with a properly integrated ASW outfit. The problem of a quarterdeck limited in size by the closeness of the after gun mounting to the stern was resolved by the ingenious solution of housing the heavy depth charges in stern chutes located beneath the quarterdeck, with remote-controlled launch using an endless chain system similar to minelaying systems of the period. The chutes could be replenished from a reload magazine deep in the hull, and were to be complemented by four depth charge throwers mounted abeam the funnels and Ginocchio towed A/S torpedoes. There was passive listening apparatus in the form of two Walser 'sound lenses', and there was also provision for an active ultrasound sensor that could be lowered in a tube in a special hull compartment forward of the bridge. However, when prototypes for the latter failed to live up to their early promise, the French were left without an effective underwater detection system. Moreover, topweight and stability problems in the early *torpilleurs* and *contre-torpilleurs* led to the removal of the throwers, thereby weakening the depth charge patterns that had originally been contemplated.

When war broke out in Europe in 1939 it quickly became apparent that the large fleet actions for which the interwar destroyers had been primarily designed were unlikely to materialise. The German fleet projected in the ambitious 'Plan Z' was in the early stages of construction, and Mussolini would wait a further year before

Depth Charge Mechanism: *Le Malin*

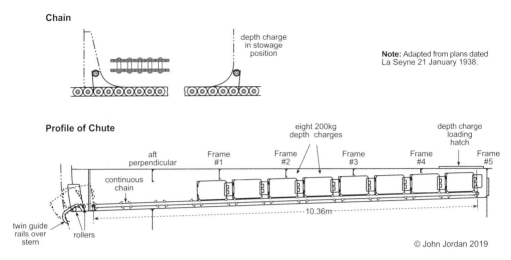

Chain

depth charge
in stowage
position

Note: Adapted from plans dated
La Seyne 21 January 1938.

Profile of Chute

eight 200kg
depth charges

depth charge
loading
hatch

aft
perpendicular

Frame
#1

Frame
#2

Frame
#3

Frame
#4

Frame
#5

continuous
chain

10.36m

twin guide
rails over
stern

rollers

© John Jordan 2019

French destroyers of the interwar period carried their depth charges in angled chutes beneath the quarterdeck. The depth charges were stowed in line on rollers of lignum vitae secured to an endless chain, and were dropped over rails set into the stern.

committing the Italian fleet to the fray, by which time the position of the French fleet built specifically to oppose it had been fatally undermined by the defeat of the French Army. Germany would again resort to submarine warfare to defeat Britain, and when the British Mediterranean Fleet eventually came face to face with the Italians it was confronted not only by a conventional surface fleet, but by large groupings of land-based level bombers and torpedo planes, and by an impressively large submarine force. The British destroyers designed during the interwar period generally had the after torpedo mounting (50 per cent of their torpedo capability) replaced by a single 4in HA gun, and were compelled to embark additional light AA weapons, depth charges and DCTs.

Once it became clear that war in the Pacific would not be following its anticipated course, similar modifications became necessary both in the US Navy and the IJN. The large US Navy Leaders quickly lost one of their twin 5in single-purpose mountings to enable their AA capabilities to be boosted, and most of the IJN destroyers lost the second of their three 12.7cm gun mountings later in the war. When the smaller US destroyers embarked the ASW weaponry for which they had been designed they became seriously overloaded, and many later had a 5in single mounting and/or torpedo tubes disembarked in compensation for depth charge throwers and additional light AA mountings.

The British in particular, but also the Americans and the Japanese, had opportunities during the war to use their destroyers in the way they intended, and the ships generally performed well on these occasions. However, these opportunities were few and far between, whereas virtually all destroyers had to defend themselves and their consorts against aircraft and submarines, often on a daily basis. The restrictions on displacement enshrined in the London Treaty certainly made it difficult to fit the additional AA and ASW capabilities when it became clear that these qualities would be essential in a modern destroyer. However, the primary barrier to a well-balanced ship was essentially conceptual; even if the London Treaty had permitted larger destroyer displacements, there is every reason to believe that the major navies would simply have opted for more main guns and more torpedoes (*cf* the US Navy's Leaders, which on 1,800 tons did not even have a dual-purpose main armament).

Chapter 6

SUBMARINES 1930–36

T HE POST-WASHINGTON TREATY PERIOD was characterised by a move towards the construction of very large submarines, many of which were modelled on the German *U-Kreuzer* completed or projected during the last two years of the war. These submarines were particularly attractive to the two Pacific powers,

US submarines moored alongside the tender *Holland* (AS-3) during the mid-/late-1930s. Note the large size of the two 'cruiser' submarines, *Nautilus* (SS-168) and *Narwhal* (SS-167) Outboard of them are the early 'fleet' submarines *Shark* (SS-174: P3); *Dolphin* (SS-169: D1), *Porpoise* (SS-172: P1), *Pike* (SS-173: P2), and *Tarpon* (SS-175: P4). (NHHC, NH 3036)

the United States and Japan, because of their exceptional endurance, which enabled them to conduct lengthy patrols in waters dominated by the navy of the other power. The US Navy's 'cruisers' could operate for several weeks in the western Pacific, in waters dominated by the Japanese surface fleet, while their IJN counterparts could monitor American surface activity in the waters around Hawaii and off the US West Coast, with the Panama Canal one of several possible areas of interest.

The Italian *Regia Marina* also invested heavily in 'cruiser' submarines, which were in theory capable of operating 'outside the Straits', in the Atlantic or the Indian Oceans. While the Italian boats were by no means as large as the American and Japanese boats, they were much larger than earlier submarines designed to operate in the Mediterranean and the Adriatic.

The French *Surcouf*, laid down in 1926, exceeded even the US Navy boats in size and power. Unlike the cruiser submarines being built for the other four Washington navies, which were intended for long-range strategic scouting and the prosecution of warship contacts in enemy waters, *Surcouf* was designed for commerce warfare within the constraints of current international law, and her large size was necessary not only for long endurance but to enable her to accommodate prisoners from the merchant ships she sank.

After the single experimental *X 1*, which had been designed and laid down before the Washington Conference, the British Royal Navy built no further cruiser submarines. A ten-year programme drawn up by the Admiralty in late 1923 included twelve cruisers, alongside no fewer than sixty submarines of the Overseas Patrol type and eight Fleet submarines, but with finances increasingly tight during the mid/late-1920s the cruiser programme was abandoned in favour of the other two types.

The rationale for the British Overseas Patrol Submarines (OPS) of the 'O', 'P' and 'R' classes was little different from that for the large American and Japanese cruisers. Built specifically for overseas deployment, these boats were designed to operate from Hong Kong and from the new base at Singapore in the seas south of Japan. Because of the worldwide network of British bases, endurance for transit was less of an issue than for the American and Japanese submarines, but once deployed they would need to conduct lengthy patrols at relatively long range and transmit the composition, speed and course of Japanese surface forces back to their base. Although more a development of the wartime submarines of the 'E' and 'L' classes than a copy of the German *U-Kreuzer*, the 'O's and their successors were large boats comparable in size to the Italian cruisers, which they matched in general capabilities if not in endurance.

The other major line of large submarine development during the period 1920–30 was that of the 'fleet' submarine, which was pursued by all except the Italian Navy. Submarines large enough and fast enough to accompany the battle fleet on deployment and to operate in advance of it or on the flanks immediately prior to action were favoured by the United States (*V1–3*), Japan (the KD3, KD4 and KD5 classes, comprising fifteen boats), France, which authorised no fewer than 31 submarines of the *1,500 tonnes* type between 1924 and 1930, and ultimately Britain (the 1,800-ton *Thames* class, the legend of which had been approved prior to the London Conference).

Both the 'cruiser' and the 'fleet' submarine concepts were dependent on large, high-powered, lightweight diesel engines. These were at an embryonic stage of development at the end of the First World War, and the most powerful German MAN models to date were still being built and yet to be installed in a submarine. These large diesels were to prove the Achilles heel of all the cruiser and fleet submarines built during the 1920s. They were unreliable and prone to breakdown, required extensive and regular maintenance (often requiring dockyard support), and in the case of the American boats were incorporated into composite drive systems that were complex, heavy and space-intensive, generally requiring two separate engine rooms to accommodate them. None of the fleet boats managed to sustain the high speed for which they had been designed for long periods, and although it was initially anticipated that these early problems would be resolved by advances in diesel technology, it was increasingly accepted that an engine based on pistons and cylinders would always be happier operating below its nominal maximum power, and was not therefore well-suited to sustained high-speed performance.

By 1930, when many of these large cruiser and fleet submarines were coming into service, other problems were becoming apparent. They were not handy boats, particularly when running submerged, and were not popular with the submariner community; some designs experienced stability problems, and all were relatively slow to dive, making them increasingly vulnerable to attack from the air. They were also over-complex both in terms of their construction and their equipment; this made them very costly and unattractive to governments operating on increasingly restricted budgets.

The London Treaty of 1930 placed new limits on unit size (2,000 tons standard) and overall tonnage (52,700 tons for each of the three major powers). This served to put a premium on submarines of moderate displacement. The US Navy in particular was quick to see that if it insisted on building the largest submarines permissible under the Treaty, this would result in a fleet of only twenty-six boats, of which a maximum of seven to nine could be on patrol at any given time. Such a decision would also mean the scrapping of the smaller 'S' class, which were useful for protecting forward bases, without replacement. The large US Navy cruiser submarines of the 1920s would not be repeated, and there would be a self-imposed ceiling of 1,500 tons on new construction.

The Japanese were more reluctant to abandon the large submarine. The IJN still wanted 2,000-ton cruisers for long-range scouting and the monitoring of enemy bases, and were now committed to providing these with aircraft to extend their effective scouting radius. The cruisers would continue to be complemented by fast fleet submarines of around 1,600 tons. However, the Japanese had no forward bases to defend – the Washington Treaty had prohibited the militarisation of the Protectorates in the central Pacific – so there was little interest in coastal patrol submarines. Japan secured parity in overall submarine tonnage with Britain and the

USA at the London Conference (despite a 5:3 ratio for capital ships and 8in-gun cruisers and a 10:7 ratio for light cruisers), but the IJN could continue to build the large submarines it wanted only if it scrapped large numbers of coastal submarines when these became due for replacement.[1]

Although the British were quick to abandon the cruiser submarine, the Royal Navy would persist for a little while yet with its vision of a fast fleet submarine. Twenty fleet submarines of the *Thames* class had been projected prior to the London Conference, but the programme was abandoned after only three units had been laid down when it became apparent that they would be unable to match the speed of the new generation of fast capital ships inaugurated by the French *Dunkerque*. In their place there would be a new, smaller overseas patrol type, the first of which would be authorised under the 1935–36 Estimates.

The *Regia Marina* would continue to build cruiser submarines alongside its 800-ton sea-going patrol types. However, the Italians were not bound by the terms of the London Treaty, so there was no limit on overall tonnage; moreover, the Italian cruisers were of relatively modest displacement.

The French *Marine Nationale*, which had been compelled by international pressure to put a premature end to the *Surcouf* programme, nevertheless continued its love affair with the fleet submarine: the latest variants of the *1,500-tonnes* type were powered by diesels with a nominal rating of 4,000bhp for a maximum surface speed of 20 knots. However, the large programme embarked on during the mid-/late-1920s had all but ground to a halt due to shipyard overload; the last of the units authorised in 1930 would not be completed until 1939, and construction of a new, even more powerful design would have to be abandoned following the German invasion of 1940.

Smaller Submarines

In 1922 all five of the major navies had a substantial stock of small or medium-sized coastal submarines, many of which had been laid down or completed during the First World War. Small submarines for coastal defence had therefore not been a priority during the period 1922–30. Only the French *Marine Nationale* had laid down submarines of this type in large numbers, and the reasons for this were both strategic and technical; they were also related to the unusual budgetary arrangements of the French Republic.

In strategic terms the coastal submarines were necessary to ensure that the British fleet, which under the terms of the Washington Treaty would now possess three times the number of capital ships permitted to the *Marine Nationale*, could not impose its will on France by blockading French ports as it had done during past conflicts. The construction of large numbers of these submarines was therefore extremely popular with the French parliament, many of whose members were incensed by what they considered to be Anglo-Saxon arrogance and intransigence at the Washington Conference.[2]

Although France already had a substantial number of boats of this type in commis-

Galatée was one of a series of small, powerfully-armed coastal submarines built for the French *Marine Nationale* during the 1920s. Note the external *tubes-canons* angled out abaft the bow. *(DR, courtesy of Jean Moulin)*

sion at the time of the Washington Conference, the designs generally dated from before the First World War, so that by 1922 most were obsolescent. Nor were they particularly successful in service, so a renewal of the French submarine fleet was a matter of urgency.

The third factor that favoured the construction in France of large numbers of coastal submarines was that they were funded not from the Navy budget, but from a separate budget allocated to the *préfectures maritimes*, a regionally based home defence organisation with its own command structure, responsible for defence of the ports and their associated shipping channels.

The only other major navy to show much interest in the coastal submarine before 1930 was the Italian Navy, which had continued to operate large numbers of small coastal boats after the First World War, but which now felt it needed to respond to the large French programme of more capable, modern submarines. Seven units of the 600-ton *Argonauta* class were laid down from 1929. These would be followed during the early 1930s by larger numbers of similar submarines of the *Sirena*, *Perla* and *Adua* classes.

During the same period it became apparent to the British that they would need to replace the coastal submarines of the war-built 'H' class, both to provide ASW targets and for operations in the relatively shallow waters of the North Sea and the Mediterranean. The result would be the 640-ton 'S' class, followed by the even smaller 'U' class.

Only the Japanese and the Americans held out against the trend towards smaller submarines, preferring to keep the elderly medium coastal boats completed just after the First World War in service to defend their coasts and, in the case of the Americans, their forward bases. However, the Japanese would build two prototype medium submarines of the RO type to provide a basis for wartime construction during the period 1930–36.[3]

Royal Navy Submarines of the Early 1930s

In June 1928 the Royal Navy's Plans Division had established a requirement for sixty-four large and fifteen small submarines. In order to achieve and maintain this force level it was proposed to build five large submarines of the Overseas Patrol type (see *WAW* Chapter 9) and one small (new 'S' type) per year then, once the design for a new, fast fleet type (the 1,800-ton 'G') slated to replace the OPS was finalised, four of the latter boats per year plus two smaller. However, these plans soon ran into difficulties. Due to budgetary problems, in 1929 two of the six Overseas Patrol submarines (*Rainbow* class) belonging to the 1928–29 programme were suspended, then cancelled.

The following year's programme included a single fleet submarine of the 'G' type plus two small patrol submarines of the 'S' class, but in the run-up to the London Conference, at which Britain would again push for the complete abolition of the submarine, the construction of these three boats was suspended. They would be authorised in May 1930 following the signing of the Treaty, and the Director of Plans set out a new long-term programme of construction taking into account the treaty provisions. It was calculated that on 31 December 1936 (the date of the treaty's expiry) the Royal Navy would have 34,009 of 'under-age' tonnage, including the 2,680tW cruiser *X1*, leaving a maximum of 18,691 tons that could be laid down between 1929 and 1933. This made for an average of 3,700 tons per annum, which implied a single large submarine and two small in most years, with two large submarines and a single small boat in others. The long-term target established for the Royal Navy was a force of twenty fast fleet submarines of 1,800 tons, twelve small submarines each of 650 tons, and six minelayers each of 1,480 tons, for a total tonnage of 52,680 tons. The origins of these three submarine types are outlined in *Warships After Washington*, Chapter 9.

The Fleet Submarines of the 'River' Class

The legend for the new fleet submarine – subsequently the 'River' class – had been approved by the Admiralty Board in October 1929, but with the London Conference intervening the first unit, *Thames*, was not laid down until January 1931. These large, powerful submarines were intended, like their OPS predecessors of the 'O', 'P' and 'R' classes, for deployment to the Far East, and endurance and long-range W/T capabilities (1,500nm) were again prioritised. However, whereas the patrol submarines were relatively slow (15 knots maximum on the surface), the 'Rivers' had a new and powerful 10-cylinder, 4-stroke diesel with supercharging that could propel them at speeds in excess of 22 knots. This, it was hoped, would enable them to operate in company with the fleet and to form part of the advance scouting

Thames (GB)

The powerful 10-cylinder supercharged diesels propelled the British fleet submarines of the 'River' class at a speed in excess of 22 knots on the surface. Note the auxiliary 400bhp diesel generators that powered the mechanical superchargers, and which increased the 8,000bhp delivered by the main diesels to 10,000bhp. The volume aft occupied by the propulsion machinery precluded the fitting of stern torpedo tubes.

line that would intercept Japanese surface forces. They were to be armed with a 4.7in shielded deck gun that could be used against enemy transports, but had only six bow torpedo tubes (each with two torpedoes), the after part of the boat being occupied by the auxiliary diesel generators employed to supercharge the main engines.

Thames was completed by Vickers in June 1932, only eighteen months after the keel was laid. Considering the size and complexity of the design, she performed well

HMS *Severn*, one of three fast fleet submarines built for the Royal Navy during the early 1930s. The second and third boats had a 4in QF Mk XII gun fitted in place of the shielded 4.7in of the lead boat, *Thames*. *(Leo van Ginderen collection)*

on trials, achieving a speed of 22.6 knots on the surface. However, stability was poor on surfacing; additional free-flood holes were cut in the upper casing, and the original 4.7in gun would later be replaced by the standard 4in model, thereby saving 6 tons in topweight. These modifications were incorporated into the second and third boats while building, and they also had their engine rooms lengthened to incorporate two escape chambers; additional buoyancy tanks in the superstructure further improved stability. Although a reduced diving depth of 200ft had been accepted for these submarines in order to reduce weight and maximise speed, the bulkheads in the two later boats were strengthened to 70lb/in².

Standard displacement was now 1,830 tons, which effectively meant that the original programme of twenty units would have accounted for 70 per cent of the overall submarine tonnage permitted under the London Treaty. The cost of these submarines was enormous in comparison to earlier Royal Navy types: £500,000 per unit – more than twice the cost of the smaller 'S' – for a weapons payload of six 21in torpedo tubes and a single 4in gun. Moreover, the year 1933, when the fourth unit of the class would have been due for authorisation, saw a number of important new developments. An increasingly unstable political situation in Europe meant a new emphasis on smaller patrol submarines designed for operations in the North Sea and the Mediterranean; and the construction in France of the fast battleship *Dunkerque*, which would shortly be answered by similar developments in the Italian *Regia Marina*, meant that the 'River' class would be unable to keep pace with the new generation of capital ships. Construction was therefore terminated after only three units had been laid down, and the Royal Navy would not lay down another 'fleet' submarine until 1959, when the advent of compact nuclear propulsion systems would make possible a submarine capable of sustained high underwater speed.

Minelayers

Although studies for the construction of a series of modern, purpose-built minelaying submarines had been proceeding throughout the 1920s, and a prototype conversion of a submarine of the 'M' class (*M3*) successfully trialled (see *WAW* Chapter 9), the design for the first production unit, the 1,500-ton *Porpoise*, was not approved until October 1930, six months after the signing of the London Treaty. She would not be laid down until September 1931, which resulted in the second boat being shunted back into the 1933–34 programme alongside the third boat.

Porpoise was completed in April 1933. Trials proved generally successful – the 'external' endless-chain minelaying system was particularly reliable and simple to operate – but she experienced the same stability problems as the other Royal Navy submarines of her generation, and the original 4.7in gun was replaced, as on *Thames*, with a 4in/40 QF gun in 1934. The five follow-on boats, authorised in 1933–36, had a modified hull design in which the saddle tanks were extended around the bottom to make a partial double hull. At the same time the raised upper casing, which in *Porpoise* enclosed only the mines, was continued to the bow. Besides improving stability, this configuration meant that all fuel oil could be stowed inter-

Table 6.1: Royal Navy Submarine Designs 1930–1936

	Thames class	Porpoise class	Shark ('S') class	Triton ('T') class	Undine ('U') class
Type:	fleet	sea-going minelayer	medium patrol	large patrol	coastal
Built:	three 1931–35	six 1931–39	eight 1933–38	fifteen 1936–41	three 1937–38
Displacement:	1,805tW	1,500tW	670tW	1,090tW	540tW
Dimensions:	345ft × 28ft (105m × 8.6m)	289ft × 30ft (88m × 9.0m)	209ft × 24ft (64m × 7.3m)	275ft × 26ft (84m × 8.1m)	191ft × 16ft (58m × 4.9m)
Machinery:	2-shaft diesel-electric; 10,000bhp/2,500hp = 22 / 10 knots	2-shaft diesel-electric; 3,300bhp/1,630hp = 15.5 / 8.5 knots	2-shaft diesel-electric; 1,550bhp/1,300hp = 14 / 10 knots	2-shaft diesel-electric; 2,500bhp/1,450hp = 15 / 9 knots	2-shaft diesel-electric; 615bhp/825hp = 11 / 10 knots
Range:	10,000nm at 8kts	11,500nm at 8kts	3,800nm at 9kts	8,000nm at 10kts	4,050nm at 10kts
Armament:	6 – 21in TT (6B: 12 torpedoes) 1 – 4.7in/40	6 – 21in TT (6B: 12 torpedoes) 1 – 4in/40 50 mines	6 – 21in TT (6B: 12 torpedoes) 1 – 3in/45	10 – 21in TT (6B+4Ext: 16 torpedoes) 1 – 4in/40	6 – 21in TT (4B+2Ext: 8/10 torpedoes) 1/0 – 3in/45

Note:
The extensive range of Royal Navy submarine designs that spanned the period 1930–36 was a reflection of the changes in policy that took place in the wake of the London Treaty. Construction of the expensive, high-performance 'fleet' submarines of the Thames class, on which so much design effort had been expended, was abandoned in favour of smaller types of patrol submarine designed for endurance rather than high tactical speed.

HMS *Cachalot*, one of a series of six specialised minelaying submarines completed during the 1930s. Note the high outer casing housing the fifty mines, which were stowed atop the pressure hull and launched using an endless chain mechanism. *(Leo van Ginderen collection)*

nally, thereby reducing the risk of leakage in the event of depth charging, and that the capacity of the main ballast tanks could be increased to 100 tons. Much attention was given to rapid diving – not an easy matter with the massive external casing – and a time of one minute fourteen seconds was achieved with one of the later boats.

The Royal Navy was very satisfied with the performance of the *Porpoise* and *Grampus* classes, but the advent of mines designed to be laid from torpedo tubes (two per tube, plus two stowed in place of each spare torpedo) during the late 1930s would weaken the case for further specialised minelaying submarines.

The Medium Patrol Submarines of the 'S' Class

Designed for offensive patrols in confined waters such as the North Sea, the medium patrol submarines of the 'S' class were intended to replace the war-built 'H' class. Compared with the latter, they were to have a heavier torpedo armament, a higher surfaced speed and longer range both surfaced and submerged, while at the same time retaining the short diving time and underwater manoeuvrability of the latter type. Delayed by the London Conference, *Swordfish* was laid down only in December 1930, but was completed in less than two years. On a standard displacement of 640tW she was armed with six torpedo tubes (two torpedoes per tube) and a 3in HA gun in a 'disappearing' mounting. She was designed for a modest speed of 13.75 knots on the surface, but for 10 knots submerged.

The 'disappearing' mounting was not successful; the housing did not significantly reduce drag and contributed to stability problems experienced with the first pair. There was a permanent list when in the normal surfaced condition, and additional free-flooding holes were cut in the hull and bridge casings to remedy this. The fittings of these submarines also proved complex and unreliable, and accommodation was cramped. The breakwater forward of the bridge was suppressed in the second pair of boats ordered, and the 3in HA gun replaced by a low-angle model. These modifications were subsequently extended to the first two boats.

When these defects became apparent during trials with *Swordfish*, the orders for the third pair of submarines (authorised in 1931–32) were deferred so that they could incorporate improvements planned for the two 1932 boats, and the eight 'S'-class submarines authorised 1931–35 became a separate class (*Shark* class). Redesign included simplified fittings and a lengthening of the pressure hull amidships by 6ft (1.8m). The machinery arrangements were also radically revised: there were now two motors coupled to each shaft and the rate of battery charging was doubled. The original auxiliary motors were removed, thereby simplifying machinery control and freeing up additional accommodation aft. External fuel tanks, which it was now feared would be vulnerable to depth charging, were dispensed with altogether, and the internal bulkheads strengthened.

Construction of the 'S' type was halted after 1935, but the twelve boats completed proved so successful during the early months of the Second World War that the design was revived, and a further thirty-two boats of an improved design would be ordered under the War Emergency and 1941 programmes.

HMS *Swordfish* running on the surface in December 1937. The 3in HA gun was in a 'disappearing' mounting, which was found to have little advantage. It was subsequently replaced by an LA model mounted directly on the deck casing. *(Leo van Ginderen collection)*

British Submarines 1930–1936

Thames (fleet)
1805tW
105m x 8.6m
22 knots surfaced
10 knots submerged

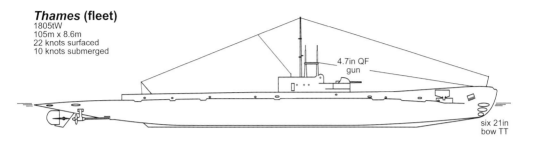

4.7in QF
gun

six 21in
bow TT

Seal (minelayer)
1520tW
89m x 7.8m
15.5 knots surfaced
8.5 knots submerged

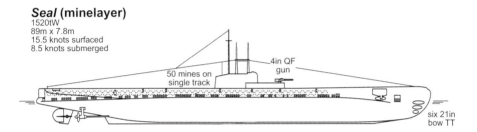

50 mines on
single track

4in QF
gun

six 21in
bow TT

Swordfish (medium patrol)
640tW
62m x 7.3m
13.75 knots surfaced
10 knots submerged

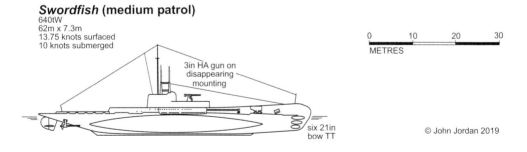

3in HA gun on
disappearing
mounting

six 21in
bow TT

0   10   20   30
METRES

© John Jordan 2019

Triton (large patrol)
1090tW
84m x 8.1m
15 knots surfaced
9 knots submerged

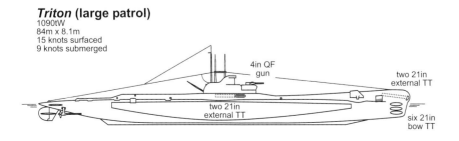

4in QF
gun

two 21in
external TT

two 21in
external TT

six 21in
bow TT

The 'T' and 'U' classes of 1935–36

With the premature termination of the fleet submarine programme, the Royal Navy looked towards a smaller type of submarine capable of overseas patrol. High speed on the surface was no longer a primary requirement, making it possible to design a boat with a useful torpedo battery and sufficient endurance for Pacific operations on little more than 1,000 tons standard displacement. Rather than conducting long-range observation – a role that would be increasingly performed by land-based aircraft, it was envisaged that the new submarines would be positioned at 'choke points' and lie in wait for the approaching IJN fleet. The new overall tonnage limit imposed by the London Treaty also favoured a smaller submarine design, as did developments in submarine detection. The result was the 'T' class, the first unit *Triton* being included in the 1935–36 Estimates, with four more boats authorised in 1936–37.

The 'T' class was designed at a time when the Admiralty had high hopes for Asdic, which held out the promise of making the previously impenetrable oceans more transparent. New and improved Asdic sets were being fitted in all British fleet destroyers from the early 1930s, and there was increasing confidence in the ability of escorts to detect submarines as they approached a surface force, before they were in a position to attack. These hopes would turn out to be misplaced: the presence of a submerged submarine during the Second World War would be generally announced by the sighting of torpedo tracks, and Asdic (and its US counterpart Sonar) would

In addition to their six internal bow torpedo tubes, for which reloads were provided, the submarines of the 'T' class were fitted with four external tubes in the outer casing at the bow and amidships. In this unidentified unit of the class, the tubes abreast the fin have been realigned to fire aft. *(NHHC)*

be useful primarily for directing depth charge attacks and to ensure that the submarine, once detected, was not able to escape. However, claims for the new technology would influence not only escort tactics but the design and tactical procedures of Royal Navy submarines of the period.

Given that the primary targets for submarines were enemy warships, in particular 'heavy' units such as capital ships and cruisers, and that these ships would be accompanied by escorts that in future would be equipped with underwater detection sensors, it might prove difficult for a submarine to penetrate that screen. This meant that the submarine would have to fire its torpedoes at longer ranges than previously anticipated; a larger salvo would therefore be essential to give the required spread that would ensure a hit, regardless of the evasive manoeuvring of the target. The other possibility was that a submarine equipped with its own Asdic detection set could determine a firing solution based on acoustic data alone, without the need to expose a periscope above water in proximity to an enemy force, thereby inviting early detection. Again this implied a large salvo to compensate for any inaccuracy in target bearing data.

Whereas earlier British post-war submarines had generally been fitted with six internal bow torpedo tubes, the 'T' class added a further two external tubes in the bow, plus two external tubes amidships, which were angled outwards from the centre line in the manner of the 'tube–canons' of the early French 600-tonnes type (see WAW Chapter 9).[4] This in theory made possible a ten-torpedo salvo, with reloads being provided for each of the six internal bow tubes.

High tactical speed was unimportant, so the main propulsion units were two 6-cylinder Vickers diesels with a combined rating of 2,500bhp (ie one quarter the brake horsepower of the supercharged 'River' class), which provided a sustained speed on the surface of 15 knots. All oil fuel was carried internally (at the cost of trim tank space) in order to preclude telltale leakage from external tanks under depth-charging. After the reduction of diving depth from 300ft to 200ft in the 'River' class, the 'T's would revert to the same 300ft standard as the Overseas Patrol Submarines of the 'O', 'P' and 'R' classes.

The major problem experienced with these submarines on completion was the adverse effect of the bluff bow on sea-keeping, making the submarines difficult to handle at periscope depth and causing some loss of surface speed in a seaway. In later boats the upper (external) torpedo tubes were moved 7ft (2.2m) aft to allow the bow to be fined. The hull configuration also appears to have been responsible for a particularly wet bridge.

The other submarine design developed for the Royal Navy during the period 1930–36 was a small coastal type intended to replace the ageing war-built submarines of the 'H' class in the anti-submarine training role. The 'U' class was originally to have been a simple unarmed target boat, but the design was subsequently developed to embrace coastal and harbour defence, including the defence of overseas bases, and short-range offensive operations in the shallow waters of the North Sea and the Mediterranean.

Originally intended for anti-submarine training, the submarines of the 'U' class were redesigned to enable them to undertake local patrols. There was no gun, and two of the six torpedo tubes were external. The bluff bow proved unsatisfactory in a seaway and led to modifications. This is *Unity* in November 1938. *(Leo van Ginderen collection)*

The 'platform' was as basic as possible: a single hull with a diving depth of 200ft and a designed speed of only 11.5 knots on the surface.[5] Unusually, diesel-electric drive was adopted, with the main diesels driving the electric motors via generators when the submarine was running on the surface. Submerged speed as designed was an impressive 10 knots, although 8.6 knots was the maximum achieved by the lead boat on trials.

For a submarine with a standard displacement of only 540 tons, the 'U' class was unusually well armed. In the final design there were four internal bow tubes each with a single reload, plus two external bow tubes located, as in the larger 'T' class, above the internal tubes. In this configuration there was no deck gun, but a 3in gun could be fitted forward of the conning tower if two of the reload torpedoes were landed in compensation.

The bluff bow was responsible for the same sea-keeping problems in these boats as in the 'T' class; if anything the problem was exacerbated by the small size of the 'U's. Later units were given a finer bow form, and the two external tubes were omitted in favour of a 3in deck gun. Early modifications as a result of trials included the addition of a quick-diving ('Q') tank for salvo compensation, and the removal of the torpedo shutters, which caused difficulties with discharge and maintenance.

Only three 'U'-class submarines were authorised pre-war, all in 1936, but forty-six boats of a slightly modified design would be ordered under the War Emergency, 1940 and 1941 programmes, with a further twenty-two units of a 'long hull' variant ordered under the 1941 and 1942 programmes. Small, manoeuvrable and packing a formidable punch for their size, the 'U' and 'V' classes were to provide valuable war service, particularly in the narrow waters of the central Mediterranean where they obtained most of their successes – and suffered most of their losses.

A Change of Direction for the US Navy

The London Treaty led to a radical rethink of the US Navy's post-Washington submarine policy. Although both the General Board and the Naval War College continued to favour large submarines with a trans-Pacific capability, the restrictions on overall tonnage imposed by the London Treaty clearly presented a dilemma: the US Navy had already expended 16,000 tons of its 52,700-ton total on only seven ocean-going submarines (*V1–7*), leaving just under 37,000 tons available for new construction even if all of the large coastal 'S' boats, which were still useful for forward base defence, were to be scrapped. If the US Navy opted for the largest submarines permitted under London (2,000 tons standard) this meant a further eighteen hulls, to be distributed between the Atlantic and the Pacific. Even if it opted for a repeat of the 1,500-ton *V7*, only twenty-four more submarines could be built (for a total of thirty-one).

The large cruisers of the *V4–6* type had been designed for an endurance of ninety days patrol, permitting two three-week transits from Hawaii to the western Pacific plus a forty-eight-day patrol. In *V7* this figure had been reduced to seventy-five days, which allowed a thirty-three-day patrol. The seventy-five-day figure was considered to be the minimum for any new class of submarine. Endurance was dependent not only on fuel stowage and provisions but on the number of torpedoes available for attacks, so the US Navy still wanted three torpedoes for each of four bow tubes and two for each of two stern tubes, even if that meant that some reloads were stowed externally in watertight containers.

Speed was set by the primary mission of attack on the enemy main body. Since the cruising speed of the US fleet as it crossed the Pacific would be limited to 12 knots by the fleet train, a sustained speed of 15 knots would give an accompanying submarine the necessary margin for keeping station and for manoeuvre. A higher maximum speed of 17–18 knots, to be sustained only for short periods, would be useful for manoeuvre prior to action, and diesel propulsion machinery capable of providing this would comfortably deliver the desired 15 knots cruising speed.

In the wake of London, the General Board wanted the smallest possible submarine compatible with these requirements in order to deliver the largest number of hulls. It was estimated by the Naval War College that a total of forty-seven submarines would allow twenty-one boats to be kept continuously on patrol, and this translated into a standard displacement of 1,140 tons. This figure was well below the displacement even of *V7*, which had previously been regarded as a small 'mobilisation' prototype by the General Board, so considerable ingenuity would need to be applied by C&R to produce a satisfactory design to the new requirements.

The most promising line of approach seemed to be a US Navy variant of the

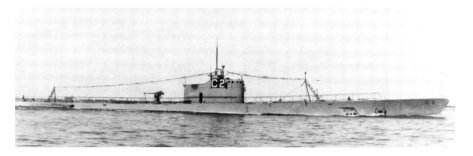

USS *Cuttlefish* (SS-171) under way in 1934, shortly after her completion. *Cuttlefish* and her sister, *Cachalot* (SS-170), were the last of the 'V' boats. They proved too small and cramped for trans-Pacific operations and were relegated to training duties during the Second World War. *(NHHC, NH 14770)*

German *U-135*, for which the submarine community had lobbied for some time. All the initial C&R sketch designs featured a German-style double hull, and designs 'A' and 'B' closely resembled *U-135* herself. Design 'C' had new lightweight diesels, which were subsequently incorporated into later sketch designs.

The General Board was eventually compelled to accept a 1,100-ton design with only two diesel engines – previously thought insufficient for maintenance during transit and patrol – and a small-calibre (3in) deck gun. There were four bow tubes and two stern tubes for 'short' torpedoes, of which a total of sixteen could be carried internally and in the tubes, and endurance was 11,000nm at 10 knots. A new lightweight German diesel with a nominal rating of 1,400bhp was finally adopted, giving a top speed of 17 knots on the surface.

The design was approved by the Secretary of the Navy in August 1930, and the last two 'V' boats, *V8* and *V9* (subsequently *Cachalot* and *Cuttlefish*) were duly laid down in 1931 and completed in 1934. Extensive use of welding was made in their construction. However, when they entered service they were found to be too small and too cramped for trans-Pacific operations, as the General Board had initially feared. Their MAN diesels vibrated badly, and had to be replaced by 4-stroke GM diesels in 1938, only four years after the submarines entered service. *Cachalot* and *Cuttlefish* were used to test the new Torpedo Data Computer (TDC), but after only three (unsuccessful) war patrols they would be relegated to training.

The Early 1,500-ton 'Fleet' Boats

Following the authorisation of funding for the last two 'V'-boats there was a two-year hiatus in US Navy submarine construction, due in large part to the worst financial effects of the Depression. The next four boats would be funded under the National Industrial Recovery Act of June 1933, and full advantage was taken of this enforced delay to re-evaluate the future direction of the submarine programme. Neither C&R nor BuEng were at all happy with the *Cachalot*s, which they considered too small and too cramped for trans-Pacific operations and whose restricted displacement and two-engine direct-drive configuration had been imposed on them for political reasons in the face of operational requirements. Following a series of conferences with submarine officers and the Electric Boat company – which besides building submarines for the US Navy had its own design team – a set of proposed characteristics was agreed at a final meeting in May 1933.

There was to be no significant change in the 'military' characteristics of the new submarines, which were to have the same armament of six torpedo tubes (four bow, two stern) with the same number of reloads (ten), the same 3in/50 deck gun, and would be designed for the same seventy-five-day endurance. Where the new design would differ from the *Cachalots* would be in its propulsion system. In place of the paired diesels of the *Cachalots*, which were coupled directly to the shafts, there would be four 1,250bhp diesels of modern design driving the electric motors via generators. This 'all-electric' arrangement, which was favoured by the General Board, had a number of advantages, including the ability to shut down each of the diesels in turn for maintenance during the lengthy transits and patrols for which these submarines were designed; it also eliminated the torsional problems that had plagued earlier multiple-engine configurations. However, the penalty was a larger and more complex propulsion plant, which required more engine-room space and a larger complement; the latter would in turn need additional bunk-space, fresh water and provisions. The General Board therefore had to accept that standard displacement would be close to 1,300 tons, thereby reducing the number of hulls that could be built under current treaty limits from thirty-five to thirty-one. However, as the General Board expected these overall limits to be reviewed at the London Conference of 1935, this was not a major concern.

The original design for the *Porpoise* class featured a double riveted hull, and the two units awarded to the Portsmouth Navy Yard were built to this configuration, using conventional construction techniques. However Electric Boat, who were to build the other two, offered a modified design with single-hull ends and an all-welded pressure hull, and these submarines subsequently became a separate sub-

Porpoise (US)

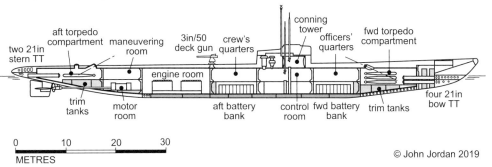

© John Jordan 2019

Porpoise was the prototype for the new US 'fleet' submarines. Her innovative diesel-electric propulsion system featured four diesel engines with associated generators powering electric motors which drove the shafts. This meant that each of the diesels could be shut down in turn for maintenance during the lengthy transit from Pearl Harbor to the western Pacific.

Tarpon (SS-175), built by Electric Boat, was similar to *Porpoise* but had a welded pressure hull and single-hull ends. All four boats of the class had a novel diesel-electric propulsion plant based around the new fast-running diesels. *(NHHC, NH 41924)*

group designated the *Shark* class. The latter design was to prove more successful in service, the double-hull 'ends' of the Portsmouth-built boats proving difficult to access for maintenance.

The *Porpoise* and *Shark* classes were the first US submarines to benefit from a new generation of lightweight, fast-running diesels derived from those developed for the American railways. Both General Motors and Winton (later absorbed by GM) offered prototypes suitable for mass production in response to a US Navy initiative, and these two manufacturers would subsequently be joined by HOR (Hooven, Owens, Rentschler) and Fairbanks Morse so that a choice of four suitable engines was available within a broad manufacturing base. For the *Porpoise* and *Shark* classes the propulsion plant selected comprised four Winton type 201A diesels rated at 1,150bhp, three 100kW diesel generators, and two high-speed geared 1,075hp motors coupled to each shaft (one for surface, the other for submerged running) in a separate compartment abaft the single engine room.

The principal defect of the new submarines was that the forward torpedo room was too short, making it difficult to remove the torpedoes from the forward tubes for servicing and to handle the reloads. However, they were otherwise successful and were followed by a repeat class of six boats (the *Perch* class) authorised under FY1935. All of these were built to the Electric Boat partial double-hull design, although the three units built in Portsmouth Navy Yard still had riveted hulls. They were powered by Winton, Fairbanks Morse or HOR diesels driving either four or eight electric motors from competing manufacturers via diesel generators, and were the first US Navy submarines to be fully air-conditioned – a major advantage when operating in Pacific waters.

Improvements considered for the next class focused on two key areas: high tactical surface speed and a proposed increase in the number of torpedo tubes and reloads. The General Board, ever conscious of developments abroad, appears to have been particularly impressed by the Royal Navy's new fleet submarines of the *Thames* class, with their high tactical speed of 22 knots and their six bow torpedo tubes. While it was now accepted in the US Navy that 22 knots was not a practical proposition in a submarine designed primarily for endurance, the General Board wanted to get as close to 20 knots as possible, arguing that a submarine whose propulsion machinery was capable of this speed could comfortably sustain 15 knots for transit to the western Pacific or when cruising with the fleet, and would also enjoy a 5-knot margin for manoeuvre in company with the fleet or when making an approach to a potential target.

With regard to torpedo tubes, earlier US Navy submarines had been fitted with a maximum of four bow tubes. It had long been considered that four torpedo hits would be necessary to sink a capital ship and it was anticipated, given the short-range attacks prescribed by US submarine doctrine, that all four torpedoes in a salvo would either hit or miss, so there was little point in increasing the number of bow tubes to six, which would have implications for the configuration of the bow and would in all probability increase displacement. By the same token, the value of fitting only two stern tubes was increasingly questioned. By late 1934 the development of the new Torpedo Data Computer (TDC) was well under way,[6] and there was the promise of new solutions to the problem of underwater target engagement. Using data inputs from sonars and other submarine sensors, the TDC could display the relative range and bearing of a target at any moment, and featured a torpedo ballistic computer that remotely set the torpedoes via power gyro-setters in the tubes. Since US submarine gyros were probably in advance of any in the world by this time,[7] this meant that a 'double-ended' submarine could engage a target at any angle. There was also interest in the tactic of approaching the target from ahead and firing the stern tubes in passing, thereby permitting a high-speed escape.

These discussions resulted in a decision to fit four bow and four stern tubes in the *Salmon* class of FY1936. Three torpedoes per tube were to be provided, so the total number of torpedoes carried was increased by 50 per cent to twenty-four. Accommodating the reloads for the stern tubes presented a problem because of the finer lines of the stern, so four of the eight were carried externally in watertight containers housed within the outer casing, the other four being stowed internally in the after torpedo room.

These and other modifications raised the displacement by more than 100 tons standard, so more powerful propulsion machinery was needed to meet the General Board's requirement for higher speed. The all-electric plant of the earlier boats proved difficult to accommodate, and there were also concerns about the ability of an all-electric plant to withstand action damage, so a return was made to a 'composite'

Table 6.2: US Navy's Submarines 1930–1936

	V8-9 (>Cachalot class)	Porpoise class	Perch class	Salmon class
Type:	ocean-going	fleet	fleet	fleet
Built:	two 1931–34	four 1933–36	six 1935–37	six 1936–38
Displacement:	1,120tW	1,320tW	1,330tW	1,450W
Dimensions:	271ft × 25ft (83m × 7.5m)	301ft × 25ft (92m × 7.6m)	301ft × 25ft (92m × 7.7m)	308ft × 26ft (94m × 8m)
Machinery:	2-shaft diesel-electric; 3,070bhp/1,600hp = 17 / 8 knots	2-shaft diesel-electric; 5,200bhp/2,080hp = 19 / 8 knots	2-shaft diesel-electric; 5,200bhp/2,370hp = 19 / 8 knots	2-shaft composite; 6,140bhp/2,660hp = 21 / 9 knots
Range:	11,000nm at 10kts 50nm at 5kts (dived)	11,000nm at 10kts 50nm at 5kts (dived)	11,000nm at 10kts 50nm at 5kts (dived)	11,000nm at 10kts 50nm at 5kts (dived)
Armament:	6 – 21in TT (4B+2S: 16 torpedoes) 1 – 3in/50	6 – 21in TT (4B+2S: 16 torpedoes) 1 – 3in/50	6 – 21in TT (4B+2S: 16 torpedoes) 1 – 3in/50	8 – 21in TT (4B+4S: 24 torpedoes) 1 – 3in/50

Note:
In contrast to developments in Europe, which continued to be focused on different types of submarine for widely differing missions in a variety of operational theatres, the design policy of the US Navy during the post-London period focused on a single type of large patrol submarine that would have the capacity to undertake lengthy patrols on station, having first transited the Pacific Ocean from its advanced base at Pearl Harbor. The adoption of diesel-electric propulsion, using lightweight, fast-running diesels derived from those developed for the American railways, would be a game-changer, allowing one or more of the diesel engines to be stood down for maintenance during the lengthy transit.

USS *Skipjack* (SS-184) on trials on 14 May 1938. These boats reverted to composite drive, which was less volume-intensive but also proved less successful. *(NHHC, NH 19023)*

power plant based on four identical 9-cylinder HOR or GM diesels, in which two were coupled to the shafts via reduction gearing (to compensate for the high speed of the new diesels) with the other two driving generators that powered the electric motors; the latter were coupled to the shafts via the same reduction gearing to produce the 5,300hp required for a designed surface speed of 21 knots. Although more compact than the diesel-electric arrangement of the *Porpoise* and *Perch* classes, the plant was more complex and less flexible, and by 1936 BuEng was already pushing for a return to the earlier arrangement. The *Sargo* class of FY1937, essentially a repeat of the *Salmon*, would be the last US submarines to have composite drive.

The Enforced Contraction of the IJN Submarine Fleet

In focusing on the cruiser issue, which was undoubtedly the focal point of discussions during the London Conference of 1930, many commentators have underestimated the significance of the decisions made regarding the overall tonnage limits to be applied to submarines. While on the face of it Japan achieved parity with the other two major powers in this arm (parity that was denied in all other categories), the IJN regarded this as a significant political defeat.

In the immediate post-war period the Imperial Japanese Navy had laid down forty-five medium patrol submarines, generally of 750–900 tons unit displacement (surfaced), and which had been completed between 1919 and 1927. After Washington it had embarked on the construction of no fewer than twenty-six large ocean-going submarines belonging to the 1923 and 1927 Programmes: the five cruisers each had a surfaced displacement of 2,150 tons, the seventeen fast fleet submarines of the KD type displaced around 1,750 tons, and the four ocean-going minelayers just under 1,400 tons. The total submarine tonnage in service or on order for the IJN when the London Conference began was almost 83,000 tons (see table), and although the 7,350 tons of new construction would be partially balanced by the decommissioning of some of the older medium boats when the J1M and the KD5s were delivered in 1932, the IJN insisted that 78,000 tons was the *minimum* figure that could be agreed if its Pacific strategy was not to be seriously undermined.

The reason the figure was so high was that Japan, like France, had seen a large post-Washington submarine programme as essential in order to compensate for her statutory inferiority in capital ships. The Japanese tonnage figure was still below that authorised by the French parliament during the period 1922–30. However,

Table 6.3: **IJN Submarine Tonnage: Submarines Laid Down or Completed by April 1930**

Programme	Submarines	Tonnage	Completed	Replacement
1915–16	2 × K1	1,470t[1]	1919	1932
	2 × F1	1,434t	1920	1933
1917–18	3 × K2	2,265t	1920–21	1933–34
	6 × L1/L2	5,412t	1920–22	1933–35
	3 × F2	2,220t	1922	1935
	10 × K3	7,550t	1920–23	1933–36
	4 × KT	2,660t	1923–27	1936–40
1919–21	1 × **KD1**	1,500t	1924	1937
	1 × **KD2**	1,500t	1928	1941
	4 × **KRS**	5,532t	1927–28	1940–41
	3 × L3	2,691t	1922–23	1935–36
	3 × K4	2,310t	1923–24	1936–37
	9 × L4	8,964t	1923–27	1936–40
1923	4 × J1	8,540t	1926–29	1940–42
	12 × **KD4**	21,360t	1927–30	1941–43
1927	1 × **J1M**	2,243t	1932	1945
	3 × **KD5**	5,115t	1932	1945
Total tonnage[1]	First Class:	45,790t		
	Second Class:	36,976t[2]		
	Overall:	**82,766t**		

Notes:
[1] All figures are based on the official surfaced displacement, which included fuel oil, lubrication oil, and fresh water. Standard displacement for these submarines had to be calculated retrospectively after it was defined in the London Treaty, and it was calculated only for those submarines it was planned to retain. Figures in published sources lack consistency and are probably unreliable.
[2] Some of the small Second Class submarines of the 'F' and 'K' types would probably have been stricken in 1932, when the large submarines of the J1M and KD5 types were due to enter service, regardless of the provisions of the London Treaty.

there were two important differences: much of French post-Washington construction had been focused on small submarines for coastal defence that were of little interest to the IJN; and the French refused point blank to reduce their 90,000-ton target for submarine tonnage, and were therefore unwilling to sign up to any of the overall tonnage restrictions embodied in Part III of the London Treaty, whereas Japan felt compelled to sign up to its provisions to avoid political isolation and a further deterioration of its relationships with the two major powers. For the US Navy, which had laid down only seven submarines since 1922, and for the Royal Navy, much of whose submarine tonnage was of First World War vintage, an overall submarine tonnage allocation of 52,700 tons was no great hardship. For the IJN, however, it undermined yet another of the cornerstones of its attempt to compensate for the US Navy's numerical superiority in capital ships.[8] It was calculated that the loss in tonnage was equivalent to two entire squadrons of fleet submarines (sixteen boats).

The first step taken by the IJN to reduce the disparity in actual and permitted tonnage was the early disposal of some its older medium patrol submarines. Between 1930 and 1932 all but four of the fifteen Schneider–Laubeuf 'K'-type boats were stricken, together with all five of the Fiat–Laurenti 'F' series and a single boat of the British-derived 'L' series. This saved almost 13,000 tons. However, further second-class submarines would have to be disposed of before December 1936 if new first-class boats were to be built. There was also a problem with the age of the IJN's submarines. Under the London Treaty rules existing submarines could be replaced only after thirteen years had elapsed from the time of their completion. The most recent second-class boats of the KT and L4 types had been completed only in 1927, so it would be the late 1930s before replacements could be laid down.

The other measure that would reduce the current total further was a recalculation of the unit displacement of the submarines currently in service to take into account the new definition of standard displacement introduced by the London Treaty, which excluded fuel oil, lubricating oil and fresh water. This reduced individual displacement by less than 100 tons for the second-class submarines, which were designed for relatively short patrols of up to twenty days; however, for the large cruisers and fleet submarines the reduction was 250–300 tons per unit.[9] On this basis there would have been a saving of 2,500–3,000 tons for the twenty-seven second-class boats and almost 7,000 tons for the twenty-six first-class boats. By the end of 1932 this meant that the overall tonnage of submarines in service with the IJN was just under 60,000 tons (of which 40,000 tons of first-class submarines), a major reduction from the 1930 figure but still well above the 52,700-ton limit that would have to be achieved by 31 December 1936.

Curiously, little attempt was made to further reduce the tonnage taken up by medium patrol submarines during the Treaty period. For example, the three British-derived L3 boats, which had been completed in 1922–23, remained in active service until 1941, when they were finally relegated to training, and the six remaining boats of the K4 and KT classes would have a similar service history, while the nine submarines of the L4 class, with a collective tonnage of more than 8,000 tons standard, were still active units when the Pacific War began in December 1941. Five of the older boats were stricken in 1936 and a further five during 1938–40, but given Japan's imminent withdrawal from the Treaty these were 'operational' rather than political decisions. Despite this, construction of new fleet and cruiser submarines, authorised under the 1931 and 1934 programmes, would continue unabated during the remainder of the Treaty period.

According to Article 20 of the London Treaty, Japan was permitted to lay down 19,200 tons of 'replacement' submarine tonnage before 31 December 1936, of which 12,000 tons could be completed before that date. The First Fleet Replenishment ('Circle 1') Programme of 1931 therefore featured nine submarines to be completed by 1937: a cruiser of 1,900 tons standard displacement, six fleet submarines of 1,400 tons, and two medium submarines of 700 tons (total tonnage: 11,700); two further cruisers and two fleet boats would follow under the 1934 'Circle 2' Programme, for a grand total of 18,300 tons.

The 1931 Programme

The single cruiser (*Junsen*)) of the J2 type, *I.6*, was essentially a redesigned J1 with purpose-built aviation facilities. It had the twin retractable hangars of the modified J1M (see *WAW* Chapter 9), and these were complemented for the first time by a catapult using compressed air, which ran along the port side of the after casing abaft the hangars. The catapult effectively replaced the after 14cm deck gun, and reduced the time spent on the surface while the submarine readied its reconnaissance aircraft; however, a minimum of twenty minutes was required for this operation, during which time the submarine was vulnerable to hostile aircraft.

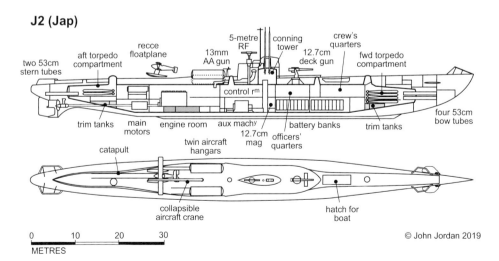

J2 (Jap)

I.6 was the first of the IJN's *Junsen*-type submarines to be equipped with a catapult for a reconnaissance floatplane. The aircraft was stowed broken-down in twin hangars that were retracted into the outer hull casing when the boat dived.

The IJN fleet submarine *I.68* of the KD6A type on trials in 1934. *(NHHC, NH 73054)*

The *I.6* was the first of the Japanese cruisers to have diesels of Japanese design and manufacture. The Kampon Type 1a Mod 7 was rated at 4,000bhp, so maximum speed on the surface was 2 knots faster than for the J1M, which had German MAN 3,000bhp diesels built under licence. A further modification was the replacement of the forward 14cm low-angle gun by a 12.7cm/40 model.

The six fleet boats (*Kaigun-dai*) of the KD6A type were likewise a development of the earlier KD5, and earlier units were fitted with the 10cm HA gun of the latter; later units had a 12cm LA deck gun. They were powered by Kampon Type 1b Mod 8 diesels with a unit rating of 4,500bhp, which raised maximum speed on the surface from 20.5 knots in the KD5 to an impressive 23 knots. This new generation of Japanese-designed diesels, incorporating the most advanced features of their Sulzer and MAN predecessors, were particularly sophisticated for their time; they employed double-action, two-cycle technology with air injection, and would be followed by even more powerful models. Despite the (understated) official standard displacement of 1,400 tons, these submarines were 8m longer than their immediate predecessors, the additional hull length being utilised to increase range from 10,000nm to 14,000nm at 10 knots.

Stern tubes were abandoned in the later KD-type submarines, but new and more powerful torpedoes were now available for firing from their six bow tubes. The standard Type 89 53cm model (in service 1931), powered by kerosene fuel and compressed air, had a range of 5,500m at 45 knots and was armed with a 300kg warhead. It would shortly be complemented by the Type 92 electric (*ie* wakeless) torpedo, based on a successful German submarine torpedo of the First World War, with a similar warhead and a range of 7,000m at 30 knots. And 1935 would see the introduction into service of the Type 95 oxygen torpedo, the 53cm (21in) submarine counterpart of the 'Long Lance', with a range of 9,000m at 49 knots and a

Table 6.4: IJN Submarines 1930–1936

	KD6A/B	J2	K5	J3
Type:	fleet	cruiser	medium patrol	cruiser
Built:	eight 1931–38	one 1932–35	two 1933–37	two 1934–38
Displacement:	1,400tW	1,900tW	700tW	2,230tW
Dimensions:	105m × 8.2m	98.5m × 9.0m	73m × 6.7m	109m × 9m
Machinery:	2-shaft diesel/electric; 9,000bhp/1,800hp = 23 / 8 knots	2-shaft diesel/electric; 8,000bhp/2,600hp = 20 / 7.5 knots	2-shaft diesel/electric; 3,000bhp/1,200hp = 19 / 8 knots	2-shaft diesel/electric; 11,200bhp/2,800hp = 23 / 8 knots
Range:	14,000nm at 10kts 65nm at 3kts (dived)	20,000nm at 10kts 60nm at 3kts (dived)	8,000nm at 12kts 90nm at 3.5kts (dived)	14,000nm at 16kts 60nm at 3kts (dived)
Armament:	6 – 53cm TT (6B: 14 torpedoes) 1 – 10cm/12cm	6 – 53cm TT (4B+2S: 17 torpedoes) 1 – 12.7cm/40 DP 1 floatplane	4 – 53cm TT (4B: 10 torpedoes) 1 – 8cm/40	6 – 53cm TT (6B: 20 torpedoes) 1 – 14cm/40 1 floatplane

Note:
The Imperial Japanese Navy, like its US counterpart, continued to focus on the construction of large 'fleet' or 'cruiser' submarines during the post-London period. The primary missions of these boats were long-range reconnaissance of US naval bases and movements, and attrition of the large expeditionary fleet that would need to be despatched across the Pacific to defend the Philippines and to defeat the Japanese battle fleet in its own waters. The only exception to this policy was the K5 medium patrol submarine, which was to be the prototype for a 'mobilisation' type that could be forward deployed to the Mandates in wartime and would provide local area defence against hostile surface units.

405kg warhead. A new torpedo fire control system would be fitted from 1931, although it lacked the technical sophistication of the US Navy's TDC and relied heavily on human observation for its data inputs.

Finally, in addition to the seven fleet and cruiser submarines of the 1931 Programme, there were two medium patrol submarines of the K5 type – the first to be ordered for more than ten years. They were intended as mobilisation prototypes, with a view to replacing the IJN's older medium boats in the homeland and local area defence role. Developed from the earlier K4 type, *RO-33* and *RO-34* had improved

A view from aft of *I.71*. Note the retention of the flat wood deck atop the outer casing derived from that of the German *U-Kreuzer*. *(NHHC, NH 73055)*

Mitsubishi single-action, 4-cycle diesels, which gave them a top surface speed of 19 knots. They proved successful and provided the basis of the larger K6 design that was put into series production shortly before the Second World War.

The 1934 Programme

For the supplementary 'Circle 2' Programme of 1934 there were to be only four new submarines: two cruisers and two fleet boats. The two fleet boats of the KD6B type were essentially repeats of the KD6A boats authorised under the previous programme, the only difference as completed being an additional 13mm AA gun mounting.

The two cruisers of the J3 type, however, although superficially similar to *I.6*, were much larger boats with a new mission. Although officially stated to have a standard displacement, like the J2, of 1,900 tons, this figure would be exceeded by almost 350 tons on completion. *I.7* and *I.8* would have a hull more than 10 metres longer than *I.6*, and would be fitted with more powerful Kampon Type 1a Model 10 diesels with a unit power rating of 5,600bhp, giving them a maximum speed on the surface of 23 knots – the same speed as the latest fleet boats of the KD6 type. They would have similar aircraft facilities to *I.6*, but with a longer catapult on an after casing that was angled upwards towards the stern to improve 'lift' on take-off. The single deck gun forward of the conning tower would again be of the larger 14cm calibre that was a feature of the earlier IJN cruisers, and would be complemented by a light AA battery comprising two twin and one single 13mm AA guns.

Every bit as significant as these other modifications was the fitting of extensive

One of two command submarines of the J3 type, *I.8*, shortly after her completion; the photo was taken on 12 February 1939. Note the angled ramp for the floatplane catapult abaft the conning tower, and the large 14cm deck gun forward. (*Fukui Shizuo collection*)

communications equipment to enable these submarines to serve as flagships for submarine squadron commanders. Previously this co-ordinating role had been performed by light cruisers, as with the destroyer squadrons, the difference being that the cruisers serving as destroyer squadron flagships were expected to accompany and lead their squadrons into battle, whereas those serving as submarine squadron flagships were to accommodate the flag staff and to act as a communications relay for High Command instructions to the submarine squadrons at their forward operating bases. The fitting out of *I.7* and *I.8* as command submarines was therefore evidence of a new tactical doctrine that envisaged the actions of groups of submarines being co-ordinated while operating on the surface at sea.

The justification for the new submarine flagships can be seen in the IJN Battle Instructions of 1934, which stated that the squadron flagship would act as a communication control station *after the submarines had deployed* (Paragraph 11) – though with due regard for the need to avoid enemy interception of radio transmissions. The Battle Instructions further stated that when the submarine flagship's services were no longer required or when the other submarines were outside communications range, the flagship was to *join the main force or operate independently* (Paragraph 12), and that when a major redeployment of the submarine squadron became necessary, the flagship should *proceed in advance of the remainder of the squadron* to the forward area (Paragraph 13). [All italics are the author's.]

Clearly the IJN, which intended to set up submarine patrol lines in strategic positions close to enemy bases and straddling the anticipated trans-Pacific route of the US battle fleet, envisaged that these lines would need to be adjusted in the light of reconnaissance and contact data, and that only a specially equipped command submarine at sea with the force could receive this data and transmit revised instructions to its squadron. This tactical philosophy would be embodied in the grouping of Japan's most modern and capable submarines into an expeditionary force (the Sixth Fleet) intended for forward deployment to the Mandates when war was imminent – in 1941 it would be based at Kwajalein in the Marshalls. With a conventional cruiser as flagship for the Vice Admiral commanding the fleet, the force would by 1941 comprise three submarine squadrons, each with two or three divisions of fleet/cruiser submarines, and each with a large submarine flagship that would exercise command and control once the squadron had deployed. The submarine flagship would be expected to use its reconnaissance aircraft to scout for the squadron, and to co-ordinate operations at sea.

The essential problem with this set-up was recognised in the rider to Paragraph 11 of the Battle Instructions. How could a submarine flagship operating in a forward area close to the enemy fleet or enemy bases be expected to transmit to other submarines without those transmissions being intercepted? Such interceptions would inevitably alert the enemy to the presence of the command submarine, and unless in secure code any transmission could give away the deployment stations of the entire squadron or patrol line. Moreover, the scouting aircraft could be used only during daylight, when a submarine operating close to enemy bases or the enemy fleet would be particularly vulnerable to anti-submarine patrols. The flawed nature of Japanese strategic and tactical thinking with regard to the deployment of its submarine arm would, in the event, be ruthlessly exposed by the Second World War.

France

Despite the French delegation's refusal at the London Conference to discuss overall tonnage limitations for categories other than those covered by the Washington Treaty (*ie* capital ships and aircraft carriers), France was a signatory to the agreement on the individual displacement and maximum gun calibre on submarines (Part II, Article 7), and to Article 22 (Part IV), which proscribed unrestricted submarine warfare on merchant shipping. It was further stated that, as a gesture of conciliation,

Due to bottlenecks in the shipyards, the final six fleet submarines of the *1,500-tonnes* type were not authorised until 1930. This is *Agosta* running her trials in July 1938. She was powered by two powerful Sulzer two-stroke diesels each rated at 4,000bhp, and had a maximum speed on the surface in excess of 20 knots. The last of these boats entered service in 1939. *(NHHC, NH 88956)*

France was also prepared to keep overall submarine tonnage within the levels currently projected. More than 82,000 tons (surfaced displacement) of submarine tonnage had been laid down or authorised since Washington, including the current 1930 tranche of the 1924 Naval Programme, and even if this figure were to be recalculated taking into account the new definition of standard displacement it remained 50 per cent higher than the overall tonnage agreed for each of the three major powers. However, the French could argue that almost 20,000 tonnes was accounted for by submarines intended purely for coastal defence and funded accordingly, whereas the United States and Japan, and to a lesser extent Great Britain, were interested only in building sea- and ocean-going submarines that could be used aggressively against enemy warships in their home waters.

In the same spirit of conciliation the French stated that no submarines would be authorised under the 1931 and 1932 Estimates. The submarines projected for these years were further fleet and coastal boats intended to bring France's overall tonnage up to its planned 96,000-tonne ceiling, so this was an important concession. However, it was one that was relatively easy to make, given the production bottlenecks that by the late 1920s were having a major impact on the ambitious French construction programmes. There had already been considerable slippage, resulting in the postponement of the entire 1928 tranche, which included the 10,000-ton cruiser *Dupleix*, the *contre-torpilleurs* of the *Vauquelin* class (see *WAW* Chapter 8) and six fleet submarines of the *1,500-tonnes* type, to the following year. Late delivery of equipment, particularly diesels, was plaguing the completion of the submarines currently on the stocks or fitting out, so the 1931–32 'submarine holiday' would be welcomed by the hard-pressed naval dockyards. Of the six 1,500-tonne boats in the 1930 tranche, none would be laid down in that year, three would be laid down in 1931, and three in 1932; it was a similar picture with the four 630-tonne boats of the *Amirauté* type (see *WAW* Chapter 9), with only *Minerve* being laid down before 1932.

There were other advantages in this hiatus in French submarine construction. France, like the other major world powers, was feeling the effects of the general depression in the world economy. In France's case there was the added complication of the major inflation of the 1920s, which had resulted not only in new submarines costing three or four times what they had in the immediate post-Washington period, but had led to further delays in construction and additional expenditure beyond that originally budgeted for when prices had to be renegotiated. Moreover, the prolonged construction periods meant that even the first *1,500-tonnes* of the 1924 *Statut Naval*, *Redoutable* and *Vengeur*, were still fitting out at the time of the London Conference – they would enter service in October and December 1931 respectively – so the enforced break would enable designs for new classes to take into account the experience with earlier boats. Finally, and perhaps most important of all, funds and manpower would be released for the design and construction of the new generation of capital ships (see Chapter 2) and the fast fleet torpedo boats needed to escort them (see Chapter 5).

The launch of the second-class submarine *Vénus* on 6 April 1935 at the Ateliers & Chantiers de la Seine-Maritime. After a period of experimentation in which the private shipyards were permitted a degree of latitude in the design of the submarines and the equipment installed, the *Marine Nationale* moved to a policy of standardisation, with the plans provided by the *Service Technique*. Four boats were authorised in 1930 and a further two in 1936. *(NHHC, NH 86125)*

This last consideration undoubtedly influenced the decision not to proceed with any further units of the *Surcouf* class. Under the terms of the London Treaty all the high contracting powers were permitted three 'oversize' submarines of more than 2,000 tons standard displacement with guns of a maximum 6.1in calibre, but although the French naval staff briefly considered modifying the two projected sisters of the *Surcouf* to conform to the new limits – they would have been armed with a twin 155mm turret derived from that of the cruisers of the *Duguay-Trouin* class – this proposal was abandoned. A design for a *sous-marin canon*, armed with either 130mm or 155mm guns in a twin turret, was drawn up as late as 1936 (design 'W'), but by this time it was being acknowledged that submarines of the 1,500-tonne type operating from Saigon would be just as effective in defending French overseas territories in the Far East.

The quest for a fast fleet submarine able to operate with and to scout for the battle fleet continued. Although the latest 1,500-tonne variants of the *Agosta* sub-group were capable of 20 knots, it was recognised that they would be able to maintain this speed for only short periods, giving them little or no margin over the existing capital ships when action was joined. Communication with surface units remained a barrier to integrating submarines tactically with the fleet. A prototype periscopic radio mast entered service, but the problem of ship-to-submarine communications was never satisfactorily resolved, so the proposed deployment of fleet submarines on the wings of the fast surface squadrons of the new *Marine Nationale* continued to be problematic. Manoeuvres in poor visibility (including night-time operations) or with the submarine at periscope depth proved hazardous in the extreme.

Following trials with the first two *1,500 tonnes* in 1932 it was reported to the Naval Staff that they were able to operate with the battle fleet in fine-weather peace-time conditions, but that in wartime there was a risk that damage would be sustained to the forward diving planes, which unlike those of their British and USN counter-parts were non-retractable. The *1,500 tonnes* were otherwise considered to have better sea-keeping qualities on the surface than the torpedo boats of the same displacement built during the 1920s. They could also dive in less than a minute and handled well when dived.

These considerations all came together in a new series of studies designated 'Z', culminating in the adoption of design Z2 in 1934–35. The new submarine, although derived from the *1,500 tonnes*, was significantly larger and faster than the *Agosta*s, and was clearly influenced by the British fleet submarines of the 'River' class, the first of which had entered service in 1932. Almost identical in length and displacement to the British boats, *Roland-Morillot* was powered by two enormous 10-cylinder Sulzer 2-stroke diesels, each rated at 6,000bhp for a maximum speed of 22–23 knots (21 knots at ¾ power).

Other improvements over the *1,500 tonnes* were largely incremental, but there were attempts to iron out some of their more obvious defects. The 400mm torpedo tubes were eliminated, giving the submarine a homogeneous armament of ten 550mm tubes (four fixed bow tubes, plus two trainable triple mountings abaft the conning tower). There were eight reserve torpedoes for the bow tubes as compared

Roland-Morillot (Fr)

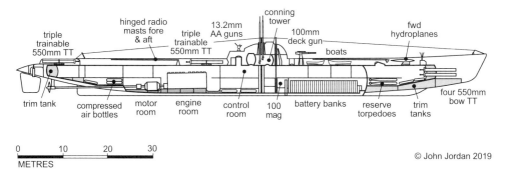

© John Jordan 2019

Roland-Morillot was the last French attempt at a fast 'fleet' submarine. The power for a designed surface speed of 23 knots was provided by two powerful 10-cylinder Sulzer 2-stroke diesels each with a nominal power rating of 6,000bhp. These submarines retained the trainable external torpedo mountings characteristic of French interwar designs, but the torpedoes carried had a uniform 550mm diameter, the earlier 400mm type having been discarded..

Table 6.5: French submarines 1930–1936

	Agosta class	Minerve class	Roland-Morillot class	Aurore class
Type:	fleet	coastal	fleet	medium patrol
Built:	six 1931–39	six 1931–39	five 1937 onwards[1]	eight 1935 onwards[2]
Displacement:	1,380tW	600tW	1,605tW	805tW
Dimensions:	92m x 8.1m	68m x 5.6m	103m x 8.3m	74m x 6.5m
Machinery:	2-shaft diesel/electric 8,000bhp/2,000hp = 20 / 10 knots	2-shaft diesel/electric; 1,800bhp/1,230hp = 14 / 9 knots	2-shaft diesel/electric; 12,000bhp/2,300hp = 22 / 9.5 knots	2-shaft diesel/electric; 3,000bhp/1,400hp = 15 / 9 knots
Range:	10,000nm at 10kts 100nm at 5kts (dived)	3,000nm at 10kts 85nm at 5kts (dived)	10,000nm at 10kts 100nm at 5kts (dived)	3,200nm at 10kts 85nm at 5kts (dived)
Armament:	9–550mm, 2–400mm TT (4B+7T; 13 torpedoes) 1 – 100mm/40	6–550mm, 3–400mm TT (4B+2S+3T: 9 torpedoes) 1 – 75mm/35	10–550mm TT (4B+6T: 18 torpedoes) 1 – 100mm/40	9 – 550mm TT (4B+5T: 11 torpedoes} 1 – 100mm/40

Notes:

[1] Only three submarines of the *Roland-Morillot* class had been laid down before the Armistice of June 1940, and the hulls were destroyed at Cherbourg with the approach of the Germans.

[2] Of the *Aurore* class only the name-ship had been completed by June 1940.

with only two in the *1,500 tonnes*. Internal fuel stowage was increased, thereby reducing the dependence on vulnerable external bunkers and giving the submarines an endurance of 10,000nm at 10 knots. Welding was adopted for the pressure hull for the first time, and the auxiliary machinery was located in a special compartment with improved access for maintenance. Improvements were made in the location of the control surfaces: the forward diving planes, which were above the surfaced water-line, were fully retractable, and the after hydroplanes were forward of the propellers. Superior sea-keeping should have resulted, enabling the submarines to maintain a high surfaced speed even in heavy seas.

The smaller counterpart of the *Roland-Morillot* was the *Aurore*, a larger, much-improved *Amirauté* type with a maximum diving depth of 100m, superior hydrody-namic features, and more powerful diesels, which gave it a designed surface speed of 15.5 knots with ¾ power. Operational radius was increased, and the armament was simplified, as in *Roland-Morillot*, by eliminating the 400mm torpedo tubes in favour of a trainable triple 550mm mounting abaft the conning tower and a trainable twin mounting above the stern. With a surfaced displacement of 860 tonnes, this was not a coastal defence boat in the traditional French tactical mould, but a medium patrol submarine capable of operating aggressively in hostile waters in the North Sea, the Mediterranean and the Adriatic.

The lead units of each of the new types were authorised in 1934, but budgetary pressures resulting from the rapid expansion of the surface fleet meant that there was to be a three-year gap in authorisations before the second *Roland-Morillot* and four further units of the *Aurore* class were authorised, together with the lead boat of an improved *Saphir*-class minelayer, the *Emeraude*.

In 1935 a new system of classification was introduced: the *sous-marins de grande patrouille* became *sous-marins de première classe*, and the *sous-marins de moyenne patrouille* became *sous-marins de deuxième classe*. The smaller French submarines were no longer regarded as a separate type intended for the less glamorous duties of coastal defence and blockade; they were now less capable versions of the first-class boats, with sea-going capabilities but with less endurance and with speed sufficient only for transit to their designated patrol areas. The first-class submarines, on the other hand, with the exception of the older and slower *Requin* class (soon to undergo a major refit and modernisation), were intended for operation with the fleet and for overseas deployment.

The pattern of submarine construction established during this period continued up to the outbreak of war, further units of the *Roland-Morillot*, *Aurore* and *Emeraude* types being authorised in 1938. However, due to the production bottlenecks already noted, which were exacerbated by industrial unrest in the dockyards and private industry from 1936 until 1938, only *Aurore* was to be completed prior to the armistice of June 1940. Many incomplete submarine hulls, including the first three units of the *Roland-Morillot* class, under construction at Cherbourg, were to be sabo-taged on the building ways; others were still incomplete at the end of the war, their construction being slowed or halted altogether for want of essential components.

Expansion in the *Regia Marina*

During the period 1922–30 the Italian Navy had laid down or completed 30,100 tonnes of submarines, a respectable figure but one that failed to match the ambitious French programme of 84,200 tonnes over the same period.

Any comparison of numbers and capabilities is complicated by the very different types of submarine the Italians opted to build. Four small cruiser-type submarines of the *Balilla* class had been completed for operations outside the Straits and a fifth, the *Fieramosca*, was fitting out; in contrast, France had only the giant *Surcouf* fitting out. There was no Italian counterpart to the thirty-one fast fleet submarines of the French *1,500-tonnes* type. Instead, the Italians had preferred to invest in sea-going patrol submarines of moderate displacement (850–950 tonnes in the surfaced condition), and had laid down and completed eighteen of these; the only French counterpart of these submarines was the slightly larger *Requin* class, of which nine had been completed during the late 1920s.

The two Italian minelayers of the *Bragadin* class had been derived from the sea-going patrol type, whereas the six French minelayers of the *Rubis* class were modified coastal boats. The small coastal type had seen a particularly heavy investment from the French, with no fewer than thirty-two boats being authorised. The *Regia Marina*, on the other hand, retained a large force of small coastal submarines from the First World War, and had only recently felt the need to begin replacing them; seven 640-tonne submarines of the *Argonauta* class (see *WAW* Chapter 9), comparable in size and capabilities to the latest French coastal submarines of the *630-tonne* and *Amirauté* types, had been authorised under the 1929 Estimates.

The new generation of submarines embarked on following the Washington Conference had not been an unqualified success. The *Regia Marina* had little experience of building large submarines, and encountered a number of technical problems with both the cruisers and the sea-going patrol boats, of which perhaps the most serious was the stability issue experienced with these double-hull (or partial double-hull) designs. Most had to be taken in hand for modifications immediately after trials, and the additional saddle tanks fitted externally to improve stability had reduced surfaced speed and endurance. The larger Italian submarines also suffered from the same machinery reliability and internal layout problems as their French counterparts. However, by 1930 many of these problems were being resolved; the two medium patrol submarines of the *Settembrini* class laid down in 1928 were particularly successful, as were the coastal submarines of the *Argonauta* class.

Whereas the other four major navies were compelled to re-evaluate their submarine building programmes after the London Conference of 1930, Italy saw no reason to change and opted for more of the same. Even the cruiser submarines of the *Balilla* and *Fieramosca* classes were well within the qualitative limits agreed at London, and overall tonnage was not an issue: following the French refusal to reduce submarine force levels below those currently projected, Italy was not bound by any overall tonnage limit.[10]

Cruiser Submarines

During the early 1930s two new types of cruiser submarine were laid down for the *Regia Marina*. The first was an experimental submarine designed by Cavallini as a cruiser/minelayer capable of operating outside the Straits. The *Pietro Micca* had an unusual 'figure 8' arrangement of the pressure hulls amidships, the smaller upper cylinder being given over to command and control while the lower cylinder housed the minelaying system; the twenty mines were laid via twin chutes on either side of the keel. This ingenious arrangement freed up the after part of the submarine for a full-sized propulsion system (the *Micca* had a designed surface speed of 15.5 knots) and two torpedo tubes, for which four reloads were provided. There were also two 120/45 deck guns, making the submarine fully effective in the conventional 'cruiser' role.

The *Micca* was the largest submarine built for the Italian Navy during the inter-war period. Her design was a success; sea-keeping qualities were good, and manoeuvrability was exceptional for a boat of this size. However, there would be no further submarines of this type because of the huge cost; it was decided that in future the *Regia Marina* would opt to build simpler submarines for the minelaying role.

The other type of cruiser built for the *Regia Marina* during the 1930s was an improved variant of the *Balilla* class (see *WAW* Chapter 9) designed, like the earlier boats, by OTO. The three submarines of the *Calvi* class were given an improved hull form with greater beam to improve stability, and the power of the propulsion machinery was reduced from 4,900bhp to 4,400bhp in order provide the necessary space and weight for two additional stern tubes and a second 120mm gun (both guns were of the newer 45-calibre model).

Although they failed to attain their designed speed of 17 knots, the *Calvi*s still proved faster than the *Balilla*s in service. And although the auxiliary diesel used for long-range cruising in the earlier boats was not installed, larger fuel bunkers ensured that the *Calvi* class had a more-than-adequate operational radius of 11,400nm at 8 knots. The large-diameter pressure hull was fully utilised to provide comfortable accommodation for the crew, with improved stowage for provisions and fresh water, giving these submarines a designed endurance of eighty days. They proved well-suited to commerce raiding, although their large size made them less handy in the confined waters of the Mediterranean.

Patrol Submarines

The primary focus of submarine construction for the *Regia Marina* during the period 1930–36 was the small coastal type derived from the 600tW *Argonauta*, of which seven had been laid down by the end of April 1930. The need to replace the war-built submarines of the Italian 'F' and 'N' classes and the Canadian-built boats of the 'H' class, while at the same time providing an effective force of modern coastal submarines as a counterweight to those being built for the French Navy, meant that a large programme was required. All would be of the Bernardis single-hull type, with a diving depth of 80m.

The twelve units of the *Sirena* class, laid down in 1931 and completed in 1933–34, were built to a modified *Argonauta* design. They had a slightly enlarged hull form and the bow was raised to improve sea-keeping; the older-model 102mm deck gun of the *Argonauta* was replaced by a 100/47 model, and there were other incremental improvements including more modern diesels and updated control systems. After a gap of four years, which corresponded with the French self-imposed submarine construction hiatus and also with the worst effects of the world recession, a further ten units of the *Perla* class were laid down, and reduced building times meant that most were completed within twelve months of the keel being laid.

By 1935, the international situation had deteriorated but more money was available. A further twenty boats of the *Adua* class were laid down in 1936–37 (three were sold to Brazil before launch). Improvements included new diesels and a modified conning tower, which now housed an MF/DF aerial at its after end. The fuel load was increased, raising endurance to a respectable 3,200nm at 10.5 knots. During the Second World War some of these boats were deployed outside the Mediterranean, where they performed remarkably well, even in a tropical climate.

Inevitably, the *Regia Marina*'s focus on building up a modern force of coastal submarines during the early 1930s meant that authorisations of large sea-going submarines were relatively few. The only units of this type laid down in the aftermath of the London Treaty were the four 970-tonne boats of the *Archimede* class. A Cavallini partial double-hull design, the *Archimede* was effectively an improved

The launch of the submarine *Anfitrite* (*Sirena* sub-group of the '600' type) at CRDA, Monfalcone, on 5 August 1933. Note the four bow 533 mm torpedo tubes; there were two further tubes astern. During the early 1930s the Italians invested heavily in coastal submarines, which were later to prove very effective in the Mediterranean. *(Maurizio Brescia collection)*

Archimede (second from the right) moored alongside other Italian large patrol submarines. A second boat of the class is on the extreme right, two submarines of the *Settembrini* class are in the centre, and there are two units of the *Mameli* class on the left; all were Cavallini/Tosi partial double-hull designs. The two deck guns of the *Archimede* class were of 100mm calibre. *(NHHC, NH 111495)*

Settembrini, with greater endurance and superior sea-keeping qualities. There was a second 100/43 deck gun and sixteen torpedoes (versus twelve). Designed specifically for ocean service, these submarines were classified *grande crociera* or *oceanica*. Two of the four would later be secretly transferred to fascist Spain.

The only other submarines of the 'oceanic' type laid down during this period were the two 1,050-tonne boats of the *Glauco* class. These were Bernardis single-hull submarines originally laid down for Portugal in 1931 but taken over by the *Regia Marina* in 1932. Like the *Archimede* class, they had a second gun and good endurance, and they proved so successful in service that the design formed the basis of the *Marcello* class that was ordered in numbers for the *Regia Marina* in 1936.

Also ordered for Portugal at the same time were the two smaller 780-tonne sea-going boats of the *Argo* class. Following the cancellation of the contract the *Regia Marina* took it over in 1935 and the two submarines were completed in 1937. This CRDA partial double-hull type proved particularly successful, and despite the relatively small size of the *Argo*s their impressive endurance (10,200nm at 8.5 knots) led to subsequent deployments in both the Red Sea and the Atlantic.

When submarine construction for the *Regia Marina* resumed in earnest in the mid-1930s, three submarines of the *Brin* class were authorised in 1936, with a further two units authorised the following year to replace the submarines transferred to Spain. Although derived from the *Archimede* class, they had a finer hull, giving them a slightly higher surfaced speed for the same horsepower. Only a single 100/43

Table 6.6: Italian Submarines 1930–1936

	Micca	Calvi class	Archimede class	Sirena class[1]	Foca class
Type:	cruiser	cruiser	medium patrol	coastal	minelayer
Built:	1931–35	three 1932–36	four 1931–35	twelve 1931–34	three 1936–39
Displacement:	1,570mt surfaced[1]	1,550mt surfaced	985mt surfaced	680mt surfaced	1,320mt surfaced
Dimensions:	90m × 7.7m	84m × 7.7m	71m × 6.9m	60m × 6.5m	83m × 7.2m
Machinery:	2-shaft diesel/electric; 3,000bhp/1,500hp = 15.5 / 8.5 knots	2-shaft diesel/electric; 4,400bhp/1,800hp = 17 / 8 knots	2-shaft diesel/electric; 3,000bhp/1,100hp = 17 / 7.5 knots	2-shaft diesel/electric; 1,350bhp/800hp = 14 / 7.5 knots	2-shaft diesel/electric; 3,000bhp/1,300hp = 16 / 8 knots
Range	6,400nm at 9kts 60nm at 4kts (dived)	11,400nm at 8kts 120nm at 3kts (dived)	10,300nm at 8kts 105nm at 3kts (dived)	4,800nm at 8.5kts 72nm at 4kts (dived)	7,800nm at 8kts 120nm at 3kts (dived)
Armament	6 – 533mm TT (4B+2S: 10 torpedoes) 2 – 120mm/45 (2 × 1) 20 mines	8 – 533mm TT (4B+4S: 16 torpedoes) 2 – 120mm/45 (2 × 1)	8 – 533mm TT (4B+4S: 12 torpedoes) 2 – 100mm/43 (2 × 1)	6 – 533mm TT (4B+2S: 6 torpedoes) 1 – 100mm/47	6 – 533mm TT (4B+2S: 8 torpedoes) 1 – 100mm/43 36 mines

Notes:
1 Figures for Washington standard displacement are not available, and were perhaps not calculated. The fuel tanks of the *Calvi* class had a capacity of 250 metric tons. Assuming a figure of 75mt for lube oil and fresh water, standard displacement of these submarines would have been 1,325 metric tons (1,305tW).
2 The *Sirena* class was followed by ten nearly identical boats of the *Perla* class (built 1935–36) and twenty repeat boats of the *Adua* class (1936–38).

Italian Submarines 1930–1936

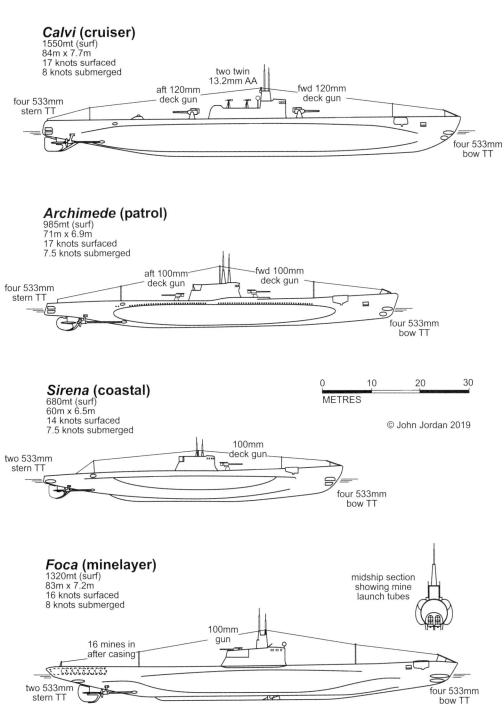

Calvi (cruiser)
1550mt (surf)
84m x 7.7m
17 knots surfaced
8 knots submerged

two twin 13.2mm AA

aft 120mm deck gun

fwd 120mm deck gun

four 533mm stern TT

four 533mm bow TT

Archimede (patrol)
985mt (surf)
71m x 6.9m
17 knots surfaced
7.5 knots submerged

aft 100mm deck gun

fwd 100mm deck gun

four 533mm stern TT

four 533mm bow TT

Sirena (coastal)
680mt (surf)
60m x 6.5m
14 knots surfaced
7.5 knots submerged

100mm deck gun

two 533mm stern TT

four 533mm bow TT

0 10 20 30
METRES

© John Jordan 2019

Foca (minelayer)
1320mt (surf)
83m x 7.2m
16 knots surfaced
8 knots submerged

midship section showing mine launch tubes

100mm gun

16 mines in after casing

two 533mm stern TT

four 533mm bow TT

vertical launch tubes for 20 mines

gun was retained, and this was now located atop the after end of a much-enlarged conning tower. This measure, taken together with the reduced beam, had the unfortunate effect of reducing stability, and even following modifications these boats were less successful in service than their predecessors.

Minelayers

Having decided that the large submarine cruiser/minelayer *Micca* was far too costly to repeat, the *Regia Marina* opted for a smaller specialised minelaying submarine derived from the *Marcello* class. The pressure-tight central minelaying cylinder of the *Micca*, with two vertical launch-tubes set into the keel amidships, was fitted in the lower half of the large-diameter pressure hull; capacity was twenty mines. The number of after torpedo tubes was reduced from four in the *Marcellos* to two, and two free-flooding horizontal mine tubes, each containing a further eight mines, were located side by side in the upper part of the casing.

The result was a substantial increase in the number of mines carried (thirty-six as compared with only twenty in the larger *Micca*), albeit at the expense of two torpedo tubes and the after reloads. The sixteen mines carried in the free-flooding after casing were also subject to corrosion and could not be reset during transit, thereby making the additional cost and complexity of the internal minelaying system difficult to justify. Like the contemporary oceanic submarines of the *Brin* class, the single

The Italian submarine *Otaria*, one of two boats (*Glauco* class) ordered for Portugal and laid down in 1931 but completed for the *Regia Marina* in 1935–36. Of the Bernardis single-hull type, they were otherwise similar in size and capabilities to *Archimede* and mounted two 100mm deck guns. *(Erminio Bagnasco collection)*

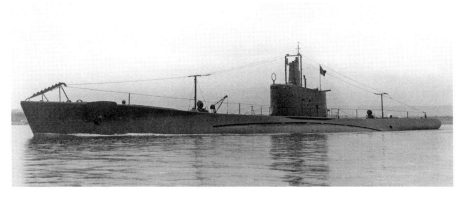

The Italian submarine *Zoea* in the spring of 1938, soon after commissioning. The three large minelayers of the *Foca* class (*Atropo*, *Foca* and *Zoea*) were partial double-hull boats of the Cavallini type, fitted with a central compartment from which 20 twenty mines were laid vertically and with two horizontal tubes in the stern, each capable of stowing a further eight mines. In addition, the *Foca* class were armed with six 533mm bow torpedo tubes. The 100mm gun was later relocated to the deck casing forward of the conning tower. *(Erminio Bagnasco collection)*

100/43 gun was initially mounted atop the after end of the conning tower; this arrangement proved equally unsatisfactory, and the gun was later to moved to the casing forward of the conning tower. Three units of the *Foca* class were laid down in 1936 and 1937, and these would be the last minelaying submarines built for the *Regia Marina*.

Conclusions

The impact of the London Treaty on the three major naval powers was considerable; its impact on France and Italy, whose delegations refused to take part in any agreement on overall tonnage limits, was negligible. The French agreed to suspend the construction of submarines over the next two years as a conciliatory gesture, but declined to reduce overall submarine tonnage below current levels that, even after recalculation to take into account the new definition of standard displacement, were at least 50 per cent greater than the 52,700-ton figure limit agreed by Great Britain, the United States and Japan. Even had France not offered this voluntary hiatus, submarine construction for the *Marine Nationale* during the early 1930s would have been stymied by production bottlenecks in the shipyards and the collapse of the French economy.

Italy had failed to keep pace with the French submarine programmes of the 1920s; the *Regia Marina* therefore had plenty of room for further expansion before it reached the magical 52,700-ton figure. The Italians would be equally affected by world economic problems during the early 1930s, but from 1934–36 would embark on a major submarine construction programme that aimed to establish parity with France. The submarines of the new programme would benefit from remarkably short construction times: generally little more than a year for the smaller coastal submarines, eighteen months for the ocean-going boats. By contrast, French

Table 6.7: Submarine Authorisations 1930–1936

Programme	Great Britain	USA	Japan	France	Italy
1930	1 *Porpoise* (1931–33) 2 'S' (1931–33)			6 *1,500-tonnes* (1931–39) 4 *Minerve* (1931–36) 1 *Saphir* (1931–36)	1 *Micca* (1931–35) 3 *Calvi* (1932–36) 4 *Archimede* (1931–35) 12 *Sirena* (1931–34)
1931	1 *Thames* (1933–35) 2 'S' (1933–34)	V8–9 (1931–34)	1 J2 (1932–35) 6 KD6A (1931–37) 2 K5 (1933–37)		
1932	1 *Thames* (1933–35) 2 'S' (1933–35)				(2 *Glauco*: 1931–35)
1933	2 *Porpoise* (1934–37) 1 'S' (1934–36)				
1934	1 *Porpoise* (1935–37) 2 'S' (1935–37)	4 *Porpoise* (1933–36)	2 J3 (1934–38) 2 KD6B (1934–38)	*Roland-Morillot* (1937–) *Aurore* (1935–40)	2 *Foca* (1936–38)
1935	1 *Porpoise* (1936–38) 1 'T' (1936–38) 1 'S' (1936–38)	6 *Perch* (1935–37)			10 *Perla* (1935–36)
1936	1 *Porpoise* (1936–39) 4 'T' (1936–39) 3 'U' (1937–38)	6 *Salmon* (1936–38)		2 *Minerve* (1936–39)	9 *Marcello* (1937–38) 3 *Brin* (1936–38) (2 *Argo*: 1935–37) 20 *Adua* (1936–38) 1 *Foca* (1937–39)
Total	7 Large 10 Medium 3 Small **6 M/L**	18 Large	11 Large 2 Medium	7 Large 1 Medium 6 Small 1 M/L	4 Large 16 +4 Medium 42 Small **3 M/L**

submarines of the new generation authorised in 1934 were still on the stocks when war broke out in September 1939, and the incomplete hulls of the large fleet submarines of the *Roland-Morillot* class were scuttled on the slipways at Cherbourg when the Germans captured the port in June 1940.

The Imperial Japanese Navy was angered by the constraints on overall tonnage imposed by Part III of the London Treaty. Having embarked on the construction of a powerful fleet of large submarines as a specific counterweight to the US Navy's numerically superior battle fleet, the Japanese felt overwhelmingly frustrated that they had again been painted into a corner by the two major Anglo-Saxon powers. However, beyond the premature retirement of a handful of obsolescent small submarines and the imposition of tight standard displacement margins on the new classes of submarine to be built under the 1931 Programme, the IJN seems to have made little effort to adhere to the 52,700-ton limit due to come into force by 31 December 1936. The production of large fleet- and cruiser-type submarines similar in size and capabilities to those built during the 1920s continued unabated throughout the London Treaty period, and older, smaller boats that should have been discarded were retained.[11]

The British Royal Navy had three new submarine designs recently approved at the time of the London Conference, and the first exemplars of two of these – the large fleet submarines of the 'River' class and the medium patrol submarines of the 'S' class – had already been authorised under the 1929 Estimates. All three of the new types were comfortably within the limits established for unit displacement and gun calibre by the London Treaty, which had to take into account the larger American and Japanese boats designed for long-range operations in the Pacific. However, the Royal Navy was now compelled to face up to the dynamic between the qualitative and the quantitative restrictions; opting to build large submarines in numbers would inevitably restrict the numerical size of Britain's submarine fleet, and with a far-flung empire to protect the same issue inevitably arose as in the cruiser category of surface warships. There can be little doubt that the overall quantitative restrictions embodied in the London Treaty hastened the demise of the large fleet submarines of the 'River' class, construction of which was prematurely terminated after only three units had been authorised. They also encouraged a trend towards a reduction in the unit displacement of the new generation of submarines authorised from the mid-1930s. The standard displacement of the new overseas patrol submarines of the 'T' class was 1,090 tons; this compared with 1,475 tons for the earlier overseas patrol submarines of the 'O', 'P' and 'R' classes (a reduction of 26 per cent), and 1,800 tons for the 'Rivers' (a reduction of 40 per cent).

There can be little doubt, however, that the major impact of the London Treaty was felt by the US Navy, which up to this point had been pursuing a programme of very large submarine cruisers and minelayers that approached 3,000 tons in their surfaced displacement. Due to the cost and complexity of these giant submarines, only three had so far been authorised by Congress, and construction time was similar to that for a large surface warship. The exceptions to the new qualitative limits on submarine size and gun calibre in Article 7 of the London Treaty had to be framed to take account of them. This programme was now at an end, and the US Navy would have to rethink its submarine strategy and come up with a new design with trans-Pacific operational capabilities that was small enough to be built in the required numbers. After an abortive attempt at a 1,120-ton design (*Cachalot* and *Cuttlefish*), which proved too small and cramped for trans-Pacific operations, the US Navy would settle on a submarine of 1,320 tons with diesel-electric drive, using lightweight, high-speed diesels derived from railroad models, which would become the basis of the mass-produced war-built 'fleet boats' of the *Gato*, *Balao* and *Tench* classes. Once again the US Navy would prove the benefits of harnessing technical innovation to the resolution of strategic problems.

Chapter 7

SMALL COMBATANTS AND AUXILIARY VESSELS

O NE OF THE PROBLEMS with extending the two categories of warship subject to quantitative and qualitative limitation covered by the original Washington Treaty (Capital Ships and Aircraft Carriers) to five in the London Treaty was that there remained a host of other miscellaneous vessels that varied in shape, size and purpose according to national preference and which fell outside these categories. While the primary focus of the naval arms limitation treaties was on 'fleets' and 'fleet units', it was felt important that at least qualitative constraints should be imposed on these vessels in order to prevent any of the five powers from circumventing the London Treaty by exploiting any legal loophole. The other benefit of formally recognising categories of vessel that could be built legitimately outside the quantitative limits imposed on the other, more closely defined categories was that this would go some way towards recognising the 'special' requirements of powers with large empires to police.

For Britain this meant an opportunity to build large numbers of anti-submarine sloops and ocean-going minesweepers for convoy escort while retaining fleet parity with the United States. Britain also hoped that the establishment of a new and unlimited 'auxiliary' category would persuade France, with extensive imperial and colonial interests that reinforced its claims for special treatment, to accept fleet parity with the Italians. Both the Americans and the Italians had overseas interests for which locally based gunboats and other ancillary craft would be of value, and the Japanese needed craft to protect their home waters and sea communications with their interests on the Asian mainland. Moreover, the US Navy strategy of an 'expeditionary' fleet that needed to cross the Pacific in order to protect its legitimate interests required the construction of large numbers of support ships to provide base and repair facilities for destroyers and submarines, fuel and stores for the battle fleet itself, and transports for troops deployed overseas.

The sheer variety of the types of warship to be covered by this new 'treaty-exempt' category initially posed a problem, but this was quickly resolved by dividing it into three distinct sub-categories: 'coastal' combatants too small to operate with the fleet;

medium-sized warships for the defence of overseas territories or the trade routes; and large auxiliary craft (generally based on mercantile types, although often armed, manned by naval crews and built to naval standards) intended to support the fleet.

All five of the major powers had completed ships in this auxiliary, 'non-fleet' category during the period 1918 to 1930, and these had to be taken into account in the framing of the qualitative limitations, which were outlined under Article 8 of the Treaty. At the same time it was considered that if all previous developments were 'legitimised' this would be responsible for an escalatory trend similar to that which ensued following the establishment of a 10,000 ton/8in gun qualitative limit for 'auxiliary vessels' at Washington in 1922. The agreed constraints were therefore accompanied by a listing, by country, of existing ships that fell within the broad ambit of one of the three sub-categories in terms of their function, but which breached the new qualitative limits in any one respect (Annex III 'Special Vessels'). It was anticipated that once these vessels became due for replacement they would be replaced either by ships within the treaty-limited categories (Aircraft Carriers, Cruisers, etc) and which would count against that navy's tonnage allocation, or by vessels that conformed to the limits agreed for the 'treaty-exempt' category.

Article 8 of the London Treaty of 1930 defined the three sub-categories as follows:

(a) Naval surface combatant vessels of 600 tons (610 metric tons) standard displacement and under.

(b) Naval surface combatant vessels exceeding 600 tons (610 metric tons), but not exceeding 2,000 tons (2,032 metric tons) standard displacement, provided they have none of the following characteristics:

– Mount a gun above 6.1 inch (155 mm) calibre.
– Mount more than four guns above 3 inch (76 mm) calibre.
– Are designed or fitted to launch torpedoes.
– Are designed for a speed greater than twenty knots.

(c) Naval surface vessels not specifically built as fighting ships which are employed on fleet duties or as troop transports or in some other way than as fighting ships, provided they have none of the following characteristics:

– Mount a gun above 6.1 inch (155 mm) calibre.
– Mount more than four guns above 3 inch (76 mm) calibre.
– Are designed or fitted to launch torpedoes.
– Are designed for a speed greater than twenty knots.
– Are protected by armour plate.
– Are designed or fitted to launch mines.
– Are fitted to receive aircraft on board from the air.
– Mount more than one aircraft-launching apparatus on the centre line; or two, one on each broadside.

– If fitted with any means of launching aircraft into the air, are designed or adapted to operate at sea more than three aircraft.

Sub-category (a) imposed no qualitative restrictions whatsoever other than displacement. It therefore covered coastal torpedo boats, small gunboats, coastal and inshore minesweepers, MTBs, etc. These were all considered legitimate weapons of self-defence; they were too small to operate effectively on the high seas, and could therefore not be used to threaten or coerce another power.

Sub-category (b) was intended to provide for larger gunboats, (slow) coastal minelayers and convoy escort ships. These could displace up to 2,000 tons and could carry up to four guns of 6.1in/155mm calibre. However, they were not permitted to carry torpedoes, and maximum speed was 20 knots. Although in terms of their displacement they were capable of oceanic operations, they were not 'fleet' units, and could be employed only for defensive purposes: for policing a power's overseas possessions, and to protect its ports or its sea lines of communication. Minelayers deemed capable of offensive operations in hostile waters were specifically excluded by the speed limitation; these operations would have to be performed by ships in the categories subject to quantitative and qualitative limits (*ie* Cruisers and Destroyers).

Sub-category (c) embraced all types of armed naval auxiliary. There was no limit on displacement, but the rules applied to sub-category (b) naval combatant vessels also applied to these ships. It was made equally clear that mercantile-type vessels could not be adapted either for minelaying or as ancillary aircraft carriers. Even seaplane carriers or tenders were restricted to carrying a maximum of three aircraft, to be launched by one or two catapults; more capable ships would have to be classified as 'aircraft carriers' and be counted against that particular allocation.

The existing ships listed under Annex III because they breached the above rules were a very mixed bunch (see Table 7.1 for a full listing). The newly defined category effectively prohibited large minelayers, and these featured strongly in the listings. However, with the sole exception of the purpose-built British cruiser/minelayer *Adventure*, completed in 1927, they were conversions of merchant ships or of elderly armoured or protected cruisers. In view of this the Japanese insisted on being permitted to replace their two elderly minelaying cruisers, *Aso* and *Tokiwa*, both of which dated from the turn of the century, before 31 December 1936, and this was duly acknowledged in Article 12 of the London Treaty.

Three existing seaplane carriers – one for the British Commonwealth of Nations, one for Italy and the French *Commandant Teste* – were also inscribed, as were a number of 15in-gun monitors in service with the navies of Britain and Italy. Several large US Navy auxiliary vessels had to be 'declared' simply because of their large gun armament of eight 5in guns, and the British listed the newly completed submarine depot ship *Medway* for similar reasons. Most of the remaining units were sloops, gunboats or yachts that exceeded either the tonnage limitation (600/2,000tW) or the speed limitation (20 knots).

Table 7.1: **Special Vessels Listed in Annex III**

UNITED STATES

Name & Type of Vessel	Displacement
Aroostook – Minelayer	4,950 tons
Oglala – Minelayer	4,950 tons
Baltimore – Minelayer	4,413 tons
San Francisco – Minelayer	4,083 tons
Cheyenne – Monitor	2,800 tons
Helena – Gunboat	1,392 tons
Isabel – Yacht	938 tons
Niagara – Yacht	2,600 tons
Bridgeport – Destroyer Tender	11,750 tons
Dobbin – Destroyer Tender	12,450 tons
Melville – Destroyer Tender	7,150 tons
Whitney – Destroyer Tender	12,450 tons
Holland – Submarine Tender	11,570 tons
Henderson – Naval Transport	10,000 tons
Total	**91,496 tons**

FRANCE

Name & Type of Vessel	Displacement
Castor – Minelayer	3,150 tons
Pollux – Minelayer	2,461 tons
Cmdt Teste – Seaplane Carrier	10,000 tons
Aisne – Despatch Vessel	600 tons
Marne – Despatch Vessel	600 tons
Ancre – Despatch Vessel	604 tons
Scarpe – Despatch Vessel	604 tons
Suippe – Despatch Vessel	604 tons
Dunkerque – Despatch Vessel	644 tons
Laflaux – Despatch Vessel	644 tons
Bapaume – Despatch Vessel	644 tons
Nancy – Despatch Vessel	644 tons
Calais – Despatch Vessel	644 tons
Lassigny – Despatch Vessel	644 tons
Les Eparges – Despatch Vessel	644 tons
Remiremont – Despatch Vessel	644 tons
Tahure – Despatch Vessel	644 tons
Toul – Despatch Vessel	644 tons
Epinal – Despatch Vessel	644 tons
Liévin – Despatch Vessel	644 tons
(–) – Netlayer*	2,293 tons
Total	**28,644 tons**

* To be named *Le Gladiateur*

Two interesting observations emerge from a detailed analysis of these lists. The first is that the total tonnage declared by the US Navy (91,496 tons – more than twice the British total of 49,561 tons) is inflated by the use of gross tonnage for the six fleet auxiliary vessels in preference to 'standard' tonnage; figures for the latter appear to have been calculated only after the London Treaty. Thus the Destroyer Tender *Dobbin* is registered at 12,450 tons, whereas subsequent published figures give standard displacement as only 8,325 tons.

BRITISH COMMONWEALTH OF NATIONS

Name & Type of Vessel	Displacement
Adventure – Minelayer (UK)	6,740 tons
Albatross – Seaplane Carrier (Aus)	5,000 tons
Erebus – Monitor (UK)	7,200 tons
Terror – Monitor (UK)	7,200 tons
Marshal Soult – Monitor (UK)	6,400 tons
Clive – Sloop (Ind)	2,021 tons
Medway – Submarine Depot Ship (UK)	15,000 tons
Total	**49,561 tons**

ITALY

Name & Type of Vessel	Displacement
Miraglia – Seaplane Carrier	4,880 tons
Faà di Bruno – Monitor	2,800 tons
Monte Grappa – Monitor	605 tons
Montello – Monitor	605 tons
Monte Cengio – ex-Monitor	500 tons
Monte Novegno – ex-Monitor	500 tons
Campania – Sloop	2,070 tons
Total	**11,960 tons**

JAPAN

Name & Type of Vessel	Displacement
Aso – Minelayer	7,180 tons
Tokiwa – Minelayer	9,240 tons
Asama – Old Cruiser	9,240 tons
Yakumo – Old Cruiser	9,010 tons
Izumo – Old Cruiser	9,180 tons
Iwate– Old Cruiser	9,180 tons
Kasuga – Old Cruiser	7,080 tons
Yodo – Gunboat	1,320 tons
Total	**61,430 tons**

The second surprising feature of the listings is the named vessels on the French list. The latter included no fewer than seventeen sloops of around 600 tons; all fell comfortably within sub-categories (a) and (b), so there was no compelling reason for them to be listed. On the other hand, the list omits the minelaying cruiser *Pluton,* a smaller version of the British *Adventure,* and which would now (in theory at least) have to count under France's light cruiser allocation. These anomalies suggest that the French delegation had little interest in the details of this submission because they had no intention of submitting to any quantitative limits on warship categories other than for capital ships and aircraft carriers, in which case the exclusion of *Pluton* from the list had little relevance.

It was intended from the outset that Article 8 would give the five Washington powers *carte blanche* to build the ships that best met their broader, and more parochial, international security obligations outside the five 'fleet' categories of warship. It is therefore unsurprising that the five navies concerned opted to build quite different types of vessel within this 'treaty-exempt' category.

The Seaplane Carriers of the 1920s

The list of 'Special Vessels' that were exempted from the qualitative limitations of the London Treaty included three 'seaplane carriers'. The French *Commandant Teste*, designed to operate a squadron of large amphibian torpedo bombers in addition to her lighter reconnaissance floatplanes, has been described in *Warships After Washington* Chapter 7 in the context of the post-Washington aircraft carrier programme of the *Marine Nationale*. The other two ships, more traditional in conception, were the Royal Australian Navy's *Albatross* and the Italian *Giuseppe Miraglia*, both of which were completed during the late 1920s.

The 4,800-ton *Albatross* was built from the keel up by the Cockatoo Dockyard, Sydney. Laid down in May 1926, she entered service in January 1929, twelve months

HMAS *Albatross* in Port Phillip Bay during her one and only commission as an Australian warship, 1929–33. Built at the Cockatoo dockyard, Sydney, she would be transferred to the Royal Navy as part-payment for the three cruisers of the Modified *Leander* class. *(Allan C Green collection, State Library of Victoria)*

The seaplane carrier *Giuseppe Miraglia* leaves the naval base at Taranto in 1935. The Hein Mat device is clearly visible above the stern, while the two seaplanes on the after catapult are Macchi M. 18 AR with folding wings. *(INHO)*

before the opening of the London Naval Conference. She had an unusual configuration, with the hangar built into a prominent raised forecastle and the machinery aft. There was a single catapult driven by compressed air forward atop the hangar, which had sufficient space for nine seaplanes; initially *Albatross* operated six Seagull spotter/reconnaissance aircraft. Maximum speed was 21 knots and the ship was armed with four single 4.7in QF high-angle guns – the same model fitted in the battleships of the *Nelson* class and the converted carriers *Courageous* and *Glorious*.

Table 7.2: **Seaplane Carriers**

	Albatross (Aus/GB)	*Giuseppe Miraglia* (It)
Built:	1926–28	converted 1924–27
Displacement:	4,800tW	4,880tW
Dimensions:	444ft × 61ft (135m × 18.6m)	121m × 15m
Machinery:	4 Yarrow boilers; 2-shaft geared turbines, 12,000shp = 21kts	8 Yarrow boilers; 2-shaft geared turbines, 16,700shp = 21kts
Armament:	4 – 4.7in/40 HA (4 × 1) 4 – 2pdr (4 × 1) 9 floatplanes	4 – 102mm/35 HA (4 × 1) 11 (+6) floatplanes

The Italian *Giuseppe Miraglia* was a former merchant ship (the *Citte di Messina*) converted from 1924 to 1927 at La Spezia. Although similar in overall dimensions and displacement to *Albatross*, she had a very different configuration and could accommodate twice the number of aircraft. A broad hangar was constructed atop the original hull amidships, the hangar roof was extended fore and aft to form a double-ended 'flight deck', and there were fixed catapults above the bow and stern. One of the more ingenious aspects of the design was the arrangement made for recovery of the aircraft: doors in the upper sides of the hull fore and aft gave direct access to the hangar deck, the aircraft being lifted aboard by hinged cranes mounted above the doors.

The *Miraglia* was designed to operate eleven seaplanes, and carried a further six aircraft broken down. Like *Albatross*, she was driven by steam turbines for a maximum speed of 21 knots, and she was armed with four 102mm guns for self-defence.

Unlike the French *Commandant Teste,* both these ships were designed primarily to provide long-range reconnaissance and spotting for squadrons of surface ships while operating at sea; *Albatross* was designed to support Australian cruisers operating in the South Pacific, and the *Miraglia* was to have a similar function in support of the Italian battle fleet in the Mediterranean. As more and more cruisers equipped with their own reconnaissance floatplanes entered service the importance of the seaplane carriers declined; their relatively low speed limited their value for fleet air reconnaissance, particularly with the advent of the 28/30-knot battleship during the late 1930s. Only the Japanese would persist with the seaplane carrier as a fleet vessel after the London Conference, but the two ships of the *Chitose* class (see below) would be much faster ships, easily capable of keeping station with the battle fleet.

Escort Vessels for the Royal Navy

During the late 1920s Britain had embarked on the construction of a series of 'sloops' based on the 'Flower' class of the First World War and intended for foreign

The sloops *Sandwich* (nearer the camera) and *Bridgewater* at Port Said en route to the Far East in September 1929. Beyond them is the survey ship *Ormonde. (Leo van Ginderen collection)*

Yarra, one of four Australian sloops of the *Grimsby* class built at the Cockatoo dockyard, fitting out at Sydney in late 1935. The Australian ships were armed with 4in HA guns in place of the 4.7in low-angle guns of the earlier British units of the class. *(Conrad Waters collection)*

service. Two ships of the *Bridgewater* class were authorised under the 1927–28 Estimates, followed by four similar ships of the *Hastings* class under the 1928–29 Estimates and eight improved ships of the *Shoreham* class under the 1929–30 and 1930–31 Estimates. Two modified units of the *Hastings* class were also built for India.

All sixteen of these ships displaced just over 1,000 tons; they were capable of a maximum speed of 16.5 knots, which enabled them to keep company with the fastest mercantile cargo vessels, and were fitted for minesweeping. Armament comprised two single 4in guns in open mountings,[1] one or both of which was capable of HA fire, and in wartime they would have been fitted for anti-submarine warfare.

The London Treaty had no impact on this programme, as the British sloops fell well within the qualitative limits imposed by sub-category (b). From 1931 to 1934 eight units of a new type, the *Grimsby* class, would be authorised, together with four for the Royal Australian Navy. Although slightly smaller than the earlier types, they would carry a heavier gun armament for the convoy escort role: two single 4.7in guns in shielded mountings and a single 3in HA gun. Several of these ships were fitted with a uniform armament of three 4in HA guns, and the last-built, *Fleetwood*, would introduce the twin 4in HA mounting fitted in later sloops.

The final class of sloop authorised for the Royal Navy during the Washington Treaty period was the three-ship *Bittern* class, of which the first, *Enchantress* (authorised 1933), was completed as Admiralty yacht with an armament similar to the *Grimsby* class, and the second, *Stork* (authorised 1934), as an unarmed survey vessel. Shaft horsepower was increased from 2,000shp to 3,300shp for a maximum speed of almost 19 knots. The third ship, *Bittern* (authorised 1935), became the prototype for a long and particularly successful series of convoy escort sloops with well-developed anti-submarine and air defence capabilities. The first British sloop to be built around Asdic, *Bittern* was armed with three twin 4in HA mountings (two forward and one aft) plus depth charge racks and throwers.[2]

Close contemporaries of the *Bittern*-class sloops were the six small patrol vessels of the *Kingfisher* class, of which the first was authorised under the 1933 Estimates with the others ordered in 1934–36. Like *Bittern*, these ships were also designed around Asdic, and their depth charge racks could accommodate thirty to sixty depth charges. However, they were significantly smaller – only just over 500 tons standard – and were intended for coastal escort work, in which role they replaced the P and PC gunboats of the First World War. Maximum speed was 20 knots, but there was only a single 4in gun for self-defence.

The third element in the First World War triad of British escort and patrol vessels was the 'Hunt'-class minesweeper, which had proved to be a useful all-purpose vessel whose size and endurance made it well-suited to the ocean escort role. Many had been built, but by the 1930s all except the later units were on their last legs and in need of replacement. The *Halcyon*-class minesweepers, the first pair of which was authorised under the 1931 Estimates, was essentially an updated 'Hunt', with a standard displacement of 800 tons and an armament of two single 4in guns in shielded mountings, of which one (later both) was capable of anti-aircraft fire. Early ships were unusual in having three-cylinder VC or VTE triple-expansion engines, while steam turbine machinery was adopted for the later units; speed was similar to that of the larger contemporary sloops, 16.5 knots. Twenty-one ships of the *Halcyon* class would eventually be built at the rate of two to four per year, of which five would initially be completed as survey ships.

Depot Ships

The new strategic situation after Washington, in which Japan was a potential adversary rather than an ally, compelled Britain to focus on the logistics of fighting a major war in the Pacific. During the mid-1920s it was decided to develop an operational base at Singapore, but it would be many years before this would be completed, and even then it would be difficult to provide the scale of logistical support necessary for the deployment of an entire battle fleet. When the first batch of Overseas Patrol Submarines of the 'O' class was authorised in 1926–27, the same Estimates included a large Submarine Depot Ship, subsequently named *Medway*, to provide support for them. At the same time, a large Fleet Repair Ship, *Resource*, was ordered. It was envisaged that a second, smaller Submarine Depot Ship, *Maidstone*, would be built under the 1928–29 Estimates, but the latter was delayed by the budgetary crisis and was finally cancelled in 1929.

The submarine depot ship HMS *Medway* at Hong Kong in 1931, with four of the overseas patrol submarines (OPS) alongside.

It was ships such as these that sub-category (c) of Article 8 was designed to embrace: large auxiliary armed warships with a primary role of fleet support. The Submarine Depot Ship *Medway*, which was completed just before the London Conference in September 1929, displaced 14,650 tons, was propelled by diesels at a maximum speed of 15.5 knots,[3] and was armed with two single 4in low-angle guns and four single 4in HA guns. She was designed to be a base ship for eighteen over-seas patrol submarines of the 'O'/'P'/'R' classes in peacetime and twenty-one in wartime. In addition to her own fuel oil she had additional tank capacity for 1,880 tons of diesel for the submarines in her care (the tanks of each OPS held 160 tons), and carried no fewer than 144 21in torpedo reloads and three spare 4in/40 QF submarine deck guns in her holds and magazines.

Medway, unlike the ex-mercantile 'tenders' previously in service with the Royal Navy and the other major navies, was purpose-built to full military specifications, and could not therefore be replicated under the London Treaty of 1930. She had internal bulges similar to those in the battleships of the contemporary *Nelson* class, and had the same liquid-loaded underwater protection system, with a mix of void and water-filled compartments – the weight of water was 1,375 tons – backed up by a 1.5in torpedo bulkhead that was 13ft inboard of the outer hull plating amidships. The upper deck was reinforced by 1.5in plating over the holds and magazines. The ship had extensive accommodation for the crews of the submarines, and workshops included a foundry, a machine shop, a plate shop, a torpedo shop, a plumbers' shop and a smithy.

In service the ship was found to roll excessively (42 degrees was recorded) due to excessive metacentric height (GM), and the depth of the bilge keels – originally restricted to 12in (0.3m) to avoid damage to submarines alongside – was subsequently increased to 36in (0.9m). *Medway* served throughout the 1930s as submarine depot ship for the China Station.

The Fleet Repair Ship *Resource* was equally impressive. She was only slightly smaller than *Medway*, and had a similar hull and protection system; geared steam turbines gave her an identical speed of 15.5 knots, and she was likewise armed with four single 4in HA guns. She could be distinguished externally from *Medway* by the heavy-lift crane forward of her bridge and the less extensive accommodation structures, but the main differences were internal, with a much greater emphasis on maintenance and repair shops. There was extensive stowage for spare parts, and additional oil fuel capacity of 350 tons to top up the tanks of smaller vessels when they were alongside for maintenance. *Resource* operated mainly in the Mediterranean after her completion in 1930.

Following the London Treaty of 1930, the trend was towards smaller depot ships of 8,000–9,000 tons. The Destroyer Depot Ship *Woolwich*, authorised under the 1932 Estimates, displaced 8,750 tons. She had no special anti-torpedo protection, but had 1in plating over her machinery and 2in plating over her magazines, and was armed with four single 4in HA guns. She could stow seventy-two 21in destroyer torpedoes and 200 depth charges, and the customary complement of workshops was enhanced by what was described at the time as 'a full outfit of machine tools of the latest type'.

Woolwich would be followed by the Submarine Depot Ship *Maidstone,* authorised under the 1935 Estimates and completed in May 1938. Similar in size and overall dimensions, the latter would be distinguished by her much-enhanced anti-aircraft capabilities, comprising four twin 4.5in DP guns and two quadruple 2pdr pom-poms.[4] This would set the pattern for further submarine/destroyer depot ships authorised under the 1937 Estimates. The trend towards a greater number of specialised depot, maintenance and repair ships would be reinforced by the increasing complexity of the weapons and electronic systems being fitted in submarines and flotilla craft of the mid/late-1930s, together with the need for large-scale Royal Navy deployments to the Mediterranean, the Indian Ocean and the Pacific in a rapidly deteriorating international situation.

Defending France and the Empire

The other major Washington power with extensive imperial commitments overseas was France. *La France d'outre-mer* stretched from the Caribbean to the South Pacific, and it was the perceived need to police these overseas territories that was at the root of the French refusal to accept parity with Italy. A study emanating from the Ministère de la Marine in 1930 that was used by the Navy Minister Georges Leygues to put the Navy's case to the French Foreign Office gave comparative figures as follows:

	France	Italy
Length of national coastline:	4,300km	4,000km
Length of colonial coastlines:	30,000km	9,860km
Area of colonial empire:	11m km²	1m km²
Population of colonies:	60m	1.8m
Length of sea lanes:	63,000km	9,000km
Value of maritime traffic:	83 billion FF	49 billion FF[5]

Article 8 of the London Treaty of 1930 at least made some concession to these responsibilities, and its provisions were exploited by the French to the extent that funding permitted. The *avisos coloniaux* (Colonial Sloops) of the *Bougainville* class were in some respects similar to the sloops built by the British from the late 1920s. They were capable of escorting small mercantile convoys, but they were also designed for an important 'presence' mission within the colonies or island groups to which they were deployed. They were significantly larger than the British ships – indeed it was the 2,000-ton displacement of the four units authorised during the late 1920s that was one of the influences on the upper limit for ships in sub-category (b) of Article 8.

The colonial sloops were specifically designed for operation in the tropics, and particular attention was paid to habitability. They were powered by diesels on two shafts that gave them a sustained speed of 14 knots (they were designed for

Bougainville (Fr)

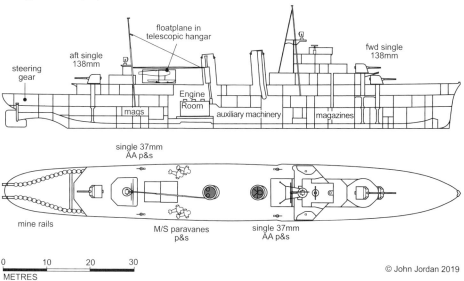

The drawing shows *Bougainville* as designed. The telescopic hangar was never fitted and the aircraft, when carried, were stowed on the open deck with wings deployed and covered with a canvas 'tent'. The main and auxiliary diesels exhausted through the second funnel; the first funnel served two conventional auxiliary watertube boilers for ship's services.

15.5 knots, which they exceeded by a large margin in trials), and endurance at 10 knots was an impressive 9,000nm. Three diesel generators each rated at 125kW provided the electrical power necessary to provide air conditioning throughout the ships, and they had an open shelter deck that extended to the sides of the hull from the forecastle to the quarterdeck to provide protection from the sun for a ship's complement of 135–140. All were fitted as flagships, with spacious and well-appointed accommodation for an admiral and his staff.

The main armament comprised three single 138.6mm mountings – the same model as in the *contre-torpilleurs* of the *Bison/Valmy* classes[6] – and there were four single 37mm guns for defence against aircraft. The broad shelter deck abaft the second funnel permitted the embarkation of a reconnaissance floatplane, which was handled by a derrick hinged from the base of the mainmast,[7] and there was light plating for the bridge. The unobstructed quarterdeck could be fitted with rails for fifty mines, and during wartime depth charge racks would be fitted.

The French colonial sloop *Amiral Charner* on a visit to Melbourne during her first deployment to the Far East. The powerful 138.6mm gun was the same model mounted in the early *contre-torpilleurs*. (*Allan C Green collection, State Library of Victoria*)

Two units were authorised under the 1927 Estimates, two under the 1928 Estimates and three under the 1930 Estimates, and there would be repeat orders for a further three in 1937/38. They proved to be extremely successful ships in service.

The large 'colonial sloops' of the *Bougainville* class were to be complemented, as in the Royal Navy, by smaller minesweeping sloops (*avisos dragueurs de mines*) of just over 600 tons. These were intended primarily for the protection of coastal traffic and of mercantile convoys plying between metropolitan France and North Africa; three of the earlier ships would be fitted specifically for colonial service. The *Elan* and *Chamois* classes were identical in design except for the raised forecastle of the latter, which improved sea-keeping and made them better suited to deployment overseas and in the North Atlantic. They were powered by Sulzer diesels that gave them a maximum speed of 20 knots and an endurance of 10,000nm at 9 knots.

Both types were armed with two single 100mm DP guns and several 13.2mm Hotchkiss MG. The early units were fitted with minesweeping gear on the stern, but in wartime this would generally be replaced by depth charge racks and two throwers. *Elan* was authorised under the 1934 Estimates; she was laid down in August 1936 but was not completed until 1939; four more units were authorised under the 1936 Estimates, and a further eight under the 1937 Estimates. The first three units of the *Chamois* class were authorised under the 1935 Estimates; two further units would be authorised under the 1937 Estimates and four more under the 1938 *bis* Estimates. Construction was protracted, and the latter ships were completed only in 1942.

Coastal Torpedo Boats

France had long believed in the potential of small surface and submersible craft armed with torpedoes to protect its coasts, ports and harbours against blockade or invasion. Article 8 of the London Treaty permitted the design and construction of an unlimited number of such 'defensive' craft under sub-category (a). The *Marine Nationale* had built up a large force of coastal submarines during the 1920s, and it made sense to complement these with conventional torpedo boats, thereby reviving the theories of the *Jeune Ecole* that dominated French tactical thinking in the late nineteenth century. The only restriction placed on torpedo boats by Article 8 was their displacement. There was no restriction on speed, so the French drew up a design in which high speed, manoeuvrability and a low silhouette were prioritised; a raised forecastle was adopted to permit the ships to operate effectively in heavy seas, but freeboard amidships and aft was extremely low.

The twelve 610-tonne torpedo boats of the *La Melpomène* class were laid down from 1933 to 1935; eight were authorised under the 1931 Estimates, and the remaining four in the following year. With a length of 80m (little more than the *avisos-dragueurs* of the *Elan* and *Chamois* classes) and two-shaft steam turbine propulsion machinery that drove them at a designed speed of 34.5 knots – 36.5 knots was attained in trials – they were armed with two 100mm Model 1930 guns in low-angle shielded mountings, two twin Hotchkiss 13.2mm MG, and two

The 610-tonne torpedo boat *Branlebas* on her full-power trials in the summer of 1937, when she attained a maximum speed of 36.5 knots; she has yet to receive her armament. The French torpedo boats proved poorly suited to escort missions due to their light construction, low freeboard and limited endurance; *Branlebas* foundered in a gale off the south-west of the UK in December 1940. *(Courtesy of A D Baker III)*

550mm torpedoes in a twin mounting. From the outset they suffered from severe stability problems due to being overweight; their low freeboard made them poor sea-boats, and these defects were compounded by structural problems.[8]

In the absence of any seaward threat to the French coast in 1939–40, these small torpedo boats would be employed as coastal convoy escorts, a role for which they were fundamentally unsuited due to their inadequate endurance: although in theory they had a range of 1,000nm at 20 knots, in wartime conditions 750–800nm was the maximum to be expected.

Once the Treaty restrictions no longer applied, a torpedo boat with almost twice the displacement, the *Le Fier* class, would be designed. Although only three hulls had been launched by the time of the Armistice in June 1940, these ships would have had twice the firepower and twice the endurance of the 610-tonne type, and would have had far better sea-keeping qualities.

New Torpedo Boats for the *Regia Marina*

Prior to and during the First World War the Italian Navy had built large numbers of torpedo boats, primarily for operations in the Adriatic. By the 1930s these were ageing fast, and Article 8 of the London Treaty permitted their replacement without any regard to quantitative limits provided displacement was kept to 600 tons standard. The Adriatic was no longer likely to be a major theatre of operations, so the role of these vessels had to be rethought. Like the French, the Italians were interested in fast, manoeuvrable ships armed with torpedoes that could protect Italian ports and bases, but which would also be capable of defending Mediterranean convoys from surface and submarine attack. These two primary missions would prove to be incompatible; as with the French *La Melpomène* class, high speed equated with low endurance, and the ships were too small and lacked the firepower to deal with attacks by surface units of destroyer size and above, while their anti-surface armament left insufficient space and weight available for anti-submarine sensors and weaponry.

In appearance the new Italian torpedo boats resembled the single-funnelled destroyers of the *Freccia* class, although displacement was only half that of the fleet vessels. They were armed with four of the traditional 450mm torpedoes, initially in one twin and two single mountings, later in four single mountings, and three single 100/47 guns. They were also fitted with depth charge racks and throwers, and there was provision for minelaying. The new torpedo boats were designed for a maximum speed of 34 knots but this was largely exceeded on trials. Additions post-completion would raise displacement by almost 250 tons by 1940, which made the ships top-heavy and reduced sea speed to below 30 knots.

The two prototype units of the *Spica* class were laid down in 1933. There was then a short hiatus until 1935–36, when fourteen slightly improved units of the *Cimene* and *Perseo* groups were laid down. A further sixteen units would be laid down in 1937–38 to become the *Alcione* sub-group.

When it became clear that quantitative limits would be abandoned when the Washington/London Treaties expired at the end of 1936, work began on a larger

The Italian torpedo boat *Libra* in 1939. Although well-armed and of sound design, these ships were of little tactical value and were reassigned to anti-submarine duties during the Second World War. *(NHHC, NHI11428)*

Italian torpedo boats of the *Spica* series at their moorings in 1939. From left to right: *Altair, Aldebaran, Antares, Andromeda, Perseo* and *Sagittario. (NHHC, NH111480)*

design intended primarily for convoy escort work. The *Orsa* class, which were initially rated as 'escort sloops' (*avvisi scorta*) but were later re-rated as 'escort torpedo boats', had a displacement of 840 tons standard, and were armed with only two single 100/47 guns, thereby freeing up the quarterdeck for anti-submarine weapons – no fewer than six depth charge throwers were fitted. The *Orsa*s continued to mount a strong anti-surface armament of four 450mm torpedoes, disposed as two twin mountings in the waist, but shaft horsepower was reduced from 19,000shp to 16,000shp, giving a maximum speed of only 28 knots. On the other hand, the capacity of the fuel tanks was more than doubled to 520 tonnes to raise endurance to an impressive 5,000nm at 14 knots. Only four ships of the class were ordered initially, but they were to prove so successful that a further sixteen units of an improved design would be built during the Second World War.

Similar in conception and capabilities to the French Colonial Sloops of the *Bougainville* class was the *Eritrea*, intended to show the flag in peacetime and to serve as an escort in war. Ordered in May 1935, *Eritrea* had a displacement of 2,165 tons standard, slightly above the London limit, and in addition to accommodation for troops was equipped with hospital facilities. The propulsion system was unusual in that it combined conventional FIAT diesels with Marelli electric motors driven by a pair of diesel generators, the three types of unit being located in three separate compartments. It was adopted during the ship's construction, together with a small

The sole Italian colonial sloop, *Eritrea*. She was specially fitted to serve as a tender for a maximum of four submarines in the Red Sea. *(USMM)*

but well-equipped workshop, to permit *Eritrea* to act as a tender for up to four submarines. Maximum designed speed was 20 knots, and range was 7,000nm at 12 knots on electric motors and 5,000nm at 15 knots on diesels. As with her French counterparts *Eritrea* was designed specifically for tropical climates – she was to be deployed to the Red Sea – and considerable attention was paid to habitability.

Eritrea was armed with two twin 120mm/45 mountings – the same model as that installed in the older destroyers of the *Leone* class. The close-range anti-aircraft armament was a mix of the elderly 40mm Vickers gun and twin 13.2mm MG – both were later replaced by a uniform AA armament of two twin 37mm/54. The ship was also fitted for minelaying. A second ship of an improved type with diesel propulsion, *Etiopia*, would feature in the 1938–39 Estimates but was not built.

Forward Support for the US Navy

The US Navy's attempts to establish itself as an oceanic force during the early years of the twentieth century focused on the creation of a battle fleet composed almost exclusively of battleships; large size effectively equated with long range, making the capital ship the unit *par excellence* for a major power with few forward bases capable of providing coal and stores, repair or maintenance. European navies of the same period, however, were beginning to complement their own battle fleets with large numbers of destroyers and torpedo boats, together with small, fast cruisers for scouting.

With the major fleet expansion programme of 1916, the US Navy was compelled to confront the issue of how to support and sustain a modern, 'balanced' battle fleet overseas, and in particular the large numbers of flotilla craft projected. The response

The US destroyer tender *Dobbin* in 1937, with five destroyers alongside. From left to right: : the Leader *Phelps* (DD-360) and the *Farragut*-class destroyers *Worden* (DD-352), *MacDonough* (DD-351), *Dewey* (DD-349) and *Hull* (DD-350) *(NHHC, NH 54527)*

The submarine tender *Holland* at San Diego in December 1934, with the two 'cruiser' submarines *Narwhal* and *Nautilus* close alongside. Outboard are five out of seven remaining 'V'-boats. From left to right: *Cachalot, Dolphin, Barracuda, Bass* and *Bonita. (NHHC, 80-G-63334)*

was a large programme of auxiliary vessels to augment the existing fleet of large colliers and oilers. The years 1919–20 saw the launch of no fewer than thirty-four such vessels displacing between 10,000 and 15,000 tons (gross) – later recalculated as 4,000–9,000 tons standard: the aircraft tender *Wright*, three destroyer tenders, two submarine tenders, two ammunition transports, three stores ships, fourteen fleet oilers, seven cargo ships, a hospital ship and a large troop transport. Each was given a defensive armament of either two or four 5in low-angle guns plus two or four 3in HA guns – the unarmed hospital ship *Relief* and the troop transport *Chaumont* excepted.

The decision to forward-base the bulk of the US Pacific Fleet at Pearl Harbor during the 1920s resulted in the construction of a new generation of destroyer and submarine tenders, this time designed from the keel up rather than mercantile conversions, together with a purpose-built repair ship. The destroyer tenders *Dobbin* and *Whitney* were designed to support two destroyer flotillas each comprising a flotilla leader and two four-ship divisions of destroyers (*ie* eighteen ships). With a gross tonnage of 12,450 tons (8,325tW) and a maximum speed of 16 knots, the new destroyer tenders had depot, repair and hospital facilities, and were fitted as flagships. *Dobbin* was launched in 1921, *Whitney* in 1923. They were followed by the submarine tender *Holland* (launched 1926), which was similar in design and equipped to support three divisions each of six submarines.

The orders for the new destroyer and submarine tenders were accompanied by an order for a purpose-built repair ship, *Medusa*, launched in the spring of 1923. Similar in size to her contemporaries, she was equipped to make both temporary and permanent repairs; there were two 8-ton derricks and shear legs with 20-ton, 10-ton and 8-ton capacities for lifting heavy items of equipment, together with medical and hospital facilities.

Dobbin, *Whitney* and *Holland*, together with the older destroyer tenders *Bridgeport* and *Melville*, had to be registered as 'Special Vessels' under the London Treaty because of their relatively heavy defensive armament of eight 5in/51 low-angle guns and between one and four 3in HA guns, which breached the limits for auxiliary vessels in sub-category (c). The war-built naval transport *Henderson* (launched 1916) had also to be registered for the same reason; the repair ship *Medusa*, which had the standard US auxiliary armament of four 5in/51 guns, did not.

The Gunboats of the *Erie* Class
The 2,000-ton *Erie*-class gunboats have the distinction of being the only completely new type of vessel to emerge from the Article 8 provisions. A large sea-going gunboat was seen as useful for protecting US interests in the Caribbean and SE Asia, and since the cruising speed of the Battle Fleet was only 15 knots, rising to 20 knots at most in combat, it was clear that a ship designed up to the qualitative limits of sub-category (b) could be utilised for screening duties in wartime, as the maximum permitted armament of four 6in guns would be invaluable for fending off destroyer attacks. The ships could also be useful as convoy escorts; their main armament would be

Table 7.3: Sloops and Gunboats for Overseas Deployment

	Shoreham class (GB)	Bougainville class (Fr)	Eritrea class (It)	Erie class (US)
Built:	8 ships 1930–33	10 ships 1929–40	1 ship 1935–37	2 ships 1934–36
Displacement:	1,100tW	1,970tW	2,165tW	2,000tW
Dimensions:	281ft × 35ft (86m × 10.7m)	104m × 12.7m	97m × 13.3m	328ft × 41ft (100m × 12.6m)
Machinery:	2-shaft geared turbines, 2,000shp = 16.5kts	2-shaft diesel, 3,200bhp = 15.5kts	2-shaft diesel-electric, 8,300hp = 20kts	2-shaft geared turbines, 6,200shp = 20kts
Armament:	2 – 4in/45 (2 × I)	3 – 138.6mm/40 (3 × I) 4 – 37mm (4 × I) (50 mines) 1 floatplane	4 – 120mm/45 (2 × II) 2 – 40mm (2 × I) (100 mines) (1 floatplane)	4 – 6in/47 (4 × I) 16 – 1.1in (4 × IV) (1 floatplane)

Note:

Although the US gunboats Erie and Charleston were remarkably similar in size and capabilities to the French 'colonial sloops' of the Bougainville class and the later Italian Eritrea, they were designed with a very different set of missions in mind, which included convoy escort and even fleet escort duties. The British sloops of the Bridgewater, Hastings, Shoreham and Grimsby classes, on the other hand, were intended for basic trade protection duties operating from foreign stations. They were robust, inexpensive and only half the size of their foreign counterparts, which were primarily for the policing and 'presence' missions.

Erie (PG-50), one of two 'gunboats' built for the US Navy in the aftermath of London, is seen here on 19 October 1936. *Erie* and her sister *Charleston* (PG-51) were built as 'treaty-exempt' vessels to conform with the cruiser sub-category (b) restrictions. *(NHHC, NH 54262)*

effective against armed merchant surface raiders, and depth charge racks and throwers could easily be accommodated in a ship of this size.

A flush-deck hull-form with pronounced sheer and a clipper bow reminiscent of the 'treaty' cruisers of the *Pensacola* class was adopted, but draught was kept to a minimum to enable the ships to navigate in shallow waters close to the coast so they could give fire support to the US Marines when required. The broad transom stern was designed to accommodate either depth charge racks or mine rails. A maximum speed of 20 knots meant that shaft horsepower could be reduced to little over 6,000shp, thereby compressing the length of the machinery spaces; there was only a single raked funnel.

The main armament comprised four single 6in/47 guns; this was the same gun fitted in the *Brooklyn* class (see Chapter 4), but elevation was limited and there was insufficient weight available to provide power loading or fully enclosed shields for the gun mountings. Because the 6in guns were low-angle weapons it was decided to fit no fewer than four of the new 1.1in quad light AA mountings. There was stowage space and a lifting derrick for a reconnaissance aircraft aft – considered essential for peacetime operations – but there was insufficient space or weight available to fit a catapult, and it was envisaged that in wartime the aircraft and its handling gear would be disembarked.

Protection was similar to that of the early 'treaty' cruiser *Pensacola*, but as with the carrier *Wasp* (see Chapter 3) the 3.5in main armour belt was to have been fitted only in wartime in order to save weight and to keep displacement within treaty limits.[9] To the evident disappointment of the CNO, Admiral William V Pratt, only two ships of this type, *Erie* and *Charleston,* were built; authorised under the FY1933 Programme, they were laid down in late 1934 and completed two years later.

The Imperial Japanese Navy

The strategic situation of Japan was subtly different to that of the other major naval powers. The IJN needed to protect the home islands against seaborne attack and, like Italy and France, ensure the security of its ports and coastal mercantile traffic. Like the latter countries, it also needed to protect its sea lines of communication with an adjacent continent – in this case Asia rather than Africa. It had no distant overseas imperial commitments to match those of France and the UK, but given the most likely scenario of having to face an expeditionary fleet despatched to the western Pacific by either Britain or the United States, long-range reconnaissance was required, together with some ability to forward-deploy submarines both to provide intelligence and to whittle down the enemy fleet prior to the 'decisive battle'.

The key elements of the naval forces outside the major categories of warship built for the IJN during the 1920s were, on the one hand, subchasers and small surface minelayers to protect the approaches to ports and harbours and, on the other, depot ships that could double as forward-deployed flagships for the submarine flotillas. Following the London Treaty the coast defence forces would be supplemented by 600-ton torpedo boats similar in conception to those built for the French and Italian Navies.

The submarine depot ships *Jingei* and *Chogei* had been authorised under the 1920 programme and were completed between 1922 and 1924. Not only were they the first purpose-built submarine depot ships to be built for the IJN, but they were designed for a unique role: that of operational submarine flagship. Unlike the American submarine tenders of the period and the later British submarine depot ships, which were essentially mercantile designs built to naval standards, *Jingei* and *Chogei* were hybrid cruiser-type warships, with a conventional bridge structure, a tripod foremast, and a powerful gun armament. They were designed to operate at sea with the fleet, providing command facilities, support and reconnaissance for a flotilla of submarines.

Jingei and her sister displaced 5,160 tons standard when completed, and were driven by steam turbines at a maximum speed of 18 knots – sufficient to keep pace with the battle fleet when the latter was cruising at around 15 knots, and more than sufficient to keep pace with the fleet submarines of the day. They were armed with four 14cm/50 guns in twin mountings fore and aft plus two single 8cm HA guns, and there was space on the after superstructure to accommodate a reconnaissance floatplane, which was handled by a derrick hinged from the base of the pole mainmast.

In service they proved less successful than hoped: they rolled badly and suffered from serious stability problems. During the late 1930s they were bulged and received permanent ballast, standard displacement rising to 6,600 tons. By this time the role of operational flagship of the elite long-range submarine flotillas was being taken on by the large cruiser submarines *I.7/I.8* and their successors (see Chapter 6), and *Jingei* and *Chogei* became flagships for submarine flotillas comprising older fleet boats and RO-type medium submarines deployed to Southeast Asia and the Mandates.

More closely comparable to the submarine depot ships built for the Royal Navy during the interwar period was *Taigei*, built under the 1931 First Fleet Replenishment ('Circle 1') Programme. Completed in 1933–34, *Taigei* had a standard displacement of 10,000 tons and was powered by diesels that gave her a speed of 20 knots – the maximum permitted under the London Treaty. The 'cruiser' armament of *Jingei* and *Chogei* was abandoned in favour of a pair of 12.7cm/40 DP guns disposed fore and aft, together with several of the new twin 13.2mm MG. The rules for sub-category (c) vessels in Article 8 permitted a maximum of three aircraft and two catapults, and full advantage was taken of this provision in order to provide reconnaissance for *Taigei's* flotilla of submarines.

A combination of shallow draught[10] and high superstructures, adopted in order to provide maintenance workshops and temporary accommodation for 400 submariners, resulted in stability problems and poor sea-keeping qualities. *Taigei* also experienced the welding and structural problems of the other IJN ships of her generation. During 1936–37 she would be taken in hand for hull strengthening and the addition of bulges; displacement would increase by 500 tons. War in the Pacific in 1941 would find her forward-deployed as a depot ship for one of the three flotillas of the elite Sixth (Submarine) Fleet based at Kwajalein atoll in the

The submarine depot ship *Taigei* was authorised under the IJN's First Fleet Replenishment Programme of 1931. Speed and armament were the maximum permitted by the London Treaty. *(Fukui Shizuo collection)*

Marshalls; she would subsequently be taken in hand for conversion to a light carrier (she became *Ryuho*).

The construction of *Taigei* would be followed by two similar ships of modified design, authorised under the 1934 'Circle 2' Programme. *Tsurugisaki* and *Takasaki* were laid down in 1935, and their design took into account the stability problems experienced with *Taigei* following her completion. However, an equally important consideration was the prospective end to the Washington Treaty regime. Japan was increasingly planning for war mobilisation at some time in the not-too-distant future, and it was considered desirable that some larger auxiliary and mercantile vessels have the potential for conversion to 'light fleet' or 'auxiliary' aircraft carriers. The design of the two new submarine depot ships took this into account; superstructures were designed for ease of replacement by a hangar and flight deck, and much larger machinery spaces were provided; shaft horsepower was quadrupled to give a maximum speed of 29 knots – an unprecedented figure for a depot ship and one that contravened existing treaty provisions. *Tsurugisaki* was completed as a depot ship in January 1939, but would subsequently be taken in hand for conversion to the light carrier *Shoho*. With relations between Japan and the United States deteriorating rapidly, her sister would be taken in hand for a similar conversion while fitting out; she became the light carrier *Zuiho*.

At approximately the same time that *Tsurugisaki* and *Takasaki* began construction, two purpose-built 'seaplane tenders' of military design, *Chitose* and *Chiyoda*, were

Chitose, seen here running trials, and her sister *Chiyoda* were laid down as seaplane tenders, but were subsequently developed as fully-fledged seaplane carriers capable of operating twenty to twenty-four floatplanes. The design provided for the ships' conversion to midget submarine carrier or aircraft carrier. *(Kure Maritime Museum)*

This photo of *Chiyoda* was taken at Woosung, China, in April 1940. The distinctive central platform mounted on four corner pillars served both to conceal a large hatch for the embarkation of midget submarines and as an embryonic carrier flight deck. *(NHHC, NH 82451)*

laid down for the IJN. Similar in overall dimensions and displacement to the submarine depot ships, these ships would likewise eventually undergo conversion to light fleet aircraft carriers. Unlike the depot ships, which as completed were powered exclusively by diesels, *Chitose* and *Chiyoda* had a hybrid propulsion plant with a set of steam turbines and a diesel engine (the latter for long-range cruising) combined on each of the two shafts using a Vulkan clutch. Total shaft horsepower was almost identical to *Tsurugisaki* and *Takasaki*, and maximum speed was again 29 knots, enabling them to operate in advance of the battle fleet, for which they were intended to provide long-range reconnaissance. Their main armament of two twin 12.7cm/40 mountings was also identical to that of the depot ships, although both mountings were forward of the bridge in order to free the after part of the ship for the extensive aviation facilities.

A capacious hangar for twelve floatplanes occupied the after part of the hull directly above the machinery spaces, with a single lift connecting it with the upper ('flight') deck. The floatplanes were moved around the deck on a system of rails that could be used to stow a further eight/twelve aircraft, and were raised via ramps equipped with electrically powered winches to the level of the four catapults[11] available for launch. There were aircraft handling cranes at either end of a prominent gantry structure amidships, and for recovery while under way a canvas ribbed Hein 'mat' was adopted, deployed from the stern, and the aircraft were lifted on board by a stern crane. The prototype Hein mat installation in *Chitose* appears not to have been a success, and *Chiyoda* was never so fitted.

A third ship of a modified design propelled exclusively by diesels, *Mizuho*, would be laid down in 1937. Slower,[12] but with a heavier anti-aircraft armament, *Mizuho* would have a similar complement of seaplanes. Like *Chiyoda*, she would later undergo conversion to enable her to deploy midget submarines.

The submarine depot ships and seaplane carriers (initially designated 'tenders') of the 1934 Programme were all built in contravention of the London Treaty. Although the displacement of armed, purpose-built auxiliary naval vessels was not limited under Article 8, all five of these ships violated the 20-knot ceiling imposed on maximum speed, and the seaplane carriers largely exceeded the limits of two catapults and three aircraft specified for sub-category (c). The violations were considered permissible because of the imminent expiry of the Washington/London Treaties; by the time these ships were completed in 1938–39 the Treaty provisions would be long dead, at least in so far as they applied to the IJN.[13]

Minelayers

Defensive minefields had traditionally been a speciality of the Russian Navy, and many of the most significant losses experienced by the IJN during the Russo-Japanese war of 1904–05 had resulted from ships deployed for blockade or bombardment of mainland ports striking Russian mines. The IJN learned the value of defensive mining during this conflict, and subsequently set out to develop effective minelaying and sweeping capabilities to ensure the security of the coastal waters around the Japanese islands and of the sea routes that connected Japan to the mainland.

A series of small 'second-class' minelayer/netlayer types were built under the 1923 and 1927 naval programmes, and these were complemented by larger 'first-class' types that would become subject to Article 8 of the London Treaty and would influence the formulation of the qualitative limitations.

There were two distinct strands to the IJN's first-class minelayer programme. The first was the minelayer/netlayer type, represented by the *Shirataka* of the 1923 Programme and the *Yaeyama* of the 1927 Programme. These were ships with the displacement of a large destroyer but the hull of a small cruiser, with high freeboard amidships and a distinctive squared-off stern with a prominent overhang, optimised for the laying of mines from tracks on the upper deck. They were powered by reciprocating machinery that gave them a maximum speed of 16–20 knots. *Shirataka* was armed with three single 12cm/45 low-angle destroyer-type guns, whereas the later ship had two single 12cm/45 high-angle mountings. The former had a capacity of 100 mines; the latter 185.

The other strand was a minelayer derived from the British *Adventure*, in which the mines were carried internally within the hull and discharged via doors in a square transom stern. *Itsukushima* was authorised under the 1923 Programme and completed during 1928–29. There were six mine tracks running throughout the after part of the ship at the level of the main deck, for a capacity of 300–500 mines. Unusually, the ship was powered by three MAN diesels each rated at 1,000bhp and driving three shafts; maximum speed was only 17 knots but endurance was impressive for a ship of this size. Stowing the mines between decks had the advantage of maximising upper deck space, and *Itsukushima* was armed with three 14cm/50 low-angle cruiser-type guns as well as two 8cm/40 HA guns. There were two depth charge throwers, and the ship was also fitted for net laying.

Despite the adoption of minelaying arrangements similar to those of HMS *Adventure*, *Itsukushima* was smaller and slower than her British counterpart, which would have to be registered as a 'Special Vessel' under the London Treaty because of her elevated displacement (6,740 tons standard) and speed (28 knots). With a standard displacement of just under 2,000 tons and a speed of 17 knots, *Itsukushima* fell just within the qualitative limits agreed for sub-category (b) vessels under Article 8, and was one of the vessels taken into consideration when formulating the wording for that article.

In order to gain acceptance for the general provisions of Article 8, it had been agreed that the IJN should be permitted to replace the elderly converted armoured cruisers *Aso* and *Tokiwa* with two new minelayers with a maximum displacement of 5,000 tons before 31 December 1936, provided that their other characteristics conformed to the provisions of Article 8 paragraph (b). The ex-Russian *Aso* was duly stricken as soon as the conference ended, and a replacement was included in the 1931 'Circle 1' Programme. The new ship, *Okinoshima,* would be laid down in 1934 and completed in 1936. She had a standard displacement of 4,400 tons and was powered by geared steam turbines; maximum speed was restricted to 20 knots in accordance with the agreement, and the gun armament of four 14cm guns in twin low-angle mountings and two 8cm HA guns was also well within treaty limits.

Okinoshima could carry a maximum of 500 mines, stowed both between decks (as in *Itsukushima*) and on additional twin mine tracks that ran for most of the length

The IJN minelayer *Okinoshima* was laid down in 1934 as a replacement for one of the two converted armoured cruisers *Aso* and *Tokiwa* She had a displacement in excess of that permitted for the other high contracting powers, and could carry a maximum of 500 mines. *(Fukui Shizuo collection)*

of the upper deck. Her large size and powerful gun armament made her suitable for use a convoy escort, and she was credited with an endurance of 9,000nm at 10 knots. Large size also made it possible to equip her with a catapult for a reconnaissance aircraft, which was handled by a derrick attached to the foot of a *Mogami*-type tripod mainmast.

Completed in 1936, *Okinoshima* proved successful in service and a similar ship of modified design, *Tsugaru*, would be built under the 1937 Programme. Although intended as a replacement for the elderly *Tokiwa*, the latter ship was retained following the expiry of the Washington/London Treaties, and was re-boilered and generally upgraded in a refit in 1937–38.

New Torpedo Boats

Thwarted in its attempt to secure a 10:7 ratio in major warships in the London Treaty, the IJN was keen to exploit any possibility to enlarge the Navy within the permitted limits. It therefore opted, like the French *Marine Nationale* and the Italian *Regia Marina*, to build a series of 600-ton torpedo boats that were in effect small destroyers. The Japanese constructors, goaded by the unrealistic demands of the Naval Staff, again produced an over-ambitious design whose serious design flaws would all too quickly become apparent.

Whereas both the French and the Italians had opted for lightweight 100mm guns, the IJN insisted on standard 'destroyer' 12.7cm/50 weapons. These were, moreover, not in simple open mountings, but in enclosed gunhouses similar to those in the destroyers of the 'Special Type' and *Hatsuharu* classes: a single forward and a twin mounting aft. The twin mounting weighed 32.5 tonnes and the single 18.7 tonnes; the weight of the single alone was equivalent to that of the three 100mm single mountings on the Italian *Spica* class! There were also two twin trainable mountings for 53cm torpedoes on the centre line amidships, and as in the *Hatsuharu* class there was a tall bridge structure. Despite this relatively heavy armament, hull weight was

Table 7.4: **Torpedo Boats 1930–1936**

	Chidori class (Jap)	*La Melpomène* class (Fr)	*Spica* class class (It)
Built:	4 ships 1931–34	12 ships 1933–38	16 ships 1933–37
Displacement:	600tW (designed)[1]	600tW (designed)	600tW (designed)
Dimensions:	82m x 7.4m	81m x 7.7m	80m x 8.2m
Machinery:	2-shaft geared turbines, 11,000shp = 30kts	2-shaft geared turbines, 22,000shp = 34.5kts	2-shaft geared turbines, 19,000shp = 34kts
Armament:	3 – 12.7cm/50 (1xII, 3xI)[2] 1 – 40mm (1 x I) 4 – 53cm TT (2 x II) 1 DCT	2 – 100mm/40 (2 x I) 4 – 13.2mm MG (2 x II) 2 – 550mm TT (1 x II)	3 – 100mm/47 (3 x I) 2 – 40mm (2 x I) 4 – 450mm TT (4 x I) 2 DCT

Note:
1 When completed, all of these ships exceeded their designed displacement, often by a considerable margin.
2 Later revised to 3 – 12cm/45 (3 x I), 2 –13mm MG (1 x II), 2 – 53cm TT (1 x II)

Chidori Class (Japan)

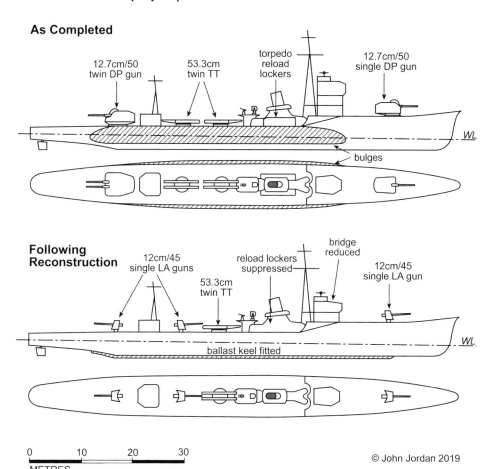

As Completed

12.7cm/50
twin DP gun

53.3cm
twin TT

torpedo
reload
lockers

12.7cm/50
single DP gun

WL

bulges

**Following
Reconstruction**

12cm/45
single LA guns

53.3cm
twin TT

reload lockers
suppressed

bridge
reduced

12cm/45
single LA gun

WL

ballast keel fitted

0   10   20   30
METRES

© John Jordan 2019

The upper drawing shows the bulges fitted shortly after completion to improve stability. The lower drawing shows the class following their major reconstruction, which involved the suppression of the bulky 12.7cm gun mountings, replaced by simple open 12cm centre pivot mountings, and one of the two twin torpedo mountings; the bridge was also lowered by one deck and permanent keel ballast added.

reduced to a minimum by the extensive use of welding, with the result that the standard displacement of the name-ship *Chidori* was below 600 tons as designed. Stability and structural problems were the inevitable consequence.

On 12 March 1934, barely two weeks after her completion, *Chidori*'s sister, *Tomozuru*, capsized in a storm with heavy loss of life. The incident would be a wake-up call to the Imperial Japanese Navy, resulting in major changes in design practice together with a programme of remedial work for ships in service or under construction that would occupy the Japanese naval dockyards for several years. *Tomozuru* herself would be salvaged and rebuilt, and her three sister-ships would undergo a similar radical reconstruction. The second of the two twin torpedo mountings would

The torpedo boat *Chidori* shortly after her commissioning in November 1933. Note the heavy 12.7cm gun mountings, which were similar to those fitted in the 1,700-ton destroyers of the 'Special Type'. Following the capsizing of her sister *Tomozuru*, *Chidori* would be completely rebuilt. *(Fukui Shizuo collection)*

be removed and the enclosed 12.7cm gun mountings replaced by three single 12cm/45 centre pivot mountings with light shields; the bridge structure was lowered by one deck, the hull strengthened and permanent keel ballast added.

Four torpedo boats had been authorised under the 1931 Programme, and a further sixteen larger units of a modified design would be authorised under the 1934 Programme. Eight of these would be completed as the *Otori* class, the remainder being re-ordered as subchasers. The *Otori* class would be armed as the reconstructed *Tomozuru*-class ships, the only modification being that the twin torpedo mounting would be replaced by a triple. They had a larger, stronger hull and more powerful propulsion machinery. However, it was now increasingly acknowledged that the fleet torpedo boat was a dated concept that had little relevance to modern naval warfare, and the linear successors of these ships would exchange their torpedoes for depth charge racks and throwers, and their high speed for endurance.

Conclusions

The qualitative limits established by the London Treaty for ships outside the five principal categories of warship had an undoubted impact on the building policy of most of the navies concerned. They permitted the construction of many small combatants and auxiliary vessels that would see valuable service during the Second World War, and which would form the basis for subsequent successful designs produced after the treaty system had finally lapsed; they were, however, equally responsible for some very poor, unseaworthy ships.

Chidori running trials after her reconstruction; she now has the older-model 12cm guns in three single open mountings and only one twin torpedo mounting. *(Fukui Shizuo collection)*

Sub-category (b) was undoubtedly the most fruitful. The French and Italian 'colonial sloops' were particularly successful; designed with tropical conditions in mind, they were well-armed and well-equipped to provide support to local ground forces, shipping and – in the case of the Italian *Eritrea* – submarines. The British 'trade' sloops, although more modest in conception, were equally successful in their own way and, more importantly, provided the basis for the improved escort sloops and frigates built in numbers during the Second World War for oceanic convoy escort. The American *Erie*-class gunboats, closely tailored to the new treaty limits, were a moderate success in that they performed largely as expected. However, they were clearly not the ships the US Navy would have chosen to build had there been no treaty constraints; only two prototype ships were built, and there were to be no successors.

Few large auxiliary warships were built under sub-category (c) during the early 1930s. There were two principal factors responsible for this: the poor state of most economies during this period, which meant that navies faced with budgetary constraints preferred to spend their limited funds on front-line vessels; and, in the case of the US Navy, the considerable investment made at the end of the First World War, which meant that there were large numbers of vessels capable of forward-based support of relatively recent construction. By the mid-1930s, with their economies in better condition and a deteriorating international situation, both Britain and Japan embarked on new programmes of large depot ships to support forward-based submarines and destroyers.

The third factor, at least during the early 1930s, was the constraints imposed on sub-category (c) vessels, which effectively precluded the construction of large seaplane carriers or minelayers. The Japanese authorised the first of the two large replacement minelayers they were permitted to build under Article 12, but were compelled to wait until the Washington Treaty was on the point of expiry before laying down the fleet seaplane carriers *Chitose* and *Chiyoda*.

Sub-category (a), which was limited only by displacement, was a 'catch-all' category intended to embrace all small combatants with a primarily defensive role such as sub-chasers, minesweepers and torpedo boats. Virtually all existing craft were of First World War construction, and would therefore shortly need replacing. The US Navy, primarily preoccupied with power projection, built virtually nothing in this category during the period of the London Treaty, while Royal Navy construction was limited to a handful of coastal escorts (designated 'patrol vessels') of 510–530 tons. However, the French, the Italians and the Japanese attempted to revive the torpedo boat, which proved to be a serious error. All of these ships were seriously overloaded, and in the French and the Japanese ships this was compounded by structural problems resulting from defective design and construction. Their high speed was purchased at the expense of endurance, which meant that they were poorly suited to the convoy escort role, and their heavy armament of guns and torpedoes left no space or weight margin for an adequate provision of anti-submarine weaponry. Moreover, only the IJN's *Chidori* and *Otori* classes, which were in essence 'second-class destroyers', could have hoped to engage any potential convoy attacker with any hope of success. The French *avisos-dragueurs*, designed to escort coastal convoy traffic, would prove too small and fragile to escort troop and supply convoys between metropolitan France and North Africa, particularly on the Atlantic side of the Gibraltar Straits. The Italian escorts of the *Pegaso* class were better, but these were significantly larger ships, with a standard displacement of 840 tons.

Whereas the torpedo boats suffered badly from a 600-ton displacement limit that was unavoidable, there was no similar restriction on an escort ship provided it carried no torpedoes and its speed was limited to 20 knots. There can be little doubt that the Royal Navy was right to opt for a 1,000-ton vessel with good sea-keeping qualities from the outset; later Italian and Japanese ships designed for the same purpose would more closely approach this size, while the US Navy's war-built destroyer escorts (DE) would have a standard displacement of 1,200–1,400 tons.

Chapter 8

POSTSCRIPT: THE LONDON TREATY OF 1936

T HE WASHINGTON TREATY, as modified by the London Treaty of 1930, was due to expire on 31 December 1936. The intention had always been that it would be superseded by a new naval arms limitation treaty, to be discussed during late 1935. However, tensions between the high contracting powers had been building for some time, and had been aggravated by what was seen by two of the five powers, Japan and France, as high-handed behaviour on the part of Britain and the United States at the London Conference. The French had responded by withdrawing from Part III of the London Treaty, which imposed strict quantitative limits on each of the 'categories' of warship defined, and although it had signed up to the remaining four parts, the French parliament had failed to ratify the Treaty. The Japanese, on the other hand, fearful of being held responsible for the failure of the conference and also of the decline in prestige that would result from Japan's exclusion from future international arms limitation agreements with the major western powers, signed and – despite bitter domestic opposition – ratified the Treaty.

During the early 1930s the stresses on the treaty system would be exacerbated by international developments. The Manchuria Incident of 18 September 1931, which was followed by a Japanese military invasion of that country, led to Japan's diplomatic isolation and withdrawal from the League of Nations in March 1933. By the spring of 1934, Japan was becoming increasingly concerned by the forward deployment of US and British naval and air assets made possible by the development of Pearl Harbor and of Singapore, and March 1934 also saw the passing in the US Congress of the Vinson-Trammel Act, which decreed that the US Navy build-up to existing treaty limits in all the defined categories: no fewer than 102 ships and 1,184 aircraft were to be authorised over eight years. The IJN responded with its Second Fleet Replenishment ('Circle 2') Programme of 1934, but Japan was still nominally constrained by the London Treaty provisions.

During 1934 informal talks on the new treaty that would follow on from Washington began in earnest. The Japanese delegation, headed by Admiral Yamamoto Isoroku, demanded parity with Britain and the United States; additional proposals included the abolition of all 'offensive' categories of warship, including aircraft carriers, which could be used to spearhead US operations against Japan in the western Pacific, and of qualitative limits. The one aspect linking these muddled and apparently incoherent proposals was that the Japanese knew them to be totally unacceptable to Britain and the United States. When, as fully expected, they were rejected out of hand, Japan announced its withdrawal from the Washington Treaty on its expiry at the end of 1936.

Further attempts would be made to bring Japan to the conference table and to breathe new life into the Treaty during 1935, and on 9 December of that year the Second London Naval Disarmament Conference was convened, attended by the representatives of all five Washington powers. The British wanted new limits on the displacement and gun calibre of capital ships and on the displacement of cruisers (already limited to 6.1in guns); however, in the current deteriorating international climate, they were not prepared to accept overall limits on the number of cruisers. The Americans were now (reluctantly) prepared to accept a lower displacement limit on cruisers, but although they were willing to agree a reduction in the gun calibre of capital ships they would insist on retention of the 35,000-ton upper displacement limit; and in the interests of parity of status, every effort was to be made to prevent the expansion of the British cruiser force to seventy ships.

Although the Japanese had agreed to participate in the conference, they had made it clear that any new treaty would start with a 'clean sheet' and that they intended to press for numerical parity with Britain and the United States – an 80 per cent ratio was regarded domestically as a bare minimum. Once it became clear that Japan's demands would be rejected, the Japanese delegation withdrew from the conference on 15 January 1936, leaving Britain, the United States and France – Italy declined to take part in the conference following international condemnation of her invasion of Abyssinia – to decide how best to proceed. This posed a problem for the British and American negotiators, in that anything they now agreed could effectively be undermined by the subsequent actions of Japan.

The resulting London Treaty, agreed in signed on 25 March 1936, was but a shadow of its Washington predecessor. In place of the noble ambition to secure world peace by a combination of limitations on naval armaments and collective security, there was a paranoid feel to its wording, with each of the signatories concerned primarily that neither of the other two powers – or, worse, one of the two major naval powers outside the Treaty – would steal a march on the others. There were new qualitative limits on the calibre of guns to be mounted in battleships (14in, down from 16in) and on the displacement of cruisers (8,000tW, down from 10,000tW), but although the overt intent behind these measures was de-escalatory, the abolition of quantitative limits simply meant that more ships in each of the defined categories could be built at lower cost.

There was a strong emphasis on early notification of the characteristics of ships to be laid down by the high contracting powers, and the notifiable characteristics were now extended to include type of machinery, designed horsepower and speed, and the number of light AA guns. No fewer than twenty-two of the thirty-two articles were devoted to 'Advance notification and exchange of information' and to 'General and safeguarding clauses'. This emphasis on early notification was tied in with various 'escalator' clauses (Article 25, paragraphs 1–6) that enabled any of the signatory powers to bypass the qualitative limits in order to match ships laid down by a power outside the Treaty, provided there was prior discussion and formal notification to the other signatories. This was a treaty with limited ambitions, doomed to irrelevance and failure as the co-signatories progressively chipped away at the edges.

Ultimately it was the failure to agree quantitative ceilings for the various categories of warship that sounded the death knell to the Treaty system. This was inevitable in the circumstances, given a fraught international situation and significant changes in the balance of power. Up until the early 1930s, British naval planning was under-pinned by the concept of a single fleet that in peacetime would be based in European waters but which in the event of war with Japan would be transferred to the Far East via the Mediterranean and based on Singapore. However, the Abyssinia crisis of 1935, which introduced the prospect of a hostile Italy, and the resurgence of Germany under Chancellor Adolf Hitler meant that Britain would effectively have to build up her naval forces to a two-ocean standard, so that they were able to protect not only the UK and trade in the North Atlantic, but British interests in the Mediterranean, the Indian Ocean and the Far East.

A clumsy, panicked attempt at a unilateral accommodation with Germany, the Anglo-German Agreement of June 1935, only served to exacerbate the breakdown in global security. It allowed the Germans 35 per cent of British tonnage in surface ships and 45 per cent in submarines. This constituted a major political success for Hitler, who for reasons of military–industrial infrastructure could not hope to build up a fleet of even this limited size until the early 1940s, and antagonised the French. The agreement rode roughshod over the Versailles Treaty of 1919, which had previously been used to keep German naval capabilities in check, and allowed Germany to build battleships of 35,000 tons and cruisers of 10,000 tons – Versailles had limited the Germans to 10,000 tons in the former category and 6,000 tons in the latter.

The agreement failed to resolve Britain's strategic difficulties and created new problems for the French who, in the absence of security guarantees from Britain or the USA, could now find themselves in a war on two fronts (and two seas) against Germany and Italy. The French response was to lay down two new battleships of 35,000 tons in October 1935 and December 1936 respectively. The first of these, *Richelieu*, took France 18,000tW above her permitted ceiling under Washington. Britain protested that the laying down of *Richelieu* was escalatory and demanded that work on the ship be slowed, but failed to see that French actions were a direct consequence of her own failure to consult with France, one of the two major co-signatories of the Treaty of Versailles, when conducting separate negotiations with Hitler's Germany.[1]

Given the early withdrawal of Japan from the London conference, the United States was equally keen to abandon quantitative limits. Although the Americans currently had no intention to increase the size of their fleet and had traditionally been reluctant to spend more than strictly necessary on naval armaments, they would need to be in a position to respond to any new construction authorised by Japan. The Japanese had made it plain that even a 10:7 ratio was unacceptable to them, so the clear message was that they intended to embark on a large programme of new construction.

In March 1937, prompted by naval intelligence suggesting that Japan was building battleships armed with 16in guns,[2] the United States invoked the 'escalator' clause (Article 25) and announced that the new battleships of the *North Carolina* class would likewise be armed with 16in guns, not 14in guns as originally planned. A further exchange of notes with Britain and France in the spring of 1938 led to a protocol signed on 30 June raising the maximum permitted displacement of future battleships from 35,000tW to 45,000tW. The treaty system was now effectively dead.

Appendix

International Treaty for the Limitation and Reduction of Naval Armament – London, 22 April 1930

Part I

Articles

1 The high contracting parties agree not to exercise their rights to lay down the keels of capital ship replacement tonnage during the years 1931–36 inclusive, as provided in chapter II, part 3, of the treaty for the limitation of naval armament, signed between them at Washington on the 6th February, 1922, and referred to in the present treaty as 'the Washington Treaty'.

This provision is without prejudice to the disposition relating to the replacement of ships accidentally lost or destroyed, contained in chapter II, part 3, section I, paragraph (c), of the said treaty.

France and Italy may, however, build the replacement tonnage which they were entitled to lay down in 1927 and 1929 in accordance with the provisions of the said treaty.

2 (1) The United States, the United Kingdom of Great Britain and Northern Ireland and Japan shall dispose of the following capital ships as provided in this article:

– United States: *Florida, Utah, Arkansas* or *Wyoming*.

– United Kingdom: *Benbow, Iron Duke, Marlborough, Emperor of India, Tiger*.

– Japan: *Hiyei*.

(a) Subject to the provisions of sub-paragraph (6), the above ships, unless converted to target use exclusively, in accordance with chapter II, part 2, paragraph II (c), of the Washington Treaty, shall be scrapped in the following manner: One of the ships to be scrapped by the United States and two of those to be scrapped by the United Kingdom shall be rendered unfit for warlike service, in accordance with chapter II, part 2, paragraph III (b), of the Washington Treaty, within 12 months from the coming into force of the present treaty. These ships shall be finally scrapped, in accordance with paragraph II (a) or (b) of the said part 2, within 24 months from the said coming into force. In the case of the second of the ships to be scrapped by the United States, and of the third and fourth of the ships to be scrapped by the United Kingdom, the said periods shall be 18 and 30 months respectively from the coming into force of the present treaty.

(b) Of the ships to be disposed of under this article, the following may be retained for training purposes:

– By the United States: *Arkansas* or *Wyoming*.

– By the United Kingdom: *Iron Duke*.

– By Japan: *Hiyei*.

These ships shall be reduced to the condition prescribed in section V of annex II to part II of the present treaty. The work of reducing these vessels to the required condition shall begin, in the case of the United States and the United Kingdom, within 12 months, and in the case of Japan, within 18 months from the coming into force of the present treaty; the work shall be completed within 6 months of the expiration of the above-mentioned periods.

Any of these ships which are not retained for training purposes shall be rendered unfit for warlike service within 18 months, and finally scrapped within 30 months, of the coming into force of the present treaty.

(2) Subject to any disposal of capital ships which might be necessitated, in accordance with the Washington Treaty, by the building by France or Italy of the replacement tonnage referred to in article 1 of the present treaty, all existing capital ships mentioned in chapter II, part 3, section II, of the Washington Treaty and not designated above to be disposed of may be retained during the term of the present treaty.

(3) The right of replacement is not lost by delay in laying down replacement tonnage, and the old vessel may be retained until replaced, even though due for scrapping under chapter II, part 3, section II, of the Washington Treaty.

3   (1) For the purposes of the Washington Treaty, the definition of an aircraft carrier given in chapter II, part 4, of the said treaty is hereby replaced by the following definition:

The expression 'aircraft carrier' includes any surface vessel of war, whatever its displacement, designed for the specific and exclusive purpose of carrying aircraft, and so constructed that aircraft can be launched therefrom and landed thereon.

(2) The fitting of a landing-on or flying-off platform or deck on a capital ship, cruiser or destroyer, provided such vessel was not designed or adapted exclusively as an aircraft carrier, shall not cause any vessel so fitted to be charged against or classified in the category of aircraft carriers.

(3) No capital ship in existence on the 1st April, 1930, shall be fitted with a landing-on platform. or deck.

4 (1) No aircraft carrier of 10,000 tons (10,160 metric tons) or less standard displacement, mounting a gun above 6.l-inch (155mm) calibre, shall be acquired by or constructed by or for any of the high contracting parties.

(2) As from the coming into force of the present treaty in respect of all the high contracting parties, no aircraft carrier of 10,000 tons (10,160 metric tons) or less standard displacement, mounting a gun above 6.1-inch (155mm) calibre, shall be constructed within the jurisdiction of any of the high contracting parties.

5 An aircraft carrier must not be designed and constructed for carrying a more powerful armament than that authorised by article 9 or article 10 of the Washington Treaty, or by article 4 of the present treaty, as the case may be.
Wherever in the said articles 9 and 10 the calibre of 6 inches (152 mm) is mentioned, the calibre of 6.1 inches (155mm) is substituted therefor.

PART II

6 (1) The rules for determining standard displacement prescribed in chapter II, part 4, of the Washington Treaty shall apply to all surface vessels of war of each of the high contracting parties.

(2) The standard displacement of a submarine is the surface displacement of the vessel complete (exclusive of the water in non-watertight structure), fully manned, engined, and equipped ready for sea, including all armament and ammunition, equipment, outfit, provisions for crew, miscellaneous stores, and implements of every description that are intended to be carried in war, but without fuel, lubricating oil, fresh water or ballast water of any kind on board.

(3) Each naval combatant vessel shall be rated at its displacement tonnage when in the standard condition. The word 'ton', except in the expression 'metric tons', shall be understood to be the ton of 2,240 pounds (1,016 kilos).

7 (1) No submarine, the standard displacement of which exceeds 2,000 tons (2,032 metric tons) or with a gun above 5.1-inch (130mm) calibre, shall be acquired by or constructed by or for any of the high contracting parties.

(2) Each of the high contracting parties may, however, retain, build or acquire a maximum number of 3 submarines of a standard displacement not exceeding 2,800 tons (2,845 metric tons); these submarines may carry guns not above 6.l-inch (155mm) calibre. Within this number, France may retain one unit, already launched, of 2,880 tons (2,926 metric tons), with guns the calibre of which is 8 inches (203mm).

(3) The high contracting parties may retain the submarines which they possessed on the 1st April, 1930, having a standard displacement not in excess of 2,000 tons (2,032 metric tons) and armed with guns above 5.1-inch (130mm) calibre.

(4) As from the coming into force of the present treaty in respect of all the high contracting parties, no submarine the standard displacement of which exceeds 2,000 tons (2,032 metric tons), or with a gun above 5.1-inch (130mm) calibre, shall be constructed within the jurisdiction of any of the high contracting parties, except as provided in paragraph (2) of this article.

8 Subject to any special agreements which may submit them to limitation, the following vessels are exempt from limitation:
(a) Naval surface combatant vessels of 600 tons (610 metric tons) standard displacement and under.
(b) Naval surface combatant vessels exceeding 600 tons (610 metric tons), but not exceeding 2,000 tons (2,032 metric tons) standard displacement, provided they have none of the following characteristics:
  (1) Mount a gun above 6.1-inch (155mm) calibre.
  (2) Mount more than four guns above 3-inch (76mm) calibre.
  (3) Are designed or fitted to launch torpedoes.
  (4) Are designed for a speed greater than 20 knots.
(c) Naval surface vessels not specifically built as fighting ships which are employed on fleet duties or as troop transports or in some other way than as fighting ships, provided they have none of the following characteristics:
  (1) Mount a gun above 6.1-inch (155mm) calibre.
  (2) Mount more than four guns above 3-inch (76 mm.) calibre.
  (3) Are designed or fitted to launch torpedoes.
  (4) Are designed for a speed greater than 20 knots.
  (5) Are protected by armour plate.
  (6) Are designed or fitted to launch mines.
  (7) Are fitted to receive aircraft on board from the air.
  (8) Mount more than one aircraft-launching apparatus on the centre line; or two, one on each broadside.
  (9) If fitted with any means of launching aircraft into the air, are designed or adapted to operate at sea more than 3 aircraft.

9 The rules as to replacement contained in annex I to this part II are applicable to vessels of war not exceeding 10,000 tons (10,160 metric tons) standard displacement with the exception of aircraft carriers, whose replacement is governed by the provisions of the Washington Treaty.

10 Within 1 month after the date of laying down and the date of completion respectively of each vessel of war, other than capital ships, aircraft carriers and the vessels exempt from limitation under article 8, laid down or completed by or for them after the coming into force of the present treaty, the high contracting parties shall communicate to each of the other high contracting parties the information detailed below:
(a) The date of laying the keel and the following particulars:
– Classification of the vessel.
– Standard displacement in tons and metric tons.
– Principal dimensions, namely: length at water-line, extreme beam at or below water-line.
– Mean draft at standard displacement.
– Calibre of the largest gun.
(b) The date of completion together with the foregoing particulars relating to the vessel at that date.
The Information to be given in the case of capital ships and aircraft carriers is governed by the Washington Treaty.

11 Subject to the provisions of article 2 of the present treaty, the rules for disposal contained in annex II to this part II shall be applied to all vessels of war to be disposed of under the said treaty, and to aircraft carriers as defined in article 3.

12 (1) Subject to any supplementary agreements which may modify, as between the high contracting parties concerned, the lists in annex III to this part II, the special vessels shown therein may be retained and their tonnage shall not be included in the tonnage subject to limitation.
(2) Any other vessel constructed, adapted or acquired to serve the purposes for which these special vessels are retained shall be charged against the tonnage of the appropriate combatant category, according to the characteristics of the vessel, unless such vessel conforms to the characteristics of vessels exempt from limitation under article 8.
(3) Japan may, however, replace the minelayers *Aso* and *Tokiwa* by two new minelayers before the 31st December, 1936. The standard displacement of each of the new vessels shall not exceed 5,000 tons (5,080 metric tons); their speed shall not exceed 20 knots, and their other characteristics shall conform to the provisions of paragraph (b) of article 8. The new vessels shall be regarded as special vessels, and their tonnage shall not be chargeable to the tonnage of any combatant category. The *Aso* and *Tokiwa* shall be disposed of in accordance with

section I or II of annex II to this part II, on completion of the replacement vessels. (4) The *Asama, Yakumo, Izumo, Iwate* and *Kasuga* shall be disposed of in accordance with section I or II of annex II to this part II when the first three vessels of the *Kuma*. class have been replaced by new vessels. These three vessels of the Kuma. class shall be reduced to the condition prescribed in section V, sub-paragraph (b) 2, of annex II to this part II, and are to be used for training ships, and their tonnage shall not thereafter be included in the tonnage subject to limitation.

13 Existing ships of various types, which, prior to the 1st April, 1930, have been used as stationary training establishments or hulks, may be retained in a non-seagoing condition.

Annex I – Rules for Replacement:

Section I

Except as provided in section III of this annex and part III of the present treaty, a vessel shall not be replaced before it becomes 'over-age'. A vessel shall be deemed 'over-age' when the following number of years have elapsed since the date of its completion:

(a) For a surface vessel exceeding 3,000 tons (3,048 metric tons) but not exceeding 10,000 tons (10,160 metric tons) standard displacement:
    (i) If laid down before the 1st January, 1920: 16 years.
    (ii) If laid down after the 31st December, 1919: 20 years.
(b) For a surface vessel not exceeding 3,000 tons (3,048 metric tons) standard displacement:
    (i) If laid down before the 1st January, 1921: 12 years.
    (ii) If laid down after the 31st December, 1920: 16 years.
(c) For a submarine: 13 years.

The keels of replacement tonnage shall not be laid down more than 3 years before the year in which the vessel to be replaced becomes 'over-age'; but this period is reduced to 2 years in the case of any replacement surface vessel not exceeding 3,000 tons (3,048 metric tons) standard displacement:
The right of replacement is not lost by delay in laying down replacement tonnage.

Section II

Except as otherwise provided in the present treaty, the vessel or vessels, whose retention would cause the maximum tonnage permitted in the category to be exceeded, shall, on the completion or acquisition of replacement tonnage, be disposed of in accordance with annex II to this part II.

Section III

In the event of loss or accidental destruction a vessel may be immediately replaced.

Annex II – Rules for Disposal of Vessels of War
The present treaty provides for the disposal of vessels of war in the following ways:

(i) By scrapping (sinking or breaking up).

(ii) By converting the vessel to a hulk.

(iii) By converting the vessel to target use exclusively.

(iv) By retaining the vessel exclusively for experimental purposes.

(v) By retaining the vessel exclusively for training purposes.

Any vessel of war to be disposed of, other than a capital ship, may either be scrapped or converted to a hulk at the option of the high contracting party concerned.

Vessels, other than capital ships, which have been retained for target, experimental or training purposes, shall finally be scrapped or converted to hulks.

Section I – Vessels to be scrapped
(a) A vessel to be disposed of by scrapping, by reason of its replacement, must be rendered incapable of warlike service within 6 months of the date of completion of its successor, or of the first of its successors if there are more than one. If, however, the completion of the new vessel or vessels be delayed, the work of rendering the old vessel incapable of warlike service shall, nevertheless, be completed within 4½ years from the date of laying the keel of the new vessel, or of the first of the new vessels; but should the new vessel, or any of the new vessels, be a surface vessel not exceeding 3,000 tons (3,048 metric tons) standard displacement, this period is reduced to 3½ years.

(b) A vessel to be scrapped shall be considered incapable of warlike service when there shall have been removed and landed or else destroyed in the ship:

(1) All guns and essential parts of guns, fire control tops and revolving parts of all barbettes and turrets.

(2) All hydraulic or electric machinery for operating turrets.

(3) All fire control instruments and rangefinders.

(4) All ammunition, explosives and mines and mine rails.

(5) All torpedoes, war heads, torpedo tubes and training racks.

(6) All wireless telegraphy installations.

(7) All main propelling machinery, or, alternatively, the armoured conning tower and all side armour plate.

(8) All aircraft cranes, derricks, lifts and launching apparatus. All landing-on or flying-off platforms and decks, or, alternatively, all main propelling machinery.

(9) In addition, in the case of submarines, all main storage batteries, air compressor plants and ballast pumps.

(c) Scrapping shall be finally effected in either of the following ways within 12 months of the date on which the work of rendering the vessel incapable of warlike service is due for completion:

(1) Permanent sinking of the vessel.

(2) Breaking the vessel up; this shall always include the destruction or removal of all machinery, boilers and armour, and all deck, side and bottom plating.

Section II – Vessels to be converted to hulks

A vessel to be disposed of by conversion to a hulk shall be considered finally disposed of when the conditions prescribed in section I, paragraph (b), have been complied with, omitting sub-paragraphs (6), (7) and (8), and when the following have been effected:

(1) Mutilation beyond repair of all propeller shafts, thrust blocks, turbine gearing or main propelling motors, and turbines or cylinders of main engines.

(2) Removal of propeller brackets.

(3) Removal and breaking up of all aircraft lifts, and the removal of all aircraft cranes, derricks and launching apparatus.

The vessel must be put in the above condition within the same limits of time as provided in Section I for rendering a vessel incapable of warlike service.

Section III – Vessels to be converted to target use

(a) A vessel to be disposed of by conversion to target use exclusively shall be considered incapable of warlike service when there have been removed and landed, or rendered unserviceable on board, the following:

(1) All guns.

(2) All fire control tops and instruments and main fire control communication wiring.

(3) All machinery for operating gun mountings or turrets.

(4) All ammunition, explosives, mines, torpedoes and torpedo tubes.

(5) All aviation facilities and accessories.

The vessel must be put into the above condition within the same limits of time as provided in Section I for rendering a vessel incapable of warlike service.

(b) In addition to the rights already possessed by each high contracting party under the Washington Treaty, each high contracting party is permitted to retain, for target use exclusively, at any one time:

(1) Not more than three vessels (cruisers or destroyers), but of these three vessels only one may exceed 3,000 tons (3,048 metric tons) standard displacement.

(2) One submarine.

(c) On retaining a vessel for target use, the high contracting party concerned undertakes not to recondition it for warlike service.

Section IV – Vessels retained for experimental purposes

(a) A vessel to be disposed of by conversion to experimental purposes exclusively shall be dealt with in accordance with the provisions of section III (a) of this annex.

(b) Without prejudice to the general rules, and provided that due notice be given to the other high contracting parties, reasonable variation from the conditions prescribed in Section III (a) of this annex, in so far as may be necessary for the purposes of a special experiment, may be permitted as a temporary measure.

Any high contracting party taking advantage of this provision is required to furnish full details of any such variations and the period for which they will be required.

(c) Each high contracting party is permitted to retain for experimental purposes exclusively at any one time:

(1) Not more than two vessels (cruisers or destroyers), but of these vessels only one may exceed 3,000 tons (3,048 metric tons) standard displacement.

(2) One submarine.

(d) The United Kingdom is allowed to retain, in their present conditions, the monitor *Roberts*, the main armament guns and mountings of which have been mutilated, and the seaplane carrier *Ark Royal*, until no longer required for experimental purposes. The retention of these two vessels is without prejudice to the retention of vessels permitted under (c) above.

(e) On retaining a vessel for experimental purposes the high contracting party concerned undertakes not to recondition it for warlike service.

Section V – Vessels retained for training purposes

(a) In addition to the rights already possessed by any high contracting party under the Washington Treaty, each high contracting party is permitted to retain for training purposes exclusively the following vessels:

– United States: 1 capital ship (*Arkansas* or *Wyoming*).

– France: 2 surface vessels, one of which may exceed 3,000 tons (3,048 metric tons) standard displacement.

– United Kingdom: 1 capital ship (*Iron Duke*).

– Italy: 2 surface vessels, one of which may exceed 3,000 tons (3,048 metric tons) standard displacement.

– Japan: 1 capital ship (*Hiyei*), 3 cruisers (*Kuma* class).

(b) Vessels retained for training purposes under the provisions of paragraph (a) shall, within 6 months of the date on which they are required to be disposed of, be dealt with as follows:

Capital ships

The following is to be carried out:

(1) Removal of main armament guns, revolving parts of all barbettes and turret machinery; machinery for operating turrets; but 3 turrets with their armament may be retained for each ship.

(2) Removal of all ammunition and explosives in excess of the quantity required for target practice training for the guns remaining on board.

(3) Removal of conning tower and the side armour belt between the foremost and aftermost barbettes.

(4) Removal or mutilation of all torpedo tubes.

(5) Removal or mutilation on board of all boilers in excess of the number required for a maximum speed of 18 knots.

Other surface vessels retained by France, Italy and Japan
The following is to be carried out:
   (1) Removal of one-half of the guns, but four guns of main calibre may be
   retained on each vessel.
   (2) Removal of all torpedo tubes.
   (3) Removal of all aviation facilities and accessories.
   (4) Removal of one-half of the boilers.
(c) The high contracting party concerned undertakes that vessels retained in accordance with the provisions of this section shall not be used for any combatant
purpose.

Annex III – Special Vessels
[The names, type and displacement of the special vessels listed in this annex are
detailed in Chapter 7, Table 1.]

PART III
The President of the United States of America, His Majesty the King of Great
Britain, Ireland and the British dominions beyond the Seas, Emperor of India, and
His Majesty the Emperor of Japan, have agreed as between themselves to the provi-
sions of this part III.

14 The naval combatant vessels of the United States, the British Commonwealth of
   Nations and Japan, other than capital ships, aircraft carriers and all vessels exempt
   from limitation under article 8, shall be limited during the term of the present
   treaty, as provided in this part III, and, in the case of special vessels, as provided
   in article 12.

15 For the purpose of this part III the definition of the cruiser and destroyer categories shall be as follows:
   Cruisers
   Surface vessels of war, other than capital ships or aircraft carriers, the standard
   displacement of which exceeds 1,850 tons (1,880 metric tons), or with a gun
   above 5.1-inch (130mm) calibre.
   The cruiser category is divided into two sub-categories, as follows:
   (a) Cruisers carrying a gun above 6.1-inch (155mm) calibre.
   (b) Cruisers carrying a gun not above 6.1-inch (155mm) calibre.
   Destroyers
   Surface vessels of war the standard displacement of which does not exceed 1,850
   tons (1,880 metric tons), and with a gun not above 5.1-inch (130mm) calibre.

16 (1) The completed tonnage in the. cruiser, destroyer and submarine categories
   which is not to be exceeded on the 31st December, 1936, is given in the following table:

Categories	United States	British Common-wealth of Nations	Japan
Cruisers:			
(a) with guns of more than 6.1-inch (155mm) calibre	180,000 tons (182,880mt)	146,800 tons (149,149mt)	108,400 tons (110,134mt)
(b) with guns of 6.1-inch (155mm) calibre or less	143,500 tons (145,796mt)	192,200 tons (195,275mt)	100,450 tons (102,057mt)
Destroyers	150,000 tons (152,400mt)	150,000 tons (152,400mt)	105,500 tons (107,188mt)
Submarines (53,543mt)	52,700 tons (53,543mt)	5:2,700 tons (53,543mt)	52,700 tons

(2) Vessels which cause the total tonnage in any category to exceed the figures given in the foregoing table shall be disposed of gradually during the period ending on the 31st December, 1936.

(3) The maximum number of cruisers of sub-category (a) shall be as follows: for the United States, 18; for the British Commonwealth of Nations, 15; for Japan, 12.

(4) In the destroyer category not more than 16 per cent of the allowed total tonnage shall be employed in vessels of over 1,500 tons (1,524 metric tons) standard displacement. Destroyers completed or under construction on the 1st April, 1930, in excess of this percentage may be retained, but no other destroyers exceeding 1,500 tons (1,524 metric tons) standard displacement shall be constructed or acquired until a reduction to such 16 per cent, has been effected.

(5) Not more than 25 per cent of the allowed total tonnage in the cruiser category may be fitted with a landing-on platform or deck for aircraft.

(6) It is understood that the submarines referred to in paragraphs (2) and (3) of article 7 will be counted as part of the total submarine tonnage of the high contracting party concerned.

(7) The tonnage of any vessels retained under article 13 or disposed of in accordance with annex II to part II of the present treaty shall not be included in the tonnage subject to limitation.

17 A transfer not exceeding 10 per cent of the allowed total tonnage of the category or sub-category into which the transfer is to be made shall be permitted between cruisers of sub-category (b) and destroyers.

18 The United States contemplates the completion by 1935 of 15 cruisers of sub-category (a) of an aggregate tonnage of 150,000 tons (152,400 metric tons). For each of the three remaining cruisers of sub-category (a) which it is entitled to

construct, the United States may elect to substitute 15,166 tons (15,409 metric tons) of cruisers of sub-category (b). In case the United States shall construct one or more of such three remaining cruisers of sub-category (a), the sixteenth unit will not be laid down before 1933 and will not be completed before 1936; the seventeenth will not be laid down before 1934 and will not be completed before 1937; the eighteenth will not be laid down before 1935 and will not be completed before 1938.

19 Except as provided in article 20, the tonnage laid down in any category subject to limitation in accordance with article 16 shall not exceed the amount necessary to reach the maximum allowed tonnage of the category, or to replace vessels that become 'over-age' before the 31st December, 1936. Nevertheless, replacement tonnage may be laid down for cruisers and submarines that become 'over-age' in 1937, 1938 and 1939, and for destroyers that become 'over-age' in 1937 and 1938.

20 Notwithstanding the rules for replacement contained in annex I to part II:
(a) The *Frobisher* and *Effingham* (United Kingdom) may be disposed of during the year 1936. Apart from the cruisers under construction on the 1st April, 1930, the total replacement tonnage of cruisers to be completed, in the case of the British Commonwealth of Nations, prior to the 31st December, 1936, shall not exceed 91,000 tons (92,456 metric tons).
(b) Japan may replace the *Tama* by new construction to be completed during the year 1936.
(c) In addition to replacing destroyers becoming 'over-age' before the 31st December, 1936, Japan may lay down, in each of the years 1935 and 1936, not more than 5,200 tons (5,283 metric tons) to replace part of the vessels that become 'over-age' in 1938 and 1939.
(d) Japan may anticipate replacement during the term of the present treaty by laying down not more than 19,200 tons (19,507 metric tons) of submarine tonnage, of which not more than 12,000 tons (12,192 metric tons) shall be completed by the 31st December, 1936.

21 If, during the term of the present treaty, the requirements of the national security of any high contracting party in respect of vessels of war limited by part III of the present treaty are, in the opinion of that party, materially affected by new construction of any Power other than those who have joined in part III of this treaty, that high contracting party will notify the other parties to part III as to the increase required to be made in its own tonnages within one or more of the categories of such vessels of war, specifying particularly the proposed increases and the reasons therefore, and shall be entitled to make such increase. Thereupon the other parties to part III of this treaty shall be entitled to make a proportionate increase in the category or categories specified; and the said other

parties shall promptly advise with each other through diplomatic channels as to the situation thus presented.

PART IV

22 The following are accepted as established rules of international law:

(1) In their action with regard to merchant ships, submarines must conform to the rules of international law to which surface vessels are subject.

(2) In particular, except in the case of persistent refusal to stop on being duly summoned, or of active resistance to visit or search, a warship, whether surface vessel or submarine, may not sink or render incapable of navigation a merchant vessel without having first placed passengers, crew and ship's papers in a place of safety. For this purpose the ship's boats are not regarded as a place of safety unless the safety of the passengers and crew is assured, in the existing sea and weather conditions, by the proximity of land, or the presence of another vessel which is in a position to take them on board.

The high contracting parties invite all other Powers to express their assent to the above rules.

PART V

23 The present treaty shall remain in force until the 31st December, 1936, subject to the following exceptions:

(1) Part IV shall remain in force without limit of time.

(2) The provisions of articles 3, 4 and 5, and of article 11 and annex II to part II, so far as they relate to aircraft carriers, shall remain in force for the same period as the Washington Treaty.

Unless the high contracting parties should agree otherwise by reason of a more general agreement limiting naval armaments, to which they all become parties, they shall meet in conference in 1935 to frame a new treaty to replace and to carry out the purposes of the present treaty, it being understood that none of the provisions of the present treaty shall prejudice the attitude of any of the high contracting parties at the conference agreed to.

24 (1) The present treaty shall be ratified by the high contracting parties in accordance with their respective constitutional methods, and the ratifications shall be deposited at London as soon as possible. Certified copies of all the *procès-verbaux* of the deposit of ratifications will be transmitted to the Governments of all the high contracting parties.

(2) As soon as the ratifications of the United States of America, of His Majesty the King of Great Britain, Ireland and the British dominions beyond the Seas, Emperor of India, in respect of each and all of the members of the British Commonwealth of Nations as enumerated in the preamble of the present treaty, and of His Majesty the Emperor of Japan have been deposited, the treaty shall come into force in respect of the said high contracting parties.

(3) On the date of the coming into force referred to in the preceding paragraph, parts I, II, IV and V of the present treaty will come into force in respect of the French Republic and the Kingdom of Italy if their ratifications have been deposited at that date; otherwise these parts will come into force in respect of each of those Powers on the deposit of its ratification.

(4) The rights and obligations resulting from part III of the present treaty are limited to the high contracting parties mentioned in paragraph (2) of this article. The high contracting parties will agree as to the date on which, and the conditions under which, the obligations assumed under the said part III by the high contracting parties mentioned in paragraph (2) of this article will bind them in relation to France and Italy; such agreement will determine at the same time the corresponding obligations of France and Italy in relation to the other high contracting parties.

25 After the deposit of the ratifications. of all the high contracting parties, His Majesty's Government in the United Kingdom of Great Britain and Northern Ireland will communicate the provisions inserted in part IV of the present treaty to all Powers which are not signatories of the said treaty, inviting them to accede thereto definitely and without limit of time.

Such accession shall be effected by a declaration addressed to His Majesty's Government in the United Kingdom of Great Britain and Northern Ireland.

26 The present treaty, of which the French and English texts are both authentic, shall remain deposited in the archives of His Majesty's Government in the United Kingdom of Great Britain and Northern Ireland. Duly certified copies thereof shall be transmitted to the Governments of all the high contracting parties.

[Signatures]

In faith whereof the above-named plenipotentiaries have signed the present treaty and have affixed thereto their seals.

Done at London, the 22nd day of April, 1930.

[Signed on behalf of the United Kingdom and parts of the British Empire not separate members of the League of Nations, Australia, Canada, Irish Free State, New Zealand, South Africa, India, France, Italy, Japan and United States.]

NOTES

Introduction

1. This proved more difficult to implement with regard to the other powers; Italy and Japan both named serving admirals as delegates.

2. Prior to the conference the Japanese Naval General Staff had established three inalienable principles: a 10:7 ratio in overall tonnage, a 10:7 ratio in large cruisers, and an allocation of 78,000 tons of submarines.

3. The Chief of the Naval Staff, Kato Kanji, resigned in protest, and Premier Hamaguchi would succumb to an assassination attempt by an ultranationalist later in the year.

4. The chief US naval delegate, Admiral William V Pratt, received a volley of criticism from the US naval establishment when he returned from the conference; the Japanese delegation to the conference all but imploded and came to blows.

5. Only eight had been laid down by the opening of the London Conference; two further ships, *Portland* and *Indianapolis* (FY1929) would be begun during its deliberations. The first ship of the radically redesigned *New Orleans* class, *Astoria*, would be laid down only in September 1930, five months after the conference ended.

6. This was not a serious problem, as the US Navy was already becoming disillusioned with the type (see *WAW* Chapter 9).

Chapter 1

1. See Roskill and Maurer & Bell, *op cit.*

2. Rear Admiral William A Moffett, head of the Bureau of Aeronautics (BuAer), was particularly scathing about them.

Chapter 2

1. A British Naval Intelligence report of 1933 claimed the United States had so far spent £16 million on capital ship reconstruction, as compared with £9 million for Japan and only £3 million for Great Britain. Even taking into account the differences in shipyard costs (US costs were higher, perhaps by a factor of two), this was an impressive figure.

2. Other navies generally raised the height of the trunnions, a much simpler operation.

3. Like the original bulges, these retained the steel 'crushing' tubes common in Royal Navy capital ships of the late war period.

4. Because of the additional work involved her refit took four years, as compared with around two years for each of her sisters.

5. *Hiei* would trial a new bridge tower intended for the battleship *Yamato*.

6. Even the British, who had protested vigorously to the United States about this during the mid-1920s, were currently increasing the elevation of the main guns of their older battleships from 20 to 30 degrees.

7. Later published in book form by Arms & Armour Press (London 1987).

8. This solution would have to wait until after the Second World War, which neither *Dunkerque* nor *Strasbourg* survived.

9. SURAL was an abbreviation of '*Suralimenté*' (forced circulation).

10. This was a factor in the French decision to opt for two quadruple turrets in *Dunkerque* and *Richelieu*.

11. The first torpedo struck aft, severely damaging the bracket for the port outer propeller shaft, and the distorted shaft (which was still being driven by its turbines) opened up the hull and all the watertight bulkheads throughout its passage.

12   The German Navy, which stayed with what it regarded as a 'tried-and-tested' concept of armouring that dated from before Jutland, never adopted the inclined belt.

Chapter 3

1   The American and the Japanese spotter aircraft, which were considerably smaller than their British counterparts, were embarked in their battleships and cruisers, not in their carriers, which were not expected to survive long enough to take part in the decisive battle fleet engagement.

2   The 13,500-ton *Langley* has been omitted because under Washington she could be replaced at any time, and since she was simply a 'development' carrier this was the US Navy's current intention.

3   A gaming exercise at the US Naval War College in which six smaller carriers were opposed by two larger ships with a similar combined air complement appeared to establish that while the offensive strikes mounted by the larger carriers were twice as effective, it was likely that following an all-out air assault by both sides both the large carriers would be out of action, whereas two of the smaller ships would remain operational and could continue to support the battle fleet. See Hone, Friedman & Mandeles, *op cit.*

4   At one point in the early/mid-1930s it was being predicted in some quarters that the increasing size and weight of modern aircraft might spell the end of the aircraft carrier altogether.

5   Delays in the development of the arrester gear meant that *Eagle* was not so fitted until 1936–37, but bomb magazine capacity was enlarged during her refit 1932–33 to enable her to support an air group comprising twelve torpedo bombers (T/B), twelve spotter/reconnaissance aircraft (S/R) and six fighter/reconnaissance aircraft (F/R) – a total of thirty.

6   This was a 'wartime' figure, as experience with *Courageous* and *Glorious* suggested that the maximum number of aircraft that could be operated efficiently using current practices was forty-two, and it was acknowledged that it would be difficult to secure funding for such a large number of aircraft in peacetime.

7   A 900ft length comparable to that of the *Lexingtons* was briefly considered, presumably with a view to adopting the US-style deck park, but was scaled back once the deck park idea was abandoned primarily because of docking considerations.

8   Ultimately, due to maintenance concerns, the maximum air complement was set at sixty aircraft.

9   The maximum size of air group was estimated in 1938 to be forty-two TSR Albacore and eighteen FDB Skua for a total of sixty, with forty-eight aircraft thought to be the 'operational' maximum. At this time *Ark Royal*'s US Navy counterparts were operating seventy-two aircraft in four eighteen-plane squadrons (one fighter, two scout/dive bomber, and one torpedo attack).

10 A 60-degree angle could be accepted for a carrier because it was not designed to stand and fight in line of battle, and shells would generally be fired by ships in pursuit.

11 *Yorktown* was dispatched by *I.168*, which fired four torpedoes at her target on the afternoon of 6 June; two struck the carrier and a third the destroyer *Hammann* (DD-412), which was lying along-side.

12 *Wasp* was sunk by the IJN submarine *I.19* in the Eastern Solomons on 13 September 1942; the submarine fired six Type 95 torpedoes in a devastating strike that also damaged the battleship *North Carolina* and the destroyer *O'Brien* (DD-415).

13 The Japanese Naval General Staff still considered anti-cruiser guns essential in a fleet carrier, and continued to argue for their inclusion in the face of strenuous opposition from officers fiercely committed to naval aviation.

14 Note the disparity between these two figures, which is frankly not credible. A ship of 17,500 tonnes 'normal' (*ie* trial) displacement would have had a standard displacement of c.15,000tW.

15 This figure appears in both *Jane's Fighting Ships* and in the US Naval Intelligence handbook *ONI 41-42* of 1942. As completed in 1933 with a double hangar, *Ryujo* had a standard displacement of 9,577tW.

16 It was also when operating close to maximum speed that the worst effects of the funnel arrangement were experienced.

17 What the British and the Americans did not, and could not know was that the 'official' displace-ments of the latest IJN carriers were well below the actual figures on completion. However, the real

irony of the limits agreed at the Second London Conference was that the first pair of carriers laid down by Japan after the expiry of the Washington Treaty, *Shokaku* and *Zuikaku* ('Circle 3' Programme 1937), would have a standard displacement of 25,700 tons, and would outclass their British and US contemporaries in a number of respects.

[18] Originally these ships were to have had the same 5.25in dual-purpose gun to be fitted in the new battleships of the *King George V* class, but it was decided that the mounting would not available in time. In all probability it would also have proved to be too large to be successfully accommodated, and its performance in the anti-aircraft role was undeniably inferior.

[19] The Navy would also take over the French order for the US F4F Wildcat, which would be rechristened Martlet in British service, and would place an additional order for a more powerful variant. All these high-performance monoplane fighters needed to be kept on deck.

[20] The contrast between British and American interwar developments in naval aviation, and the organisational and institutional differences which underpinned them, are further explored in Hone, Friedman and Mandeles, *American & British Aircraft Carrier Development 1919–1941* (US Naval Institute Press, Annapolis 1999).

Chapter 4

[1] The IJN, which adopted a fleet structure similar to that of the US Navy, referred to the battle force as the 'main force'. The Italian and French fleet structures were also a virtual mirror image of one another: the French equivalent of the battle force was designated the '*1re Escadre de ligne*', while its scouting force counterpart was the '*1re Escadre légère*'; in the *Regia Marina* they were designated '*1a Squadra*' and '*2a Squadra*' respectively.

[2] For the Royal Navy a combination of direction finding (DF) and patrol submarines with long-range wireless transmission capabilities seems to have remained the preferred method of locating enemy forces at longer ranges, with reconnaissance closer to the fleet being performed by aircraft operating from the decks of carriers, which were less constrained by sea state and weather conditions when launching and recovering aircraft than cruisers. The US Navy would later favour large reconnaissance seaplanes, operating either from land bases or from sheltered anchorages, to secure first contact with the enemy fleet. The IJN favoured the monitoring of enemy bases by large cruiser submarines, the latest of which could operate floatplanes (see Chapter 7).

[3] The US Navy was of the opinion that the British could only contemplate building 7,000-ton cruisers because of their extensive network of overseas bases, which they claimed to be worth an extra 2,000–3,000nm of endurance.

[4] The length of the hull, however, was increased by only 12ft, making for a cramped ship.

[5] The three units of the 'K' class and *Leipzig*.

[6] Literally, 'cartoon ships'.

[7] A British paper dating from the late 1920s, in which the DNC pressed for the Royal Navy to adopt larger, high-performance boilers and lighter machinery, gave a figure of 68shp/ton for the *Di Giussano*s against only 45.3shp/ton for the projected 'treaty' cruisers of the *Surrey* class.

[8] When completed, *Emile Bertin* would become the flagship of the group of *contre-torpilleurs* based at Brest, and new combat orders (under the direction of Admiral Darlan) would be drawn up that envisaged her leading and supporting the *contre-torpilleurs* in much the same way that the British *Arethusa*s would lead and support the Royal Navy's destroyer flotillas.

[9] *Gloire* broke down while in company with the cruiser *Australia*, and was compelled to return to Casablanca after temporary repairs instead of proceeding to Dakar.

[10] Technical advisors to the US delegation included both Admiral William A Moffett of the Bureau of Aeronautics, a keen proponent of the flying deck cruiser, and the C-in-C Battle Fleet (later CNO) Admiral William V Pratt, likewise an enthusiast.

[11] The official designations of IJN cruisers following the London Treaty were 'A-class' and 'B-class'.

[12] The new machinery seems to have been generally successful and was adopted for the medium fleet carriers of the *Soryu* and *Amagi* classes as well as for subsequent classes of cruiser.

[13] The shell and its propellant were stowed separately, but were assembled before loading; this simplified the loading process and reduced the firing cycle.

14 In the second batch of ships there would be a third installation aft capable of directing both low- and high-angle fire, plus an upgrade to HACS IV.

15 In the event the first two ships, *Newcastle* and *Southampton*, were completed at 9,080–9,090 tons, while of the 1934 batch the last two units completed at 9,020 tons. The modified ships were completed remarkably close to their designed displacement of 9,400 tons. These figures reveal how successful the British were at keeping control of weights while ships were under construction. The Japanese were clearly less successful in this respect, largely because of the pressures on their constructors from the Naval Staff to attempt far too much on a given displacement.

16 A design similar to the Japanese and American ships with five triple turrets was also considered, but a 635ft length would have restricted the number of docks available, particularly overseas.

17 The result of this was an informal agreement between the major powers that 300 tons overweight was permissible for reconstructed 'treaty' cruisers, which would need to be brought up to date to deal with an increasing aerial threat.

18 The reconstruction of the *London* class was to have been even more radical, being based on the configuration of the latest 6in-gun cruisers of the *Fiji* class.

19 See Evans & Peattie, *Kaigun*, p. 273ff, for a full account.

20 Currently authorised, building or in service were eighteen 10,000-ton, 8in-gun cruisers; nine 10,000-ton, 6in-gun ships of the *Brooklyn* class, and ten 7,000-ton, 6in-gun ships of the *Omaha* class. Of the latter, *Omaha* and *Milwaukee* could be replaced in 1939, the others not until 1943–45 (see Table 1.2).

21 A subsequent report by War Plans delivered in 1937 raised this figure to 100.

22 After 31 December 1936, the expiry date for the Washington Treaty, there would be thirteen ships of the 'C' class extant, together with eight of the 'D' class.

23 The largest design, 'T', had two triple turrets.

24 Elevation was 70 degrees, and 7–8rpm the practical rate of fire.

25 It would later rise to 5,450 tons.

26 These discussions began in 1934, when the 1930 London Treaty was still in force, so there must have already been a strong feeling that overall tonnage limits would no longer apply after December 1936.

Chapter 5

1 Due to the economic situation only a 'half-flotilla' of four destroyers plus a leader had been authorised in 1929, but the programme was now back on track.

2 The Denny-built *Ardent* (launched 1913) was the only destroyer previously built using this method of construction.

3 The downside of this was that lightening the hull and increasing the weight of equipment and fittings higher in the ship would lead to stability problems if it were not carefully managed. This phenomenon was undoubtedly at the root of the problems experienced with the first generation of French post-war flotilla craft, the fleet torpedo boats of the *Bourrasque* class and the *contre-torpilleurs* of the *Tigre* class.

4 Their British counterparts were designed for 5,500nm at 15 knots, which is broadly comparable to the figure for the US destroyers.

5 One of the problems with existing ASW equipment was that the 'Y-gun' depth charge projector developed during the First World War had to be fitted on the centre line, and centre-line space in the new design was at a premium following the decision to locate both banks of torpedo tubes on the ship's axis and to fit an additional 5in gun. However, the General Board's preference for guns and torpedoes over ASW weaponry showed where its priorities lay.

6 The hazard such a manoeuvre implied both for the firing ship and for other destroyers in the same formation during a confused, high-speed action was enormous; it seems surprising in retrospect that such a proposal should have been taken seriously.

7 The new US destroyers, with their dual purpose guns, sophisticated fire control systems and high-technology machinery, cost much more to build than their more rugged and conservative British counterparts.

8 Article 21 stated that if the national security of any High Contracting Party in respect of warship

categories covered by Part III of the Treaty were to be 'materially affected' by new construction of any power outside the agreement, it was permitted to make a proportionate increase in its own strength and to inform the other powers accordingly (the implication being that those powers might choose to do the same).

9 The *Mogador*s both exceeded 43 knots for short periods on trials; *Le Hardi* achieved 39 knots and her sister *Fleuret* 40 knots.

10 The IJN's *Akizuki* class, ordered in 1939 as anti-aircraft escorts for the fast carrier task forces, displaced 2,700 tons standard; the US Navy's *Fletcher* class, which were general-purpose destroyers with a useful anti-air capability, displaced 2,325 tons. The first Royal Navy destroyers to be built specifically for Pacific operations, the 'Battle' class laid down 1942–44, had a similar displacement to the American ships. Their gun/torpedo armament was on a par with the 'A' to 'I' classes, but the 4.5in DP guns could be elevated to 80 degrees and were controlled by a purpose-designed (and heavy) HA fire control system; there was also a powerful battery of 40mm anti-aircraft guns.

Chapter 6

1 Ironically, the large IJN submarines would prove far less effective during the Second World War than the smaller British and American boats and, for that matter, less effective than had been anticipated by the Japanese High Command. While doctrine, and in particular the inflexibility of the IJN's tactical thinking, must bear a large part of the blame, it has to be said that these large boats were vulnerable to air and surface attack, and that their size and lack of manoeuvrability were a major disadvantage both in conducting torpedo attacks on escorted surface units and in dealing with the inevitable response.

2 When the Navy presented a programme of forty-six fleet, eight cruiser and thirty coastal submarines to parliament in the aftermath of Washington the *députés* insisted that the last figure be increased to forty-eight!

3 Submarines of this size would be useful for the defence of Japan's island territories and bases in the event of conflict in the Pacific.

4 The attraction of angled tubes for both the French and British was that neither had developed preset gyro mechanisms for their torpedoes that would enable them to change course after leaving the tube; the submarine's bow therefore had to be pointed at the target before firing.

5 The lead boat, *Undine*, nevertheless attained 12.5 knots on trials.

6 Development work began in 1932–33, and the first specifications were issued in February 1935. The first prototype would be installed in the spring of 1938.

7 By the end of the First World War US torpedoes could in theory be gyro-set to turn up to 90 degrees after firing.

8 The other major cornerstone was the 8in-gun cruiser (see Chapter 4).

9 Figures in English-language publications are inconsistent and unreliable. In at least one source the figure given for standard displacement is the same as that published in another source as the lower of two figures for surfaced displacement (the higher figure being the one for the submarine with the external oil tanks full).

10 Even if France could be persuaded to reduce its submarine tonnage to the 52,700 tons agreed between the three major powers, this figure would still have left Italy plenty of room for expansion.

11 The last pre-London fleet variant, the KD5, which had a length of 98m and a surfaced displacement of 1,705 tons, was declared to have a standard displacement of 1,575 tons. Its post-London successor, the KD6, was declared as having a standard displacement of 1,400 tons, but was in fact even larger, with a length of 105m and a surfaced displacement of 1,785 tons. Little credence can be placed on the displacement figures declared by Japan in their construction programmes of the 1930s, which were never amended upwards to the correct figure when the ships were completed.

Chapter 7

1 The second of the ships built for India, *Indus*, was armed with two single 4.7in guns as in the contemporary RN *Grimsby* class.

2 Note that this main gun armament was permissible only after the Treaty expired in December 1936.

3   The choice of diesel over more conventional steam turbine machinery was not unusual for ships of the period intended to support submarines – see also the Italian colonial sloop *Eritrea* and the IJN's *Taigei*. Diesels could power generators to provide electricity when submarines were alongside without the need to fire up boilers, and could also be used to recharge the submarines' batteries; a further advantage was that the engineering personnel of the Depot Ship would be equally comfortable dealing with repairs and maintenance of the submarine engines.

4   Permissible only now that the London Treaty of 1930 had expired.

5   Figures from du Ravray, *Vingt Ans de Politique Navale (1919–1939)*.

6   The guns were originally ordered to replace the 130mm guns of the *Jaguar* class, but were not fitted once the stability problems with the latter ships became apparent (see *WAW* Chapter 8).

7   The original design featured a fixed, telescopic hangar (see drawing), but this was never fitted.

8   One unit serving with the Royal Navy, *Branlebas*, foundered off the Eddystone lighthouse in December 1940.

9   As with *Wasp* this never happened.

10   Shallow draught was adopted to permit forward deployment to the island anchorages and atolls of the Mandates.

11   There were initially only two, in order to conform to the requirements of the Treaty.

12   *Mizuho* was designed for a maximum speed of 27 knots, but the elimination of the geared steam turbines, leaving her with only two four-cylinder diesels rated at 15,200bhp, effectively ensured that she would be capable of only 22–23 knots. It was the low speed of *Mizuho* which ultimately militated against her conversion to a light aircraft carrier.

13   As late as the 1939 edition *Jane's Fighting Ships* was crediting the two *Chitose*s with a speed of 20 knots, and *Mizuho* with a speed of 17 knots, suggesting that these were the officially declared figures. No details of the air complement or the number of catapults were published, although photographs of *Chiyoda* taken by the Royal Netherlands Navy later that year clearly showed the number of catapults and aircraft. The two depot ships were credited with a top speed of 19 knots.

Chapter 8

1   The slow-down of work on these two battleships occurred anyway when the French dockyards and shipyards were hit by industrial action in 1936–37. In an ironical turnabout, by November 1939 Churchill, now First Sea Lord, was urging the French Admiral Darlan to complete *Richelieu* as soon as possible so that she could oppose the new German battleship *Bismarck*!

2   The calibre was in fact 18.1in (46cm), although this would not become known until after the end of the Second World War.

BIBLIOGRAPHY

Historical

Books

Asada, Sadao: *From Mahan to Pearl Harbor*, US Naval Institute Press (Annapolis, Maryland 2006).

Espagnac du Ravray: *Vingt Ans de Politique Navale*, B Arthaud (Grenoble, Switzerland 1941).

Evans, David C and Peattie, Mark: *Kaigun: Strategy, Tactics and Technology in the Imperial Japanese Navy 1887–1941*, US Naval Institute Press (Annapolis, Maryland 1997).

Greene, Jack and Massagnani, Alessandro: *The Naval War in the Mediterranean 1940–43*, Chatham Publishing (London 1998).

Hone, Thomas C, Friedman, Norman, and Mandeles, Mark D: *American and British Aircraft Carrier Development*, US Naval Institute Press (Annapolis, Maryland 1999).

Maurer, John H and Bell, Christopher M (Ed): *At the Crossroads Between Peace and War: The London Naval Conference of 1930*, US Naval Institute Press (Annapolis, Maryland 2014).

McIntyre, W David: *The Rise and Fall of the Singapore Naval Base*, Macmillan Press (London 1979).

Miller, Edward S: *War Plan Orange*, US Naval Institute Press (Annapolis, Maryland 1991).

Minardi, Salvatore: *Il Disarmo Navale (1919–1936)*, Ufficio Storico della Marina Militare (Rome 1999).

Peattie, Mark: *Sunburst: the Rise of Japanese Naval Air Power, 1909–1941*, US Naval Institute Press (Annapolis, Maryland 2001).

Roskill, Stephen: *Naval Policy Between the Wars*, Collins (London 1968).

Periodicals & Other Resources

Record of Meetings of the British Empire Delegation, Washington and London (1930) Conferences.

Papers and Record of Meetings of the First Committee, London Conference.

Papers and Record of Meetings of the Committee of Experts, London Conference.

Record of Plenary Sessions, London Conference.

Contemporary articles published in the following:

Annals of the American Academy of Political and Social Science (AAAPS)

Proceedings of the Academy of Political Science in the City of New York
Pacific Affairs
Pacific Historical Review
Political Science Quarterly
Foreign Affairs
Far Eastern Survey
The American Journal of International Law

Technical

General

Chesneau, Roger (Ed): *Conway's All the World's Fighting Ships 1922–1946*, Conway Maritime Press (London 1980).

Campbell, John: *Naval Weapons of World War Two*, Conway Maritime Press (London 1985).

Friedman, Norman: *Battleship: Design and Development 1905–1945*, Conway Maritime Press (London 1978).

Friedman, Norman: *Submarine: Design and Development*, Conway Maritime Press (London 1984).

Gray, Randal (Ed): *Conway's All the World's Fighting Ships 1906–1921*, Conway Maritime Press (London 1985).

Great Britain

Akermann, Paul: *Encyclopaedia of British Submarines 1901–1955*, Maritime Books (Liskeard UK, 1989).

Brown, David K: *Nelson to Vanguard: Warship Design and Development 1923–1945*, Chatham Publishing (London 2006).

Friedman, Norman: *British Carrier Aviation*, Conway Maritime Press (London 1988).

Friedman, Norman: *The British Battleship 1906–1946*, Seaforth Publishing (Barnsley 2015).

Friedman, Norman: *British Cruisers: Two World Wars and After*, Seaforth Publishing (Barnsley 2010).

Friedman, Norman: *British Destroyers: From Earliest Days to the Second World War*, Seaforth Publishing (Barnsley 2009).

Friedman, Norman: *British Destroyer & Frigates: The Second World War and After*, Seaforth Publishing (Barnsley 2006).

Friedman, Norman: *British Submarines in Two World Wars*, Seaforth Publishing (Barnsley 2019).

Hobbs, David: *British Aircraft Carriers*, Seaforth Publishing (Barnsley 2013).

Hobbs, David: *Aircraft Carrier Victorious: detailed in the original builders' plans*, Seaforth Publishing (Barnslcy 2018).

Murfin, David: 'Small Cruisers for the RN Between the Wars', *Warship 2011*, Conway (London 2011).

Raven, Alan and Roberts, John: *British Battleships of World War Two*, Arms & Armour Press (London 1976).

Raven, Alan and Roberts, John: *British Cruisers of World War Two*, Arms & Armour Press (London 1980).

Roberts, John: *Battlecruiser Repulse: detailed in the original builders' plans*, Seaforth Publishing (Barnsley 2019).

Waters, Conrad: *British Town Class Cruisers*, Seaforth Publishing (Barnsley 2019).

Watton, Ross: *The Battleship Warspite*, Conway Maritime Press (London 1986).

United States

Friedman, Norman: *US Aircraft Carriers: an Illustrated Design History*, US Naval Institute Press (Annapolis, Maryland 1983).

Friedman, Norman: *US Battleships: an Illustrated Design History*, US Naval Institute Press (Annapolis, Maryland 1985).

Friedman, Norman: *US Cruisers: an Illustrated Design History*, US Naval Institute Press (Annapolis, Maryland 1985).

Friedman, Norman: *US Destroyers: an Illustrated Design History*, US Naval Institute Press (Annapolis, Maryland 1982).

Friedman, Norman: *US Submarines Through 1945: an Illustrated Design History*, US Naval Institute Press (Annapolis, Maryland 1995).

Hone, Thomas C and Hone, Trent: *Battle Line: the United States Navy 1919–1929*, US Naval Institute Press (Annapolis, Maryland 2006).

Japan

Boyd, Carl and Yoshida, Akihiko: *The Japanese Submarine Force and World War II*, US Naval Institute Press (Annapolis, Maryland 1995).

Jentschura, Hansgeorg, Jung, Dieter, and Mickel, Peter: *Warships of the Imperial Japanese Navy, 1869–1945*, Arms & Armour Press (London 1977).

Lacroix, Eric and Wells, Linton: *Japanese Cruisers of the Pacific War*, US Naval Institute Press (Annapolis, Maryland 1997).

Lengerer, Hans: 'The Japanese Destroyers of the *Hatsuharu* Class', *Warship 2007*, Conway (London 2007).

Lengerer, Hans: 'The *Tomozuru* Incident', *Warship 2011*, Conway (London 2011).

Lengerer, Hans: 'The Light Carrier *Ryujo*', *Warship 2014*, Conway (London 2014).

Lengerer, Hans: 'The Japanese Destroyers of the *Asashio* Class', *Warship 2016*, Conway (London 2016).

Polmar, Norman and Carpenter, Dorr B: *Submarines of the Imperial Japanese Navy 1904–1945*, US Naval Institute Press (Annapolis, Maryland 1986).

France

Huan, Claude: *Les Sous-Marins Français*, Marines éditions (Bourg-en-Bresse 1995).

Jordan, John: 'The Colonial Sloops of the *Bougainville* Class', *Warship 2016*, Conway (London 2016).

Jordan, John: 'French Submarine Development Between the Wars', *Warship 1991*, Conway Maritime Press (London 1991).

Jordan, John and Caresse, Philippe: *French Battleships of World War One*, Seaforth Publishing (Barnsley 2018).

Jordan, John and Dumas, Robert: *French Battleships 1922–1956*, Seaforth Publishing (Barnsley 2009).

Jordan, John and Moulin, Jean: *French Cruisers 1922–1956*, Seaforth Publishing (Barnsley 2013).

Jordan, John and Moulin, Jean: *French Destroyers 1922–1956*, Seaforth Publishing (Barnsley 2015).

Saibène, Marc: *Les Torpilleurs Légers Français 1937–1945*, Marines éditions (Nantes 2004).

Italy

Brescia, Maurizio: *Mussolini's Navy: A Reference Guide to the Regia Marina 1930–1945*, Seaforth Publishing (Barnsley 2012).

Cosentino, Michele: 'The Colonial Sloop *Eritrea*', *Warship 2016*, Conway (London 2016).

Giorgerini, Giorgio and Nani, Augusto: *Le Navi di Linea Italiane*, Ufficio Storico della Marina Militare (Rome 1966).

Giorgerini, Giorgio and Nani, Augusto: *Gli Incrociatotori Italiani*, Ufficio Storico della Marina Militare (Rome 1964).

Pollina, Paolo M: *I Sommergibili Italiani*, Ufficio Storico della Marina Militare (Rome 1963).

Tignelli, Rear-Admiral V E (Ed): *I Cacciatorpediniere Italiani*, Ufficio Storico della Marina Militare (Rome 1966).

INDEX